‹ Designing Web Graphics.4 ›

(4TH EDITION)

Words: **Lynda Weinman**

Design: **Ali Karp**

dwg.4

LYNDA WEINMAN

New Riders Publishing
201 West 103rd Street Indianapolis, Indiana 46290
An Imprint of Pearson Education
Boston>Indianapolis>London>Munich>New York>San Francisco

International Standard Book Number: 0-7357-1079-1
Library of Congress Catalog Card Number: 00-109741
Printed in the United States of America
First printing: January 2003
07 06 05 04 03   7 6 5 4 3 2 1

Interpretation of the printing code

The rightmost double-digit number is the year of the book's printing; the rightmost single-digit number is the number of the book's printing. For example, the printing code 03-1 shows that the first printing of the book occurred in 2003.

Trademarks

All terms mentioned in this book that are known to be trademarks or service marks have been appropriately capitalized. New Riders Publishing cannot attest to the accuracy of this information. Use of a term in this book should not be regarded as affecting the validity of any trademark or service mark.

Warning & Disclaimer

Every effort has been made to make this book as complete and as accurate as possible, but no warranty of fitness is implied. The information is provided on an as-is basis. The authors and New Riders Publishing shall have neither liability nor responsibility to any person or entity with respect to any loss or damages arising from the information contained in this book or from the use of the CD or programs that may accompany it.

CREDITS

Publisher
David Dwyer

Associate Publisher
Stephanie Wall

Editor in Chief
Chris Nelson

Executive Editor
Steve Weiss

Production Manager
Gina Kanouse

Product Marketing Manager
Tammy Detrich

Publicity Manager
Susan Nixon

Senior Development Editor
Jennifer Eberhardt

Project Editor
Jake McFarland

Technical Editors
Rich Evers
Molly E. Holzschlag
Robert Reinhardt

Indexer
Cheryl Lenser

Proofreaders
Jessica McCarty
Linda Seifert

Cover Artwork
Bruce Heavin
bruce@stink.com

Designer
Ali Karp
alink newmedia
alink@earthlink.net

Manufacturing Coordinator
Dan Uhrig

lynda.com Publications Director
Garo Green

ABOUT THE AUTHOR

Lynda Weinman has been teaching computer graphics since 1984. She has worked as a faculty member at Art Center College of Design, UCLA, American Film Institute (AFI), and San Francisco State Multimedia Studies Program. Lynda has written magazine articles for *MacWorld, MacUser, MacWeek, Step-by-Step Graphics,* and *How* magazines. She has been a speaker at many industry events, including MacWorld, Seybold, Photoshop World, Thunder Lizard Web and Photoshop conferences, DV Expo, LA DV Show, SIGGRAPH, and Comdex. She has worked as a consultant for Apple, Microsoft, Oracle, and many other corporations.

Lynda formed **lynda.com, inc**. in 1997 with her husband and illustrator Bruce Heavin. Lynda.com creates training materials for creative professionals in the form of books, CD-ROMs, online tutorials, classes, and events. Lynda.com is the co-founder of FlashForward, a conference for Macromedia Flash developers. Other events, such as After Effects West and the Traveling Road Show, have been produced exclusively by lynda.com. To learn more, check out http://www.lynda.com!

TOC QT Q QLQNCE

TABLE OF CONTENTS

ACKNOWLEDGMENTS

Here I am with my other love, my new bike! I've learned that girls cannot live on all work and no play!

Lynda and daughter Jamie playing with the digital camera...

My husband, Bruce. He looks kind of serious here, but he can't fool me.

In a parallel universe, editor Jennifer lives in the Alps tending Swiss cows.

Ali, the design femme fatale. When she isn't designing books, she's reading 'em! She's outta control...

DEDICATION

Thanks to my loving family, **Bruce** and **Jamie**, for supporting and accepting me. I am very lucky to have you.

Thanks to my other family, **lynda.com**. It is an honor to work with such a great team of smart, dedicated people.

Thanks to **Garo Green**, Director of Publications at lynda.com, for believing in books and in me. Your help on this project was invaluable.

Thanks to my other other family, **New Riders Publishing**. I feel as if we've grown up together! Jen, Jake, David, Steve, and Chris, you guys all rock!

Thanks to **Ali Karp**, Book Designer Extraordinaire, for pulling off another masterpiece. You are da bomb!

Thanks to **Domenique Sillett** for examples and sushi dates!

Thanks to **Ramey** for being my friend and exercise bud. See you at our first Century!

Thanks to the **audience** for this book; you are my inspiration.

This book is dedicated to all the people who want to communicate using the Web. You are the inspiration for this book.

About The Technical Reviewers

Rich Evers Rich is a Human Factors Engineer who's been designing and coding web sites since 1994. His penchants include Dreamweaver, Photoshop, and XML/XHTML. When he's in a bad mood, he's been known to destroy mice and keyboards, throw things, and use italics. When he's in a good mood, you might find him cooking, dancing, and riding roller coasters (though not at the same time).

Molly E. Holzschlag With more than 20 web development books to her credit, Molly is a writer and speaker known for her warm voice and outspoken passion for the Web. She is also a columnist, feature writer, and editorial consultant, having published for Adobe, *Macworld*, *PC Magazine*, Builder.Com, and more. Her "Integrated Design" column was a favorite with *Web Techniques* readers. Molly has also served in an editorial capacity for *Digital Web Magazine*, *Web Review*, and was technical editor of *Eric Meyer on CSS: Mastering the Language of Web Design*. Molly is a steering committee member for the Web Standards Project (WaSP), she serves as Education Director for the World Organization of Webmasters, and she develops curricula for web-related certifications and degrees at several institutions, including the University of Arizona.

Robert Reinhardt Robert is the lead co-author of the *Flash Bible* series (Wiley), the *Flash MX ActionScript Bible* (Wiley), and *Rich Media MX: Building Multi-User Systems with Macromedia MX Software* (Macromedia Press). He is also co-principal of [theMAKERS] (http://www.FlashSupport.com), a multimedia company in Los Angeles. Robert has developed multimedia courses for educational facilities in Canada and the U.S., been a speaker at FlashForward, and presented at FlashintheCan and SIGGRAPH. With a degree in photographic arts, Robert takes a holistic approach to computer applications for the creation of provocative multimedia. Recent projects have included screen graphics for Sean Penn's film *The Pledge* (2000) and the web site for the Warner Bros. feature film *Training Day*.

TELL US WHAT YOU THINK

As the reader of this book, you are the most important critic and commentator. We value your opinion and want to know what we're doing right, what we could do better, what areas you'd like to see us publish in, and any other words of wisdom you're willing to pass our way.

As the Executive Editor for New Riders Publishing, I welcome your comments. You can fax, email, or write me directly to let me know what you did or didn't like about this book—as well as what we can do to make our books stronger. When you write, please be sure to include this book's title, ISBN, and author, as well as your name and phone or fax number. I will carefully review your comments and share them with the author and editors who worked on the book.

Please note that I cannot help you with technical problems related to the topic of this book, and that due to the high volume of email I receive, I might not be able to reply to every message.

Fax: 317-581-4663
Email: steve.weiss@newriders.com
Mail: Steve Weiss (Executive Editor)
      New Riders Publishing
      201 West 103rd Street
      Indianapolis, IN 46290 USA

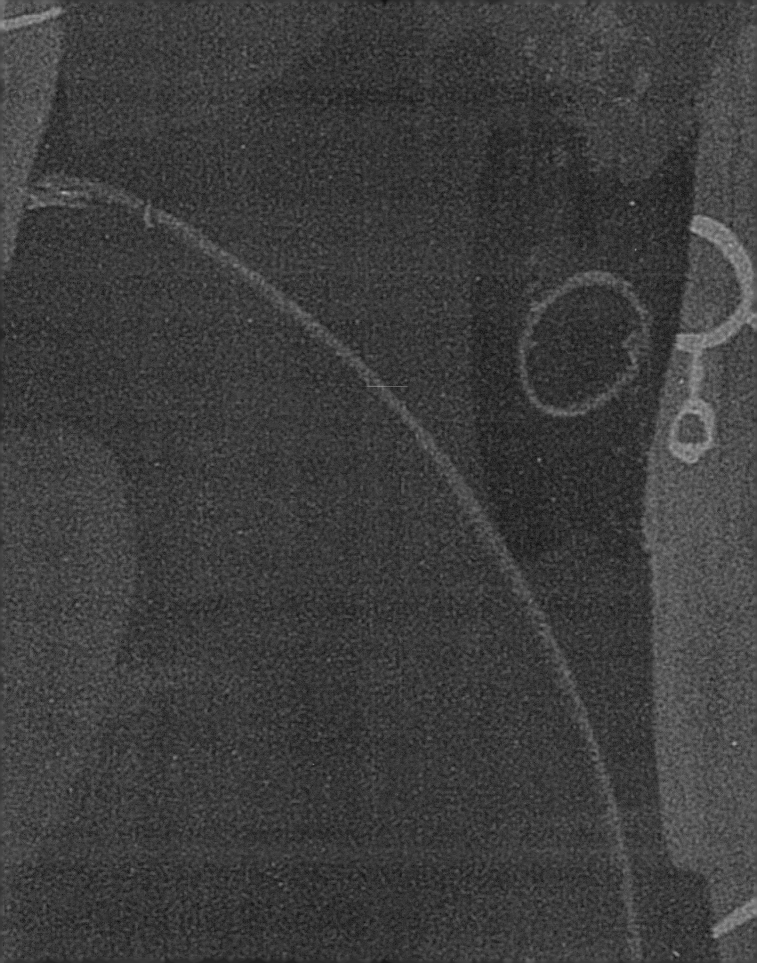

DESIGNING WEB GRAPHICS.4

INTRODUCTION

> › The Ever-Changing Web
>
> › What's New in DWG.4
>
> › What the Chapters Cover
>
> › How DWG.4 Works

Welcome to the fourth edition of *Designing Web Graphics*. It's been more than four years since the third edition hit the bookstores, and since then I have been overwhelmed by the number of readers who have written to thank me for this book. *Designing Web Graphics* is currently used by teachers at high schools, universities, and trade colleges throughout the world. It has been translated into numerous languages and is found on most professional web designers' desktops, as well as in the library of thousands of non-professional web and design enthusiasts.

THE EVER-CHANGING WEB

When I first started writing about the Web in 1995, it was brand new and not that many people yet knew about or used it. Then the boom times came, and lots of people thought if they could just become a web designer that they would make a great deal of money and retire rich and young. We're all living through the dot-bomb time right now—the "humble" economy instead of the "new" economy that was based on over-valued concepts and promises.

Today's Web is much like the old west after the bust of the Gold Rush. The Internet is littered with the remains of failed mines (closed web sites), out-of-work '49ers (high-tech workers), and bankrupt supporting companies (ISPs, hosting companies, backbone providers)—many ironically centered in and around San Francisco, California, the epicenter of the Gold Rush of 1849.

The people who were in it for the quick buck have gone away, and that's ultimately a good thing for those who are serious about this medium and profession. The medium has a bad name right now because there were bad business practices in place. The business practices of the dot-com boom age and the Web are not tied; the Web is still growing and evolving at a steady pace and will continue to do so. Its importance to our culture, economy, and community is still vital.

What compels me to stay devoted to this subject matter with as much passion and energy as I had in 1995? The Web is a phenomenon on so many levels that I still find myself awestruck by it. I am still amazed when someone from Europe or Asia enters my guest book. I am still amazed that, as an individual using a little box that shines back at me, I can communicate with others on a global level. I am still amazed when I see a URL on a billboard, the side of a truck, or a T-shirt. I am still amazed that the Web grew up to be such a big thing to so many people. I imagine that at some point, I'll become jaded by the Web but, for the moment, I think it's an exhilarating time to be alive and witnessing the emergence of this medium.

I'm an educator, and nothing pleases me more than to teach others. Teaching people about the Web is not an easy task, however, because there are so many unfamiliar constraints and rules. For me, designing for the Web is not about dogmatic ideas and rigid principles. It's about harnessing the power of design to enhance ideas and communication.

The term "web site" is a bit of a misnomer because "web site" can mean so many things. There are sites for educational, entertainment, commercial, informational, vanity, and experimental purposes, as well as sites for a hybrid of many purposes. How could you possibly apply the same rules to all these different types of sites? I wouldn't presume to know the one "right" way to make a site for all these different purposes.

Instead, I believe that knowledge is power. If I can share with you the knowledge about how to do things, the repercussions of certain decisions and strategies, or the penalties of using certain technologies, you can make decisions about what is right or wrong for your site.

I've been creating computer graphics for the past 19 years and have watched tools and computer hardware come a long way. Even so, it's truly amazing how frustrating computers can be at times and how much time can be eaten up by things that don't work right or by wrestling with inefficient tools.

My goal is to spare you some of the pain by sharing my favorite tips, tools, and techniques, as well as the ever-present "gotchas" that plague those of us doing this work. Don't forget that web design is still in its infancy. Anyone who claims to be an expert has been doing this work for less than a decade, which is a pretty short time in the scheme of things.

My attitude is that we are all new at this stuff, even those so-called "expert" folks. I consider myself both a student and a teacher of web design. There's never been a reason to understand file compression, navigational techniques, color palettes, animation, and sound in one visual design discipline. And visual design should not be entirely separated from information design and/or programming design. Great sites work on all levels, not just visual design. The Web makes it possible and necessary to combine many different disciplines at once, and it's one rare superhuman who can do it all well.

I hope this book is helpful to you. If it is, I have done my job.

WHAT'S NEW IN DWG4

If you own an older edition of this book, you might be wondering what's new in this edition and whether you should buy anew. For that reason, I thought it would be valuable to share a list of what's new so you can make your decision easily and decide if these new additions are of value to you.

> Web Aesthetics

> Establishing Goals

> Information Architecture

> Comping & Prototyping

> Accessibility Issues

> XHTML

> Creating Community

> Adding Programming Features

> Usability

> Getting Listed

HOW DWG.4 WORKS

It's always tricky to write about web design, because there are so many overlapping principles and concepts. For example, tables can be used for layout and alignment or for cutting apart images to save on file size and downloading time. Teaching about linked graphics and navigation involves both image creation techniques and HTML or CGI. Sometimes, making the decision about which chapter to put with which subject is difficult! For this reason, I have intentionally structured this book so that readers can approach it in a nonlinear manner. Whenever a subject is mentioned in more than one chapter, it is clearly noted.

Those who use the Web for information often wonder if they need to buy a book, when so much information is available for free right on the Web. Indeed, the Web is an invaluable resource, and this book is not meant to be a substitute for it. Few will dispute the advantages to having all the information you need in a compact, transportable, and easy-to-read format. Books have not lost their importance in the age of networked information, but instead must work in tandem with electronic resources to be as effective as possible. This book (of course!) has a sister web site—http://www.lynda.com/books/dwg4.

Although it might be possible to read or skim this book in a single day, the information inside is far too overwhelming to absorb in a single sitting. It took me many months to write this fourth edition. Even with that many months, I could not have possibly understood the task at hand without many more years of experience under my belt as a computer graphics artist and teacher. The task of collecting all this information in one place is enormous and, frankly, never feels finished. The Web changes and evolves constantly, but once the ink is dry on this book's pages, it will forever be there.

That's why there are many references to outside information sources in this book. Everything from other URLs, other books, magazines, conferences, newsgroups, mailing lists, and CD-ROMs are offered as support resources whenever a new subject is touched upon. I wrote this book with the full understanding that information will change and evolve, and I've given you outside channels to get to that new information. Updates and errata will be posted at my web site as well. Just remember how to spell my name—with a "y"—and you'll be able to email me or check in on my web site at any time. I can't promise to answer everyone, but I respond whenever time permits. Enjoy the book, and I hope to see you on the Web!

lynda@lynda.com | http://www.lynda.com

DESIGNING WEB GRAPHICS.4   What the Chapters Cover

dwg.4

NOTES

getting Started

introduction

This chapter takes a look at the various issues that surround the setup of a "web design studio." It also outlines the different choices for getting started. This chapter covers career decisions, pricing standards (or lack thereof), educational resources, and hardware/software guidelines.

Not all readers of this book want to be professional web designers. Many people have personal web sites and want to improve their graphics and design skills for the sole reason that it is gratifying to make a great-looking site. Some of you are already making a living through web design, or are setting up a design studio as a business for the first time. Feel free to skip around and just read the sections that apply to your interests and goals.

> Careers

> Training

> Skills Assessment

> Portfolio

> Pricing

> Hardware

> Software

Lynda's Career Counseling

If you were to take a poll of professional web designers and query them about their histories before they became involved with the Web, you would be amazed at how many disparate background specialties you would find. We're in an era where web design is so new that very few people knew this was what they wanted to be when they grew up.

Therefore, if you are new at this (and all of us are really, considering that the Web is only a few years old), you are not alone. Basically, almost everybody is in the same camp. Those who excel in this industry are always self-taught in something, be it design, programming, or project management.

Schools and universities are finally starting to offer classes, certification, and degrees in web development, but very few professionals in the workplace are products of a formal web education. Even if you have had the luxury of web-specific training, the industry is in constant flux, and the skill of teaching one's self will always be at a premium.

The questions to ask when heading down the web design career path are:

> Where do I get training?

> What skills will employers expect?

> What kind of portfolio should I build?

> How do I know what to charge?

> Should I start my own company?

> How do I find a job in this field?

The following sections will help you answer these questions and will direct you to resources for further exploration.

TRAINING

The term "training" has evolved over the years to include books, seminars, lectures, hands-on classes, certification, and online courses. Everyone has different learning styles, and it might be helpful to answer some questions about yourself before you embark on a training path.

> Do I learn best by "doing?"

> Do I learn best by "being shown?"

> Do I learn best by "studying?"

> Do I learn best by "examining other's work?"

You might learn best through combining all these means, but my experience as a teacher has taught me that most people have different learning styles. It's important to identify what type of "learner" you are and to choose training that best suits your learning style. If you can first identify what type of learner you are and accept that the most important aspect of training is that you actually learn something, then you can make intelligent choices about how to get the best training for your learning style.

If grade-point averages and/or certification are important to you, make sure they are important to your prospective employer. My experience has proven that most employers care more about the competence and quality of actual performed work than about grades or degrees. This is not to dismiss the value of a course that offers certification or grades. It is simply to forewarn you that it's often more important that you actually have a portfolio and real experience than a degree or high grade in a class.

When I taught full-time at **Art Center College of Design**, I used to tell my undergraduate and graduate students that it really didn't matter what grade they got in my class. It mattered much more if they actually learned and retained the information and could produce results in a real-world situation. Many of my students, based on a single class, went on to successful web design careers, and I'd like to think it was because the emphasis of my training was on practical results instead of grades.

Before you take a class, do a little research into the teaching methods of the teacher and see whether it fits your learning style. If it's possible, see if you can talk to other students who have taken the same class. There are lots of classes out there that aren't effective; it would be a shame to waste your time and money on one of them.

TEACH YOURSELF!

Very few people who are good at their fields learned everything they know in school. That is especially true of the Web. Here are some resources and ideas to help teach yourself web design and general design:

> Read web design and development books. It's often hard to tell the good from the bad, so try to find a review before you buy! Many online book resellers offer reader-generated reviews of books. (I also offer many personal recommendations throughout chapters of *Designing Web Graphics.4.*)

> Reverse engineer sites. If you find a site you like, view the source code! Chapter 9, *"HTML & XHTML"* will teach you how.

> Read web design magazines.

> Use Online web design and HTML resources.

> Join usenet groups or listservs.

> Attend conferences or take seminars.

IMPROVE YOUR GENERAL DESIGN SKILLS

I recently had the pleasure of interviewing Joe Sparks, creator of **Radiskull** and **Devil Doll** (http://www. joesparks.com). We had a spirited conversation about technology and, specifically, about the means to getting an education in technology. He holds a position that I agree with, which is to discourage designers from studying technology in school.

This might come as a surprise position, but his rationale struck a true chord for me. Technology, such as software, hardware, and delivery mediums (such as Web, CD-ROM, print, etc.) change often, and studying them in school is a partial waste of time. Besides, many students know more than their teachers in these areas, and learning about technology can often be more frustrating than it is productive. His point was to study with teachers who are masters in design and communication principles, as those principles rarely change. Study things like color, typography, composition, editing, story telling, and writing instead, and learn how to operate computer programs on your own if you can.

Joe's idea, which makes a lot of sense, is to tap into the instructors for what they know best and leave learning the new and ever-changing technology stuff for your own time. I thought it was an interesting perspective, which is why I shared it here.

Here's a short list of suggestions, if you don't have the luxury of attending design school. Even if you are design-school educated, you will probably still partake in the following suggestions:

> Read design books. Go to a bookstore and camp out in the design section, not the computer area!

> Read design magazines.

> Attend design conferences or seminars.

> Join a professional design association like AIGA (http://www.aiga.org).

> Go to museums and galleries for inspiration.

> Find your muse. Look to things in nature and life that inspire you artistically.

WHAT SKILLS ARE IMPORTANT?

If you want to market yourself as a web designer, you will find that almost every employer you talk to expects a different set of skills. At times, it will feel as if there is no end to what you need to know and learn in order to be marketable. In one sense, there is no end to what you could learn, but you do need to keep in mind that no one person can learn everything. So the question becomes, how high should you set your goals?

In my opinion, the following are skills that you will need day in and out as a web designer. You might notice a similarity between these lists and several more chapter names in this book! :-)

Core Skills	Additional Skills
Image Optimization	Storyboarding
Transparency	Flash
Background Tiles	Shockwave
Animation	Director
Layout	HTML & XHTML
Color	DHTML
Typography	JavaScript
Photoshop Layers	CSS
Alignment	Database & Applications

FIRST CAREER STEPS

Most first jobs in web design are what I would label as "production" jobs. You might not get asked to do anything more creative than to mass produce a bunch of images to fit into someone else's design. I highly recommend that you take these first jobs in your stride and have patience in climbing the career ladder. You will get an education you couldn't find elsewhere.

In my book *Deconstructing Web Graphics.2* (co-written with Jon Warren Lentz), one of my favorite web designers, Ammon Haggerty (http://www.qaswa.com), described his first job in multimedia design where he spent three months cutting masks in Photoshop. If you pay some dues doing grunt-like production work, you will share good company with many people like Ammon! It's a myth to think you will walk into the world and become a highly paid art director of a mainstream web site.

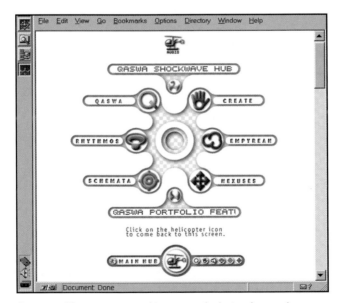

Ammon Haggerty owns his own web design firm and creates some of the coolest web graphics around (http://www.quaswa). He started his career doing production grunt work, just like you probably will!

THE IMPORTANCE OF A PORTFOLIO

Nothing is more important than a portfolio of examples to show a prospective employer. A good portfolio is more compelling than all the degrees and good grades the world has to offer. Building a portfolio can accomplish much more than good job prospects; it can also serve as an experimentation ground to teach yourself new skills.

As you read through this book, or browse the Web, you will likely get all kinds of neat ideas to try. Use your own web site as a playground for exploring this field. An employer is going to like that you are a self-starter and that you possess initiative. There will be plenty of times in your professional life when you'll get asked to do something you've never done before. Start practicing this on your own first!

If you are interested in getting hired to design rollover buttons, be sure you have a lot of different buttons on your web site. If you want projects where you get to choose the colors, experiment with different color schemes to prove this is something you're good at. If you hone into what you like to do best, and make sure you have plenty of examples that promote that skill, your chances of being hired to do what you love are much greater.

In addition to publishing your own web portfolio, nothing beats having real clients to list on a resume. If you are new at web design, see if you can design a site for a friend, relative, local company, or non-profit cause. Even if it never gets published to a real working URL, it will show a future employer that you've worked with other people's needs and ideas, and that you have some real-world experience.

KNOWING WHAT TO CHARGE

I've heard of prices for web site design ranging from $20 to $2 million. It can be that crazy; I swear! Of course, there are different levels of web sites—the cost of a two- or three-page site versus that of a thousand-page site is obviously going to be different.

A huge number of factors go into pricing. If your objective is to get a job at a web design firm, you will typically get the most money if you freelance and use your own computer. Of course, that is also the least secure method of employment! By accepting a salaried in-house position, you might make less but learn a lot more.

If you do plan to start your own company, there are lots of hidden costs. I always recommend that students get a job before they decide to start a business. You'll quickly see that there is a lot more to creating a successful company than knowing the technical or design side of web publishing. Try adding

accounting, bidding, public relations, marketing, advertising, office outfitting, business taxes, and health care costs to the list, and you'll start to get my drift!

It would be a big mistake for me to quote prices in this book because for every pricing rule, there will be always someone out there to break it. You will always have your big-name web design firms pricing their work higher than a new upstart company. You will always have famous illustrators who get paid more than recent art school graduates. There will always be inequities and a wide variation of pricing ranges.

If you're going to bid on building an entire site, it might help to know what other companies charge. Internet Service Providers (ISPs) often double as web design firms, and it's helpful to check out their pages to see what their pricing strategies are. Hint: They are often also a good source of work for freelance web designers!

For an ISP list, check out http://thelist.internet.com. It might help to find ISPs that are in your local area (or areas within which you'll be freelancing) to get a good idea of what pricing your specific market will bear.

In addition to knowing what the market rates are, it's important to understand and state your own boundaries. It's often not clear to clients that web sites are "designed," "programmed," and "maintained." You must be very clear about what services you are providing for the money, or you may discover that their expectation of what you owed them was different than yours.

Legal contracts are a very good thing. Either invest in a lawyer to write up a contract template for you, or use those that are available from professional groups, such as the **Graphics Artists Guild** (http://www.gag.org) or visit one of the many links at http://webdesign.about.com/compute/webdesign/cs/contracts/index.htm.

When I ran my own freelance motion graphics design company before my daughter was born, I learned firsthand how tricky bidding could be. It helped that I had worked in the field for many years before going out on my own. I knew how long it would take me to finish a given task and, therefore, knew how to charge so I'd be properly compensated. It took years of learning assessment skills to be good at my own business. Some clients were easy, and others were a nightmare. So many factors go into bidding—it involves good people and negotiation skills in addition to good technical skills.

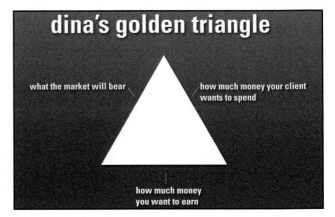

dina's golden triangle

what the market will bear

how much money your client wants to spend

how much money you want to earn

A teacher at our school, Dina Pialet, who is also the owner of **451 Advertising & Design** in Ventura, California (http://www.fourfiftyone.com), shared this bidding strategy with me: The price of a job is the result of how much money you want, what the client can pay, and what the market will bear.

PRICING RESOURCES

An established industry pricing resource can be purchased from the Graphics Artist Guild.

Graphic Artists Guild Handbook:
Pricing & Ethical Guidelines, 10th Edition
North Light Books
ISBN: 0-932102-11-5
http://www.gag.org

This book has historically set pricing guidelines for many areas of design, including print publications, merchandising, cartooning, animation, and technical illustration. They are starting to touch upon web design pricing, but this area is still too new to have reliable guidelines.

You can also visit their web site to learn about joining the Guild. They offer legal assistance for web designers and other types of artists, as well as chapter meetings, newsletters, and Guild events.

HOW TO FIND JOBS IN WEB DESIGN

Often, the best way to find a job is first to find a web design firm that you like. As you browse the Web, start visiting the "contact" or "credits" area of sites you like. Many sites post job listings or the name of the Human Resources contact.

You might also consider subscribing to a listserv related to web design. Job listings are often posted, as well as invaluable tips and commentary about web design. Important warning: If you do subscribe to a listserv, you can expect a lot (a lot) of extra email! A listserv is an email-based exchange to which many people subscribe. Some of these lists have thousands of subscribers, and hundreds of email messages are passed within a single day. You might consider subscribing to the archived versions of these lists or getting an email program that allows you to write filters so that the listserv email is stored separately from your personal email.

Favorite Web Design Listservs
http://www.babblelist.com
http://www.wwwac.org/#mailing_list
http://www.webdesign-l.com

Web/Design-Based Headhunters
http://www.aquent.com
http://www.wertco.com

Online Job Listings
http://www.monster.com

It might also help to post your resume and portfolio to your own web site. That way, you can list your URL at the bottom of a printed resume, and prospective employers can check you out online. This way, search engines can list your resume, too, if someone is doing a search for your specific skills. Which leads us directly to the next section…

USE SEARCH ENGINES!

The Web has more information and leads than any other resource in the universe. Your key to locating information about jobs, tips, techniques, software, and hardware (and just about anything else in the universe!) can be found by using search engines.

Search engines are web sites that offer URL listings to you based on keyword queries. In order to use a search engine, you must first understand that there are two different types of search engines: spider-based and directory-based.

A **spider-based search engine** gets its information from a software robot (also called a spider or crawler) that automatically visits and revisits web sites and catalogs their contents. A **directory-based search engine** gets its information from submissions (and often robots as well).

A spider-based search engine is good when you want to find every possible resource on a given subject. But sometimes, you'd rather find the information based on a more narrow search. For example, I used AltaVista, a spider-based search engine, to help my daughter research her bird report for school, which yielded a few hundred web page addresses for us to choose from. When I went to research family vacations, however, AltaVista would have yielded way too many results. I instead chose Yahoo!, a directory-based search engine. I only saw family vacation listings from companies that had submitted their URLs to Yahoo!, so there were less to choose from, and I had an easier decision.

In addition to knowing which type of search engine to use, it's also beneficial to know how to use a search engine. For example, when I typed Lynda Weinman into AltaVista, the response yielded a whopping 113,170 results! Instead, if I put Lynda Weinman in quotes ("Lynda Weinman") or placed a plus sign (Lynda+Weinman), it yielded a more accurate result of 5,392 web pages that included a reference to me.

If you'd like to learn how to use search engines (highly recommended!), visit these educational URLs:

Power Search for Anyone
By Danny Sullivan
http://searchenginewatch.com/facts/powersearch.html

Search Engines
By Bruce Grossan
http://www.webreference.com/content/search

DON'T BELIEVE EVERYTHING...

With all this talk about search engines, I thought it might be important to point out that not all information on the Web is accurate or reliable. The Web reflects many societies and cultures, many viewpoints, and ethics. You gotta be careful not to trust everything and browse the Web with a skeptical eye toward the truth. Don't believe everything you read.

HARDWARE CHOICES

In a day and age where each computer manufacturer is boasting faster, cheaper, and better computers than the next, you might wonder what type of system is suitable for your web publishing and design needs.

Macs and Windows machines are going to have the widest range of web design tools, and most of your web audience will be using one of these platforms. So, even if you're lucky enough to work on a high-end UNIX platform, you might consider getting one of these lower-end platforms to author web pages. At the very least, it will give you a reality checkpoint.

Chances are, you already have a computer. If you do not and are considering getting one to use for web design, then you have a challenging decision to make. Which flavor, Mac or Windows? Be forewarned that this is a topic of great passion and controversy. This subject is known to stir up more trouble than a political or religious debate. On the other hand, many people do regard this subject as sacred as religion!

MACS VERSUS PCS

Let me first state my own bias clearly. My first computer was an Apple II+ running CPM. My second computer was a Macintosh that I bought in May 1984. I bought my first PC in 1995, and currently own numerous Macs and PCs. (I'm a computer packrat; why sell 'em when the old ones aren't worth anything? Consider donating yours to a good cause instead!)

My bias is toward graphics and design (probably obvious), and I have taught design professionals for the past 12 years mostly using Macintosh computers. Most design professionals who have been into digital imaging for very long own Macintoshes because it used to be that it was the only computer platform that supported graphics. This is no longer true, although there is still a huge user base of Macintosh loyalists who grew up using their Macs and don't have any desire to switch to Windows.

This has created a great irony in web design: Many professional web designers and art directors use Macs, but most of the audience they design for uses Windows. I am not suggesting that you buy a Mac or that Windows machines are inferior. I'm simply stating that, for historical reasons, more visual designers use Macs.

It is a fact that there are many more PCs in circulation than Macs, and most of your audience will likely be using PCs. So, if you want to see your web site as most of your audience will see it, you will want to consider owning a PC. I think it's beneficial to have both platforms if at all possible. Virtually all professional web design firms and many independent web designers have both. Even if you buy one state-of-the-art computer for work and a used, older computer for testing, you'll be in better shape than if you only own one platform.

WHICH PLATFORM IS BEST?

There is truly no wrong or right platform. Regardless of which platform you buy, you will be able to design web pages. I strongly suggest that you try out the software and equipment you want to get before you buy it. Ask around. Find sites that you admire and ask the developers what equipment and software they recommend. There's no wrong decision here; just make sure your choice fits your budget, needs, and style.

It's always important to check your site on platforms other than that from which you authored. If you are lucky enough to own two platforms, this can be done in the luxury of your own office, studio, or home. If not, make sure you locate another system where you can preview your site. As future chapters describe in detail, what you see on one platform isn't necessarily what you see on others. This is a universal problem that you will encounter, regardless of which platform you decide to own.

tip

MAC VERSUS WINDOWS

Mac: You'll find the majority of design-based software comes out for the Mac and for Windows. Even so, most service bureaus that deal with desktop publishing are biased toward Macs. Most likely, you'll find more support among other artists and designers if you are on a Mac.

Windows: Most end users use Windows. Most browser software comes out first for Windows, and often never fully supports the Mac. Windows has a bigger market share, so equipment and peripherals are often less expensive. If you're technically inclined, you can build your own PC much easier than you can a Mac. This can not only save you money, but it allows you to put your resources into the aspects of the computer that are most important to you.

SYSTEM REQUIREMENTS

Processor speed: These days, we often hear about fast processor speeds, sometimes well in excess of 1500 megahertz. How important a factor is processing speed in terms of web design? Not very. Processing speed helps with 3D graphics rendering and the speed of rendering television or film-sized movies. It really helps when you're working with a huge, high-resolution image that's being prepped for printing. Making images for the Web requires that you work with low-resolution graphics and text files. Processing speed helps with complex, math-intensive computer operations. Unless you are planning to use your computer for those types of projects in addition to web design, a fast processor is going to buy you very little advantage.

RAM: Most computer veterans will assure you that you can never have too much RAM (**R**andom **A**ccess **M**emory). Extra RAM means that you can run simultaneous applications and with less likelihood of crashing. It lets you keep an HTML editor, imaging program, and web browser open at the same time. This will save you more time (and isn't your time worth money, too?) than you may imagine. Never skimp on RAM if you can possibly avoid it. Try to get at least 128MB, and more if possible. Seriously, you can never have too much RAM! Many web browsers require a minimum of 16 to run at all, and imaging software (especially Photoshop!) requires much more. How much do I have? 1 Gig of RAM! Do I use it? You betcha—no one will ever balk at having a lot of RAM.

Hard disk(s): This is the other resource you can never have too much of. I highly recommend getting a removable storage system in addition to a permanent hard drive. CD-ROM rewritable drives are commonplace now, and they come in quite handy to archive your work. As well, removable drives that have a hundred or more gigs now sell for a pittance

of what they used to. If you are going to be working regularly with a computer service bureau or outside company sharing files, be sure to see what they have so your removable storage system is compatible with theirs.

Video card: Most computer systems ship with a video card pre-installed. For this reason, many new computer buyers aren't even aware of their video card's features or capabilities. The video card is what dictates how many colors your monitor can display, and usually comes in 256-color versions (8-bit), thousands of colors (16-bit), or millions of colors (24-bit). Images look much better with millions (24-bit) of colors displays. If possible, go for a card with the highest bit depth (24-bit). Sometimes, it's possible to own a card that can be upgraded with additional video RAM (V-RAM) to upgrade its bit-depth capabilities.

Sound card: If you plan to work with sound, you will need a sound card. Again, many contemporary computers ship with these cards built in. The Web today offers mostly 8-bit sound because the files are smaller and faster to download. Just like with video, you'll get better results if you start with the highest quality and downscale for your audience later.

Monitor: The majority of your audience will be on standard 17" monitors. Even though we recommend that you design your site to work within a small screen (more on this in Chapter 15, *"Background Tiles"* and Chapter 21 *"Alignment & Tables"*), it's much easier to design on a larger monitor because you have more room for all the menus, windows, and palettes that most popular imaging programs sport these days. Almost any kind of monitor will do (make sure it will work with the kind of video card you get), but bigger is better for ease of use with design.

Scanner: Because you'll be working with low-resolution imagery, dots per inch and image quality are not your primary considerations when choosing a scanner for web design. Speed is the primary concern, so pick a scanner that can scan in color quickly. I used to own a multiple-pass scanner, which would take separate scans for each color channel: red, green, and blue. I finally broke down and got a one-pass scanner, and the time savings is worth every penny that I spent on it. For the resolution of web images, speed is the only factor that will make any difference in your production flow.

Digital camera: Having a digital camera is a great asset for working on web images. It's often only a matter of moments before you can transfer the image from your camera to your computer screen because both the camera and the computer deal with digital images. There is a huge range when it comes to features and quality of digital cameras. Because you're working with low-resolution images for web delivery, you do not need a high-quality digital camera—though having one is pretty cool if you can afford it. If you do other kinds of work besides web design, such as print, video, or film work, you should consider getting as good a digital camera as you can afford.

SOFTWARE

Software is a huge part of your investment in a web design studio, both in terms of money and time. If you haven't been around computers long, you might not realize that software changes all the time. If you buy version 1.0, next year you'll have to decide whether or not to upgrade to version 2.0, and that process will go on for years and years.

The truth about software is that it almost always improves with future versions. You may get along just fine with a version of software that you already own and decide against upgrading even if there are improvements. The point is that software is fluid by nature. If it stayed the same, we would complain. It doesn't make for the most comfortable purchasing decisions, however!

How many other professions or hobbies do you know of where the tools change and evolve constantly? You can bemoan this fact, or embrace it. If you plan to participate in the digital arts, though, changing software is a fact of life.

There are three categories of software: commercial software that you buy in the store, free software that you download off the Net, and shareware that you download today and pay for tomorrow (http://www. shareware.com is a great place to start).

Most likely, you will have to buy software sooner or later, even though at times it seems that everything anyone would ever want is found on the Web. The next section lists resources, makes recommendations, and helps you weigh some of these challenging software decisions.

imaging programs

To create graphics for the Web, you need some image-making software. This book concentrates primarily on Photoshop, ImageReady, and Fireworks advice. The World Wide Web has brought about a new era in software publishing, since most web imaging editors offer free trial versions from their web sites. This makes it possible for you to try tools before you buy them. Those of us who have been into computing since before the "WWW" really appreciate this fact, as I'm sure any newcomer will as well.

Adobe Photoshop (http://www.adobe.com) is the most popular imaging software among professional designers on any platform for almost any purpose—not just web design. Not surprisingly, Photoshop also has the most depth and features of all the imaging software reviewed in this book. I primarily use Photoshop, and this book is weighted in its favor. This book will show examples using Photoshop 6.0, though many exercises will work on older versions of Photoshop as well.

ImageReady (http://www.adobe.com) ships with Photoshop and is geared toward web- and screen-based imaging instead of print-based imaging. You can download a trial demo version from their site.

Fireworks (http://www.macromedia.com) is a web graphics software package that is a very strong image editor, which uses vectors and bitmaps to do the job. It also writes JavaScript rollovers and includes image optimization features. You can download a trial demo from their site.

Of course, other software tools will be mentioned in other chapters in this book, and tips, techniques, and training resources will be listed then. A discussion of HTML editors is found in Chapter 9, *"HTML & XHTML."*

---

tip

SHOP FOR DISCOUNTS

You may be frightened off by the prices of software, but don't pay retail! Look into the many mail-order catalogs for great discounts. Some of these catalogs have online resources as well:

Egghead http://www.egghead.com

Mac Zone http://www.maczone.com

PC Zone http://www.pczone.com

Also, if you take a class in Photoshop, sometimes you can get an impressive student discount. It might just cover the expense of the class and the software! Before you enroll, be sure to find out whether the school of your choice sells student-priced software and whether you qualify.

getting started

summary

Getting started in web design can present an overwhelming number of decisions and choices. This chapter focused on some guidelines to help you make those decisions. To summarize, these were the key points:

> If you're going to purchase formal training, make sure the class you choose best fits your personal learning style.

> Most great web designers are self-taught in one area or another. Learning to teach yourself is a key skill in this field.

> A web-based portfolio is more important than any grade, degree, or certification.

> Web sites are not created equally; you will find different pricing strategies for different types of sites.

> It's best to own a Mac and PC for authoring web pages and for checking compatibility.

> Try out software before you buy it by visiting software companies' web sites and downloading trial versions of their software.

Web AESTHETICS

INTRODUCTION

In the beginning, people thought that building a web site meant learning and using HTML. Then people realized they needed to learn graphics applications to make images for the Web. Then they realized they had to think about usability and navigation and accessibility. The process of making web sites has changed since the early days, which is a natural byproduct of maturity—maturity of web designers' designs, of users' tastes, and of users' expectations. Somewhere in the mix lies the importance of plain-old design: color design, typographic design, and layout design.

With all the teaching and lecturing I've done, I have met thousands of web designers and developers face-to-face. From these experiences, I have come to believe that people don't want to create bad-looking sites on purpose; they just don't know how to do better. Many people have gotten into web design without formal design training. This chapter won't be a substitute for years of training, but it is geared to help those who are seeking advice related to good design principles.

The definition of aesthetics from dictionary.com is "a guiding principle in matters of artistic beauty and taste; artistic sensibility." This definition addresses two components of aesthetics that this chapter deals with: the fact that aesthetics is about design principles and that calling something "beautiful or artistic" is a subjective judgment.

COLOR AESTHETICS

Few people are well trained in color theory, and most web developers, even seasoned artists, are insecure about their abilities to choose pleasing color schemes. You would think color theory would be a fun and creative subject. Unfortunately, it is approached in a very dry and technical manner in most color theory books. This chapter approaches color theory with a distinct web focus. It's my goal to back away from overtly technical explanations and gravitate toward easily identifiable principles and techniques.

I cannot, however, take credit for most of the ideas in this section; I can take credit only for the way in which the ideas are presented. My husband Bruce Heavin, who painted the wonderful cover to this book and all my others, is my color mentor. He has shared his color-picking methods with me, which has greatly enhanced my own color-picking abilities. I hope to pass down his pearls of wisdom to as many people as possible, hence, the approach of this chapter.

COLOR VOCABULARY TERMS

In order to describe color, we must first establish some common vocabulary terms. Here are the most important terms covered in this chapter:

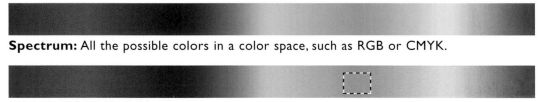

Spectrum: All the possible colors in a color space, such as RGB or CMYK.

Hue: Defines a specific location on the color wheel or in the color spectrum. In this example, a green hue has been selected.

Value: Describes the range from light to dark. In this example, a red hue is shown at varying values from dark to light.

Saturation: Defines the intensity of a color.

Muted: When people describe muted colors, they often refer to colors that have very little saturation.

Contrast: Separation between values. **Readability:** Relates to contrast.

Tint: The process of adding white to a color.

Tone: The process of adding black to a color.

CHOOSING COLOR THEMES

In order to choose pleasing color themes for your web pages and sites, it's necessary to learn a bit about color relationships. This next section will familiarize you with some terms that will later be shown in the context of web pages.

Many books on the market describe the emotion of color. Some might say that purple is for passion, red is for anger or attention, and blue is for tranquility. I don't believe anyone can or should project what a color means to someone else. It is totally subjective, regardless of what any book might tell you.

As well, color associations are cultural. To cite a specific example, someone from Israel came to our school in California and complained that the colors of our site were the same that were used by the Nazis for armbands that identified Jews during the holocaust. For this reason, he was deeply offended that the lynda.com site used yellow and black. As a person of Jewish descent, this wasn't an association I had ever made—I just liked the way yellow and black look together. I didn't change the colors of the site, because they don't carry that association for me. I would, however, be sensitive to using those colors if I were designing a Jewish web site.

Some clients might use pre-existing color schemes for their logos, printed brochures, or corporate identity. In such cases, you will need to work with their colors in a pleasing manner that is suitable for the Web.

Other times, you might have total freedom over a color scheme. Sometimes freedom is a dangerous thing in the hands of someone who doesn't know what to do with it! Rather than focus on the subjective and intangible aspects of color emotion, I've chosen here to focus on harmonic relationships of color.

COLOR RELATIONSHIP TERMS

Primary colors

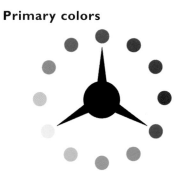

Secondary colors

Tertiary colors

Complementary colors

Split complementaries

Analogous

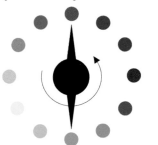
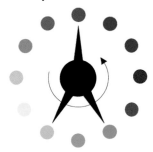

May be rotated in any direction on the wheel.

May be rotated in any direction on the wheel.

May be rotated in any direction on the wheel.

Monochromatic

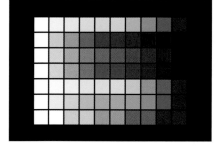

Takes a single hue and uses different values of that hue.

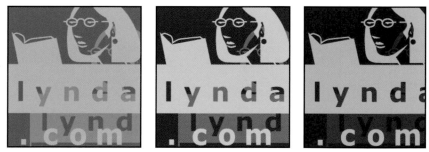

Three examples of monochromatic color schemes using (from left to right) cyan, warm colors, and cool colors.

APPLYING COLOR RELATIONSHIPS TO WEB DESIGN

Perhaps you can impress your clients or colleagues by knowing the difference between a complementary color and a tertiary color, but unless you can put that knowledge to dynamic use on your own site, it's not going to result in practical knowledge. The color relationship terms that were just established all have to do with choosing hues. But what about saturation and value? They are equally as important as hue, if not more so in most cases!

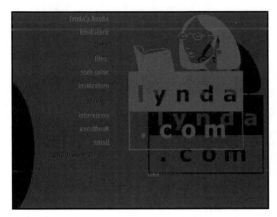

In this horrible example, the color scheme is analogous, using blue, red, and magenta hues. The readability is just plain horrible, if not impossible.

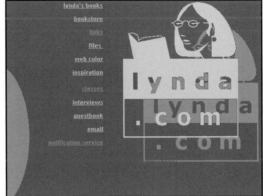

This better example uses the same analogous color scheme of blue, red, and magenta, but it also uses varied values and saturations. What a difference! It is not enough to choose a type of color palette; you must also learn to balance values and saturation of color at the same time for readable color relationships.

Looking at the horrible color combination, you'll notice that all the colors are fully saturated and close in value.

Looking at the better color combination, you'll notice that there is variety in saturation and value.

A great exercise to force yourself to think in these terms is to previsualize your web site in Photoshop, as I have, using layers. Try filling the layers with shades of gray, instead of color, to make the information you want to "pop" work correctly. After you've designed the page using grays, replace the grays with colors. You'll be amazed at how effective this is as a learning exercise.

Hues have replaced grays, and I'm getting the exact read I want with my colors.

By designing first in grayscale, you can train yourself to think of colors as values as well as hues.

tip

COLOR HARMONY PHOTOSHOP PLUG-IN

A remarkable Photoshop plug-in that came to my attention and relates to this subject is called **Hot Door Harmony**. You can download a trial version from http://www.hotdoor.com. At the time this chapter was written, the product was Mac-only, but a Windows version is on the way.

Hot Door Harmony lets you select colors through harmonic relationships. The program shows you color selections within the browser-safe spectrum. You can increase the Tint (lighten) or Tone (darken) settings to access different values, and you can copy the hexadecimal code for any color. I highly recommend that you download this tool for a test spin.

Hot Door Harmony is easy to use. Just click on which type of color scheme you want (for example, analogous) and then spin the ball.

If you understand the balance between hue, value, and saturation, you can force the read of your image to highlight what's important and subdue what isn't. It's quite empowering to grasp this concept. Applying it to your designs puts you in control of your color, so it will no longer be left to chance.

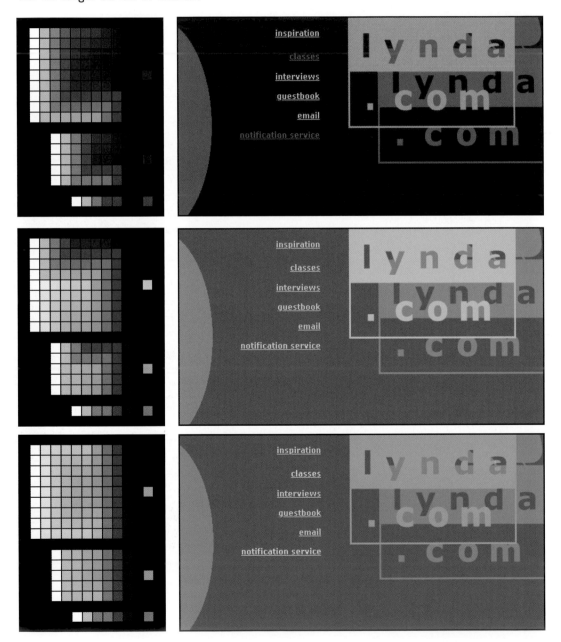

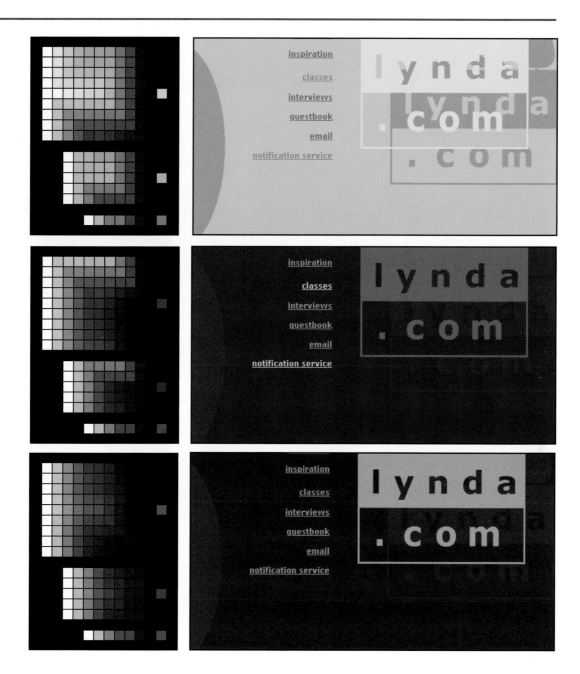

readability

Making a web page read with color the way you want is the key to effective communication. You want to draw your end user to the areas of your site that are most important, and you can do that in a variety of ways. Let's look at some examples of using color as a device for creating visual importance or hierarchy.

If I want my logo to be the most important element of this page, I can make it pop with color. If my navigation element is more important, I can choose to make that pop instead.

A very important exercise that you should try before you develop your opening page is to identify what the first, second, third, and fourth reads should be. Armed with a specific order of importance, you should be able to use many of the principles covered in this chapter to achieve your communication goals using color.

color gallery

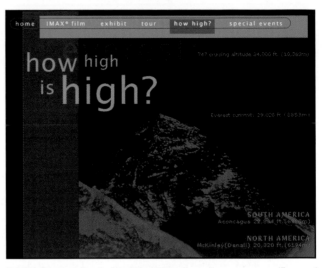

IMAX Everest: Roof of the World Film (http://www.mos.org/Everest/howhigh/howhigh.htm) is a great example of using complementary colors in an effective manner.

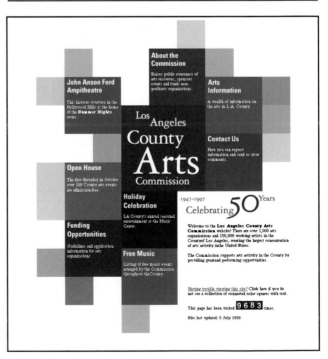

The LA County Arts Commission: (http://www.lacountyarts.org) uses a lot of colors, but they look unified because the creator paid close attention to the value of each color. Because the values are similar, even the many different hues look harmonious.

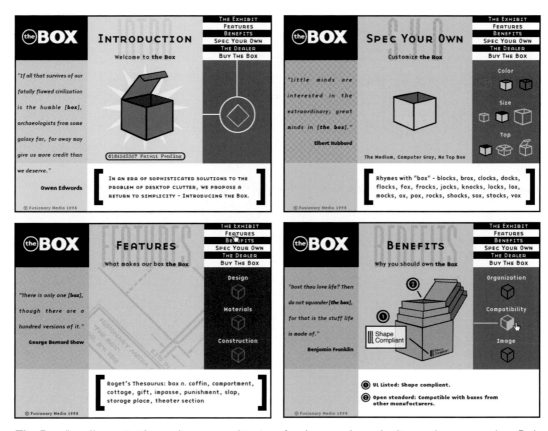

The Box (http://www.sixsides.com) uses a combination of analogous color and split complementary colors. Each area of the site is branded by color, which achieves a dual purpose of looking good and reinforcing navigation.

TYPOGRAPHY AESTHETICS

There are many limitations with typography on the Web—especially with HTML type—and many of these are discussed in Chapter 20, "HTML Type." This chapter instead focuses on the design principles of type. It also concentrates on type as an image of type, or type in a Flash movie, rather than HTML-generated type.

GLOSSARY OF KEY TYPOGRAPHIC TERMS

Before you venture too far into the subject of web type, let's establish a common vocabulary. The following examples cover many of the basics of type terminology.

> Most web browsers default to a serif typeface.
>
> This is a serif typeface!

Serif: A serif typeface has a stroke attached to the beginning or end of one of the main strokes of each letter. Many people think this style of type is the easiest to read as body copy. The default font in most browsers is a serif typeface: Times Roman on Macs and Times New Roman on PCs.

> You can specify san-serif fonts too.
>
> This is a san-serif typeface!

Sans-serif: A sans-serif typeface has no slab attached. Sans-serif type is specified with the **FONT FACE** tag, which is described fully later in this chapter.

note

CSS CAN DO

Many of the typographic functions listed in this section that are not possible with HTML are possible with CSS, which will be addressed in Chapter 23, "Cascading Style Sheets."

> monospace
> proportional

Monospace: A monospace font uses the same amount of horizontal width for every character, unlike a standard proportional font, which uses a different amount of space for each character. The top example shown here is set in Courier and could be accomplished in HTML with the **PRE** tag. You can specify monospace typefaces with the **PRE**, **CODE**, or **TT** tags.

> regular leading regular leading regular leading regular leading regular
> regular leading regular leading regular leading regular leading regular
> regular leading regular leading regular leading regular leading regular
> regular leading regular leading regular leading regular leading regular
> regular leading regular leading regular leading regular leading regular

Default leading: Leading (pronounced *ledding*) is the measurement of space between lines of type. The origin of the word "leading" dates to early days of typography when lead type was used. Blank pieces of lead were used between rows as spacers. This figure shows standard leading in HTML using no custom tags.

> looser leading looser leading looser leading looser leading looser lead
> looser leading looser leading looser leading looser leading looser lead
> oser leading looser leading looser leading looser leading looser leading

Looser leading: This design can be re-created with CSS using the line-height property. You'll learn more about CSS in Chapter 23, "Cascading Style Sheets."

> **this text has default word spacing**
>
> **this text has word spacing of 125%**

Spacing: This is the amount of space between each letter of a word. This can be managed with CSS.

DROP CAPS CAN BE KEWEL

Drop cap: A drop cap is used with all capital letters to indicate that the first letter of a word should appear in a larger size. In HTML, you can create a drop cap by using the **FONT SIZE** tag or with CSS, which is the preferred method.

> FOR HOTWIRED MEMBERS
> Test Patterns presents pet projects that kept us up nights: MiniMind, KHOT, and the amazing Beta Lounge.

Small caps: HotWired uses small caps on its front page ad. This example shows the use of small caps as a form of headline. Different sized text is best typeset using CSS.

> e palette, as I so named it, is the actual pal
> within their browsers. The palettes used by th
> . This palette is based on math, not beauty. |
> rs in this palette, but Netscape, Mosaic and |

Body text: The body text, or body copy, of a document is the main block of text.

The Browser Safe Color Palette

By Lynda Weinman

Headline text: A headline is used to break up information. It can do so by being larger in size, a different color, or a different font. It might have an underline, bold, or other visual treatment, which will cause it to stand out.

Baseline shift: Enables you to change the position of a single character up or down.

Kerning: Enables you to adjust the spacing between individual characters. This can be achieved in CSS by using the **letter-spacing** property.

Leading adjustment: Enables you to specify a particular leading by using point size measurements. This can be achieved in CSS by using the **line-height** property

Word spacing: Enables you to adjust the space between words. This can be achieved in CSS by using the **letter-spacing** property.

Tracking: Enables you to adjust the global spacing between letters.

TYPE 101

Does type design fascinate you, but you really don't know much about it? It is a fascinating subject indeed and a rather complex science. I've selected some excellent resources for you to use to train yourself in type terms and issues. There are a number of interactive, type education-based sites on the Web. Here are two of my favorites.

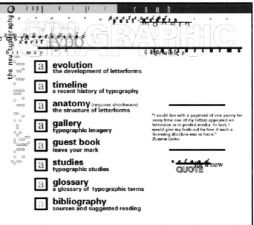

counterSPACE (http://counterspace.motivo.com).

typoGRAPHIC (http://www.rsub.com/typographic).

LEARN MORE ABOUT TYPOGRAPHY

Microsoft Typography
An excellent essay on hinting. Read all about it here!
http://www.microsoft.com/typography/hinting/hinting.htm

The Microsoft Typography Glossary
A disagreeably facetious type glossary, which includes the low-down on all the type jargon you can possibly absorb.
http://www.microsoft.com/typography/glossary/content.htm

Daniel Will-Harris
Choosing and using type and prolific verbiage.
http://www.will-harris.com/use-type.htm

webreview.com
Search the following site for "will-harris."
http://webreview.com/archives.shtml

CounterSPACE
A beautifully executed interactive study in type created in Macromedia Flash.
http://counterspace.motivo.com

typoGRAPHIC
A thorough (beautifully designed) look into the world of typography.
http://www.rsub.com/typographic

FONTS FOR THE WEB

There are two distinct ways to publish text to the Web: with ASCII text (created by coding HTML or CSS) or with pictures of text in the form of web graphics such as GIF, JPEG, or SWF (Flash).

Below is an example of two pages that use HTML-generated text. The one to the left has specified Verdana as the font, while the one to the right shows the default typeface of the Web: Times Roman. In order for visitors to see this content, they must have these fonts pre-installed on their systems. That's why your choices for HTML-generated fonts are more limited than your choices for type that you publish as a graphic.

One of the reasons designers have chosen to ignore text is that it's been really difficult to dictate the appearance and structure of text on web pages.

Verdana 8pt
aobocodoeofogohoiojokolomonopoqoro
albicldlelflglhljlklmlnlolplqlrlsltlulvlwlxl

One of the reasons designers have chosen to ignore text is that it's been really difficult to dictate the appearance and structure of text on web pages.

MS Sans
aobocodoeofogohoiojokolomonopo
albicldlelflglhljlklmlnlolplqlrlsltlulv

One of the reasons designers have chosen to ignore text is that it's been really difficult to dictate the appearance and structure of text on web pages.

Verdana 10pt
aobocodoeofogohoiojokolomonopo
albicldlelflglhljlklmlnlolplqlrlsltlulv

This site has specified Verdana as the font.

A lot of people credit me with the browser-safe palette, but it's a misplaced honor (if you can call it that!). I do have the distinction of being the first author to identify and publish the colors - but I can't take credit for creating them.

The browser-safe palette exists because it was born from a mathematical formula. Programmers who write browsers and software applications love mathematical arrays because they are logical and can be

There may be a resurgence in the need for the browser-safe palette when designing for alternative online publishing devices, such as cell phones and PDAs. Those systems are still in 1-bit (black and white) or 8-bit color. Right now, very few people are designing their web sites to work on those systems, so the need for the browser-safe color palette is definitely downgraded to a mere shadow of its former glory.

I'll venture to say it's safe to design

This example uses the pre-installed default typeface Times Roman.

When you publish HTML-generated text, it's necessary that the visitors to your page have pre-installed whatever font you specified. This limits the kinds of typefaces that you can use. You will learn how to specify different fonts for HTML-generated text in Chapter 20, *"HTML Type."*

---

default fonts for windows and macintosh

windows 12 pt type	mac 12 pt type
Arial	**Chicago**
Arial Black	Courier
Arial Narrow	Geneva
Arial Rounded MT Bold	Helvetica
Book Antiqua	Monaco
Bookman Old Style	New York
Century Gothic	Palatino
Century Schoolbook	Times
Courier	Verdana
Courier New	Georgia
Garamond	
MS Dialog	
MS Dialog Light	
MS LineDraw	
MS Serif	
MS Sans Serif	
MS SystemX	
Times New Roman	
Verdana	
Georgia	

Although the list might change with newer operating systems, this is a valuable list of fonts that come pre-installed on Windows and Macintosh machines. When working with the **FONT** tag and CSS (which you'll learn how to do in Chapters 20 and 23), this is a good list to refer to when choosing fonts for HTML-generated text delivery.

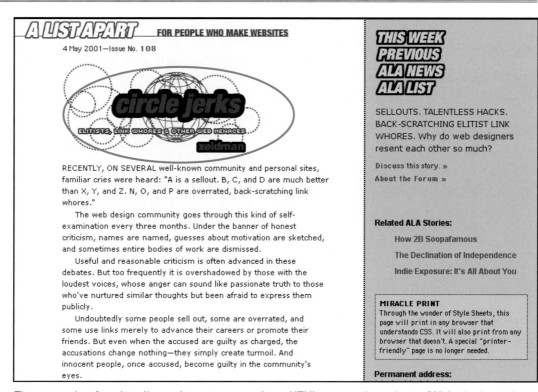

This screen shot from http://www.alistapart.com combines HTML-generated text (using CSS for leading, indents, and position, which you'll learn about in Chapter 23, "Cascading Style Sheets"). The text that is set as a graphic is circled. It's possible not only to use different fonts than what you can with HTML-generated delivery, but you can add effects to the type, such as outline colors, glows, and extra graphic elements.

note

PROS & CONS OF HTML-GENERATED & IMAGES OF TEXT

If you care about creating beautiful typography, you might think to yourself that you're never going to use HTML-generated text because it is so restrictive. CSS now offers a lot of flexibility and control, so this is no longer true. This is not to suggest that you favor one text delivery method over another—it's just to educate you regarding the trade-offs of your choices. Here are some important things to consider:

> CSS-generated type is searchable, accessible, can be translated to other languages, and is small in file size.

> Pictures of text afford more design freedom. You can use any font and style and the end user does not have to own the font to view the picture.

Legibility Issues

The issue of color readability was already addressed, but typography on the Web (and off) has many legibility issues of its own. One of these issues is whether to use serif or sans-serif type. In the olden days of type education, it was widely believed that serif typefaces were easier to read as body text and sans-serif fonts were easier to read as headlines.

Serifs become inefficient below 12 pt. digitally speaking.
12 pt. Times New Roman

Serif ASCII text on the Web.

Sans-serif fonts are clearer at these small sizes.
12 pt. Verdana

Sans-serif ASCII text on the Web.

With ASCII text, sans-serif typefaces are much easier to read than serif. This type could be created using the **FONT FACE** element in HTML (see Chapter 20, "*HTML Type*") or with style sheets (see Chapter 23, "*Cascading Style Sheets*").

Font Differences Across Platforms

You would think that an ASCII typeface would look the same between Mac and Windows platforms. Sadly, this is not the case. Have you ever gone to a site that was beautifully designed, but you couldn't read the text? It could be a cross-platform problem with the font that was chosen for the page.

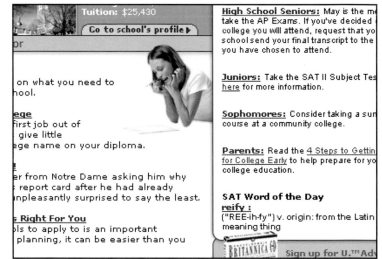

At **Colleges.com** the HTML was written to contain two ASCII fonts: Verdana (left) and Arial (right). While Verdana reads beautifully on Mac or Windows, Arial does not. If you think you'll have a Macintosh audience, don't use Arial.

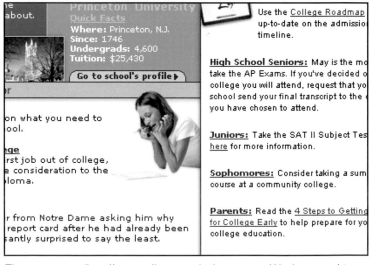

The same page (http://www.colleges.com) shown on a Windows machine—Verdana and Arial both look fine.

Browser-Safe or Not?

by Lynda Weinman

A lot of people credit me with the browser-safe palette, but it's a misplaced honor (if you can call it that!). I do have the distinction of being the first author to identify and publish the colors - but I can't take credit for creating them.

The browser-safe palette exists because it was born from a mathematical formula. Programmers who write browsers and software applications love mathematical arrays because they are logical and can be

There may be a resu for the browser-safe designing for alterna publishing devices, s and PDAs. Those sy bit (black and white) Right now, very few designing their web those systems, so th browser-safe color downgraded to a m former glory.

I'll venture to say it's

Browser-Safe or Not?

by Lynda Weinman

A lot of people credit me with the browser-safe palette, but it's a misplaced honor (if you can call it that!). I do have the distinction of being the first author to identify and publish the colors - but I can't take credit for creating them.

The browser-safe palette exists because it was born from a mathematical formula. Programmers who write

There may be a resur for the browser-safe designing for alternati publishing devices, su and PDAs. Those sys bit (black and white) Right now, very few designing their web si those systems, so the browser-safe color p downgraded to a me

The default font for the Web: Times Roman. My opinion? There are better fonts to use for readability. However, this font choice (or lack of choice, in this example) works between the platforms.

Browser-Safe or Not?

by Lynda Weinman

A lot of people credit me with the browser-safe palette, but it's a misplaced honor (if you can call it that!). I do have the distinction of being the first author to identify and publish the colors - but I can't take credit for creating them.

The browser-safe palette exists because it was born from a mathematical formula. Programmers who write browsers and software applications love mathematical arrays because they are logical and can be generated programmatically. As a designer, the web-safe color palette leaves a lot to be desired. Mostly, it's

There may be a resu for the browser-safe designing for alterna publishing devices, and PDAs. Those sys bit (black and white) Right now, very few designing their web those systems, so th browser-safe color p downgraded to a me former glory.

I'll venture to say it's without the palette. however, that many hire designers and d

Browser-Safe or Not?

by Lynda Weinman

A lot of people credit me with the browser-safe palette, but it's a misplaced honor (if you can call it that!). I do have the distinction of being the first author to identify and publish the colors - but I can't take credit for creating them.

The browser-safe palette exists because it was born from a mathematical formula. Programmers who write browsers and software applications love mathematical arrays because they are logical and can be generated programmatically. As a

There may be a resu for the browser-safe designing for alterna publishing devices, s and PDAs. Those sys bit (black and white) Right now, very few designing their web those systems, so th browser-safe color p downgraded to a me former glory.

I'll venture to say it's without the palette.

Georgia works on either platform, although it's still not as legible as a sans-serif font in my opinion. It is better than the default serif font, however, because it's slightly more legible.

Browser-Safe or Not?

by Lynda Weinman

A lot of people credit me with the browser-safe palette, but it's a misplaced honor (if you can call it that!). I do have the distinction of being the first author to identify and publish the colors - but I can't take credit for creating them.

The browser-safe palette exists because it was born from a mathematical formula. Programmers who write browsers and software applications love mathematical arrays because they are logical and can be generated programmatically. As a designer, the web-safe color palette leaves a lot to be desired. Mostly, it's contains far less light and dark colors than I wish it did, and is heavy on highly saturated colors and low on muted, tinted or toned colors.

There may be a resurg the browser-safe palet for alternative online pu such as cell phones a systems are still in 1-b or 8-bit color. Right nov are designing their web those systems, so the browser-safe color pal downgraded to a mere former glory.

I'll venture to say it's sa without the palette. Ke however, that many co designers and develop badge of Web design these colors, so you m how to use them if you point, the palette is bui

Browser-Safe or Not?

by Lynda Weinman

A lot of people credit me with the browser-safe palette, but it's a misplaced honor (if you can call it that!). I do have the distinction of being the first author to identify and publish the colors - but I can't take credit for creating them.

The browser-safe palette exists because it was born from a mathematical formula. Programmers who write browsers and software applications love mathematical arrays because they are logical and can be generated programmatically. As a designer, the web-safe color palette leaves a lot to be desired. Mostly, it's

There may be a resur for the browser-safe p designing for alternativ devices, such as cell Those systems are st white) or 8-bit color. R people are designing work on those system the browser-safe colo downgraded to a mere former glory.

I'll venture to say it's s without the palette. Ke however, that many co

Helvetica looks lousy on the Mac, even at a big size. It's very hard to read… Don't you agree? Helvetica doesn't render well on a Mac at any size. Notice how the letters touch each other, making readability difficult?

-1 Arial

As a designer, the web-safe color palette leaves a lot to be desir Mostly, it's contains far less light and dark colors than I wish it d and is heavy on highly saturated colors and low on muted, tinted toned colors.

-2

As a designer, the web-safe color palette leaves a lot to be desired. Mostly, it's contains far less light and dark colors than I wish it did, and is heavy on highly saturated colors and low on muted, tinted or toned colors.

-3

As a designer, the web-safe color palette leaves a lot to be desired. Mostly, it's contains far less light and dark colors than I wish it did, and is heavy on highly saturated colors and low on muted, tinted or toned colors.</p>

Arial works fine on a Mac as long as it isn't published at a size smaller than 12 points. Once it gets smaller, it's impossible to read on a Mac.

Browser-Safe or Not?

by Lynda Weinman

A lot of people credit me with the browser-safe palette, but it's a misplaced honor (if you can call it that!). I do have the distinction of being the first author to identify and publish the colors - but I can't take credit for creating them.

The browser-safe palette exists because it was born from a mathematical formula. Programmers who write browsers and software applications love mathematical arrays because they are logical and can be generated programmatically. As a designer, the web-safe color palette leaves a lot to be desired. Mostly, it's

There may be a resurg for the browser-safe pa designing for alternativ devices, such as cell Those systems are st white) or 8-bit color. R people are designing t work on those system the browser-safe color downgraded to a mere former glory.

I'll venture to say it's s without the palette. Ke however, that many co

Arial always looks great on Windows.

-1 Default Face

As a designer, the web-safe color palette leaves a lot to be desired. Mostly, it's contains far less light and dark colors than I wish it did, and is heavy on highly saturated colors and low on muted, tinted or to colors.

-2

As a designer, the web-safe color palette leaves a lot to be desired. Mostly, it's contains far less light and dark colors than I wish it did, and is heavy on highly saturated colors and low on muted, tinted or toned colors.

-3

As a designer, the web-safe color palette leaves a lot to be desired. Mostly, it's contains far less light and dark colors than I wish it did, and is heavy on highly saturated colors and low on muted, tinted or toned colors.</p>

Notice at the −3 size how difficult the default font, Times Roman, is to read?

-1 Georgia

As a designer, the web-safe color palette leaves a lot to be desi Mostly, it's contains far less light and dark colors than I wish it and is heavy on highly saturated colors and low on muted, tin toned colors.

-2

As a designer, the web-safe color palette leaves a lot to be desired. Mostly, it's contains far less light and dark colors than I wish it did, and is heavy on highly saturated colors and low on muted, tinted or toned colors.

-3

As a designer, the web-safe color palette leaves a lot to be desired. Mostly, it's contains far less light and dark colors than I wish it did, and is heavy on highly saturated colors and low on muted, tinted or toned colors.</p>

At the smallest size, the serifs in Georgia make it hard to read.

-1 Verdana

As a designer, the web-safe color palette leaves a lot to be desir Mostly, it's contains far less light and dark colors than I wish it di and is heavy on highly saturated colors and low on muted, tinted toned colors.

-2

As a designer, the web-safe color palette leaves a lot to be desired. Mostly, it's contains far less light and dark colors than I wish it did, and is heavy on highly saturated colors and low on muted, tinted or toned colors.

-3

As a designer, the web-safe color palette leaves a lot to be desired. Mostly, it's contains far less light and dark colors than I wish it did, and is heavy on highly saturated colors and low on muted, tinted or toned colors.</p>

Even at the smallest size, you can still read the sans-serif font. I do have a strong bias toward Verdana as the best cross-platform font for the Web.

VERDANA & GEORGIA

Until now, most web publishers and designers have lived in a chocolate and vanilla typographical world. Web browsers have defaulted to using two typefaces: a serif font for standard text and a monospace font for code.

The trouble is, the basic font choices in browsers are bland at best. Arial and Helvetica suck! They are "ugly." In fact, all the fonts that ship as default fonts on the various platforms are "ugly" What makes them ugly? Here's a short lesson in identifying the ugly factors.

Digital type is generally not well hinted (the uniform spacing between letters) for the screen. Letters often touch one another, making them hard to read—especially in very small sizes (9 pt. and below). Serifs (the slabs at the ends of lines on each type character) improve readability when printed at high resolution, but they actually interfere with readability on the screen. Italics are even more problematic and are almost illegible in many sizes and on many platforms.

For us to get a wider range of choices for type on the Web, fonts must be designed for the screen from the ground up. Microsoft took a leadership role in this endeavor by hiring renowned type designer **Matthew Carter** (ITC Galliard, Snell Roundhand, Charter, and Bell Centennial— the font used in phone books) to develop two screen-based font families for them.

Matthew Carter's two fonts (*Verdana* and *Georgia*) are beautifully designed for web delivery.

The differences between these font families make up a primer on what features work for screen-based typography. They were designed with a larger x-height (the size of ascenders, such as the letter *d*, and descenders, such as the letter *g*). Letter combinations such as *fi, fl,* and *ff* were designed clearly so they do not touch. Uppercase characters are a pixel taller than their lowercase counterparts when displayed at key screen sizes to improve readability. In addition, the spacing between characters is much looser, making it easier to scan quickly.

It took Matthew Carter two years to create these typefaces, and Microsoft gave his fonts away for free. This did the online community a great service, but giving away fonts won't work for people who earn their living designing type. You can read more about this subject later in the chapter when I cover font embedding.

One of the reasons designers have chosen to ignore text is that it's been really difficult to dictate the appearance and structure of text on web pages.

Verdana 8pt
aobocodoeofogohoiojokolomonopoqoro
alblcldlelflglhljlklmlnlolplqlrlsltlulvlwlxl

One of the reasons designers have chosen to ignore text is that it's been really difficult to dictate the appearance and structure of text on web pages.

MS Sans
aobocodoeofogohoiojokolomonopo
alblcldlelflglhljlklmlnlolplqlrlsltlulv

One of the reasons designers have chosen to ignore text is that it's been really difficult to dictate the appearance and structure of text on web pages.

Verdana 10pt
aobocodoeofogohoiojokolomonopo
alblcldlelflglhljlklmlnlolplqlrlsltlulv

This figure shows a comparison between Carter's Verdana and its counterpart, MS Sans.

One of the reasons designers have chosen to ignore text is that it's been really difficult to dictate the appearance and structure of text on web pages.

Georgia 10pt
aobocodoeofogohoiojokolomonopoqoro
alblcldlelflglhljlklmlnlolplqlrlsltlulvlwlxl

One of the reasons designers have chosen to ignore text is that it's been really difficult to dictate the appearance and structure of text on web pages.

Times New Roman 10pt
aobocodoeofogohoiojokolomonopoqoro
alblcldlelflglhljlklmlnlolplqlrlsltlulvlwlxl

One of the reasons designers have chosen to ignore text is that it's been really difficult to dictate the appearance and

Georgia 12pt
aobocodoeofogohoiojokolomonopoqo
alblcldlelflglhljlklmlnlolplqlrlsltlulvlwlxl

This figure shows Georgia compared to Times New Roman.

tip

GEORGIA & VERDANA

Verdana and Georgia
An excellent article about these two fonts written by Daniel Will-Harris.
http://www.webreview.com/1997/11_07/webauthors/11_07_97_4.shtml

Matthew Carter
An interview with the font creator.
http://www.webreview.com/1997/11_07/webauthors/11_07_97_10.shtml

FONT SIZE DIFFERENCES BETWEEN MACS & PCS

No, you are not nuts. If you have both a Mac and a PC, you might notice that standard default fonts look different on the two platforms. Fonts display larger on PCs than they do on Macs.

It looks as if Explorer, as of version 5, has dealt web design a new twist: Fonts will default to the same larger size regardless of whether they are on Mac or PC. This is not the case with Netscape, however, so there's still a discrepancy. The way around this is to use style sheets that are set to pixels. You will learn how to create such a style sheet in Chapter 23, *"Cascading Style Sheets."*

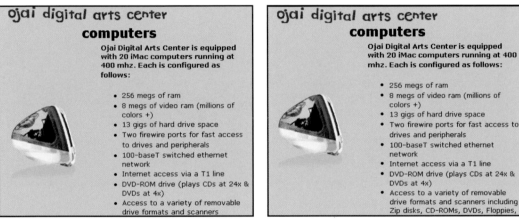

Internet Explorer 5 on Windows.

Internet Explorer 5 on Mac.

Netscape 4 on Windows.

Netscape 4 on Mac.

Note: On Internet Explorer the font size is the same regardless of whether viewed on Mac or PC. On the Mac, however, there is a discrepancy between Netscape and Explorer.

FONTS FOR DELIVERY AS WEB GRAPHICS

When designing headline type or special type elements such as navigation buttons or small amounts of body copy, it's acceptable to use graphic formats (GIF or JPEG) to publish images of type. Therefore, it's possible to use any font you want, because your end users don't have to own or install the typeface to view the content on their computers.

Therefore, in relation to producing headline text, it's possible to obtain for free or purchase as many fonts as you desire. This section will share some good resources for finding fonts on the Web—both for free and for a fee.

GREAT RESOURCES FOR ONLINE FONTS

There are tens of thousands of PostScript and TrueType fonts available to personal computer users. It's a great benefit to be able to view and order fonts online—especially during those late nights when you're designing something that's due the next day and you need a specific font you don't yet own. If you're looking for new fonts, check out the following URLs. Some of these font developers distribute their wares for free, and some do not. Regardless, all of these sites are worth visiting.

Fontastic
http://rover.wiesbaden.netsurf.de/~kikita

Chank Diesel
http://www.chank.com

Nekkton
http://www.donbarnett.com

Just van Rossum and Erik van Blokland
http://www.letterror.com

Fonthead Designs
http://www.fonthead.com

House Industries
http://www.houseind.com

Emigre Fonts
http://www.emigre.com

Handwriting Fonts
http://www.execpc.com/~adw

Letraset
http://www.letraset.com

Daniel Will-Harris' Personal Favorites
http://www.will-harris.com/faces98

ITC
http://www.itcfonts.com

Adobe's Type Browser
http://www.adobe.com/type

There are thousands of fonts available on the Web. Here are just a few: http://www.chank.com, http://rover. wiesbaden.netsurf.de/~kikita/, http://www.letterror.com, http://www.will-harris.com, http://www.emigre.com, and http://www.letraset.com.

BASIC STYLES OF TYPEFACES

When movable type was first invented, there was just one kind of typeface—a Roman face, which is characterized by its serifs. Today, there are many more styles, some of which are shown below.

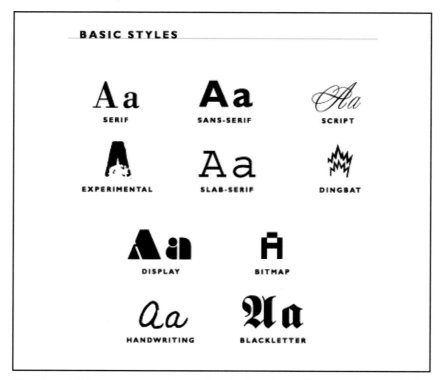

Most fonts fall into one or another of these basic styles: serif, sans-serif, script, display, bitmap, experimental, slab-serif, dingbat, handwriting, and blackletter.

DON'T USE TOO MANY FONTS

During the early days of desktop publishing, everyone who had a computer and a laser printer thought they were a designer. One of the hallmarks of "bad" design from those days was mixing too many typefaces on a single page. While this isn't as huge a problem on the Web, it still pays to know how to work artistically with few fonts. This is a case of "less is more."

WHAT IS A FONT FAMILY?

When I taught at **Art Center College of Design** in Pasadena, I remember there was a typography class (taught by someone else) that always had a wait list. During the course of this class, students worked for 14 solid weeks and were "only" allowed to use a single font! This is actually a great way to teach and learn typography. The exercise of working with a single font teaches the benefits of working with a single font family.

Triplex Condensed Serif

Triplex Condensed Serif Black

Triplex Serif Bold

Triplex Serif Extra Bold

Triplex Serif Light

A font family is a single font that comes in different styles and weights. This is an example of **Triplex**, which can be purchased at http://www.emigre.com. Here, the condensed, bold, and light faces look different enough, but related. It's possible to create a lot of different design communications using this single font.

If you visit http://counterspace.motivo.com and select the **Counterspace** menu item, you will find a wonderful Flash movie that describes the anatomy of type. Within this presentation is a section on the artist's favorite fonts. Notice how these studies are made to look so different even though each study uses a single typeface.

By varying the size, weight, and color of a single font, notice how much variation and difference can be achieved.

ALIASING OR ANTI-ALIASING

Most digital artists prefer the way anti-aliasing looks, but anti-aliasing is not always the best technique with typography. Very small type actually looks worse and quite mushy if it's anti-aliased. Think about HTML type, the type on your computer desktop, and the type in a word processor. Very small type sizes (12pt. and smaller) do not look good anti-aliased.

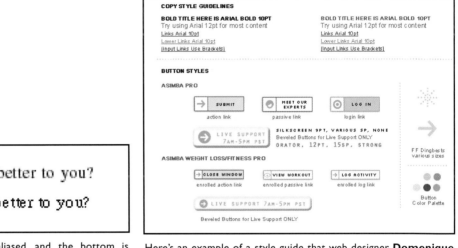

which looks better to you?

which looks better to you?

The top version is anti-aliased, and the bottom is aliased. Which looks better to your eye? I prefer aliased type at small point sizes and often find anti-aliasing difficult to read.

Here's an example of a style guide that web designer **Domenique Sillett** (http://www.littleigloo.com) created for a client to show different button styles and colors for their web site. She used an aliased font called Silkscreen, which is perfect for small buttons because it is so readable.

Font Sample

THIS IS SILKSCREEN.
THIS IS SILKSCREEN BOLD.
THIS IS SILKSCREEN EXPANDED.
THIS IS SILKSCREEN EXPANDED BOLD.

You can download the free Silkscreen font from http://www.kottke.org/plus/type/silkscreen/index.html.

Serif Type as Image

San-Serif Type as Image

Hybrid Type as Image

When type is created as an image or inside a Flash movie at larger point sizes (36 pt. shown here), it is legible regardless of whether it is serif, sans-serif, or a hybrid font.

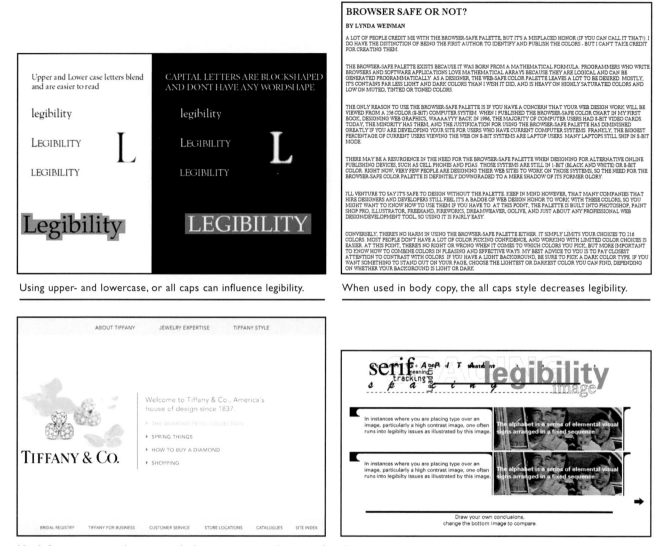

Using upper- and lowercase, or all caps can influence legibility.

BROWSER SAFE OR NOT?

BY LYNDA WEINMAN

A LOT OF PEOPLE CREDIT ME WITH THE BROWSER-SAFE PALETTE, BUT IT'S A MISPLACED HONOR (IF YOU CAN CALL IT THAT!). I DO HAVE THE DISTINCTION OF BEING THE FIRST AUTHOR TO IDENTIFY AND PUBLISH THE COLORS - BUT I CAN'T TAKE CREDIT FOR CREATING THEM.

THE BROWSER-SAFE PALETTE EXISTS BECAUSE IT WAS BORN FROM A MATHEMATICAL FORMULA. PROGRAMMERS WHO WRITE BROWSERS AND SOFTWARE APPLICATIONS LOVE MATHEMATICAL ARRAYS BECAUSE THEY ARE LOGICAL AND CAN BE GENERATED PROGRAMMATICALLY. AS A DESIGNER, THE WEB-SAFE COLOR PALETTE LEAVES A LOT TO BE DESIRED. MOSTLY, IT'S CONTAINS FAR LESS LIGHT AND DARK COLORS THAN I WISH IT DID, AND IS HEAVY ON HIGHLY SATURATED COLORS AND LOW ON MUTED, TINTED OR TONED COLORS.

THE ONLY REASON TO USE THE BROWSER-SAFE PALETTE IS IF YOU HAVE A CONCERN THAT YOUR WEB DESIGN WORK WILL BE VIEWED FROM A 256 COLOR (8-BIT) COMPUTER SYSTEM. WHEN I PUBLISHED THE BROWSER-SAFE COLOR CHART IN MY FIRST BOOK, DESIGNING WEB GRAPHICS, WAAAAYYY BACK IN 1996, THE MAJORITY OF COMPUTER USERS HAD 8-BIT VIDEO CARDS. TODAY, THE MINORITY HAS THEM, AND THE JUSTIFICATION FOR USING THE BROWSER-SAFE PALETTE HAS DIMINISHED GREATLY. IF YOU ARE DEVELOPING YOUR SITE FOR USERS WHO HAVE CURRENT COMPUTER SYSTEMS, FRANKLY, THE BIGGEST PERCENTAGE OF CURRENT USERS VIEWING THE WEB ON 8-BIT SYSTEMS ARE LAPTOP USERS. MANY LAPTOPS STILL SHIP IN 8-BIT MODE.

THERE MAY BE A RESURGENCE IN THE NEED FOR THE BROWSER-SAFE PALETTE WHEN DESIGNING FOR ALTERNATIVE ONLINE PUBLISHING DEVICES, SUCH AS CELL PHONES AND PDAS. THOSE SYSTEMS ARE STILL IN 1-BIT (BLACK AND WHITE) OR 8-BIT COLOR. RIGHT NOW, VERY FEW PEOPLE ARE DESIGNING THEIR WEB SITES TO WORK ON THOSE SYSTEMS, SO THE NEED FOR THE BROWSER-SAFE COLOR PALETTE IS DEFINITELY DOWNGRADED TO A MERE SHADOW OF ITS FORMER GLORY.

I'LL VENTURE TO SAY IT'S SAFE TO DESIGN WITHOUT THE PALETTE. KEEP IN MIND HOWEVER, THAT MANY COMPANIES THAT HIRE DESIGNERS AND DEVELOPERS STILL FEEL IT'S A BADGE OF WEB DESIGN HONOR TO WORK WITH THESE COLORS, SO YOU MIGHT WANT TO KNOW HOW TO USE THEM IF YOU HAVE TO. AT THIS POINT, THE PALETTE IS BUILT INTO PHOTOSHOP, PAINT SHOP PRO, ILLUSTRATOR, FREEHAND, FIREWORKS, DREAMWEAVER, GOLIVE, AND JUST ABOUT ANY PROFESSIONAL WEB DESIGN/DEVELOPMENT TOOL, SO USING IT IS FAIRLY EASY.

CONVERSELY, THERE'S NO HARM IN USING THE BROWSER-SAFE PALETTE EITHER. IT SIMPLY LIMITS YOUR CHOICES TO 216 COLORS. MOST PEOPLE DON'T HAVE A LOT OF COLOR PICKING CONFIDENCE, AND WORKING WITH LIMITED COLOR CHOICES IS EASIER. AT THIS POINT, THERE'S NO RIGHT OR WRONG WHEN IT COMES TO WHICH COLORS YOU PICK, BUT MORE IMPORTANT TO KNOW HOW TO COMBINE COLORS IN PLEASING AND EFFECTIVE WAYS. MY BEST ADVICE TO YOU IS TO PAY CLOSEST ATTENTION TO CONTRAST WITH COLORS. IF YOU HAVE A LIGHT BACKGROUND, BE SURE TO PICK A DARK COLOR TYPE. IF YOU WANT SOMETHING TO STAND OUT ON YOUR PAGE, CHOOSE THE LIGHTEST OR DARKEST COLOR YOU CAN FIND, DEPENDING ON WHETHER YOUR BACKGROUND IS LIGHT OR DARK.

When used in body copy, the all caps style decreases legibility.

Used for navigation elements and short sentences, the use of all caps is much more legible. **Tiffany.com** site is also a great example of sticking to one or two typefaces and varying color, weight, and size to create a beautiful, elegant look.

Putting text over image is often a challenge to legibility. This study is in the legibility section at http://www.rsub.com/typographic.

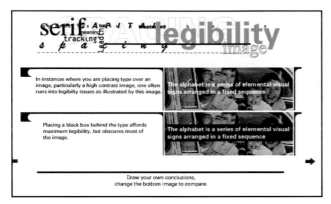

By putting a black bar between the photo and the type, the legibility is greatly increased.

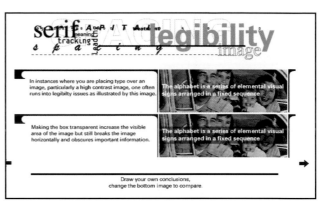

By putting a transparent black band between the white text and the black-and-white image, legibility is increased.

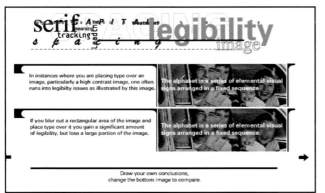

By creating a band of blurry photographic content between the white type and the black-and-white image, legibility is increased.

By creating a black outline around the white type, the legibility is increased.

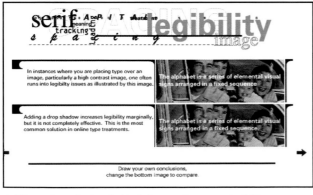

Adding a drop shadow behind the text increases legibility.

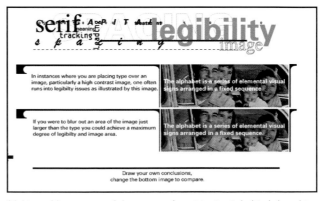

Making a blurry copy of the type and positioning it behind the white type creates greater legibility.

Body copy

I think the Web is an incredibly great way to gather information. Typically, when I find a page with a lot of text on it, though, I print the page on my printer instead of sitting and reading through the text on my screen. Who wants the light of a monitor blaring in one's face while having a recreational read? Give me crisp type on paper over that any day! I feel the same way about all computer-based text delivery systems, such as CD-ROMs and interactive kiosks. If I'm going to read a lot of text, I'd rather do so on paper. As designers, we have to recognize that computer-based presentations pose distinct challenges, and we should not treat our type-ridden web pages the same way we would print.

I advocate breaking up type into small paragraphs. Also, use different weights, such as bold and italic, to make it possible for the reader to skim the page easily and catch the important points. Adding hypertext (text that links from one spot to another, which typically appears underlined or bold depending on the the viewer's browser preferences) is another way to break up screen text into more digestible portions. The idea is to break up blocks of text as much as possible. Assume your readers are skimming, and make it easy for them.

Understand that you're asking a lot of your end user to sit and read page upon page of type on a screen. It's your job to invent ways to hold his or her interest and to bring out the important ideas. You can do so by using CSS, HTML, or graphic-based text.

Printing web pages

As if there aren't enough things to think about in web design, here is another wrench thrown your way: If you intend to have your audience print information from your pages, you should design your pages with that in mind. Many people don't realize, for example, that if they set up a dark web page background with white type, the background will not be printed with the file. What results? White type on white paper—or as some might say "a blank page."

I am not suggesting that you have to always use light backgrounds with dark type on every page, but if you know you want your audience to print a specific page, test print it yourself to see whether it is legible!

Some sites get around this issue by creating two versions of the same page—one that isn't printable and another that is. MapQuest is one of these sites.

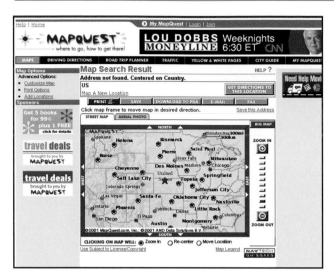

If you wanted to print a page from **MapQuest.com**, you would press the Print button.

You might think the Print button would send the document to the printer, but it does not. Instead, it sends you to another page that is suitable for printing.

If you want to create two sets of pages for your site—one that is better for viewing and one that is better for printing, you can follow MapQuest's lead. The objective is to make a page for printing that is as simple as possible—no tables, no frames, no fancy DHTML layers or CSS. While you can print more complex pages, you won't be able to preview how they will print as well as if you keep your design really simple for printing.

Creating a PDF file is another option that you might consider for pages you want to have printed. PDF stands for **P**ortable **D**ocument **F**ormat. It was developed long before the Web existed as a means of transporting documents to end users who didn't own the software applications the documents were created in. If, for example, I wanted to send a client a PageMaker document, and he or she didn't own PageMaker, my client could still see my layout with all the correct fonts and images intact.

PDF files are created with software called Acrobat, available from Adobe. Once you have the PDF authoring tool installed on your computer, you can choose to print to your printer or to a PDF document. If you print to PDF, you create a file instead of a printout. You can then upload the PDF to your web site (using the **A** tag and the extension **.pdf**), and as long as your end user has the PDF web browser plug-in called Acrobat Reader, he or she can see your document. Trouble is, the plug-in is a hefty 3–4 megabytes. If you own any Adobe products, you'll find that most of the CD-ROMs include the Reader but, nevertheless, it is hefty for those who don't already have it.

PDFs are great if you have forms or documentation that need to uphold formatting. The IRS (http://www.irs.gov) uses PDF forms to make tax reporting forms available online.

To view a series of tutorials on how to use Acrobat to create PDF files, visit http://www.adobe.com/products/tips/acrobat.html.

tip

LEARN MORE ABOUT ACROBAT

Visit http://www.adobe.com/products/tips/acrobat.html to view numerous tutorials on how to make PDF pages for your site. You can create a PDF directly from many Adobe tools, or by using Acrobat you can publish just about any other kind of document as a PDF file.

USING FIREWORKS FOR TYPE DESIGN

Macromedia Fireworks software is one of many ideal environments for creating type and graphic web elements. The various Effects settings enable you to create all kinds of special type effects for headlines that you can use on the Web. The editable text feature lets you set up one look and then change certain words that will take on the same appearance. This is great for creating navigation buttons!

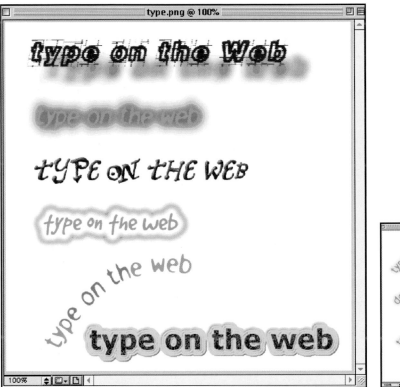

Fireworks offers a host of effects (similar to Photoshop's Layer Effect feature). The fonts shown above were all downloaded for free from the Web from Fontastic, Fonthead Designs, and Chank Diesel (http://www.fonthead.com).

Once you set up a style you like in Fireworks, you can duplicate it and change the words. You can also copy and paste appearances, which is handy if you change your mind (or if your client changes his or hers!).

HTML FOR PLACING TEXT GRAPHICS

Placing graphics on a web page is addressed in depth in Chapter 17, *"Rules & Bullets."* The most basic way to insert a graphic on a page is to use the **IMG** element. Here's how to insert the drop-shadow artwork, that you created earlier, on a page.

code

```
<html>
<body>
<img src="dropshad.jpg">
</body>
</html>
```

If you want to link the drop-shadow image to another source, combine the **IMG** element with an **A** element.

code

```
<html>
<body>
<a href="http://www.domain.com">
<img src="dropshad.jpg"></a>
</body>
</html>
```

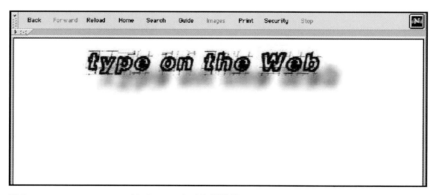

This page uses a text graphic inserted with HTML.

WHAT ABOUT FLASH?

Macromedia Flash is a vector-based authoring program and web plug-in that allows you to create animation, interactive content, and web pages. Because it works with vector data instead of bit-maps (GIF and JPEG), the information is much smaller and downloads more quickly than any other format on the Web. It is possible to create entire web sites in Flash that use any font you want, and those fonts will be accurately displayed to any visitor who has the Flash Player plug-in installed.

The authoring tool has the ability to work with any font that you have installed in your system. You can make the type animate, fade, scale, and/or rotate over time, creating much more dynamism than GIF and JPEG could ever hope to possess. The authoring tool lets you assign sounds and rollovers to type as well, and you can create links that jump to other Flash scenes (meaning your visitor might view your entire site without ever seeing a single HTML ASCII font).

One of the major drawbacks to Flash has been its reliance on a plug-in. While the plug-in is small (118K), it is still a deterrent to many. Fortunately, Netscape now includes the plug-in with its shipping version. In addition, Windows 98 supports Flash as a native file format.

I think Flash holds incredible promise as an HTML alternative. It gives designers the design control they want without forcing them to learn any programming. There is also a sister product, called Flash Generator, which allows you to use Flash with database-driven content. You could set up a template in Flash, for example, and have dynamically changing content conform to the template. Very exciting stuff.

The drawback to Flash is its reliance on a plug-in, its authoring tool (which is very deep, and has a medium–high learning curve), and the fact that Flash content is not searchable by most search engines or text readers. I think Flash is here to stay, and it offers one of the most promising multimedia technologies the Web has seen so far. To read more about it, visit http://www.macromedia.com/software/flash.

Pentagram (http://www.pentagram.com) uses typography, at large and small scale, as the subject of a dramatic introduction animation in their Flash portfolio. This would not be possible with HTML, CSS, DHTML, or any other technology on the horizon.

AESTHETICS OF LAYOUT

Another area that poses great challenges to web designers is layout. This is partially because of technical limitations of the Web. There are many techniques used to create layout, which you will learn about in Chapter 21, *"Alignment & Tables,"* and Chapter 23, *"Cascading Style Sheets."* This section addresses the visual principles of layout and composition.

AVOID RECTANGLE-ITIS

We do a lot of site critiques for students who attend our school. It didn't take long to realize that there was an undiagnosed disease on the Web—rectangle-itis! This is a result of too many rectangles on web sites. Rectangles are everywhere:

> Frames

> Tables

> Images

> Browsers

Rectangles make your users feel boxed in. They divide the small amount of real estate that you have into smaller pieces. They make everything on the page feel the same: predictable, boring, standard. Sites that use too many rectangles feel generic and templated.

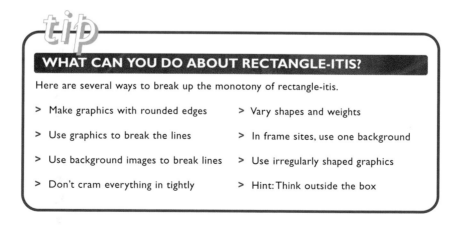

WHAT CAN YOU DO ABOUT RECTANGLE-ITIS?

Here are several ways to break up the monotony of rectangle-itis.

> Make graphics with rounded edges

> Use graphics to break the lines

> Use background images to break lines

> Don't cram everything in tightly

> Vary shapes and weights

> In frame sites, use one background

> Use irregularly shaped graphics

> Hint: Think outside the box

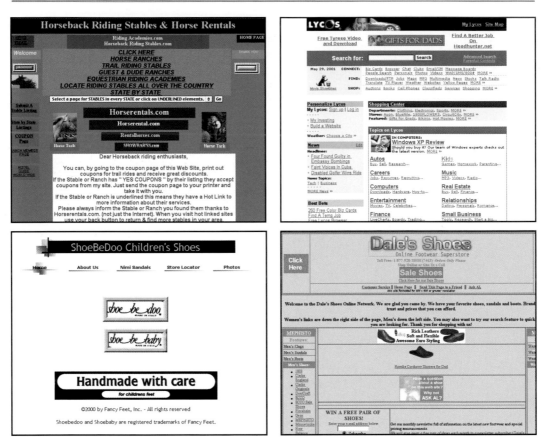

These sites (http://www.horserentals.com, http://www.lycos.com, http://www.shoebedoo.com, and http://www. dalesshoes.com) could really benefit from breaking out of the rectangular mold! Rectangles get to be pretty repetitive, boring, and annoying after a while. It's natural to use them on sites, because images, frames, browsers, and tables all come in the shape of a square or rectangle by default. Through learning a few techniques, it's possible to break out of this mold without much effort.

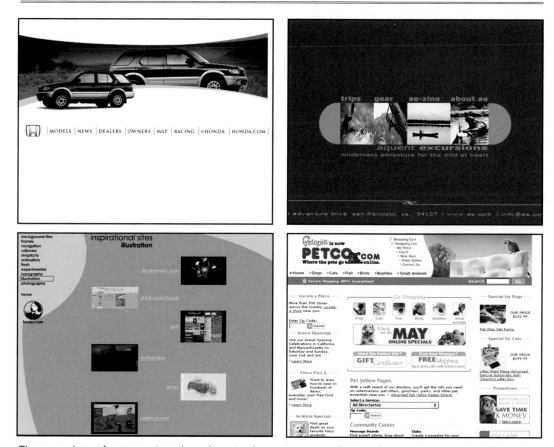

There are lots of ways to introduce dynamic shapes into your designs that aren't rectangular. These sites (http://www.honda.com, http://www.ae.com, http://www.lynda.com, and http://www.petco.com) show a few ideas.

USE A GRID

Though this might sound like I'm now encouraging rectangle-itis, I do advocate the use of a grid in your design. The grid itself is not a visible component—it just helps you align your text and images so your design has a sense of security and order. Grids are easy to implement using HTML tables (which you'll learn about in Chapter 21, *"Alignment & Tables"*).

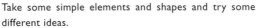

Create a simple grid like this, and try some different designs using it.

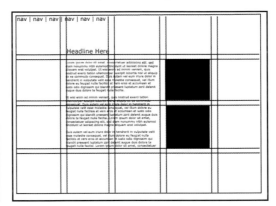

Take some simple elements and shapes and try some different ideas.

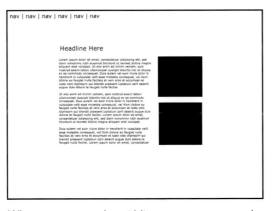

When you remove the grid lines, you start to see the beauty and purpose of a grid.

Even though these are different designs, they feel united through the invisible grid.

A Gallery of Sites That Use Grids

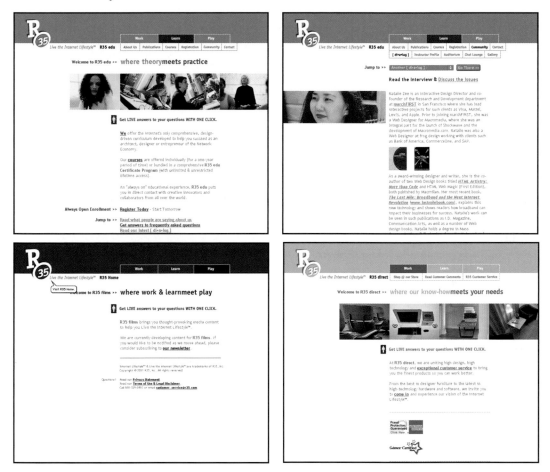

R35 (http://www.r35.com) uses a grid, as well as whitespace and clean simple design, to make the content very easy to access.

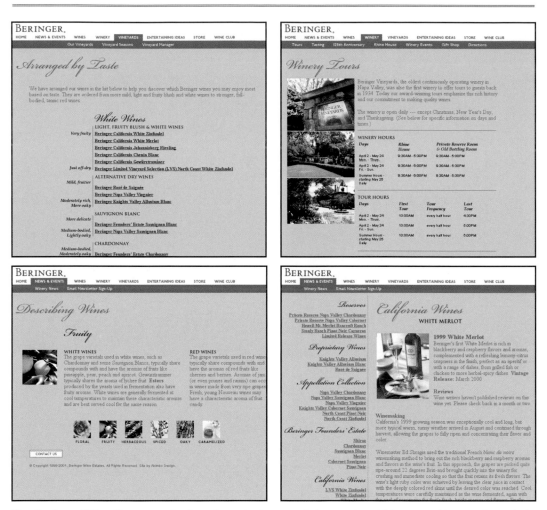

The **Beringer Wine Company** site (http://www.beringer.com) changes the grid, but everything remains orderly, aligned, and easy to get to. It is also notable for its typography and color design. Overall, a beautiful site by all the criteria of this chapter!

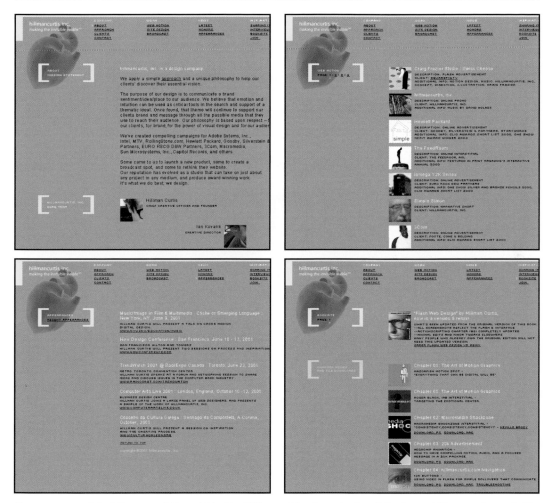

You can see and feel the use of the grid in the **Hillman Curtis** web site (http://www.hillmancurtis.com). The consistency makes for a site that is easy to navigate and understand, while the design variations hold your interest on every page.

MAKE YOUR LINE WIDTHS EASY TO READ

If you put text on an HTML page without a table, it will stretch to the width of the browser. My advice is to create tables to limit the width of text on your pages. You'll learn how to do this in Chapter 21, *"Alignment & Tables."* By looking at the following studies, you'll see why tables are so important with layout.

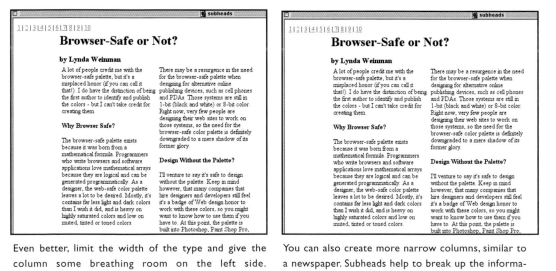

If you don't format HTML, your type will fill an entire screen; and the larger the monitor, the worse the problem. It's very tiring on one's eyes to stretch the width of a browser to read a single line of text.

By creating an HTML table, and turning off its borders to make it invisible (see Chapter 21, *"Alignment & Tables")*, you can limit the line width and make reading this text easy regardless of what size monitor you have.

Even better, limit the width of the type and give the column some breathing room on the left side. Nothing on the page feels crowded now, and nothing is in the way of you and your read.

You can also create more narrow columns, similar to a newspaper. Subheads help to break up the information as well.

WHITE SPACE IS BETTER THAN TIGHT SPACE

Using white space lets your eyes rest on different areas of a web page. It makes it more relaxing and easy to find information. Sometimes fighting for white space is a hard political battle—trust me, I've fought it myself. Many people mistakenly think that the more information you cram on a page, the more valuable the content is. This is especially difficult in companies with lots of divisions, or schools with lots of departments. Judge for yourself with the following examples—white space helps the visitor find the information. Too much information is overload and stops being effective.

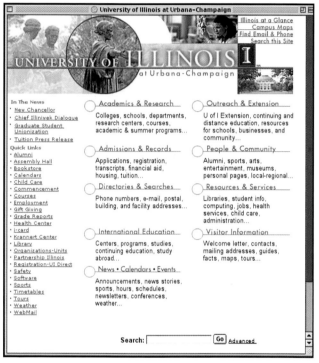

The **Arizona State University** site (http://www.asu.edu) presents a lot of information in a relatively small amount of space. It is visually very cluttered, and there is little to no white space. (It's probably a political nightmare to be the web designer for this site!) The amount of information works at a cross purpose to its intent. I would give up trying to find a link on this page, and would simply type what I was looking for into the search box! That's not necessarily a bad thing (more on this in Chapter 7, "Navigation"), but regardless, in my opinion this site suffers from information overload that probably serves fewer people than it could if it were less cluttered.

The **University of Illinois** (http://www.uiuc.edu) also has a lot of information on its site. Through the use of white space and consistent separation of information, though, I think the content is much easier to find and focus on. Lack of clutter will always prevail over clutter.

Remember the Fold

The term "fold" comes from newspaper design because newspapers are typically folded in half. The headlines and lead stories are always on the front page and above the fold. The term has come to apply to web pages as well. A single screen, without scrolling, is considered above the fold.

It's important when you design your page that your front door (usually called the home page) places important navigation items above the fold. To determine where the fold is on a web site, however, has to do with what resolution your audience is viewing the site.

When I wrote the first edition of this book, I advocated that people design their web sites for 640×480 resolution. This was standard "waaay" back in 1995 when I was writing the book. Today, you would be hard pressed to buy a computer system that displayed at lower than 1024×786 resolution. Still, a lot of laptops are set to 800×600, and many people with poor eyesight (I sadly qualify) change their resolution to 800×600 so they can see better.

The **Yahoo** site (http://www.yahoo.com) puts icons along the top, but their navigation offers so many choices that it's challenging to know where to click.

The **Google** site (http://www.google.com) cuts to the chase. It's assumed that search is more powerful than links in this approach, and they waste no space about it! This site's key navigation (the search box) would be considered "above the fold" at any resolution.

The **CNN** site (http://www.cnn.com) puts their key navigation on the left side, and it is above the fold whether the site is viewed on 800×600 or larger resolutions.

THE AESTHETICS OF ANIMATION

You will learn how to make animated web graphics in Chapter 24, *"Animation & Audio"*. Since this is the chapter on web aesthetics, the focus here will be on what works and what doesn't from a visual communication point of view.

With the exception of multimedia, the Web is the first medium to combine animation and body text on a single page. For this reason, it's no wonder that many people struggle to use animation effectively.

Adding animation to a site can be great, but it can also have the reverse effect of annoying your audience or detracting from what your page is trying to say. During a conference I once attended, Ben Olander, Creative Director at **Angry Monkey** (http://www.angrymonkey.com) commented, "Most animation you see on the Web is the equivalent of the **BLINK** tag." I agree with him, but I also see this as a natural outgrowth of artists and developers who are first working with a new tool.

Here are some very general, personal guidelines I would like to share:

> Animation calls attention to itself much more than static images on a page. Make sure that the content of your animation is, in fact, something you want the most attention called to on your page. If it isn't, the animation will effectively detract from what you're trying to communicate.

> In most instances, animation that cycles or loops endlessly will eventually become annoying.

> If you use more than one animation on a single page, the effect may be overwhelming to the end viewer instead of impressive.

> Make sure your animation loads quickly. You'll learn guidelines to achieve fast downloading speeds in Chapter 24, *"Animation & Audio."* If you make your audience wait too long for an animation to load, they'll move onward before ever seeing it.

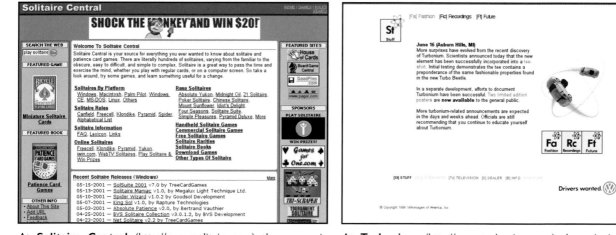

At **Solitaire Central** (http://www.solitaire.com) the screen is almost entirely surrounded by blinking, animating ad banners and sponsor banners. It makes it almost impossible to read the content in the middle.

At **Turbonium** (http://www.turbonium.com) the spinning atom animation on the right side of the screen moves so fast and furiously that it almost makes you too nauseous to stay on the page.

web AESTHETICS

SUMMARY

Good web design is the practice of using design to enhance communication. Unfortunately, design can also be counter productive to clear communication. Here are some principles to keep in mind:

> Pay closest attention to the values of the colors you pick and make sure that you chose color combinations that have enough contrast to read easily.

> ASCII type rules are different than rules for graphic type.

> With ASCII type, be sure the font and size you pick is readable on all platforms.

> With graphic type, stick to one or two font families, and use color, size, weight, and style to create different "looks" and hierarchies.

> Make sure that your layout is organized, has enough white space, has lines of text that are short and easy to read, and keeps important navigation elements above the fold.

> Animation is good when the thing that is animating is the important information to look at. Peripheral animation should not loop endlessly, or it will annoy your visitors.

Planning
Web Projects

Introduction

Whether you're bidding on a web design project or you have one in your pocket, your work is just beginning. The stages this chapter covers are how to profile a project, conduct research, obtain the necessary assets, work with milestones and project management, work with teams, and deal with contracts.

getting the job

The audience for this book is made up of all types of people, from teachers and students, to web professionals, to in-house designers and developers. Some of you don't have to worry about getting clients or jobs, and if that's the case, feel free to skip this section.

The most important advice I can give you is to build a portfolio of work to show. Very few people will hire you to develop or design a project without first seeing your work. If you don't have any paying work to show, create some pseudo-web sites or graphics so that you can show what your capabilities are.

You will likely be asked to bid on projects and/or propose creative briefs. Both of these processes are challenging because web projects are often difficult to define. Here are some strategies to keep in mind.

ASK QUESTIONS!

When I taught at **Art Center**, I sensed reluctance on the part of students to ask a lot of questions about their assignments from me, hence my concerns that they wouldn't know how to ask questions of their future clients or employers. There's a natural tendency, when you're new at something, to be afraid of "sounding stupid" by asking too many questions.

What might surprise you is that if you ask too few questions, you stand a far greater chance of looking "stupid" than if you do the proper information collecting beforehand. Being a successful web designer (or any kind of designer for that matter) doesn't just involve good design and technical skills, but good communication skills as well. Being able to communicate well means understanding your client's objectives as thoroughly as you can.

As someone who has been in the position of being an employer, I am far more confident in those around me who are bold enough to ask the hard questions than the quiet types who never say or ask much.

Sample Questions

> What is the site about?

> What are the goals of the site?

> How will we measure success?

> Who is the target audience?

> What are the audience expectations?

> Who is your competition?

> How do you want your audience to use your site?

> How will you make money on this web site?

THE CREATIVE BRIEF

Introduction: Begin with a summary of what the projects scope is. Describe the goals of the web site, define the audience, and set the scope.

Discuss Problems: Break the brief down into specific issues. Define what problems you see that are triggering the need for the web site or web site redesign.

Offer Solutions: Distinguish yourself or your firm. What needs to be accomplished? Who is the target audience? Who are the competitors? What are the measurable goals and "ROI" (**r**eturn **o**n **i**nvestment)? Why are you the right company or person to do so?

THE CREATIVE BRIEF WORKSHEET

Answering the questions on this worksheet will effectively build the skeleton for your creative brief. The information gathered in the Discovery process (Client Survey, research, interviews) will provide you with the answers.

Project Summary:

State general project information, goals, and relevant background information for the site redesign. This paragraph should be a statement overview of the project as a whole.

1. What is the basic overview of the project? Briefly include background information if relevant.

2. What is the single purpose of the new site?

3. What are the secondary goals of the new site?

4. What are the long-term goals?

Audience Profile:

Profile the target audience. Provide enough detail to enhance everyone's understanding of who the audience is. Include some user demographic information. Your goal with this section is to answer the following: Who is the target? What do these people care about? And what do they do online on a daily basis?

The website http://www.web-redesign.com offers this worksheet as a free download. This is companion documentation to the book *Web Redesign* by Kelly Goto and Emily Cotler (New Riders Publishing, ISBN: 0-7357-1062-7). If you're craving a lot more in-depth information about this subject than the chapter you're reading offers, this is the book for you! It contains lots of sample questions and worksheets, as well as many real-world examples.

THE PROJECT PROFILE

In the legal world, the process of collecting information about a case is called "discovery." There's a discovery period with every project you take on, where it's your job to figure out the right questions to ask, and to get the answers you need to go further.

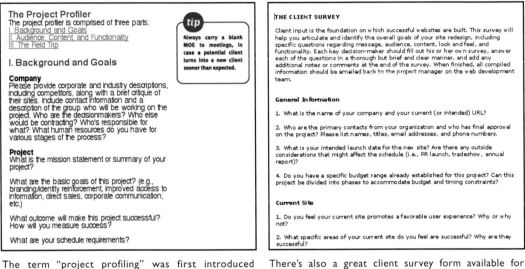

The Project Profiler
The project profiler is comprised of three parts.
I. Background and Goals
II. Audience, Content, and Functionality
III. The Field Trip

I. Background and Goals

Company
Please provide corporate and industry descriptions, including competitors, along with a brief critique of their sites. Include contact information and a description of the group who will be working on the project. Who are the decisionmakers? Who else would be contracting? Who's responsible for what? What human resources do you have for various stages of the process?

Project
What is the mission statement or summary of your project?

What are the basic goals of this project? (e.g., branding/identity reinforcement, improved access to information, direct sales, corporate communication, etc.)

What outcome will make this project successful? How will you measure success?

What are your schedule requirements?

tip
Always carry a blank MOE to meetings, in case a potential client turns into a new client sooner than expected.

THE CLIENT SURVEY

Client input is the foundation on which successful websites are built. This survey will help you articulate and identify the overall goals of your site redesign, including specific questions regarding message, audience, content, look and feel, and functionality. Each key decision-maker should fill out his or her own survey, answer each of the questions in a thorough but brief and clear manner, and add any additional notes or comments at the end of the survey. When finished, all compiled information should be emailed back to the project manager on the web development team.

General Information

1. What is the name of your company and your current (or intended) URL?

2. Who are the primary contacts from your organization and who has final approval on the project? Please list names, titles, email addresses, and phone numbers.

3. What is your intended launch date for the new site? Are there any outside considerations that might affect the schedule (i.e., PR launch, tradeshow, annual report)?

4. Do you have a specific budget range already established for this project? Can this project be divided into phases to accommodate budget and timing constraints?

Current Site

1. Do you feel your current site promotes a favorable user experience? Why or why not?

2. What specific areas of your current site do you feel are successful? Why are they successful?

The term "project profiling" was first introduced to me in David Siegel's book *Secrets of Successful Websites: Project Management on the World Wide Web* (New Riders Publishing, ISBN: 1-56830-382-3). The book's site (http://www.secretsites.com/home/set_core.html) has many great resources.

There's also a great client survey form available for download from http://www.web-redesign.com, the web site that accompanies the book *Web Redesign* by Kelly Goto and Emily Cotler.

SAMPLE CHECKLIST

Sample questions in a project profile document follow. You can download the project profile form from David Siegel's book site: http://www.secretsites.com/profiler/set_partnering.html.

Questions for the Client

What is the mission of your company?

What is the goal of your web site?

Who are the decision makers?

Will there be other contractors to work with?

Who is responsible for which areas of the site?

How will you measure the success of this project?

Who is your target audience?

Questions About the Audience

What does your audience want from your site?

What kinds of issues are important to your audience?

What platforms are they using?

Are there any hardware/software restrictions or concerns?

What kind of hardware/browser is your audience likely to have?

Questions About the Project

What is the budget?

What is the deadline?

What is the schedule?

Who is your competition?

List five sites that you aspire to compete with or surpass.

Are there any branding issues that should be incorporated into the site design?

Is there a budget for user testing?

Questions About Assets

Has any work already gone toward this site?

Is it a redesign or a site from scratch?

Do you have all the assets, or do they need to be created?

Who will be the contact person for the assets?

Who will approve the assets?

What format are the assets in?

Questions About Content

Who will create the content?

Who will update the content?

Who is the person responsible for content at your company?

How frequently will the content need to be updated?

How frequently will the content be updated?

Questions About Function

Who will host your site?

Who will handle the database or email lists?

Who will analyze the logs?

What are the security guidelines/issues?

What is your long-term objective for the site?

Are their any special technical considerations?

Questions About Budget

Who will pay for hosting?

Who will pay for maintenance?

Who will pay for the database development/maintenance?

Who will pay for the scripts and programming?

Who will pay for the visual design?

Questions About the Schedule

What is the deadline for launch?

What is the deadline for user testing?

What are the milestones within the framework of the project?

Who will pay for the scripts and programming?

Who will pay for the visual design?

DOCUMENT EVERYTHING!

As you work with clients, it is very important to document each step of the way. This can be done in an email each time you meet or come to decisions. A paper (or e-paper) trail works to eliminate any miscommunications that may occur along the way.

For a great article on clients, read "A Client's Guide to Design" at http://www.aiga.com/content. cfm?ContentID=460.

CLIENT RELATIONS

Relating to clients is hard in any medium. The need for clarity is essential, especially when it comes to web design! That's because so many clients don't understand what's involved. They're not jerks; they just don't understand. There's a big difference.

I meet so many designers and developers who resent their clients and seem to regard them as if they are stupid. It's easy to complain, but it's far harder to understand, listen, and relate. If you sincerely don't like your client, don't work for them. Disrespect has a way of being a two-way street.

Here are my top ten pearls of wisdom.

1 Be Selective (if you can!)

Interview your clients, just as they interview you. You have to develop assessment skills to make sure the match is good for your personality and resources. If you want a certain type of work, make sure your portfolio supports that.

If you need the money, or need to learn, take on some clients who don't meet your standards. Go into it with your eyes open, and try not to resent the experience. Even bad client experiences can be good if you learn from them.

2 What Is Your Job?

It's your job to be the educator, problem-solver, listener, and fixer. The better you are at those skills, the more clients you'll have.

3 Pricing

There are no standards. What is your time worth? Can you estimate how long the project will take? Find out what the budget is if you can. Make sure it's worth your while. If you aren't good at discussing this stuff—billing, collecting, and so on—then you shouldn't be in business for yourself.

4 Expect Change

If you aren't open to changes, then you will be someone your client won't want to work with in the future. Remember, they are the client. It is your job to please them, as well as execute their vision. Big egos get in the way of this process.

5 Get It in Writing

Document each step of the way, and you'll protect yourself and your client from misunderstandings.

6 Admit Fault

If you make a mistake , you're going to earn a lot more trust if you admit it than if you hide it.

7 Ask Questions

It's far better to ask too many question than not enough. The best designers predict the right questions to ask. It's very possible to complete an entire job, only to discover that you forgot to ask an essential question and the entire project has to be redone.

8 Payment Structure

Get an advance. Make sure your deliverables are very clear, so you can charge overage if something else is asked of you.

9 If You're Going to Be Late

Let your client know—don't make them chase after you. It looks far better if you come to them. Contact clients regularly. Don't let the only time you contact them be to troubleshoot problems.

10 Ask for Feedback

When a project ends, ask your client for feedback. There's always room for improvement, and you can learn from any criticism or praise.

CONTRACTS & LEGAL ISSUES

Nothing makes you feel quite more like a grownup than contract negotiations. It's a scary part of being in business, but there are a few key issues that you should educate yourself about. If you can afford it, having a lawyer spend an hour or two looking over an important contract is well worth its weight in gold.

There are times that your client will give you a contract, and other times that you will want to give them your contract. You should develop one of your own, in the event they don't have one. The following terms and issues should be considered in relation to legal contracts.

Services to Be Performed

It's a good idea to document the exact services that you are expected to perform. The more specific, the easier it is to enforce.

Payment Rate

The rate or price that you will be paid should be included in the contract.

Invoice Schedule

The schedule for invoicing should be documented in the contract.

Payment Schedule

You should not just specify how much and when you will invoice, but also when they will pay.

Copyrights

Determining who owns the copyright is sometimes negotiable and sometimes not. Web site content could conceivably lead to other projects, such as film, video, books, etc. If you can maintain the copyright, it's best for you, of course. There are going to be lots of times when this isn't possible, however. The United States Copyright Act assumes that if you are the creator of the work (your ideas, your artwork, your writing, etc.) that you own all rights unless otherwise signed away. You can expect that this is not black and white when you are creating a web site for someone else, as it most often is a collaboration of your/their ideas, your/their artwork, your/their content, etc. It's important to define who owns the copyright in the contract rather than leave this to speculation.

All-Media Rights

All-media rights is a legal term that is intended to cover a broad range of delivery mediums, such as print, video, CD-ROM, Web, handheld, etc. Each one of these separate uses could be of value to you. Contracts that ask for all-media rights are, in essence, asking you to allow the client the rights to distribute your work in all media. The clause is often added, "now known or invented in the future." It's to your advantage to keep all-media rights and to your disadvantage to give them up.

All-Rights

If you are asked to give up all-rights, what does that mean? It means that you will have no rights to your work in any form in the future. It's similar to all-media rights, and may be even more all encompassing.

Work for Hire

A work-for-hire agreement grants the copyright of your work to your client.

NDA

NDA (**N**on-**D**isclosure **A**greement). You might share proprietary information with your client, or vice-versa. NDA contracts are usually separate contract documents.

Non-Competition Clause

This clause can protect the "look and feel" you create for your client. It might be hard to hold up in court, but could discourage the client from re-using your artwork or concepts without your involvement. If this clause is in the client's contract, it is there to restrict you from using the same look and feel on other clients' web sites.

Cancellation/Kill Fee

A negotiated fee paid by the client to the designer when the client does not use the artwork. It usually means that the artwork was approved, but it could not be used for one reason or another.

Exclusive Use

No one except the client can use or publish the web site design.

Non-Exclusive Use

A non-exclusive use is a good thing, especially if you want to be able to republish the design you created in a portfolio or you want to reuse the design for other clients. When you give away the exclusive rights to you work, you might not be able to show it as a portfolio piece on your own site! Scary!

LEGAL LINKS

Internet and Intellectual Property Law
Ivan Hoffman, B.A., J.D.
http://www.ivanhoffman.com

Graphic Artists Guild Contract Monitor
http://www.gag.org/contracts/contracts.html

AIGA: A Client's Guide to Design
http://www.aiga.com/content.cfm?ContentID=460

WORKING WITH TEAMS

It's likely that if you are going to work on web sites, you are going to work with a team. If you have a small team that all works in the same office, perhaps everyone can keep track of what everyone else is doing. Chances are that you will run into communication and work-flow issues. Some likely scheduling and picture management problems are explored below.

Problem

Your programmer needs to work on the same page as your designer. One person ends up overwriting the important change that the other team member already made.

Solution

You might want to look into version-tracking software. There is a checkout service in Dreamweaver MX, a popular HTML editor, that lets you know whether or not a file is "checked out" by someone else. A more robust solution can be found with specialized version tracking software such as *WebDAV*, (**W**eb-based **D**istributed **A**uthoring and **V**ersioning). It is a set of extensions that allows users to collaboratively edit and manage files on remote web servers. WebDAV (http://www. webdav. org) is built into Adobe GoLive and Macromedia Dreamweaver MX.

Another type of software that larger working groups often turn to is called *content management software*. This type of software helps you manage your content (HTML, images, and media) and can spot and fix broken links. There are several choices of content management software. For information about the different software packages that handle content management, visit http://techupdate.zdnet.com and do a search for "content management software."

Problem

An important milestone for the site review is due tomorrow, and you just found out that the programmer has a dentist appointment and can't make the deadline.

Solution

You might want to invest in scheduling software. If you visit http://www.knowledgestorm. com and search for "project scheduling," you'll see a review of 20+ different solutions.

Problem

You know you already made a picture for that page, but what the heck did you call it and where is it on your hard drive?

Solution

You might be in need of an image database. A good article that compares the options can be found at http://www.cyberbohemia.com/Pages/Bridgepages/organizing&managing.htm.

tip

TEAMWORK RESOURCE

Collaborative Web Development:
Strategies & Best Practices for Web Teams
Jessica R. Burdman
Addison Wesley Publishing
ISBN: 0-201433-31-1

PLANNING WEB PROJECTS

SUMMARY

This chapter focused on issues related to planning and executing a web design project. Here's a brief summation:

> Analyze and define the goals carefully. Do your homework and ask a lot of questions before you begin.

> Clear and open communication skills are key with working with both clients and other team members.

> Make sure you have a contract, and that it adequately covers all the issues. Obtain the advice of a lawyer, and visit the legal resource sites listed in this chapter as well.

Establishing Goals

INTRODUCTION

At the heart of the Web is the fact that it is a publishing medium. Publishing should involve having a clear message, motive, and delivery. The goal(s) of your site should be focused around what the user wants, not just what you want to give them. Whatever you decide upon, make sure the goal(s) are clear and measurable; otherwise, you will not be able to determine whether your site is a success or a failure.

The success of a web site is not always reflected by the number of "hits" that it gets each month. The true success of a web site is determined by how well it accomplishes its goals. This chapter focuses on how to achieve better purpose with your web sites by setting careful and realistic goals.

DEFINING YOUR GOAL

Determining the goal of your web site should be the very first step you take, before you decide on architecture, look and feel, or navigation. Here is a checklist of questions to help you through this process:

> What is the objective of the site? (Sales, public relations, information, entertainment, etc.)

> Are there any special goals or needs? (The logo has to be blue, the board of director's pictures have to be on the site, etc.)

> How will you know if it succeeds? (Revenue, hits, banner ad click-throughs, etc.)

Once you answer the questions above, it's time to put them in order of importance. Here's a sample list, although your order may vary:

1 Generate revenue through sales

2 Increase awareness of your brand

3 Create community

4 Create loyalty to your product

5 Educate visitors about your product

6 Be better than your competition

identifying your audience

Here are some questions to get you thinking about your users.

> Who is my target audience?

> What will this audience want from the site?

> How can I "think like my user"?

Here is a sample list of what some of the answers might look like, based on scenarios.

SCENARIO 1

1 My audience is composed of 18- to 30-year-olds.

2 They want to come to my site because they want to have fun.

3 They care about being on the cutting edge of what is hip.

4 They enjoy meeting each other and having a destination through which they can connect.

5 They don't have a lot of money and are looking for bargains.

6 They are not likely to buy as much as they are likely to want to hang out.

SCENARIO 2

1 My audience is composed of 30- to 70-year-olds.

2 They want to come to my site to learn about investment opportunities.

3 They care about the return on their investment.

4 They care about the safety of their investment.

5 They care about their privacy.

6 They care about the security of transactions on the site.

7 They might be older and have poor eye site, so type needs to be bigger.

8 They need to have things explained in clear terms, without a lot of jargon.

SCENARIO 3

1 My audience is composed of all ages and all kinds of people.

2 They care about getting their news and weather.

3 They want easy access to information and would use a search function.

4 They are in the mood to collect information, not to buy things.

5 They want links to other sites and articles.

6 They want an opportunity to discuss the news and weather.

WHAT IS USER EXPERIENCE?

After coming up with what you think your users want, it's also important to think about their experience on your site. The term "user experience" is thrown around a lot these days—it's the study of what it is like to be a user.

There isn't some mythical user in the sky that you are targeting your site toward. You're a user—what is your experience? Query yourself about what you like and dislike about the Web. If you think about your experience on web sites, you can learn a lot about what to do and what not to do. As you go through a site, what are your emotions and inclinations? Learning to make a user-centered site means putting yourself in the shoes of the user and catering to the user experience.

What do you hate about the Web?

> Bad graphics

> Annoying content

> Bad navigation

> Under construction pages

> Content that's wrong

> Content that doesn't change

> Too slow

> Broken links

What do you like about the Web?

> Inspiring graphics

> Helpful content

> Usable navigation

> Updated, accurate information

> Global communication medium

> Personalization

> Incredible repository of information

Here are some more detailed lists. These are just some sample scenarios. Try some of your own, and see what you come up with!

What do you expect from stores?

> Privacy policy

> Security policy

> Shopping cart feedback on price

> Shopping cart feedback on quantity

> Shopping cart feedback

> Ability to change mind

> Ability to return to shopping experience

> Suggestions for related products

> Mailing list form for information on future products

What do you expect from review sections?

> Read other people's reviews
> Add reviews
> Rate reviews
> Rate reviewers
> Ability to reject reviewers

What do you expect from discussion boards?

> Read threads
> Contribute to threads
> Delete threads
> Add threads
> Rate threads
> Rate contributors to a thread

What do you expect from content designed to entertain?

> Is it entertaining?
> Rate its value
> Skip it quickly
> Ability to launch or close it quickly

What do you expect from informational pages?

> See a synopsis
> Read a longer version
> Understand how much information is there
> Rate the information

What do you expect from a list of resource links?

> View the list
> Add to the list
> Delete from the list
> Rate the list
> Launch the link in a new browser window

WHAT IS YOUR SITE'S GOAL?

To learn how to establish a goal, let's walk through an example. Let's say your goal is to provide information about one of your hobbies: native plant gardening.

Again, these are just some sample strategies to help get your juices flowing about features to add to your web site. See if you can make a similar list to what is more suited to your own content.

Goals

> Encourage people to learn about native plants.

> Share resources for buying and planting native plants.

> Include a store for books on the subject.

> Have a discussion board on the subject.

The User

Visitors are coming to this site about native plants. Do they feel like they've come to the right place? Do you provide the security that users will find what they want? Are the navigation buttons meaningful?

Make clear labels versus buttons that look like native plants that you have to roll over to see what they contain (mystery meat buttons).

> Break information into small bytes: less is more.

> Use page numbers, such as 1 of 3, to show how much there is to read.

The Store

> Offer more than just the book's title. How about some advice or personal recommendations? Even better, let your visitors review and/or recommend their favorite books on native plants.

> Make the privacy policy visible.

> Make it easy to switch between the shopping cart and browsing.

The Discussions Area

> Make it a friendly space. Choose colors and graphics that relate to the subject matter. Suggest discussion topics.

> Make it easy for readers to navigate the discussions area (i.e. retrieve, post, and delete messages).

The Links Area

> Keep it updated.

> Accept submissions for links to involve your user.

note

BOOKS ON SETTING GOALS & USER-CENTERED DESIGN

Web Navigation
Jennifer Flemming
O'Reilly
ISBN: 1-5659-2351-0

Web ReDesign
Kelly Goto and Emily Cotler
New Riders Publishing
ISBN: 0-7357-1062-7

Information Architecture
Louis Rosenfeld
O'Reilly
ISBN: 1-5659-2282-4

MTIV: Making **T**he **I**nvisible **V**isible
Hillman Curtis
New Riders Publishing
ISBN: 0-7357-1165-8

establishing goals

summary

This chapter offered strategies for developing clear goals and targeting a defined audience. Here's a brief summary:

> Balance your personal goals with the potential goals of your end user. Make sure that both sets of goals are considered and weighed carefully, in order of importance.

> Define a profile for your audience, and think about what they would be looking for when they come to your site. Think like a user, and you are much more likely to satisfy one!

> Make clear labels that accurately reflect the navigation choices on your site. Use simple language—don't rely on icons or insider terminology.

> Based on the content, see if you can come up with features to match, such as discussion boards or resource links. Be sensitive to your goals, your user, and your content, and you'll succeed at reaching your objectives.

04

Comping & Prototyping

Introduction

In reality, your web design skills don't mean anything if you don't have strong ideas and concepts. The amount of time that you spend up front planning your ideas will pay off royally in the end.

MINING CREATIVE IDEAS

If you are new (or even old) to design, you will likely find yourself creatively blocked from time to time. There are a variety of ways to gain inspiration, and not all of them obvious.

Most professional designers keep a tickler file of ideas. This can consist of magazine cut-outs, photographs, articles, and keepsakes. Looking through design annuals is one way to see what ideas others have had, but sometimes looking to things unrelated to web design per se—nature, fashion, science, and news—can trigger ideas that are more original than just copying what you've already seen.

It's very important to connect with the subject matter at hand. If you are doing a site about one thing, there are usually lots of related peripheral ideas that might support an interesting creative direction. It's a great idea to free associate and make a list of quick ideas.

Let's say that you were creating a site for a wedding photographer. I'm simply going to type out any thought that comes into my mind that's related. Some of the ideas might not make any sense—that's almost the point!

Photo paper	White	Cake
Cameras	Sheer fabric	Dancing
Hearts	Bridal bouquet	Celebration
Flowers	Promise	Friends
Darkroom processing	Sunset	Barbie and Ken
Lips	Sunrise	Lovebirds
Holding hands	Happiness	Ribbon
Rings	Locket	Eyelet
Lace	Security	Pink
Eyes	Family	Silhouette

With this collection of ideas, try to hone in on the ones that resonate most. Whether you chose one or a select few concepts, think of how that idea relates to a type choice, a color scheme, or a layout. The more attention you pay to the concept up front, the more developed your idea will ultimately become.

WHY CREATE A PROTOTYPE?

The prototype process addresses many different purposes. It can establish the look and feel of the web site, determine what colors, typefaces, and image button treatments are to be used, and determine the different compositions for different levels of the site. Creating sample pages in an imaging program can point out design flaws or help a client buy off on a design direction for the web site. This process is usually conducted in an imaging tool, such as Photoshop or Fireworks.

Tool Considerations

I recommend either Photoshop or Fireworks because they are flexible design tools. You want to use a tool that makes it easy to swap a color, change some text, and move images around. Standard page layout tools such as QuarkXPress, InDesign, or PageMaker are not ideal for this purpose. Photoshop and Fireworks allow you to do more than move blocks of text around on the page—you can also create the graphics and final typography from your prototypes once they are approved. Layout tools are intended to go to a printer or printing press; Photoshop and Fireworks are geared to create images for the computer screen.

Size Considerations

One of the problems of designing a prototype for a web page is making sure that you work 1:1 for the final output. In order to do this, you need to make a decision about how big to target your web pages. For example, there are many different computer resolutions. The majority of people have their resolution set to 800×600 or 1024×768. Older machines might be set to 640×480; newer machines might be set to 1600×1200. Here's a chart that lists the common resolution settings:

Resolution	Comment
640×480	Most older computers were set to this resolution. This has not been a standard resolution since 1997.
800×600	Many laptops ship at this resolution in 2002; however, the current trend is toward support for higher resolutions.
1024×768	The most common resolution for machines that ship today.
1600×1200	A lot of computers are shipping today with this capability, but it is not as standard as 1024×768.

The decision to target a specific size screen resolution can be challenging! It's best to err toward the lowest common denominator because something that is too large for your visitors' screens will cause them to have to use scrollbars. For this reason, I recommend the conservative 800×600 resolution for most web presences.

BROWSER CHROME

Once you decide on a target resolution, it's important to shave some pixels off to make room for something called browser chrome. Browser chrome is the space that is used by the required buttons, scrollbars, and title area of a web browser.

In this 800×600 resolution example, the browser chrome takes up 47 pixels right to left, and 173 pixels top to bottom. That leaves a usable area of 753×427! If you create a prototype that doesn't account for the browser chrome, you still might cause your visitor to scroll to see your important content.

Browser chrome can take up more or less space, depending on how your end users have set their preferences. Here's a case in which the browser chrome takes up quite a bit less space. It's best to err to the worst-case scenario, however, so most web designers usually don't design for this best-case scenario.

SKETCHES HELP!

It's a great idea to sketch your idea first before you venture into an image editor. These kinds of roughs don't need to be beautiful—they just need to loosen up your brain for design ideas and directions.

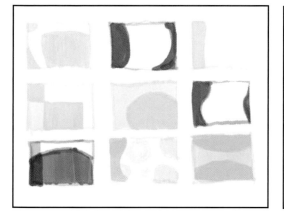

Start with a rough composition and create a bunch of fast design ideas.

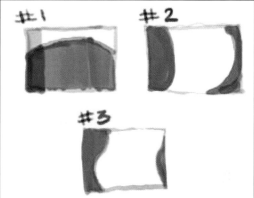

Hone in on what you like, and pick three.

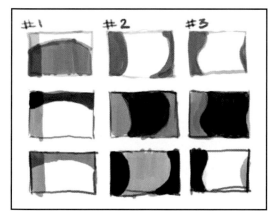

With the three ideas that you like, try different variations by using a range values from light to dark.

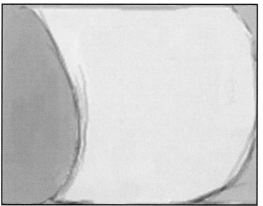

Hone in on what value and shape you like.

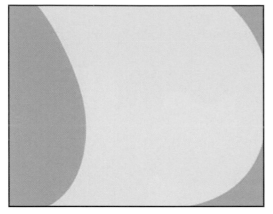

Convert the values to color choices.

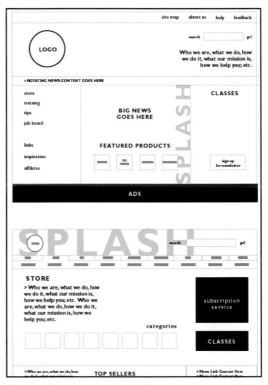

Start laying your text and other graphic elements on top of your background image.

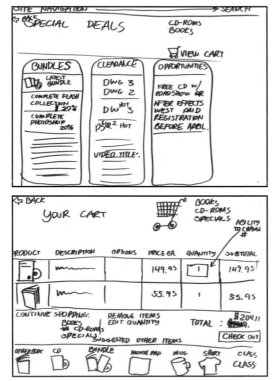

Rough your ideas out on paper before you open a graphics program. These sketches don't have to be beautiful or polished—they just loosen your mind up as you're problem solving.

Many designers create a wireframe version of the site before they introduce color or final graphic/text elements. This was created in Adobe Illustrator. The idea is to figure out the composition and layout before you start developing final artwork.

START WITH A DUMMY

Once you've determined which resolution you want to target, create a dummy file in Photoshop or Fireworks. You can open this dummy and resave it with a different name so it can serve as a template for your web projects.

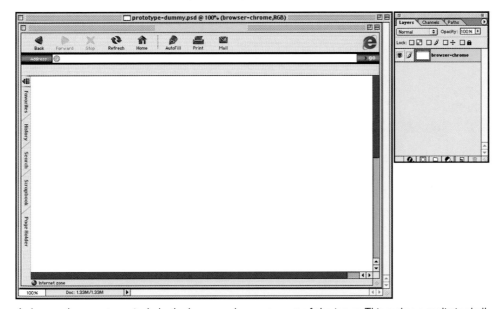

A dummy document can include the browser chrome as part of the image. This makes a realistic shell for your design roughs, so you are certain not to extend beyond the right amount of space.

I created this document by taking a screen shot. On a Mac, use the keyboard shortcut *Cmd+Shift+3*. This will create a file titled "Picture 1" on your hard drive. You can open this file in Photoshop or Fireworks to clean up the content so it appears as a generic window. On Windows, use the *Print Screen* key. This will copy the screen shot into your computer memory so that when you open a new file in Photoshop or Fireworks, the Paste command will paste the screen shot into the new document. From there, you can edit the image to remove specific content so it can become a generic shell for your prototyping needs.

Here's where you can find more sophisticated screen capture software:

Snapz Pro (Macintosh only**)**
http://www.AmbrosiaSW.com/utilities

Snag-It (Windows only**)**
http://www.techsmith.com

USING LAYERS

When creating a prototype, it's best to separate content onto layers. This helps you isolate areas that you want to change. It also makes it easier to export images as final documents once you've settled on an approved prototype.

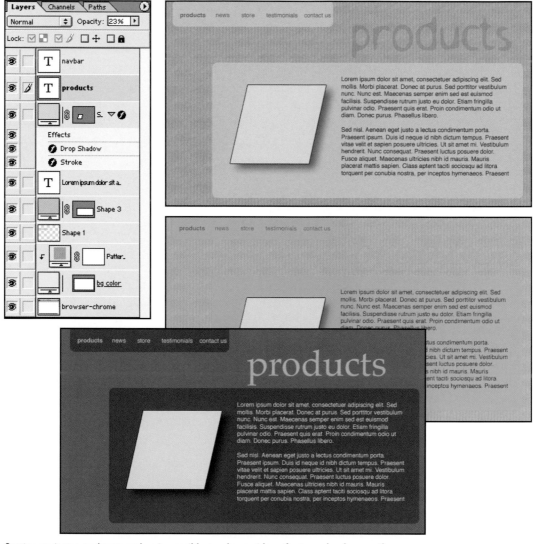

Setting up items on layers makes it possible to change ideas, fonts, and colors easily.

Once you've set up your prototype, you can turn layers on and off to isolate artwork for the final web page. This is when layers really come in handy! As well, both Photoshop and Fireworks allow you to slice images and export individual slices. All of these techniques combined are used to produce the final artwork for the site.

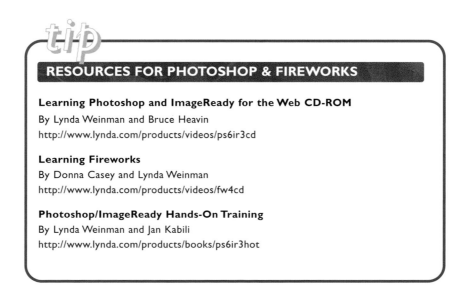

By turning off isolated layers and using a slice tool, it is possible to cut apart the prototype to produce final images. After they are sliced, they need to be optimized. Read Chapter 11, *"Speedy Graphics"* to learn about the criteria with which to optimize your graphics.

RESOURCES FOR PHOTOSHOP & FIREWORKS

Learning Photoshop and ImageReady for the Web CD-ROM
By Lynda Weinman and Bruce Heavin
http://www.lynda.com/products/videos/ps6ir3cd

Learning Fireworks
By Donna Casey and Lynda Weinman
http://www.lynda.com/products/videos/fw4cd

Photoshop/ImageReady Hands-On Training
By Lynda Weinman and Jan Kabili
http://www.lynda.com/products/books/ps6ir3hot

Making Style Guides

A style guide is useful for prototyping because it reinforces what the format should be for different design elements. This guide can also help other team members know how to create sub-pages for the site, or it can help clients understand how the web site relates to other identity elements in their own branding system.

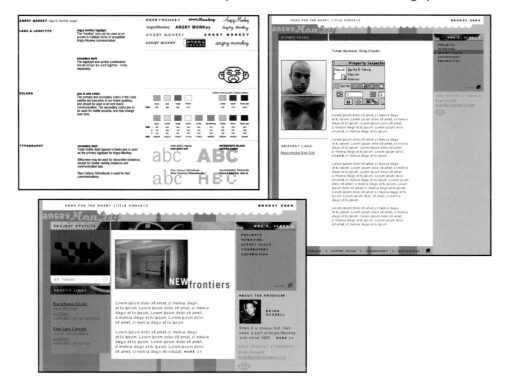

While working at Angry Monkey, a web design firm that unfortunately is no longer in business, Domenique Sillett created this style guide for their web site. You can see here how the style guide relates to a finished web page with the applied styles.

DANGERS OF PROTOTYPING

Without understanding how web pages are constructed or optimized, it's entirely possible to design something that is difficult or impractical to execute. Here are some pitfalls to be aware of:

Can't be done in conventional HTML.

When images overlap, or edges of text intersect with other page elements, you might be forcing your design to be constructed as an image instead of in conventional HTML. In general, if you avoid overlapping shapes and text, you have a better chance of using standard HTML. If accessibility isn't an issue (see Chapter 8, *"Accessibility Issues"*), then publishing a lot of images might not be a problem.

Need to generate a transparent.

In the event that you have a non-rectangular shape for your graphic, you will likely want to create a type of graphic that can include a mask. The most common format for this type of graphic is a transparent GIF. Read Chapter 16, *"Transparent GIFs"* to learn how to make these critters.

Background image will repeat.

Whatever graphic you insert into the background element in HTML will repeat unless you use CSS techniques to prevent this. To learn more about background images, read Chapter 15, *"Background Tiles."*

Graphics can't compress well.

There are two primary types of graphics on the Web: GIFs and JPEGs. Understanding how the file format is affected by the type of images you create can help reduce the file size of your graphics. To learn about optimizing graphics, read Chapter 11, *"Speedy Graphics."*

---

tip

HOW MUCH DETAIL?

Prototypes usually begin with little detail and slowly evolve toward a final result. There are different levels of prototypes that you'll create at different stages. Don't make your initial efforts too detailed, as you can expect they'll need to be changed over and over again. You shouldn't be doing finals until the necessary people have gone through the review process with you.

comping & prototyping

summary

Prototypes help you work out your ideas and allow you to troubleshoot potential problems. Here's a short list that outlines the workflow advocated in this chapter:

> Use a flexible image editor, such as Photoshop or Fireworks, to create your prototypes.

> Establish a target size before you begin, and take browser chrome into account.

> Set up artwork on layers for maximum flexibility.

> Develop a style guide.

> Be aware of authoring pitfalls and don't design yourself into a corner that you can't work your way out of.

Information Architecture

Introduction

Determining the information architecture of your site is a process upon which many other processes hinge. At its most simple form, information architecture outlines the structure of your web site. It's the process of developing categories and labels, and deciding where all the pieces of your web site belong, and in what order.

Because hyperlinks are non-linear, mapping the order of your pages is not often a straightforward process. Planning the information architecture of your site is one of the most important aspects of developing your web site content, even though it has nothing to do with graphics, color, animation, or typography.

This chapter covers how to organize your web site into an architecture that will best suit your subject matter and your visitor's needs. By sticking to the user-centered design techniques that are discussed throughout this book, you can develop an organizational system that works for your content, your message, and your end user.

WHAT IS INFORMATION ARCHITECTURE?

Information architecture is a term that stands for the organization of information. This can be the process of determining how many categories your web site will contain or what they will be called. The objective of information architecture is to organize information to make your content easy to find.

In libraries in the U.S., we have an organizational system called the Dewey Decimal System. This classification system assigns a book to one of 10 main topic categories, each of which is further broken into 10 sub-categories; each of those subcategories is broken down into even more categories, and so on. This classification number is then referenced to the book's title, author, and subject matter. This system works well because it is the same in all libraries, and most Americans learn to use it from the time they enter grade school.

Books use information architecture. You know to look to the Table of Contents, to chapter numbers, to page numbers, and to the index in the back. Books have an established navigation and organization system. Web sites do not!

It is helpful when determining what type of information architecture to choose for your site to look at other established systems.

COMMON ORGANIZATIONAL SYSTEMS

> Alphabetical

> Geographical

> Chronological

> Audience-specific

> By metaphor

> By topic

> By importance to developer

> By importance to user

> Custom

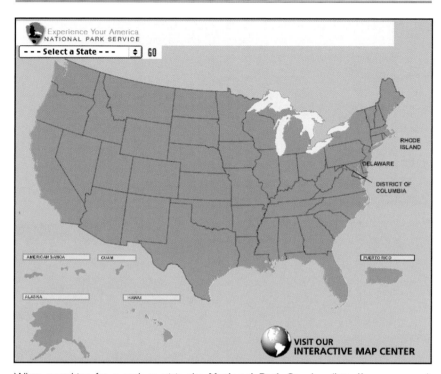

When searching for a park to visit, the **National Park Service** (http://www.nps.com) sensibly organizes the information by geography.

Macromedia (http://www.macromedia.com) offers the link to a designer/developer section. This section is organized by audience-specific information.

COMMON NAVIGATIONAL SYSTEMS

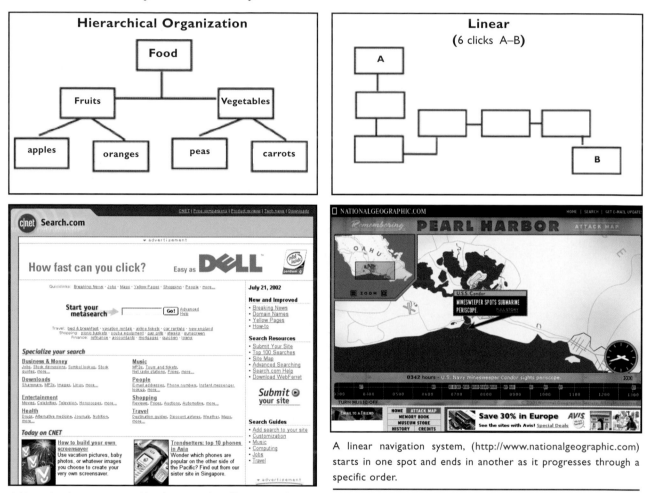

A hierarchical site structure, like the one at http://www.search.com, builds off ideas and sprouts new children as it grows in complexity.

A linear navigation system, (http://www.nationalgeographic.com) starts in one spot and ends in another as it progresses through a specific order.

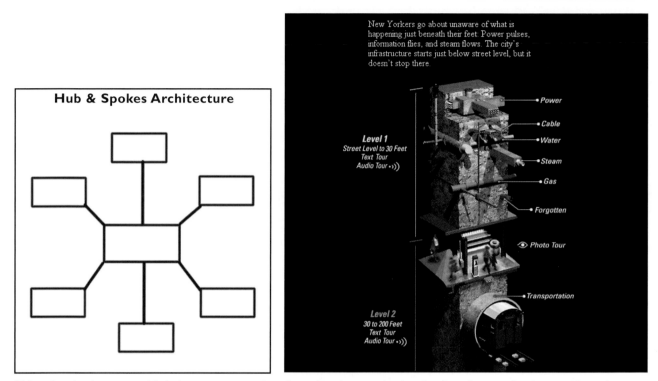

Hub & Spokes Architecture

Hub-and-spokes has a central hub that you return to in order to launch to another location (http://www.nationalgeographic.com).

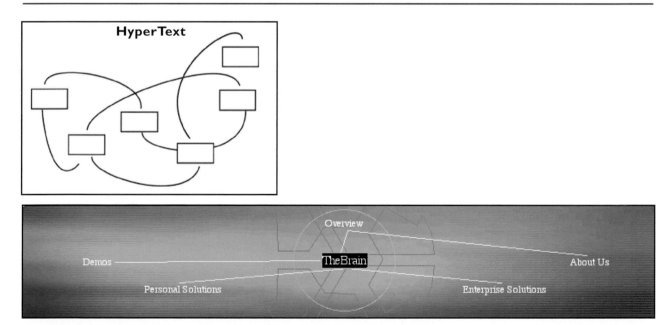

HyperText navigation has no start or end point—everything is launched from any direction.

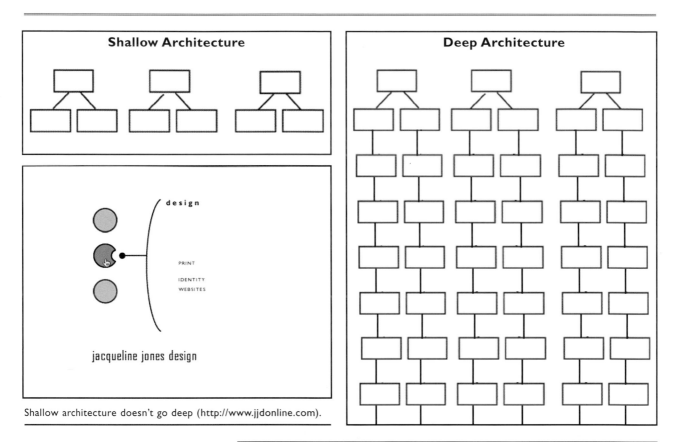

Shallow Architecture

Deep Architecture

Shallow architecture doesn't go deep (http://www.jjdonline.com).

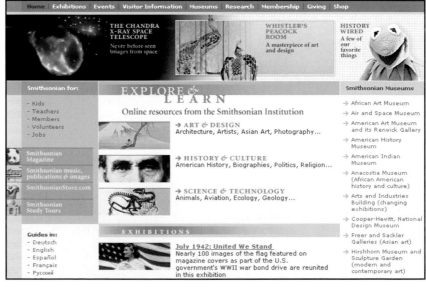

Deep architecture has levels that go very deep (http://www.smithsonian.org).

THE PROCESS

The first step to determining your site's architecture is to decide what category names will be for each section, as well as the number of sections that you want. It's good to think about what areas will need to be persistent versus what areas will change.

For example, many sites that use ecommerce will have persistent links for the shopping cart, tracking, shipping, and/or billing information. Many people use index cards or sticky notes to write down category ideas. This is a great technique because it allows you to move subjects around easily and change your mind. Plan to spend at least a day or two on a small site—or weeks on a larger site—to make sure you've tried every possibility and scenario. This is a case when it's really great to encourage others to contribute their ideas.

Just as you would conduct user testing of a finished web site, it's a good idea to test your information architecture ideas on a few trusted colleagues or potential end users. There are many tools like Adobe Illustrator or Macromedia Freehand that help you organize ideas. Here are some other alternatives:

Visio

http://www.microsoft.com/office/visio

Inspiration

http://www.inspiration.com

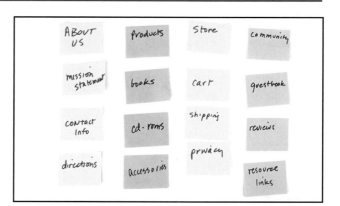

Index cards or sticky notes work well because you can change your mind and rearrange topics easily.

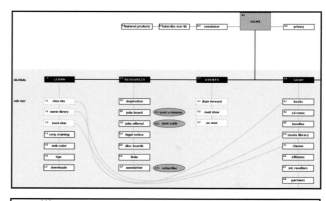

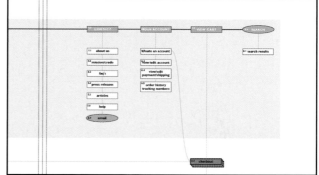

This site map was laid out in Adobe Illustrator and was wider than a single screen to map out.

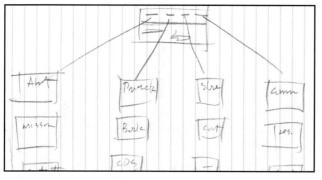

Scribbles do fine as well. Most of the time people map ideas out on paper before they make a more formal site map.

HOW MANY CATEGORIES?

There are some experts who say that you should never have more than 6–8 links from your front page. Others say that if you rely on allowing your users to use a search box, that your navigation system has failed. Every site is ultimately different, but it is a good rule of thumb to try to limit your categories to as few as possible, without compromising usability. This is a delicate line to cross, and is easier said than done. Is less more, or is more more? Both the sites below are extremely popular, even though the approaches are different.

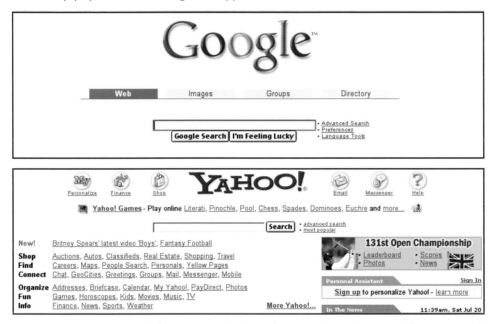

Although **Google.com** and **Yahoo.com** are both search engines, they take a very different approach to categories. Google offers five categories and a giant search box. Yahoo! has numerous other links, inviting people to either browse or search. Yahoo! also offers a lot of other services such as email and personalization.

CATEGORY CASE STUDIES

This section looks at four different major software companies and shows how different information architectural approaches were taken with each site.

In all of these examples, each site has similar offerings. How they have chosen to structure their content is what differs. You can see what a difference the structure makes by studying web sites that have a similar purpose (these are all software sites) but different approaches. As you are developing your own content, try to find at least four other sites that are similar to yours and compare what works and what doesn't.

Corel.com attracts the most attention to its tag line and mission statement. This assumes that the visitor coming to this site doesn't know what Corel offers and needs to be sold on them as a company. If you were looking for product support or to upgrade, you would have to search a bit harder for that information within this architectural shell. The categories Products and Support exist, but they're pretty low in the visual hierarchy. The next read is on the potential user categories: Small Business, Enterprise, or Creative Pro. The assumption is that either you are new to Corel altogether or that you want to identify what kind of software suits your business or creative needs. Again, it's an approach that assumes a novice visitor and offers less support for the existing customer. Notice that there isn't a search box! If you were coming to Corel to find a specific item, you would have to click through a lot of links and not feel very secure that you might find what you were looking for quickly enough.

The **Microsoft.com** main categories are easy to find, and the search box is prominent. If you wanted to meander around and look through different sections, you'd have lots of options from the front page. A lot of visual attention is given to a series of images on the top that contains the tag line MSN: Put your PC to bed at night. This is a link to an article on MSN, but that's not clear from the graphic at all. Still, this doesn't comprise the ability of new or frequent Microsoft vistors to find what they're searching for. There's no attempt to identify the potential user as a business, creative, enterprise, or anything else.

Adobe.com places a lot of attention on the main navigation categories, even offering sub-categories on the front page. Search isn't at the top level, since it requires that you click on a link to reach it. There is no attempt to identify what type of user is interested in what type of product, such as whether you're a creative, business, or enterprise user. Product announcements and advertisements are given great prominence, which makes sense since this is a software company. Still, the lack of an easy-to-find search box on the top level is a frustrating choice to those visitors who want to use the search feature.

Macromedia.com has clear main and persistent navigation. Search is easy to find and is usable right from the front page. They choose to prominently promote a different single product on the upper right. Below that, they have lots of other links and categories for people who want to browse around. They have one main navigation link that allows visitors to identify themselves as designers or developers.

Labels

Once you establish what categories you need, there is a challenge to choose a usable "label." For example, here are similar words for the same thing:

> Product

> Offerings

> Merchandise

> Descriptions

> Stuff

> Gear

It's very important to create labels that make sense to your visitor—avoid "insider" terminology or cutesy verbiage that can potentially confuse outsiders. As well, for those international visitors to your site, labels that are unclear may not translate well.

Do you know the store **Abercrombie & Fitch** (http://www.abercrombie.com) as A&F? Do you know where a link called Lifestyle would take you? Abercrombie sells women's clothes as well as men's and kid's. Do you know how to get there? This site has beautiful graphics and photography, but its site architecture and labeling is challenging to use. It shows that beauty alone doesn't cut it. Good site architecture and labeling practices can cause all your hard work on aesthetics to fail.

Labeling Case Study

The following examples showcase different labeling systems.

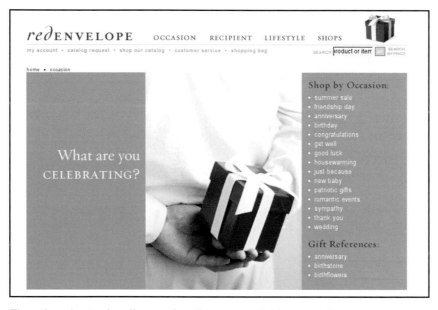

The gift web site http://www.redenvelope.com is broken into four main navigation categories: Occasion, Recipient, Lifestyle, and Shops. By clicking on each section, a list of subcategories appears on the right.

This is the *Recipient* section. I might have chosen a less impersonal word than Recipient, such as "Person" or "For Whom?"

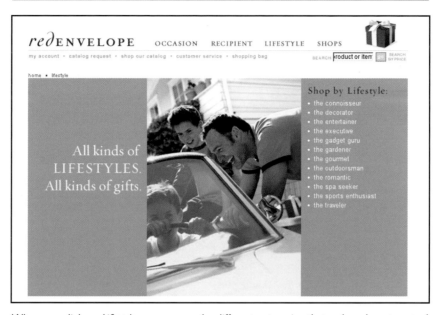

When you click on *Lifestyle*, you can see the different categories that redenvelope targets. I think the term "Interests" or "Specialties" might be more descriptive and easily understood than Lifestyle.

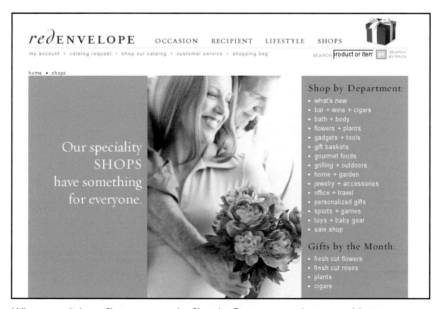

When you click on *Shops*, you get the Shop by Department subcategory. It's important to keep your labels consistent! I think "Department" might be a better label than Shops. It's more descriptive of what you'd find when you get to the link.

INFORMATION ARCHITECTURE

SUMMARY

Site architecture requires careful planning and sensitivity to your user's objectives. Here are some key points found in this chapter:

> Information architecture relates to how you organize the content on your site. There are numerous methods to choose from, and you will need to invest serious time and inquiry into the process.

> The number of categories that you use on your site is determined in the information architecture process. Most developers err toward fewer links, but some sites thrive on offering lots of links and choices, too. There is no one right way, so you have to rely on your user's preferences in relationship to the content you are presenting.

> The way you label your categories can make a huge difference to the success of your information organization. Try to pick words that are meaningful to your end user, and stay consistent from label to label.

06

Navigation

Introduction

Navigating is something we do in everyday life without really thinking about it. We know how to read a book by looking at a Table of Contents and page numbers. We know to cross the street when the light turns green. We know to turn on a light by flipping a switch. These tasks are simple because the "interface" to accomplish them is understood by everyone in our culture.

In the case of a book, a traffic light, or a light switch, the navigation objective is fairly simple. A web site's objective has many more problems to solve. The fact that a web site does not necessarily present information in a linear manner is problem number one. A link on one page might take you to 10 links that spawn 100 more pages. It is impossible to thoroughly index all the pages as you would in a book, or use a simple on off switch to signal go forward or backward, or jump to a new location or to stop.

This chapter focuses on the challenges of navigation, planning for navigation, different types of graphics for navigation, and examples of successful and unsuccessful navigation.

THE PURPOSE OF NAVIGATION

Your navigation system is the guide that allows your audience access to your information. Developing a navigation system can be thought of as creating an educational system for your end users. You are educating them about how to use your site, and creating a visual and functional vocabulary that contains words, pictures and, possibly, sound and motion. Sometimes you want to communicate that something on your site is a link. Sometimes you want to communicate that something is a final static destination. This process takes tremendous thought and care.

PLANNING YOUR NAVIGATION

The navigation system that you design for your site should answer the following general questions for your audience:

> Where am I?

> What's here?

> Where else can I go?

> How do I go forward?

> How do I get back?

More specific navigation challenges come with more specific tasks. For an ecommerce system, letting your users know how to order, how to check out, how something will be shipped, that the site is secure, and what the shipping charges will be are all specific navigation challenges.

With a book site like http://www.barnesandnoble.com, for example, visitors want to find books. They might want to search by author, title, subject, bestsellers, reviews, or by impulse. The navigation for this specific task has to offer alternative ways to achieve the same objective. The more versatile the navigation, the more successful it will be because it will serve the greatest variety of users.

EVERYONE WANTS SOMETHING

People come to your site wanting something. They have different needs and expectations, but they nevertheless want something. If you provide that "something," they will want to come back. If you don't, they won't. This is a simplistic summary but, nevertheless, very true.

Since most sites offer more than one "something," it's helpful to make a list of what you think people who come to your site might want. Depending on the scope of your site, this list will be short or long. Every web site scenario will be different. Here are some general examples of what potential visitors might want:

> To find something	> To auction something
> To see something	> To purchase something
> To learn about something	> To sell something
> To compare something	> To publish something
> To refer someone to something	> To find someone
> To trade something	> To interact with someone
> To read what someone else thinks about something	> To lurk around other people who interact

Next, you should make a list of what you want. Here are some typical examples of what you might want.

> To make money	> To get attention
> To share information	> To teach something
> To get feedback	> To communicate

By assessing what it is that people want and weighing that with what you want, you can then go about the business of designing the visual hierarchy for your navigation.

DEVELOPING VISUAL HIERARCHY

As the site designer, you have a lot of control over how people interact with your site. You can and should make certain aspects much more prominent than others. Visual hierarchy can be established using visual design techniques such as color, shape, size, transparency, typography, and composition.

Shutterfly.com has a simple, targeted approach. Its visual hierarchy clearly illustrates what the site is about.

You have the power to draw in your visitors and guide them with your design. If you give everything equal importance, you make no assumptions about what your audience wants or what you want them to accomplish. Sometimes this is a positive approach, but most often it is not.

Sites, like **Kodak.com**, that offer a lot of services have a much harder time creating a targeted visual hierarchy.

THE IMPORTANCE OF SEARCH

All sites do not have search capabilities, and some sites don't need them. But if you have much content to offer at all, there is probably is no greater service than to provide a search function. Most buttons contend to send you only to a single destination; however, a search button is the portal to many potential links.

If I wanted to use Yahoo! to find a bicycle club in Ventura County, I could choose two different methods of getting there: clicking on links or using the search capability. Clicking on links could easily take forever. Scanning the front page, my eyes quickly dart over hundreds of different words and links. Let's see… What category is it? Health > Fitness?

Once I've clicked on Fitness at http://www.yahoo.com, I am presented with fitness categories, but none of them says biking. Maybe it would be under Physical Education? Or Aerobics? I'm already stumped and thinking I'd better use my Back button.

What person in his or her right mind wouldn't use Search at this point instead? If you have a site with any depth at all, make sure your Search button is prominent and easy to find. To learn about adding search functionality to your site, read Chapter 26, *"Adding Programming Features."*

PERSISTENT NAVIGATION

Some navigation is page-specific, and some is persistent throughout the entire web site. The page-specific navigation is something that will change depending on the context of the page. In a store, the navigation choices might have to do with shipping, privacy, security, and schedule. In a product section, the navigation choices might have something to do with pictures, information, reviews, price, etc.

There are certain aspects of the site that people might want to get to from any page. Typically, these navigation choices include the major categories of your site (i.e. store and products) as well as contact information. Without persistent navigation on your site, you create dead-ends. Some visitors might come to your site via a referral link and enter through a side or back door. If this happens, they won't know what else you offer unless you provide persistent links on that page.

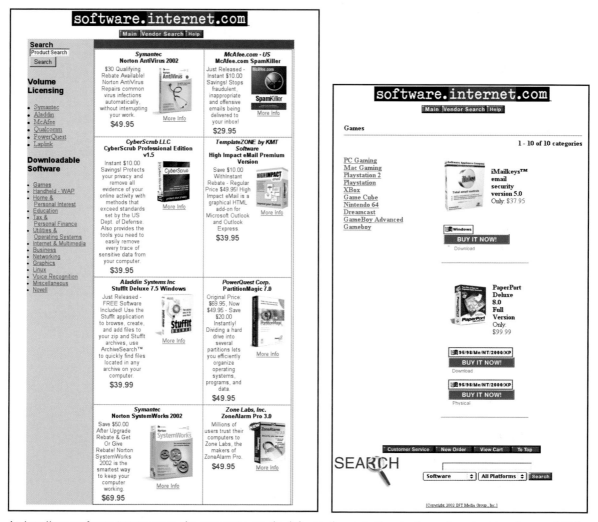

At http://www.software.internet.com, the categories on the left are the navigation to the main categories. As you drill in, however, you lose all contact with the main categories of the site. This page is a great candidate for persistent navigation.

This software site (http://www.zones.com) takes a different approach. It keeps navigation persistent on every page. On which site do you think it is easier to find your way around?

ISSUES RELATED TO NAVIGATION

Navigation is not an island unto itself. You cannot develop successful navigation without addressing the following related issues.

Planning: You would develop a different navigation system for a children's site than you would for a commerce or information site. You shouldn't begin to develop the navigation graphics or look and feel for a project until you have come up with a profile for your audience. You will find information about developing a strategy in Chapter 4, *"Establishing Goals."*

Architecture: You wouldn't build a house without plans, and you can't build a web site without them either. Setting up the architecture beforehand lets you know what kind of navigation components you'll need to design. For more information, read Chapter 6, *"Information Architecture."*

Comps: Developing a "look and feel" for your navigation requires that you first prototype how the artwork is going to look. For more information on this process, read Chapter 5, *"Comping & Prototyping."*

Accessibility: Every web site should have a plan for making it accessible to as many people as possible. Read more about this essential practice in Chapter 8, *"Accessibility Issues."*

Usability: After you've designed the site navigation, you'll need to test it to see how successfully it meets your goals. Learn more about this in Chapter 27, *"Usability."*

NAVIGATION GRAPHICS & INDICATORS

This section offers a library of common styles of navigation graphics and systems for describing navigation.

HTML or XHTML Link

An HTML link typically has an underline. The advantage of an HTML link over an image-based link is that it can be indexed by search engines and it's accessible to visually impaired users with a screen reader. You can make images and imagemaps accessible with a little know-how, which you'll learn in Chapter 8, "*Accessibility Issues.*"

CSS Rollover

A rollover made with CSS can change color on rollover, and the underline for a link can be programmed to be on or off. This kind of rollover still has the advantage of being searchable by a search engine because it is in ASCII text.

Dropdown Menu

Dropdown menus are a great navigation device because they don't take up a lot of room, yet can contain a lot of contextual information. For those people who don't need to see the extra info, they don't have to; and for those who do, it's a beautiful thing. Dropdown menus are created many different ways: in Flash, using DHTML, or with JavaScript. They are usually quite complex to program but very handy and useful!

Sitemap

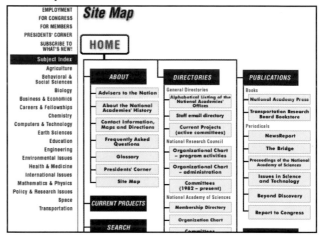

The National Academies (http://www.nationalacadamies.org) sitemap shows a flowchart of the entire site and is a good alternative navigation system. Often, users will discover a part of the site they did not know existed by looking at a map of the entire site.

Breadcrumb

Directory Topics		New! Submit a Site
You are here: Home > Entertainment > Celebrities > Artists > Painters		
Painters A	Painters H-I	Painters P
Painters B	Painters J	Painters R
Painters C	Painters K	Painters S
Painters D	Painters L	Painters T
Painters E-F	Painters M	Painters V
Painters G	Painters N-O	Painters W

A breadcrumb shows the path to and from the page you are currently on.

Imagemap

cd-roms & online movie library

learning **Mac OS X**
learning **Photoshop Elements**
learning **QuarkXPress 5.0**
learning **Illustrator 10**
learning **Director 8.5**
1624+ movies and growing in our online training movie library!
Only $25 per month!

An imagemap is a single graphic that contains multiple links. It is a good way to have multiple links represented with graphics, but without downloading a lot of pictures inside complicated table structures.

Persistent Navigation

Home | Accessories | Books | CD-ROMs | Classes | DVDs | Satellite Classes | Special Bundles | Videos
All Products | Cart | Checkout | Customer Registration | Customer Menu

Persistent navigation is usually created entirely in XHTML, HTML, or CSS and is located at the bottom of every web page. The advantage to using persistent navigation is that users who enter your site via a back or side door (through a referral link, for example) still see the scope of what it offers. Persistent navigation should be used in conjunction with other, easier to find and use, navigation methods.

Remote Rollovers

A remote rollover, like the one at http://www.altoids.com, means that when you roll over one part of the screen, another part of the screen updates. Like a dropdown menu, this saves space because the new image is only shown in context of its rollover. You don't have to leave the page to see or obtain new information. This kind of rollover can be accomplished with JavaScript, CSS, or Flash.

Graphic Rollovers

Rollovers indicate that something is a link much more clearly than static graphics do.

Forms Navigation

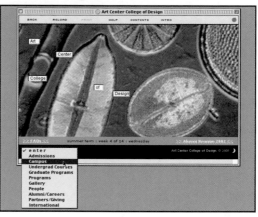

Simple form menus work as well as elaborately designed menus with graphics. At http://www.artcenter.edu, **Art Center** makes extensive use of forms-based navigation and still manages to look very highly designed.

Frames

The Art Center site (http://www.artcenter.edu) uses frames to show wide graphics of their student gallery. This is an unconventional use of frames, yet it succeeds to show the gallery space in a much more compelling manner than with smaller, individual images.

BAD & GOOD NAVIGATION GRAPHIC PRACTICES

This section showcases a variety of common navigation challenges and solutions.

Marking the Spot

The interface for **Design For Life** (http://ndm.si.edu/dfl) uses a frameset at the bottom for its navigation and in the central area for its main navigation topics. This is a site that houses an exhibit from the Cooper-Hewitt National Design Museum in New York. There is a duplication of topics in the text-based bottom navigation and the graphics-based main navigation. This has become a common practice, and it offers two different ways to navigate to the same information. In this example, the designer has given precedence to the graphic links in the center of the screen over the text-based links at the bottom. As you drill into the site, the text links at the bottom become your main source of navigation.

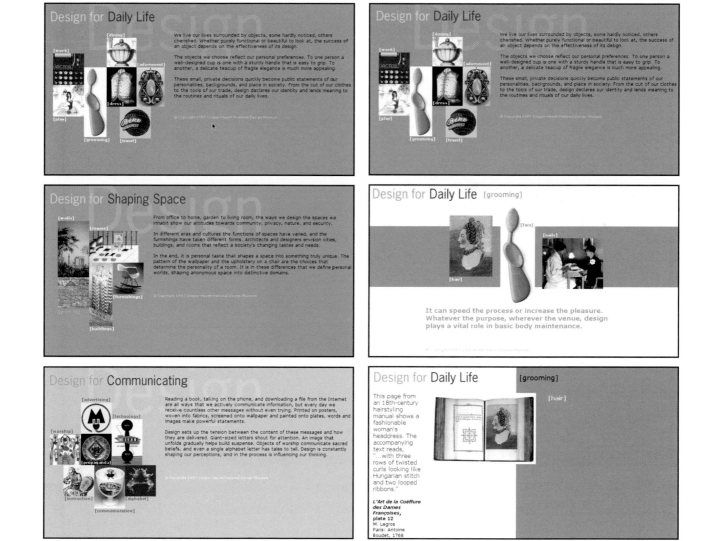

The **Cooper-Hewitt National Design museum** uses a frameset for its navigation. This allows you to click on a link at the bottom of the screen, and then the top of the screen switches to that location. The site marks each section clearly with a beautiful graphic treatment showing clearly where you are. In addition to using word markers to identify each section, the site brands each area with a different color.

As you drill into the site, you'll find that there are levels of information, and the layout reflects the levels. When you drill in to look at a category, there is a horizontal band across the page. Drilling in deeper shows a vertical band and more focused layout.

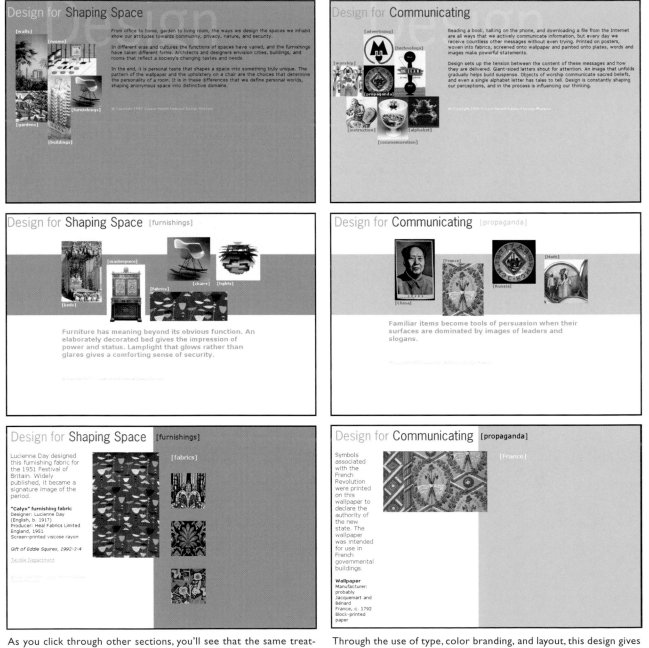

As you click through other sections, you'll see that the same treatment has been used consistently throughout the site.

Through the use of type, color branding, and layout, this design gives the visitor lots of consistent clues about navigation.

Navigation Level

Target's site (http://www.target.com) offers four alternative ways to navigate through the site. The persistent navigation on top takes visitors to areas that are commonly referenced, yet not central to the store experience. The search box allows shoppers to go to a specific product or area of interest. The shopping navigation at the left takes visitors to departments within the store. The impulse shopping links take visitors to a specific product.

Once you've clicked on a department (this is showing Bed and Bath), the navigation changes subtly, yet dramatically. Where the department navigation area was before is now replaced by a text-based navigation to the specific areas within a department. To return to the department list, you would use the form-based menu called More Departments. While this might seem like it lacks consistency, it works. Visitors were taught on the first page where to look on the screen for key navigation decisions. As the decision choices change, their location does not, which allows the site design to respond contextually to what the customer is trying to accomplish.

Clicking on a specific section of Bed and Bath (Bath), the navigation bar still offers excellent feedback support that tells you where you are, where you've been, and how to get to other departments. Now, fewer products are shown, allowing you to click on one that interests you.

As you get to a specific area, the focus becomes extremely narrow, allowing you to examine that one product more closely.

Next Buttons

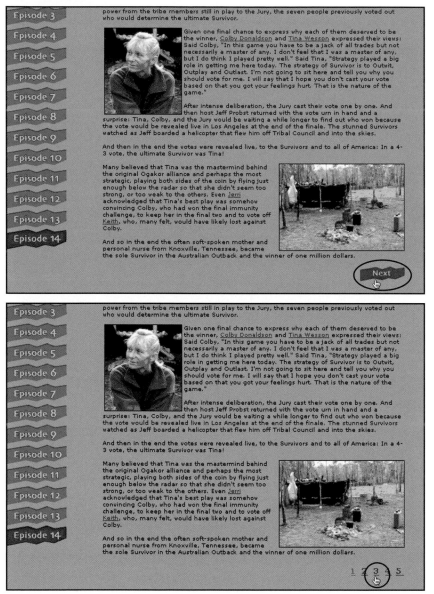

The use of a *Next* button is common on the Web. The problem with a Next button is that it doesn't tell you how many pages are yet to come. This page is from http://www.cbs.com/primetime/survivor3. It's more informative to put numbers on the page, such as this, or 1 of 5, to let the visitor know how many pages there are in all. The Next butto does not achieve this.

CONSISTENCY MATTERS

As you develop your navigation, it's important that you create a consistent visual vocabulary. Many sites break this rule on the front page, which serves as an introductory entry into the site, but then keep things consistent throughout.

Restoration Hardware (http://www.restorationhardware.com) has a different navigation approach on its front page than it does on its interior pages.

After clicking on the *Accessories* link, the context-sensitive navigation for that area appears on the left. There is a consistent approach, even though the front page was different from the interior pages.

After clicking on the *Hardware* link, the left-side navigation becomes context-sensitive to that category. All of the links that were found on the front page are suddenly at the top of this interior page.

The **Pottery Barn** site (http://www.potterybarn.com), owned by the same parent company, takes a front page approach similar to Restoration Hardware. Like the cover of a catalog, this page has a catchy image and lists all the categories for the site.

Unfortunately, once you click on an interior page, there is no way to see all the categories again without going back to the main page. This approach is called "hub and spokes," and it requires that the visitor return to the hub to find other choices. It is not nearly as practical or efficient as a "consistent navigation" scheme.

Chase the Button

In the **Six Feet Under** section of the **HBO** site (http://www.hbo. com), they have created an area called "The Wake," which contains extra information about the characters from this TV series. The menu of character names moves in 3D space, and you have to chase each picture with your cursor in order to click on it. This kind of navigation is novel for a moment, but becomes frustrating to the end user when it becomes hard to access wanted information.

Splash Screens

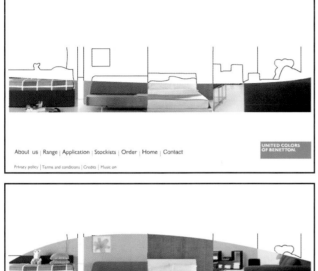

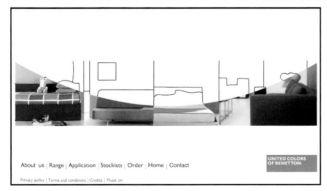

When you arrive at the **Benetton Paints** site (http://www. benettonpaints.com), the front page animates and plays music. There is no need for a "Skip Intro" button, however, because even as the animation builds and loops, the navigation is always present.

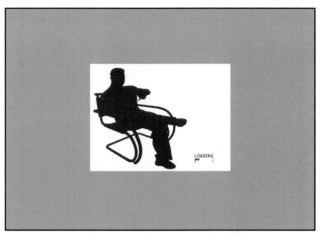

This wonderful site (http://www.iconologic.com/ff2002/neocon) has a loading screen before it can play. The man sitting in the chair keeps raising his arm to look at his watch, and the animation loops until the site loads. Consider putting navigation or useful information on your load screens as an alternative to requiring that your visitors wait at your door with nothing to do. Or, at the very least, add a "Skip Intro" button that will allow people to go to the site or a navigation page more quickly.

To Icon or Not

With the introduction of graphical user interfaces, icons and thumbnail pictures became popular in interface design. A lot of people have the preconception that an icon makes a program more friendly and easy to use. I actually don't agree with this. I think that icons should never be used as a substitute for text-based navigation. It takes a long time to establish a visual vocabulary that is understood by all people. This set of visual links was found on the front page of the **Celebrity Cruises** site (http://www.celebritycruises.com).

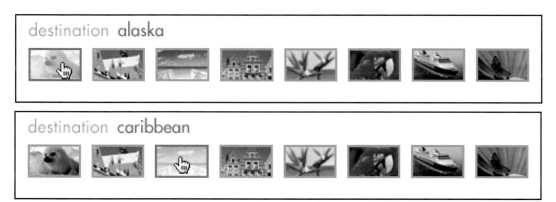

I knew that these were rollovers (big assumption!), by moving my mouse over these thumbnails I would see that they represented different cruise destinations. **Vince Flanders**, in his funny book *Web Pages That Suck*, coins a term that applies to these buttons: "Mystery Meat Buttons." If you don't know what a button means until you mouse over or click on it, it is a *mystery meat* button. While the site designer's intent was surely to create a beautiful presentation, the assumption that the visitor would know that these were icons or buttons is a big leap of faith.

While the icons on the **Yahoo!** site aren't nearly as stylish or beautiful as the thumbnails on the Celebrity Cruises site, you don't have to wonder what they mean.

NAVIGATION RESOURCES

To learn more about navigation, check out the following books and web articles:

Web Navigation, Designing the User Experience
Jennifer Flemming
O'Reilly
ISBN: 1565923510

Web Pages That Suck
Vincent Flanders
Sybex
ISBN: 0782140203

Design of Everyday Things
Donald A. Norman
Doubleday
ISBN: 0385267746

Envisioning Information
Edward Tufte
Graphics Press
ISBN: 0961392118

Web Menus with Beauty and Brains
Wendy Peck
John Wiley & Sons
ISBN: 0764536435

Web Navigation – Knowing Where You Are
http://www.emdash.com/webapps_new/nav.htm

Bad Human Factors Designs
http://www.baddesigns.com/

Where Am I? Navigation and Interface
http://www.webreference.com/authoring/design/talent/chap3/1/4.html

Designing for Navigation
http://www.wdvl.com/WebRef/Navigation/Design.html

navigation

SUMMARY

Navigation is a tricky craft that needs to be carefully planned and executed. Here are some key points that this chapter covers:

> A navigation system needs to provide a visual and functional vocabulary that teaches visitors how to use your site.

> Avoid mystery meat buttons and icons that don't have text references.

> Use persistent navigation on all pages so visitors can always get to other locations and see the scope of your site.

> Offer alternative methods to reaching a goal. Not all visitors come to your site wanting the same thing.

> The hierarchy of your site design should support navigation goals.

Accessibility Issues

Introduction

Accessibility has become one of the hottest new topics in web development. This is due to increased awareness and recent legislation that mandates that web sites work for people with disabilities, such as those who are visually, hearing, and/or cognitively impaired.

Making your web sites accessible does not "only" mean making them accessible to people with disabilities but accessible to "all" who visit your site, including those with disabilities and those without disabilities. For example, if you implement a technique that makes your site more accessible to a person who is sight impaired and the result is that your site becomes less accessible to someone who has good vision, you have failed in making your site accessible.

This chapter focuses on techniques that help you follow government guidelines and practical guidelines to make your sites usable for all people.

GOVERNMENT MANDATES

As the Web has matured, the need for accessibility has spawned legislation that protects citizens with disabilities. This section of the chapter gives you some background information into that legislation.

> The Americans with Disabilities Act (ADA) of 1990
http://www.usdoj.gov/crt/ada/adahom1.htm

The Americans with Disabilities Act of 1990 defines requirements of state and local governments and places of public accommodation to provide assistance and services, if necessary, to ensure appropriate and effective communication with disabled persons. Similar to the Rehabilitation Act, which defines the federal department and agencies' responsibilities, the Americans with Disabilities Act defines the role of states, local governments, and all other parties identified as entities under the ADA (such as city governments, businesses, etc.). If your web site contains information available to the general public and parts of it are not accessible to disabled persons, you would be in violation of the ADA. In fact, lawsuits have already been won over this very issue.

Try not to panic. This does not mean you are going to be sued tomorrow if someone cannot access your vacation photos on your personal home page. Under the guidelines of the ADA, those who are affected by these guidelines must have a web presence with information available to the general public.

> The Rehabilitation Act of 1973
http://www.ed.gov/offices/OSERS/RSA/Policy/Legislation/narrative.html

The Rehabilitation Act of 1973 is a piece of federal legislation that is intended to provide disabled persons employment, economic, and social independence. The Act contains several sections that focus on rights, advocacy, and protections for disabled persons.

> Section 508
http://www.section508.gov

Section 508 is part of the revision to the Rehabilitation Act of 1973 under the Workforce Investment Act of 1998, which addresses the needs of disabled persons and information technology. In a nutshell, this legislation outlines the responsibilities of the federal government departments and agencies in helping disabled persons become active, independent, and self-sufficient parts of society, which includes making certain information accessible to them.

SECTION 508

After reading the last section, you know where *Section 508: Electronic Information & Technology* comes from. This section of the Rehabilitation Act mandates that federal departments and agencies ensure that access to electronic and information technology is made available to disabled persons that are federal employees or part of the general public. There are two major points under this section:

> Federal agencies that develop, distribute, maintain, deliver, or use electronic information and technology must assume the responsibility for making this same information available to persons with disabilities in a manner that is comparable to those without disabilities.

> Disabled persons, who are part of the general public, who are attempting to get information from a federal agency must be able to do so in a manner which is comparable to those persons without disabilities.

Gosh, nothing like a little light reading, huh? ;-) The point of the previous section isn't to make you an expert on either of the two acts; rather, it's intended to give you a better foundation in understanding how the issue of web accessibility came to be and who is responsible for the development and monitoring of these web accessibility issues. In the next section, you will learn about the web accessibility guidelines that have been developed by the web standards committee, the **W**orld **W**ide **W**eb **C**onsortium (W3C).

W3C Accessibility Guidelines

The W3C has taken a proactive role in helping developers learn to make accessible web pages. Their web site contains a collection of documents that you should definitely know about and read carefully. These documents have been widely acknowledged as the de facto standard for understanding, creating, and developing accessible web pages. The list that follows is suggested reading:

Web Content Accessibility Guidelines 1.0

This is one of the most important documents on web accessibility. It identifies and explains the 14 guidelines, their checkpoints, and prioritizes each.
http://www.w3.org/TR/WCAG10/

Techniques for Web Content Accessibility Guidelines 1.0

This document gives you techniques and examples for making your web sites accessible. Once you understand the 14 guidelines of web accessibility, this document will help you create accessible pages by giving you sample code and different scenarios you might encounter. You will want to print and keep a copy of this one nearby.
http://www.w3.org/TR/WCAG10-TECHS/

CSS Techniques for Web Content Accessibility Guidelines 1.0

This document focuses on creating accessible web pages using Cascading Style Sheets. You will find examples using CSS in addition to deprecated code, which illustrates something developers should avoid doing. This is an important document and should be read carefully.
http://www.w3.org/TR/WCAG10-CSS-TECHS/

HTML Techniques for Web Content Accessibility Guidelines 1.0

This document focuses on creating accessible web pages using HyperText Markup Language (HTML). Similar to the CSS Techniques document, this one also provides readers with good and bad code examples, illustrating what developers should and should *not* do!
http://www.w3.org/TR/WCAG10-HTML-TECHS/

14 Guidelines of web accessibility

While the 14 guidelines of accessibility can be found online at http://www. w3c.org/TR/WCAG10-TECHS/, this chapter offers brief explanations of these points. This way, you don't have to go scouting online to find this essential information and can use this book as a resource to take with you or leave by your desk where you work. Be sure to check the W3C web site, however, as changes or additions will appear there faster than I can write another edition of this book!

Guideline 1
Provide text alternatives to auditory and visual content.

Because some people are completely blind, color-blind, or suffer from other visual disabilities, it is important to include text alternatives for non-text content, included but not limited to images, graphical representations of text (including symbols), imagemap regions, animations (e.g., animated GIFs), applets and programmatic objects, ASCII art, frames, scripts, images used as list bullets, spacers, graphical buttons, sounds (played with or without user interaction), stand-alone audio files, audio tracks of video, and video.

There are three ways to implement a text alternative:
> **ALT** attribute

> **LONGDESC** element

> **D** link

The most common example of this is adding the **ALT** attribute to the **IMG** tag in HTML. The information contained within the **ALT** attribute can be read aloud by audible screen readers, which are used by those who are blind or visually challenged in order to access information on the Web. As well as those with visual disabilities, many people view the Web with images turned off to speed up their download time. **ALT** attributes are used by all people, not just those with visual barriers.

It is imperative that the text contained within an **ALT** attribute provide the same important information as that contained within the auditory or visual content. For example, the **ALT** text might describe an image or it might describe how the navigation system on a page works, etc. The goal with writing and providing the **ALT** text is to help your visitor access information, not to simply meet the requirements of this guideline. Make your **ALT** attribute information meaningful and purposeful! The HTML for the **ALT** attribute is shown on the following page.

code

```
<img src="magnifyingglass.gif" alt="Search">
```

As well, the **LONGDESC** tag is used to provide longer, alternative content than that of an **ALT** attribute. This is accomplished by linking to another HTML page that contains the longer description. Note that the **LONGDESC** tag is not supported by many browsers, but it is supported by current and compliant screen readers that read web pages aloud to those with visual disabilities.

code

```
<img src="97sales.gif" alt="Sales for 1997" longdesc="sales97.html">
```

code deconstruction

> The **LONGDESC** tag refers the screen reader to a document called **sales97.html**. A bar chart shows shows percentage increases in sales by month. Sales in January were up 10% from December 1996, and sales in February dropped 3%.

Last is the **D** link, which is an alternative to the **LONGDESC** element. The **D** link is an old protocol for providing links to descriptions that was used before non-visual browsers started supporting the **LONGDESC** attribute. A **D** link is a link built around the letter ID.

code

```
<img src="97sales.gif" alt="Sales for 1997">
<a href="sales97.html">D</a>
```

code deconstruction

> Note: The **D** can be the letter D, or the letter D with brackets (**[D]**), or an image like a blank GIF that won't display, with the word **"D-link"** in the **ALT** attribute.

code

```
<img src="97sales.gif" alt="Sales for 1997">
<a href="sales97.html"></a>
<img src="blank.gif" border="0" alt="D-link">
```

code deconstruction

> Clicking on the **D** link will take the visitor to **sales97.html**, a chart showing how sales in 1997 progressed. The chart is a bar chart showing percentage increases in sales by month. Sales in January were up 10% from December 1996, sales in February dropped 3%.

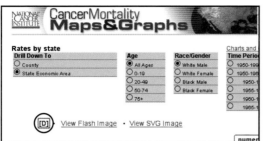

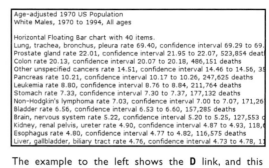

Here's a real-world example of a **D** link in action (http://cas.popchart.com/cancer).

The example to the left shows the **D** link, and this image shows the result of clicking on it.

GUIDELINE 2
Don't rely on color alone.

If you are using color as a way of communicating information on your pages, you need to make sure that the information is still received when the page is viewed without color. For example, some devices are not capable of displaying more than two colors, such as black and white. In addition, if you are using a light-colored text on a light-colored background, the text may be rendered invisible on a black-and-white display. In addition, a person who is color-blind may have a hard time making a distinction between the two light colors. It becomes more important to pay attention to the "contrast" between colors when you design for accessibility purposes.

You can check the color of your web page designs by changing your monitor to grayscale or black and white. If the information doesn't read appropriately, you will need to choose lighter or darker colors in your design. A great resource for more information about color design and accessibility is http://www.lighthouse.org/.

GUIDELINE 3
Use markup and style sheets and do so properly.

This is the one guideline that will most likely be a huge change for experienced web designers. For a long time now, some parts of the HTML specification have been used outside of their original purpose. Tables, for example, which were designed to organize data, have been used to lay out pages and images. Because this was not their intended usage, problems have come up in the different browsers. This causes serious problems with the devices, such as screen readers, used by some disabled persons. Make sure you use the markup language as it was intended, not to achieve some special effect that can cause disharmony between browsers!

For layout, the absolute position available in CSS should be used instead of tables. Other problems with HTML markup cited in the W3C guidelines include those used to emphasize text. For example, you should use **STRONG** or **EM** to emphasize text, not **B** or **I**.

If you have a headline in your document, do not simply bold the text. Use the **H1-H6** tags. If you are using an image of text for your headline, be sure to indicate that it is a headline element by using the **ALT** attribute. The same goes for lists. Use list markup, such as **DL**, **UL**, and **OL**. These list tags should not be used to indent text; instead, use CSS for that.

GUIDELINE 4
Clarify natural language usage.

code

```
<p>The young boy said to the old man on the bench &quot;
<span lang="DE">Guten Tag!</span>&quot;</p>
```

code deconstruction

Use markup (the **LANG** attribute) to make changes in the natural language of the document. This will help screen readers that are capable of changing pronunciation or language as it's reading aloud the document to a disabled person.

code

```
<html lang="DE">
. . . this page's content would be in German.
</html>
```

code deconstruction

In addition, it's considered good practice to define the natural language of the each web page. You can do this within the HTML tag itself.

For a listing of all the two-letter language codes, such as **DE** for German, visit http://www. lcweb.loc. gov/standards/iso639-2/langcodes.html#ab.

GUIDELINE 5
Create tables that transform gracefully.

Use correct markup to ensure that your tables are understood by accessible devices. For tables that contain data, for example, make sure you identify the row and column headers. This is really important for devices that let users navigate between table cells and rows. Without the proper code, this important capability is frequently not available. If your table has more than one row of headers, make sure you use the correct markup to group data cells and header cells—for example, using the **COL** and **COLGROUP** tags to group columns. Many examples of table markup are included here: http://www.w3.org/TR/WCAG10-HTML-TECHS/#identifying-table-rows-columns.

GUIDELINE 6
Ensure that pages featuring new technologies transform gracefully.

It's fine to use technologies, such as plug-ins, applets, and/or frames. However, the guidelines require that you make sure that when these newer technologies are disabled or tuned off that your pages are still accessible. For example, organizing the information on your page so that it can still be read with style sheets disabled is one way to meet the requirements of this guideline. A technique for this is included in Chapter 23, *"Cascading Style Sheets."* For pages that contain special scripts, plug-ins, applets, etc., make sure that the information on those pages is accessible on alternative pages.

GUIDELINE 7
Ensure user control of time-sensitive content changes.

You may not be aware that an unexpected movement, such as a flickering GIF animation, can induce a seizure in a person with disabilities. In less severe cases, moving information can be very difficult, if not impossible, to read by someone who has a cognitive disability. Does this mean you can't have movement or animation on your pages? No, but if your web pages contain this type of information, make sure you give the user the ability to pause or stop the moving objects. Some browsers let you click on an animated GIF to stop the animation. Because all browsers don't offer this feature, however, you should try to create animations that don't contain unnecessary screen flickering, irregular blinking or flashing, or movement that continues to loop without the ability to pause or stop the movement.

GUIDELINE 8
Ensure direct accessibility of embedded user interfaces.

If you are using a technology on your web page that has its own interface, you need to make sure that the interface is accessible and device independent. This is certainly an issue for Flash developers who create their own custom applications. When these types of objects are added to a web page, accessibility must still be considered. If it is impossible to make the interface accessible, then alternate means of accessing the same information must be provided. If this is a concern, then you should definitely consult with the Authoring Tools Accessibility Guidelines for more information: http://www.w3.org/TR/ATAG10-TECHS/. As well, Macromedia has an area on its web site dedicated to help Flash developers make more accessible content: http://www.macromedia.com/ macromedia/accessibility.

GUIDELINE 9
Design for device independence.

Your web pages should be designed so that they have device-independent access so disabled persons can use their choice of input devices. For example, if a user cannot use a keyboard because of a disability, then your page should still be accessible through other devices, such as voice, hand wand, or other types of devices. This is commonly achieved through text alternatives (**ALT**, **LONGDESC**, or **D**) for client-side imagemaps or images that are used as links. As well, you can create logical tabbing order for tables, links, and forms. Techniques for this are available at http://www.w3.org/TR/WCAG10-HTML-TECHS/#link-accesskey.

GUIDELINE 10
Use interim solutions.

This guideline identifies some things you should not do until browsers offer better support for them. For example, changing the current window or spawning new browser windows can be very confusing to a disabled person using a screen reader. Until this is supported better and can be completely disabled in browsers, alternate methods of presenting the information should be used. Problematic examples are cited at http://www.w3.org/TR/WCAG10-TECHS/wcag10-tech.html#def-until-user-agents.

GUIDELINE 11
Use W3C technologies and guidelines.

This guideline is pretty obvious. You should use the W3C technologies (as presented in the specifications) and follow the accessibility guidelines. Well, by reading this chapter you are halfway there. This guideline also states that you should provide alternate information that is in an accessible format.

GUIDELINE 12
Provide context and orientation information.

This guideline outlines some important things you can do to make it easier for the user to understand the navigation and relationships between your web pages. Most of the checkpoints in this section deal with frames and framesets. This guideline stresses the need to supply the purpose of frames and how they relate to one another. For example, carefully naming the frames within framesets is a priority #1 checkpoint. Techniques are provided at http://www.w3.org/TR/WCAG10-HTML-TECHS/#frame-names.

GUIDELINE 13
Provide clear navigation mechanisms.

This guideline stresses the need to provide consistent navigation throughout your web pages. By doing so, you will enable all users to locate the information they are looking for much more quickly and reliably. By adding navigation bars and site maps, you can make all the information on your site much more accessible.

GUIDELINE 14
Ensure that documents are clear and simple.

This guideline is a bit abstract and basically tells you to design pages well. Make sure that you have consistent page layouts, clear and understandable images, and language that benefits all users of your web pages. This will ensure that people who do not speak English as their first language will have a much better chance of understanding what you are presenting. The W3C site offers some concrete examples and scenarios at http://www.w3.org/TR/ WCAG10-CORE-TECHS/#comprehension.

USEFUL ACCESSIBILITY TECHNIQUES

In this section, you'll find useful and practical techniques that you can use for making your web pages more accessible. These techniques were derived from the various techniques documents published by the W3C and are available online. I have tried to offer more information in some places to make them easier to understand.

Use HTML heading tags to define the structure of your documents.

This is an important technique to use in long documents that contain various section, sub-sections, topics, sub-topics, etc. Using heading tags will help define the structure of your document and the importance of sections to one another. For example, a web site containing a story with several chapters might look like this:

code

```
<h1>Chapter 1</h1>
<p>Once upon a time . . .</p>
<h1>Chapter 2</H1>
<p>In the small cottage . . .</p>
```

code deconstruction

Heading tags are read through a screen reader with different emphasis and can help someone who is blind more easily navigate through the document. For example, **H1** is read with more emphasis than **H2**, etc.

Use the ALT atttribute on all your images (and other non-text elements).

All of the non-text content on your page should contain the **ALT** attribute. Note: It's equally important to make sure this alternative text is meaningful so the disabled visitor has the best experience possible.

code

```
<img src="09_01.jpg"
alt="a cappuccino cup overflowing
 with white fluffy foam"
width="150" height="150">
```

code deconstruction

Notice how the **ALT** space is used to provide a "meaningful" text equivalent. This will help a blind person understand what they cannot see with their own eyes.

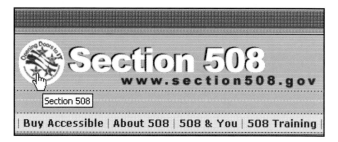

The **ALT** attribute has the added bonus of causing a small yellow tooltip to appear in some browsers. This provides a text description while the image is downloading, or in the event that images have been turned off in the browser setting.

Use style sheets to control the layout and presentation of your web page.

This is a critical step in separating the structure and presentation of your pages. It is not acceptable to use HTML (i.e. **FONT**) to format your pages. Instead, you should use Cascading Style Sheets to describe the layout, formatting, and presentation of your web pages. For example, you should not use the **FONT** tag to define the appearance of your text. Style sheets should be used instead.

code

```
h1 { font-size: 3em; }
```

code deconstruction

In the example above, the text is set to a relative size, which means it will change relative to the size of the text defined in the user's browser or style sheet. This is very helpful to persons with low vision and other visual disabilities because it gives them control over the size of the text they view while maintaining relative sizes. Be sure to read Chapter 23, *"Cascading Style Sheets,"* for a more complete examination of this subject.

Add captions and summaries to your tables and identify the header and rows.

This is important for people who are accessing your web page through a screen reader because the header is read out loud differently than the date in rows.

Product Listing by Item Number		
Item #	**Name**	**Length**
001	Learning Dreamwaver	4 hours
002	Learning Flash	6 hours
003	Learning Illustrator	8 hours

This looks like a normal HTML table, right? Well, it is, but it's also an accessible HTML table because I have added a caption and summary, and identified the header and rows.

Let's take a look at the code for this table and then you'll learn why it's so important to make this effort when building your tables.

code

```
<table width="300" border="1"
summary="This table lists all of our
products by item number, including
the name and description of each.">
<caption>Product Listing by
Item Number</caption>
<tr>
<th>Item #</th>
<th>Name</th>
<th>Length</th>
</tr>
<tr>
 <td>001</td>
 <td>Learning Dreamweaver</td>
 <td>4 hours</td>
</tr>
<tr>
 <td>002</td>
 <td>Learning Flash</td>
 <td>6 hours</td>
</tr>
<tr>
 <td>003</td>
 <td>Learning Illustrator</td>
 <td>8 hours</td>
</tr>
</table>
```

code deconstruction

Notice that I used the **SUMMARY** attribute to describe the contents of the table. This should state the purpose and overall content of the table. I also provided a **<CAPTION>** for the table, which is listed at the top visually, not the bottom like you might have assumed. And, I used the **<TH>** tags to identify the headers in my table.

Ok, so why is this such a big deal? Well, for a blind person who has this page read aloud through a screen reader, it's a *huge* deal. For example, when this page is read out loud, because of my efforts, it will be read like this:

code

```
Caption: Product Listing by
Item Number

Summary: This table lists all of our
products by item number, including the
name and description of each.

Item #: 001, Name: Learning Dreamweaver,
Length: 4 hours
Item #: 002, Name: Learning Flash, Length:
6 hour
Item #: 003, Name: Learning Illustrator,
Length: 8 hours
```

code deconstruction

Try reading the section above out loud to yourself and imagine whether you'd still be able to understand the contents of this table if you could not see the screen. Pretty cool, huh? With just a little extra time and effort, you can make a big difference for a lot of disabled web surfers!

Use the TITLE attribute to name frames.

Frames present challenges to persons who aren't disabled, so you can imagine the headaches they can cause for disabled users. One way to make them accessible is by careful use of the **TITLE** attribute. For example, the code example below uses the **TITLE** attribute to give meaningful names to the frames so the user can better understand how the frames relate to one another.

code

```
<frameset cols="15%,85%"
title="catalog of products>
<frame src="navbar.htm"
title="product navigation bar">
<frame src="content.htm"
title="product descriptions">
</frameset>
```

code deconstruction

Use client-side imagemaps instead of server-side imagemaps. While client-side imagemaps are the norm, it's still important to make this point. Server-side imagemaps require that the server process where the user clicks and what page they should be taken to. Server-side imagemaps also require a specific input device.

code

```
<img src="navigate.gif"
width="300" height="50"
usepmap="#navbar"
border="0">
<map name="navbar">

<area shape="rect" coords="10,7,77,42"
href="home.htm" alt="Home"
title="Home">

<area shape="rect" coords="87,7,153,42"
href="products.htm" alt="Product Listing"
title="Product Listing">

<area shape="rect" coords="171,10,235,43"
href="contact.htm" alt="Contact Information"
title="Contact Information">

<area shape="rect" coords="248,10,311,41"
href="map.htm" alt="Site Map"
title="Site Map">
</map>
```

code deconstruction

Make sure that your client-side imagemaps include a meaningful **ALT** attribute for each link. This is really important for people accessing the page through a screen-reading device. Above is an example of a good client-side imagemap. Notice the **USEMAP** tag; this denotes a client-side imagemap. Also notice the consistent use of meaningful **ALT** attributes for each link.

Make sure any animations or movies contain synchronized equivalent alternatives.

If your web pages contain content, such as Flash or QuickTime, you should ensure that you use captioning to provide users with a text transcript of the content. If the technology you are using does not support captioning, then make sure you have a plain-old text available, which provides the disabled person with access to equivalent information.

You should also know about SMIL (**S**ynchronized **M**ultimedia **I**ntegration **L**anguage). SMIL was created by the W3C specifically for synchronizing multimedia and text files. You can find out more about SMIL here: http://www.w3.org/AudioVideo. More specifically, you can learn more about SMIL and accessibility at http://www.w3.org/TR/SMIL-access.

code

```
[knock on door]
[knock]
[knock]
Who is it?
Hi, it's just the mailman!
```

code deconstruction

Your captioning should always be descriptive and include supporting information to understand what's being said and occurring in the movie.

---

note

MACROMEDIA & MICROSOFT CONTENT

Companies, like Macromedia and Microsoft, have published online information and tutorials for making their content accessible. You should visit the links below if you are working with Flash or Windows AVI files.

Macromedia Flash
http://www.macromedia.com/macromedia/accessibility/features/flash/overview

Microsoft SAMI
(Synchronized Accessible Media Interchange)
http://www.msdn.microsoft.com/library/default.asp?url=/library/en-us/dnacc/html/atg_samiarticle.asp

Make sure links clearly identify the target and that you provide a text equivalent when using images as links.

This might seem like Web Design 101, but it's worth stating here. Avoid using terms like "click here" for your text links, instead using something that describes the target. For example, if you were linking to a map of the 50 states, you might use something like "map of United States" as the text for that link. I know it seems elementary, but you would be shocked at the number of "click here" links on the Web! Imagine if you were site impaired (close your eyes) how meaningless the term "click here" would be all by itself without further description.

cascading style sheets & accessibility

You'll find a lot more information on the general techniques for programming CSS in chapter 23, *"Cascading Style Sheets."* Here are some golden rules that apply specifically to using CSS for accessibility purposes.

Setting Font Size

Use relative units to set the size of text, instead of **FONT SIZE="4"**, on your web pages. This lets objects have relative size to one another.

code (recommended)

```
.header { font-size: 3em }
.body { font-size: 2em }
```

code (not-recommended)

```
.header { font-size: 10pt }
```

Controlling Layout

Use style sheets to control the layout and positioning of the objects on your web pages. This is an important part of CSS and making accessible web pages. Most web designers have been taught to use tables to construct their layouts. After fighting issues in the different browsers, you can usually get things to look the way you want, but this only addresses the appearance of the tables. Visually impaired people can have lots of trouble understanding tables that are read aloud to them through a screen-reading device. By using CSS instead, you can control the visual layout and still ensure the information is accessible.

Formatting Text

Use the CSS elements **text-align**, **text-indent**, **word-spacing**, and **font-stretch** to control the amount of space between words. You can learn more about these CSS elements online or in other books.

You should not use deprecated tags, such as **FONT** and **KI**. Use relative units, such as em, instead of non-relative measurements such as pixels, to set the size of text. Use hexadecimal values instead of color names to set colors. Here is a list of the deprecated HTML tags:

Deprecated Tag	Alternative
`<APPLET>`	`<OBJECT>`
`<BASEFONT>`	Use style sheets
`<CENTER>`	Use style sheets
`<DIR>`	`<UL>`
`<FONT>`	Use style sheets
`<ISINDEX>`	`<INPUT>`
`<LISTING>`	`<PRE>`
`<MENU>`	`<UL>`
`<PLAINTEXT>`	`<PRE>`
`<S>`	`<DEL>`
`<STRIKE>`	`<DEL>`
`<U>`	Use style sheets
`<XMP>`	`<PRE>`

Creating Space

Use the CSS markup `margin`, `margin-top`, `margin-bottom`, and `margin-left` to create space around objects. You should avoid using non-breaking spaces to add more space around objects, because HTML should be used to identify structure (not presentation) and because proper accessibility practices require the separation of structure and presentation.

Setting Position

Instead of using tables to lay out your pages, use the CSS markup `float`, `position`, `top`, `right`, `bottom`, and `left` to control the position of objects. These properties let you achieve absolute positioning that would otherwise need to be created using HTML tables. Using tables for layout purposes can make it impossible for screen readers to process the page properly. These devices read from left to right and will not recognize tables, which can make your page completely inaccessible to someone using one of these devices.

Creating Borders

Use the CSS border properties to create borders around elements. Do not use nested tables to achieve similar effects. While these can be useful for persons with good vision, they serve no purpose for the blind because they are not identified by screen-reading devices.

Information Accessibility

Make sure your pages degrade gracefully if style sheets are disabled. While style sheets should be used to control the position, layout, and formatting of your document, your pages should be coded so that if style sheets are disabled, the information is still accessible to the person visiting your page. There is a great example of this in *"CSS Techniques for Web Content Accessibility Guidelines 1.0"* (http://www.w3.org/TR/2000/NOTE-WCAG10-CSS-TECHS-20000920).

note

CSS RESOURCES

There are great resources on the Web and in print for learning more about Cascading Style Sheets. You'll find a listing of some of these online resources in the following section of this book. Using CSS can make your site accessible to millions of disabled persons, so it's totally valuable to invest your time and learn as much as you can about it.

CHECKPOINTS & RATINGS OF ACCESSIBILITY

You have now read about the 14 essential guidelines of web accessibility and have been exposed to techniques that help implement these recommendations. The W3C also outlines a series of checkpoints, referred to as Priority 1, 2, or 3. A list of each checkpoint and its priority is located at http://www.w3.org/TR/2001/CR-UAAG10-20010912uaag10-chklist. These priorities help developers determine which guidelines have a greater impact on accessibility. Descriptions of the three priorities, according to the W3C, follow:

> **Priority 1:** The web developer "must" satisfy these guidelines; otherwise, one or more groups will find it impossible to access the information. You really want to ensure that you meet every one of the Priority 1 guidelines.

> **Priority 2:** The web developer "should" satisfy these guidelines; otherwise, one or more groups might find it pretty difficult to access the information within the document. You should try and satisfy as many Priority 2 guidelines as possible.

> **Priority 3:** The web developer "may" want to satisfy these guidelines; otherwise, one or more groups will find it somewhat difficult to access the information within the document. You should make an attempt to satisfy these guidelines.

THREE "A"S OF ACCESSIBILITY

In addition to the priority checkpoint rating, the W3C has identified three levels of conformance: A, Double-A, and Triple-A—for the web content accessibility guidelines. This rating system makes it easier for developers and visitors to determine how accessible a web site truly is.

Achieving a certain level of conformity allows you to use a special logo, branding your site as accessible according to the W3C guidelines. It lets your visitors know that you care about this important issue. You can download these logos at http://www.w3c.org/WAI/WCAG1-Conformance.html.

Here is what each of the levels of conformance mean:

> **(A) Level A:** The web page has satisfied all of the Priority 1 checkpoints.

> **(AA) Level Double-A:** The web page has satisfied all the Priority 1 and 2 checkpoints.

> **(AAA) Level Triple-A:** The web page has satisfied all the Priority 1, 2, and 3 checkpoints.

web site testing systems

There is an emerging software market for accessibility testing systems that evaluate your site and make suggestions or corrections that help you comply with the new standards.

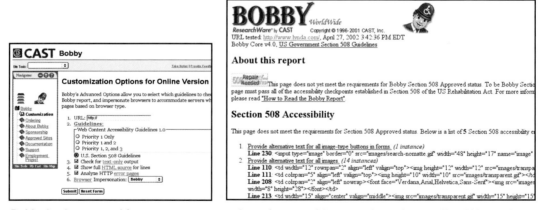

Working in conjunction with Macromedia's Dreamweaver, **UsableNet's** LIFT (http://www.usablenet.com) software contains a wizard that scans your HTML and fixes tables, images, and scripts. In addition to offering LIFT for Macromedia Dreamweaver, which is not free, they have a web-based service that will evaluate your web site for free. As you can see, lynda.com didn't fare too well!

Bobby has been around for years to test your web site for accessibility at no charge. It now offers 508 compliance evaluation. To visit this service, go to http://bobby.cast.org/bobby.

ONLINE ACCESSIBILITY RESOURCES

As with most things, you can find just about everything you want to know on the Web. This is especially true about information on web accessibility. Because the issues surrounding accessibility on the Web are changing almost daily, it's a great place to find the most current information. Oftentimes, one page will lead you to another and so on.

Here are some places that you should definitely take a look at:

Web Accessibility Initiative
http://www.w3.org/WAI

Web Accessibility Resources
http://www.w3.org/WAI/Resources

Techniques for Web Content Accessibility 1.0 Guidelines
http://www.w3.org/TR/WCAG10-TECHS

Access-Board
http://www.access-board.gov

webABLE!
http://www.webable.com

The Web Design Group
http://www.htmlhelp.com

Macromedia
http://www.macromedia.com/macromedia/accessibility

Adobe
http://access.adobe.com

Evaluation and Repair Tools
http://www.w3.org/WAI/ER/existingtools.html#Evaluation

GLOBAL ACCESSIBILITY ISSUES

As American web developers, it's easy to think that English is the only language that exists in the world. I know we don't really think this, but we rarely think about other languages because our culture is not bilingual. If you travel to Europe, you are immediately struck by how many languages you hear in the streets—people who live there *never* assume that theirs is the only language. The truth is that while English is widely used and understood throughout the world, it is not the primary language of the majority of Earth's inhabitants.

Forget Europe for a moment, and think about the immediate neighbors of the US: Mexico and Canada. Right there, you have got two languages to consider: Spanish and French. Did you know there are more Chinese-speaking people in the world than any other language? You probably don't think about this much in your daily life because you don't hear a lot of Chinese spoken in America.

The Internet as we've come to know it today is called the World Wide Web because it exists all over the world. Chances are very likely that someone for whom English is not a primary language will access your site. What can you do to make their user experience better? If you aren't concerned about their user experience, think about your income. Do you care about that? If you have something to sell on your site, you need to consider the foreign market. Otherwise, you are missing out on a potential source of revenue.

The good news is, if you abide by the accessibility practices described in this chapter, your site has a much better job of working for a non-English audience.

English to Chinese
English to French
English to German
English to Italian
English to Japanese
English to Korean
English to Portuguese
✓ **English to Spanish**
Chinese to English
French to English
French to German
German to English
German to French
Italian to English
Japanese to English
Korean to English
Portuguese to English
Russian to English
Spanish to English

You can choose to translate your web site from English to all these other languages for free at http://www.babelfish.altavista.com. I am not able to vouch for how accurate its translation service is, but it beats having to publish your site in another language if you do not have resources for translation.

This example shows how the **lynda.com** site looks in Spanish. Notice that anything that is in ASCII text has been translated to the Spanish language, and anything that is an image has stayed in English.

Altavista allows you to check and see how your site fares in another language. Just go to http://www.babelfish.altavista.com and type in your URL.

You might hear the term "localization" or "globalization" of web content. These terms relate to the process of translating your site into multiple languages. If you have the resources to hire a translator for target audiences, then you might want to offer different sites. You see this a lot with large companies that have a significant presence in multiple countries.

Levi.com has navigation choices for Europe, USA, Asia, Latin America, Canada, and South Africa. They've got the resources to develop all these sites in different languages. This is the ideal approach to creating localized content.

Chances are, you don't have the resources to create multiple sites in multiple languages. In summary, even though posting a lot of images to your site might make it look really cool, you are sacrificing the ability to translate your site by using images for mission-critical information. Something as simple as putting the content of your site into ASCII makes the difference between a non-English person understanding your site or not.

accessibility issues

summary

Accessibility has become one of the most significant issues in the web industry. In many cases, it is the law to incorporate accessibility guidelines, and if you ignore these practices, you could find yourself in violation of the Americans with Disabilities Act. Despite the law, it makes good sense to create a web site that can reach more people. In principle, making your web pages more accessible will make them more accessible to all your visitors, not just those with disabilities. The guidelines, issues, and techniques surrounding the issue are changing at a rapid rate. Keeping current on this important topic will be a valuable asset to every web designer.

> Accessibility is the practice that makes web sites work for people with disabilities, such as those who are visually, hearing, and/or cognitively impaired.

> Read the guidelines so you know what features will make your site accessible.

> Do your research so you are informed about all the latest techniques and developments in accessibility practices.

> At minimum, add **ALT** attributes to your critical graphics and headings to your tables and charts.

> Use CSS for formatting purposes and avoid deprecated tags that affect formatting but disregard structure.

> Test your site through accessibility validation services, such as UseableNet (http://www.usablenet.com).

> If you do adhere to good accessibility practices, consider putting the W3C compliance logo on your site.

08

HTML & XHTML

INTRODUCTION

I am devoting an entire chapter in this book to HTML and XHTML and their WYSIWYG (**W**hat **Y**ou **S**ee **I**s **W**hat **Y**ou **G**et) editors because these issues are as critical to a web designer's livelihood as choosing the right image editor or hardware platform. With the introduction of XHTML, the situation has gotten more complicated. Should you learn HTML and XHTML? Which one is better? What's the difference between the two? Like you, I had many of these same questions.

Many different types of people are going to read this book. Each of you will have a different level of experience with HTML and/or XHTML, while some of you won't have a clue about either. That's just fine! Most readers, regardless of skill or experience level, will find valuable information in this chapter. I find that most people who already know HTML still have lots more to learn about it, and those who are just getting started have many confusing decisions to make.

Deciding how much HTML or XHTML to learn and which, if any, HTML or XHTML editor to use is a choice you will not know how to make without understanding a few of the issues this chapter covers. Inside, you'll find a short synopsis of HTML, an explanation of why HTML is counter-intuitive to design, and an overview of the markup language. You will also find a detailed explanation of XHTML, the differences between it and plain vanilla HTML, the powerful features available in XHTML, and recommendations on using it now. And finally, I'll let you know whether or not you should learn to code from scratch, give you tips and resources for learning HTML and XHTML, and include an overview of HTML and XHTML editors.

HTML & XHTML IN A GRAPHICS BOOK?

At this point, some of you might be wondering why this book need contain any discussion of HTML and XHTML at all. Didn't you buy this book because you wanted to understand how to make graphics for the Web?

What you might not realize is that HTML and XHTML are inextricably joined at the hip with graphics. If all you learned was code, you would have boring, text-laden pages that contained no images. If all you learned about was web graphics, you'd have no understanding of how to incorporate them into a web page without HTML and XHTML.

SHOULD YOU LEARN HTML?

If you never "wanted to be a computer programmer" when you grew up, and the idea of writing HTML might be a bit intimidating, unappealing, or just plain loathsome to you, the Web might be a good reason to change your attitude. Learning HTML is a bit of a nuisance, but it isn't nearly as difficult as learning a real programming language. The rewards are much greater than the pain—I promise.

If you compare the Web to the early days of desktop publishing, HTML is a lot like the PostScript language. You used to have to write in PostScript to produce computer typesetting. Today, we have programs like InDesign, QuarkXPress, and PageMaker, which write PostScript behind the scenes, without anyone ever seeing the code or even needing to know it exists. No one, except a die-hard PostScript programmer, would need or want to learn to write PostScript today.

So how is HTML any different from yesterday's Post-Script? Because HTML has gone through several iterations and revisions, and PostScript is a stable programming language that works for any PostScript-enabled imaging device.

In the many years I've been involved with the Web, HTML has gone through some serious changes. Some of these changes were sanctioned by the W3C (**W**orld **W**ide **W**eb **C**onsortium—the official standards committee for the Web), but many were not. Browser vendors such as Netscape and Microsoft have actually changed the course of HTML development by introducing proprietary enhancements to the code, rather than focusing on implementing standards. This explains why pages look and function differently between Netscape Navigator and Internet Explorer. For these reasons, HTML cannot be compared to PostScript or any other programming or markup language because it is still in development.

So am I saying that to be a web publisher today you must learn HTML? Yes and no. Frankly, some of the best web sites I've ever seen were developed by artists who didn't understand a line of HTML code and who teamed up with an HTML programmer. It is possible to divide the line and leave art to artists and code to programmers. However, the demographics of the Web have changed significantly. Artists are now being expected to perform tasks that normally required a programmer. With the recent fallout in the web industry, designers and web developers are expected to know and do more for less. The heydays of making huge amounts of money for simply knowing HTML are gone and not likely to return. Even so, you may fall into the camp of artists who don't want to learn HTML, and that is totally valid. Just be forewarned—you will feel powerless, and it can definitely make you less competitive when you are looking for a web designer position.

Is there a middle ground? Yes. (It is discussed later in this chapter in the "HTML Editors" section.) These software programs write HTML invisibly, just like QuarkXPress and PageMaker write PostScript, and you don't have to understand a line of code to use them. With the increased demands on web designers, I would strongly recommend that you take the time to learn at least the basics of HTML. You will feel empowered and better understand the restrictions of HTML and how they affect your designs.

Most artists, by definition, are control freaks. We like to pick the exact right color, make the exact shape, and see the exact layout. Throughout this book, I will discuss when HTML affords this type of exacting precision and when to give up on the control freak stuff.

There are a few major penalties one suffers from skimping on an HTML education. The first is that someone else will be in the position to tell you whether you can or cannot do certain effects, and you will probably regard them suspiciously. The other is that if you are called upon to troubleshoot something you have designed, you will not know how. This could cause you to lose credibility in a work situation, or could simply result in being frustrating to you. With the increase in expectations of web designers, not knowing HTML can work against you when you are competing for a position or bidding on a project. If you have the time and inclination, you should at the very least get comfortable viewing HTML code and understand its basic structure.

note

SHAMELESS SELF-PROMOTION

Frankly, I didn't wholeheartedly like any of the HTML books out there, so I enlisted my programmer brother to co-author one with me. Our book is much like a class, which walks readers through hands-on exercises and contains all the necessary course materials on the CD-ROM. It only covers HTML, however, not XHTML. If you want to check out the book and read a sample chapter, check out http://www.htmlbook.com.

Creative HTML Design.2
Lynda & William Weinman
New Riders
ISBN: 0735709726 $39.95

HOW TO LEARN HTML

There are several ways to learn HTML, and many great resources exist online. You will find a list of them in this chapter.

The *View Source* command, which is found within most browsers, should be your premiere guide. If you like something you see on the Web, view its source code. You can copy and paste someone else's source code into your own word-processing program or HTML editor. This is done all the time, and is not frowned upon by the web authoring community. In fact, most of the HTML jockeys I've met tell me this is exactly how they taught themselves the markup language.

There are several software programs, available for both Mac and Windows, that let you download (referred to as "sucking down") an entire web site (HTML files, images, etc.) to your hard drive. This gives you the opportunity to open it manually or in a WYSIWYG editor and then deconstruct it in a more visual manner. This deconstruction approach to learning is one that I strongly advocate, especially for designers who have an affinity for learning from visual cues.

Here are just a few of the available programs:

Macintosh: **WebDevil**
   http://www.chaoticsoftware.com
   Web Whacker
   http://www.bluesquirrel.com/cd_macww

Windows: **Teleport Pro**
   http://tenmax.com/home.htm
   Custo
   http://www.netwu.com

Studying HTML may seem intimidating, but most people will find it very simple to learn the basics. It's not necessary to write every line of code by hand, but if you learn to write a little, it will help your comprehension of the more difficult programming tasks.

HTML can be written in a simple word processor or in a dedicated HTML or WYSIWYG editor. The key to writing HTML is that it must be saved in ASCII format *(text-only mode)* and include the file extension .html or .htm (either will work).

tip

IMPORTANT HTML TERMS

When I first learned HTML, I thought everything inside the brackets was called a tag. My brother, co-author of *Creative HTML Design.2*, corrected me. If you want to know how to speak about HTML properly, here's a handy terminology list:

Tag: Everything between the "<" and ">" symbols. For example, `<BODY>` is a tag.

Content: Everything that falls between the open and closing tags of an HTML document is called content.

Attribute: A modifier to an element. Attributes have two components: the attribute *name* and the attribute *value*. In the example `<TABLE BORDER="1">`, `TABLE` is the element, `BORDER` is the attribute name, and `1` is the attribute value.

Attribute Value: Usually follows an attribute name. In the example `<TABLE BORDER="1">`, `1` is the value of the attribute name.

Element: A tag or tagset used to describe the structure of a document and its contents. For example, the entire string `"<TABLE BORDER="1">"` is called an element.

WHAT DOES HTML LOOK LIKE?

HTML is a markup language that has a pretty simple structure. Here is a very basic example, with key elements that you should understand:

code

```
1   <HTML>
2   <HEAD>
3   <TITLE>name_of_document
4   </TITLE>
5   </HEAD>
6   <BODY>The stuff that goes on the page goes inside the body tag.
7   </BODY>
8   </HTML>
```

code deconstruction

1   All HTML documents must begin with the **HTML** tag.

2   The **HEAD** of the document contains all of the header information.

3   The **TITLE** element contains the name of the document, which will appear at the top of the browser window.

4   It's necessary to close the **TITLE** tag, which is indicated by the slash.

5   It's always necessary to close the **HEAD** tag, which is indicated by the slash.

6   Everything that is visible inside the HTML document is inside the **BODY** tag.

7   Ya gotta close the **BODY** tag.

8   And ya gotta close the **HTML** tag, too.

Of course, there are lots and lots of other tags, attributes, and values for an HTML document. This is just the absolute, most-basic page you could ask for, just to show you that it is pretty understandable if you break it down in simple chunks. Also, I should point out that even though the HTML tags in this example were capitalized, that is not a requirement of HTML; it is a personal preference and will vary among web developers.

tip

LEARN MORE ABOUT HTML

As well as the View Source trick and reading a book, there are plenty of fantastic online resources for learning HTML. Here is a list of some of my favorites:

NCSA
A Beginner's Guide to HTML
http://www.ncsa.uiuc.edu/General/Internet/WWW/
HTMLPrimer.html

HTML
An Interactive Tutorial for Beginners
http://www.davesite.com/webstation/html

HTML Writer's Guild
A Resource List
http://www.hwg.org/resources/html/intros.html

Webmonkey
An HTML Tutorial
http://www.hotwired.com/webmonkey/teachingtool/
index.html

NCDesign
An HTML Design Guide
http://www.ncdesign.org/html

Index DOT HTML
The Advanced HTML Reference
http://home.webmonster.net/mirrors/bloo-html

HTML EDITORS

There might come a day when understanding HTML is not critical to creating complex and professional web pages. That day is already here if you are a casual web publisher and don't want to exercise a great deal of control over the look and feel of your content. My father, for example, has a web page. He didn't care about learning HTML, making his own graphics, or anything beyond putting his content online (favorite TV shows, political rants, news about his cat and granddaughter, etc.). Using an HTML editor was the perfect choice for him to create a web page, and I don't think he really needed to worry about HTML.

There are all types of HTML editors—from the type that would satisfy my father to the type that would satisfy the most persnickety programmer. Some types of HTML editors allow you to work in a WYSIWYG (**W**hat **Y**ou **S**ee **I**s **W**hat **Y**ou **G**et) mode. This means that you can type directly in the editor and instead of seeing HTML code, you'll see whatever you typed. These types of editors give you the freedom to change a font style, font size, or alignment, or drag and drop images into position. If you view the source code the WYSIWYG editor produced, it will show all the HTML elements that were hidden from your view.

There are disadvantages and advantages to using HTML editors. When I taught full-time at Art Center College of Design, I used to forbid my students to use HTML editors until a few weeks had passed so they could learn to code by hand. This wasn't because I didn't think HTML editors are great; I do, and I use them all the time! It was because editors shield you from the HTML learning process, and I think it's important to understand the process before turning it over to an editor. Even the best editors at times require troubleshooting, and you will be powerless to do so if you don't understand what you're doing.

There are many varieties of WYSIWYG editors. Some are consumer-oriented, and some professional. We're entering an era of fourth- and fifth-generation HTML editors, so the software has improved tremendously and is bending to the needs of ever-changing specifications. This is good news, because, the early versions were too immature to be very useful. If you haven't tried an HTML editor in the last two or three years, try some of the new breeds. They have matured and are much better than they used to be.

The advantages of using an editor are profound. Editors can be a tremendous timesaver, allowing artists and non-programmers to easily mock up pages and get ideas out quickly. Then there are those people who just don't want to learn HTML or can't. Your ability to learn HTML has less to do with your intelligence than your aptitude for this task. I know many bona fide, brilliant individuals who cannot make their minds think in HTML. Why should they have to? They don't.

That said, the next question to ask is what type of HTML editor best suits your needs. Some are good for designing individual pages, others for site management, and still others for advanced design with DHTML using JavaScript, CSS, and/or Document Object Models.

tip

TRY BEFORE YOU BUY

One of the best things about most HTML editors is that you can typically download demo versions to "try before you buy." I highly recommend that you do this to ensure that the editor meets your needs. Often, the HTML editor's site has lots of very helpful tutorials, and sometimes even user groups that offer email-based subscription lists.

GoLive
http://www.adobe.com

Dreamweaver
http://www.dreamweaver.com

BBEDIT
http://www.barebones.com/products/bbedit.html

Homesite
http://www.macromedia.com/software/homesite

FrontPage
http://www.microsoft.com/frontpage/default.htm

HTML EDITING FEATURES

Deciding on HTML software has everything to do with the scale and scope of your web site, your budget, your programming aptitude (or lack thereof), and your expectations. I am not going to recommend any specific software, because everyone's needs will be different. Instead, I thought it would be helpful to outline some features, and then you can pick an HTML editor that contains the features you want.

Roundtrip HTML: The term "roundtrip" HTML was coined by the Macromedia Dreamweaver product team. It means that you can write custom code in the editor, and the editor won't rewrite the code for you (which all editors used to do). Adobe's GoLive has a feature called "360" that does the same thing. One of the dangers of using an HTML editor is the fact that it adds its own code to the HTML. In many HTML editors, if you remove the proprietary tags and then re-import the files for maintenance or changes, the program will re-insert them! Roundtrip, or 360 features, in an editor mean that the code stays like you typed it, regardless of whether you save the file and re-import it.

DHTML (Dynamic HTML): A collection of technologies that work together to produce more interactivity and dynamic content than HTML alone can offer. It usually involves the combined use of HTML or XHTML, CSS, scripting, and the **D**ocument **O**bject **M**odel (DOM). HTML 4.01 is the most current specification for HTML (XHTML is the successor to HTML and will be addressed later in this chapter).

Fonts: Just about all HTML editors allow you to set fonts, and change size and style. This is standard fare. (More information about font tags and workarounds are in Chapter 20, *"HTML Type."*)

CSS (Cascading **S**tyle **S**heets**):** Cascading Style Sheets are used for specifying specific layout and style properties, such as absolute positioning, font size, font family, leading, indents, and much more. Individual style sheets can be included in individual web pages, or a web site can reference a single CSS document. (More about this in Chapter 23, *"Cascading Style Sheets."*) Some HTML editors support the creation of CSS, although this is usually reserved for high-end, professional HTML editors.

JavaScript support: JavaScript is a scripting language that extends the capabilities of HTML. Popular uses of JavaScript include rollovers, specifically sized browser windows, and browser detection. (More on JavaScript can be found in Chapter 26, *"Adding Programming Features."*) Some HTML editors support the capability to add or append a JavaScript, while others actually write JavaScript functions. These features are usually found in high-end and professional HTML editors.

Plug-in support: Plug-ins are separate files that must be installed in a browser in order for plug-in content to be visible. Common plug-ins that you might be familiar with include RealPlayer, Flash, QuickTime, and Shockwave. Some HTML editors don't support the capability to code plug-in content, but most professional-level editors do.

Frames: Frames create regions of a web page that are stationary while other regions can change. If you plan to use frames, I highly recommend that you test the HTML editor for this feature before you buy it. Many HTML editors handle frames poorly, what I mean is that they are difficult to pre-visualize and set up. (For more information about frames see Chapter 22, *"Frames."*)

Alignment: Some HTML editors are better at alignment than others; again, it's always best to try before you buy! (More information about alignment can be found in Chapter 21, *"Alignment & Tables"* and Chapter 22, *"Frames."*)

Tables: Tables are very important for layout and images, and some HTML editors create tables better than others. (More information about tables can be found in Chapter 21, *"Alignment & Tables."*)

Site management: Some HTML editors will include site management features. This is extremely handy, because you can typically change a link and the change will ripple through your site.

Database integration: Some HTML editors interface well with databases. If you plan to run your site using a database, this should be a consideration.

Button rollovers: The latest and greatest HTML editors will write JavaScript rollovers for you.

Browser conversion: Some HTML editors will convert pages that utilize DHTML and CSS to alternative pages that use HTML that is supported by earlier browsers. At the time this book was written, the two most popular WYSIWYG HTML editors, Adobe GoLive 6 and Dreamweaver MX, had great support for XHTML.

Browser Feature Comparison Chart						
	GoLive 5	Dreamweaver 4	BBEdit 6	Homesite 4.5.2	FrontPage 2002	NetObjects Fusion MX
Rountrip HTML	X	X	X	X	X	
DHTML	X	X		X	X	X
CSS	X	X	X	X	X	X
JavaScript Support	X	X	X	X	X	X
Plug-in Support	X	X	X	X	X	X
Frames	X	X	X	X	X	X
Site Management	X	X		X	X	X
Database Integration	X	X		X	X	X
Button Rollovers	X	X		X	X	X
Browser Conversion	X	X		X		X
Platform	M·W	M·W	M	W	M·W	M·W

WHAT IS XHTML?

As I pointed out earlier, the current version of HTML is 4.01. There will not be a version 5 of HTML. Instead, there will be XHTML. In fact, XHTML 1.0 and 1.1 already exist as the current, formal recommendation sanctioned by the World Wide Web Consortium (the standards committee of the Web). Although HTML is still the prominent language used to create web pages and is perfectly acceptable for use, XHTML is completely usable right now. Interestingly, XHTML is readable by any web browser due to the fact that, while XHTML follows XML rules, it uses the familiar HTML elements and attributes. XTHML 2.0 is under development.

XHTML stands for e**X**tensible **H**yper**T**ext **M**arkup **L**anguage. So then, how is XHTML different from its close companion HTML? The most visible difference between the two markup languages can be seen in their syntax, with all opening tags requiring a closing tag. Here are some of the key differences:

> All element and attribute names are in lowercase. For example, `<P>` would not be valid, but `<p>` would be a valid XHTML element.

> All attribute values must be contained within quotes, single or double. For example, in HTML you can write `<TD NOWRAP>`, but in XHTML you would have to write `<td nowrap="nowrap">`. You should be consistent in your use of quotes.

> All non-empty elements must have a closing tag. For example, `<p>this is good text.</p>` is a valid XHTML element while `<p>this is bad text` is not.

> All empty tags should be written with a space and a / symbol at the end of the tag. For example, `<br />` is valid XHTML while `<br>` is not. This method of closing empty tags ensures that your pages are compatible with older browsers.

XHTML follows the XML rules and syntax guidelines. Because XML has very rigid requirements for writing code, XHTML is a more structured markup language than HTML. This more structured approach to markup languages will enable one document to be viewed on multiple devices (web browsers, cell phones, PDAs, etc.) by simply creating different style sheets for each device. In a nutshell, XHTML is basically HTML 4.01 reformulated using the syntax of XML.

If XHTML is really an XML document, then you are probably wondering what is XML? First, let me tell you right up front that you don't have to learn XML to work with XHTML. (Phew... what a relief!)

XML is a markup language that gives you that ability to create your own markup elements. This enables developers and programmers to use XML to create their own markup elements to send and receive data that HTML was never intended to handle, such as content from a database. I don't want to confuse you with a lengthy explanation of XML, so if you can hang on to that much, that's all you need to know about XML to get through this section.

Here is the XHTML acronym and a look at each component separately:

eXtensible: Extensible means that the functionality of the language can be changed by adding or modifying features. The architecture of the language has been constructed in such a way that it can be modified to meet the individual needs of its users. As you can imagine, this is a very powerful principle. This lets you basically create your own version of the language, HTML in this case, so you can have it work within your own unique environment.

HyperText: HyperText refers to the ability to quickly (**Hyper**) move to different parts of a document (**Text**) page. This is the basic premise behind the Web. The ability to click on a link and go somewhere else on the same page or to a web site on the other side of the planet is what makes it different from other communication mediums, such as a printed page. The term "HyperText" was coined by Ted Nelson in 1965, decades before the Web existed!

Markup: Markup is used to describe the content of the document being viewed. For example, the `<i>` element in the XHTML markup indicates that a part of the text should be in italics.

Language: The Language portion of the acronym means that XHTML is a markup language. Because it is part of XML, which is a computer language in its own right, this qualifies XHTML as a computer language. Unlike HTML, which is not capable of creating web applications, XHTML is capable of creating fully functional web applications.

How well will the software vendors who create web and image editors support XHTML? How well will the community accept the new markup language? Will another language be developed before this one gains prominent acceptance? Much of this is open to debate and speculation. The next few months and years will certainly determine how this language folds into the mix of the World Wide Web. Fortunately, XHTML 1.0 and 1.1 are completely supported by browsers—all browsers, even older browsers that were developed before the existence of XHTML. There is no penalty to using XHTML today for this reason.

SHOULD YOU LEARN XHTML?

I mentioned earlier that the expectations of today's modern web designer are much different than they were three years ago. Then, it was possible to exist as a successful web designer without knowing any, or very little, HTML. Most designers either teamed up with a programmer or used one of the many WYSIWYG HTML editors. Today, the requirements of the average web designer frequently include a working knowledge of HTML (and often times many other languages and technologies, such as JavaScript, CGI, PERL, etc.)

Even with an uncertain future, am I saying that you should learn XHTML? Yes, I would recommend it. XML has become a very powerful force on the Web, and it would be my guess that XHTML will become a supported web standard. Let me clarify that I don't think it's necessary to learn XHTML this weekend. But, as time progresses and its acceptance broadens, I think it's a good thing to know. Because XHTML is basically a reformulation of HTML, it should be quick to learn for those of you with prior HTML experience. If you are unfamiliar with or have no experience with HTML, learning XHTML should not take you that long to pick up because it is created using simple English. If the thought of this terrifies you, don't panic! There are numerous reference books available on this subject. (I suggest you consider the book *XHTML* by Chelsea Valentine and Chris Minnick, published by New Riders Publishing, ISBN: 0-7357-1034-1.)

As well, this book is here to help. Most of the HTML examples in this book are supplemented with an XHTML example of the same exercise.

HOW TO LEARN XHTML

As you can imagine, the Web is full of resources that can aid in learning XHTML. In addition, there are a number of books published on XHTML that can help you build a strong foundation in this markup language.

One of the most effective ways to learn XHTML is by doing. I know it sounds obvious, but nothing can beat writing the code manually.

If this sounds terrifying to you, then try using one of the editors listed at the end of this chapter and then review the XHMTL code that is generated. This deconstruction approach to learning code can be effective, but will require knowledge of the basic elements—and that's exactly what this chapter will give you.

IMPORTANT XHTML TERMS

Like HTML, there are important terms to know when you are learning XHTML. These terms will help get you started and should give you a good, solid foundation for XHTML education:

Tag: Everything between the "<" and ">" symbols is referred to as a tag. For example, **<hr>** is a tag. In XHTML all tags must be written in lowercase.

Container: All XHTML tags require containers, also known as closing tags. For example, **<title>** requires the closing tag **</title>**. An exception to this are empty tags, which can be written with a single tag. For example, **
**. Notice that there is a space between the "r" and the "/" symbol. This is to ensure that this XHTML is as backward compatible as possible.

Content: Everything that falls between the open and close tags of an XHTML document is called content.

Attribute: A modifier to an element. Attributes have two components: the attribute name and the attribute value. In the example **<table border="1">**, **table** is the element, **border** is the attribute name, and **1** is the attribute value.

Attribute Value: Usually follows an attribute name. In the example **<table border="1">**, **1** is the value of the attribute name.

Element: A tag or tagset used to describe the structure of a document and its contents. For example, the entire string **"<table border="1">"** is called an element.

Entities: Also referred to as special characters, these are standard codes used to represent a wide range of characters such as accented letters, typographic elements such as em dashes, and symbols such as copyright.

ONLINE XHTML REFERENCE

The Web, holding true to its form, holds an enormous number of resources for learning XHTML. This is one of the best ways to learn the language and get help from other XHTML pioneers. ;-) Here is a brief list of a few of my favorites:

The Formal XHTML 1.0 Recommendation
This is the formal recommendation by the WC3.
http://www.w3.org/TR/xhtml1

XHTML.org
This web site provides an incredible amount of information on XHTML.
http://www.xhtml.org

XHTML School
This is a great place to learn more about XHTML with great resources.
http://www.w3schools.com/xhtml

XHTML Guru
This site provides a listing of XHTML books and even offers book reviews.
http://www.xhtmlguru.com

WHAT DOES XHTML LOOK LIKE?

If you have ever seen HTML code, then you will find instant comfort in looking at XHTML code. Because XHTML is a reformulating of HTML, many things look the same or similar with minor differences. Even if you haven't looked at HTML code before, I think you will find XHTML code very easy to read and understand.

While there are some distinct and critical differences between XHTML and HTML, they are both markup languages and share many common traits. This is good news because it will lessen the learning curve for those of you familiar with HTML. Here are some of the basic elements of an XHTML document written in correct syntax:

code

```
 1   <?xml version="1.0"?>
 2   <!DOCTYPE html PUBLIC"-//W3C//DTD XHTML 1.0 strict//EN
     "http://www.w3.org/TR/xhtml1/DTD/xhtml1-strict.dtd"
 3   <html xmlns="http://www.w3.org/1999/xhtml">
 4   <head>
 5   <title>
 6   </title>
 7   </head>
 8   <body>
     <p>This is where the content of your page will be placed.</p>
 9   </body>
10   </html>
```

code deconstruction

1   **XML declaration:** Identifies the document as an XML document. It is recommended but not required, and because it can cause rendering problems in some browsers, most developers will leave it off.

2   **Document Type Declaration:** Declares the document as being a specific document type and conforming to a specific **D**ocument **T**ype **D**efinition (DTD). The DTD is not the declaration. It is the laundry list of allowed elements, attributes, and characters that the URI in the declaration is referring to. There are three XHTML DTDs available:

> **XHTML Transitional:** This DTD lets you maintain backward compatibility with older browsers while still providing access to HTML 4.01 elements.

> **XHTML Strict:** This DTD does not provide access to any of the HTML elements that were designed to control the appearance of a page. This is the truest form of XHTML elements.

> **XHTML Frameset:** This DTD gives you access to the HTML elements needed to create framesets.

3 **XHTML Namespace:** This URL points to a file that gives detailed information about the particular XML vocabulary, which is XHTML in this case.

4 The `<head>` tag contains all of the header information.

5 The `<title>` tag defines the page title, which appears at the top of the browser window and in the bookmark lists.

6 All XHTML tags must be closed, so this is the closing `</title>` tag.

7 You guessed it! This is the closing `</head>` tag.

8 All of your visible content will be placed inside the `<body>` tag.

9 Yup, here is another closing tag. This is the closing `</body>` tag.

10 Last, but not least, is the closing `</html>` tag.

This example represents only a smidgen of the available XHTML tags, attributes, and values. But, it covers the basics and is a great place to start your XHTML education. I will cover more examples of XHTML throughout this book where appropriate.

XHTML EDITORS

For those of you not ready to dive into coding your XHTML pages manually, there are ways to convert your existing HTML documents into valid XHTML documents. It's possible to use your existing WYSIWYG HTML editor to create your pages and then use one of the programs listed below to convert them into valid XHTML documents. I'm very sure that you will see some WYSIWYG-generated XHTML in the near future. Until then, check out the links below so you can get your hands on one of these nifty tools.

To the right is a listing of some of the available programs that will convert your existing HTML documents into XHTML documents:

Macintosh:
HTML Tidy
http://www.geocities.com/SiliconValley/1057/tidy.html
upCast
http://www.infinity-loop.de

Windows:
HTML Tidy
http://www.w3.org/People/Raggett/tidy.exe
Amaya
http://www.w3.org/Amaya
Mozquito Factory 1.5
http://www.mozquito.com

HTML & XHTML

SUMMARY

This chapter reviewed many of the issues surrounding HTML, XHTML, and their editors. Here's a synopsis:

> HTML makes it difficult to control exacting design because it was developed to be accessible to many computer platforms, languages, and devices.

> XHTML 1.1 is the most current version of the markup language for the Web. Basically, it is a reformulation of HTML 4.01 using XML rules and syntax guidelines.

> The future of XHTML is unknown. While it has many promising features and capabilities, only time will tell if it will be accepted as the de facto markup language for the Web.

> It's best to understand the basics of HTML and XHTML so that you will be able to troubleshoot problems if and when they arise. In today's competitive marketplace, it can even make you a stronger candidate for a web designer position.

> If you plan to use an HTML or XHTML editor, try it before you buy it. This chapter contains many URLs for HTML editing software. Many XHTML editors are freeware and do not cost anything to download and use.

> There are many programs available for converting HTML documents into XHTML documents. This can save you time from having to learn how to code XHTML manually.

> There is no best HTML or XHTML editor, just ones that are best for you and your needs. Read up on the features to help you decide which one is right for you. The web is full of great resources on free HTML and XHTML editors.

09

Web File Formats

Introduction

Most of us have never cared a hoot about file formats. A file format is something that is in the background of daily tasks—a formality for saving computer files, but nothing beyond that. You might be used to saving files as BMP, PICT, TIFF, EPS, or Photoshop (PSD), but it's not like any of those file types have any special place in your heart.

The Web has introduced some new file formats that, beyond formality, directly affect the performance of your web site. That starts to get a little closer to the heart, right? Maybe not, but trust me. If you understand a bit about the various web file formats, your site will perform better for it.

This chapter offers the inside scoop on web file formats, hopefully without getting too nerdy on you. As usual, I've tried to condense the information to the interesting essentials, in order to spare you from technical overload. Still, I can't in good conscience spare you entirely, or my mission to help you make faster and better-looking web sites would fail.

There are many file formats in the world to write about, but this chapter provides an overview of the main web-based file format contenders; Chapter 11, *"Speedy Graphics,"* offers detailed instruction on how to make the smallest possible graphics.

BITMAP OR VECTOR?

File formats for computer graphics typically fall under two categories: bitmap or vector. If you have worked at all in computer graphics already, some familiar bitmap formats might be Photoshop (PSD), PICT, BMP, or TIFF. Common vector formats include Illustrator (AI), QuarkXPress, FreeHand, EPS, and PostScript. None of these formats are used for the Web because they produce files that are too large to download.

The most widely supported and used image formats on the Web are GIF and JPEG. Part of the reason they are so widely supported is because these file formats are native MIME types to most browsers. This means that end viewers see these types of graphics easily, without changing any settings in their browser or doing anything special beyond typing in an URL. Web developers like us can publish GIFs and JPEGs to our hearts' content, without fear that they won't be seen. Getting a file format accepted as a recognized MIME type by the browser vendors or W3C (**W**orld **W**ide **W**eb **C**onsortium) can make or break a file format's viability.

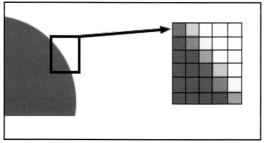

Raster, or bitmap, artwork is stored as a series of values.

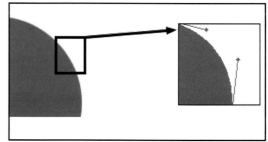

Vector artwork is stored as mathematical instructions.

GIFs and JPEGs are bitmap formats, also known as "raster graphics" in some circles. A bitmap file is stored by the computer as a series of values, with each pixel taking a set amount of memory. That is why the same exact image that is scaled at 100% will take more memory than one that has been reduced to 50%. Every pixel counts for a set amount of memory.

Vector graphics are a different story. Vector graphics contain a series of lines, curves, and splines that form different shapes through mathematical instructions. A very simplistic explanation follows: Suppose you had an image that contained a line that was 20 pixels long. In a bitmap format, this image would take 20 pixels to describe, while the same line in a vector format might only take one mathematical instruction, such as a start and end location of the line. Unlike raster formats, vector formats take the same amount of memory regardless of whether they are scaled big or small.

Vector formats are resolution-independent, meaning they will scale according to the output device, without affecting the amount of disk space they take up (or in web terms, without affecting the amount of downloading time they require or the size of the browser window!). In the print world, the same 100K vector graphic image will print at 300 dots per inch on a home printer or 2,400 dots per inch on a professional imagesetter printer. The vector format prints at whatever resolution the printing device allows, as all it really contains is a set of mathematical instructions that are interpreted by the printing device.

Bitmap files are the opposite. If any of you has ever created bitmap images for print graphics, you will testify to the need to work with huge file sizes. It is not uncommon that a Photoshop image that appears in a magazine might be over 100 megabytes. Because the file savings and device independence of vectors is indisputable, you might start to recognize the efficiency a vector format would bring to the Web.

It should be strongly noted that vector graphics are more suited for line art, illustrations, type, and flat-style artwork than bitmaps. Bitmaps are better suited for continuous-tone images, such as photographs, blurry images, soft edges, glows, and drop shadows. While you can succeed at presenting line art in a bitmap format and can attempt to simulate a continuous-tone image in a vector format (with lots of complex fills and gradients), ideally each format is best suited for specific types of content.

Later in this chapter, two vector formats for the Web will be described: Macromedia Flash and SVG. These formats require plug-ins, so they are not supported as standard MIME types such as GIF or JPEG.

Vector formats can typically scale to any dimension and still retain perfect resolution. It's because they are resolution-independent.

Bitmap formats, such as GIF and JPEG, look terrible when scaled. The number of pixels stay the same but, because they get enlarged, they look distorted and jaggy.

Since the standard web graphic file formats are bitmap formats, most vector graphics have to be rasterized before they can be viewed. Once they are scaled, they lose quality like all bitmap formats. You have probably seen GIFs or JPEGs on the Web that have been stretched using the **HEIGHT** and **WIDTH** attributes, and usually images that have been altered this way look pretty jaggy and distorted. That's because bitmaps don't scale very elegantly. The exact opposite is true of vectors!

Common imaging tools that create and export vectors include CorelDraw, Illustrator, and FreeHand. Common imaging tools that create and export bitmaps are Photoshop, Fireworks, PaintShop Pro, Image Composer, and Macromedia Director. Some programs create vector and bitmap graphics, such as Macromedia Fireworks and Adobe Photoshop, but these programs only export bitmaps. This combined capability reduces the need for separate graphics programs, which makes these tools more flexible and efficient to use for web graphics creation than other tools on the market.

There is only one vector format that is currently widely accepted and used throughout the Web. The SWF file format, produced by Macromedia Flash and other SWF authoring tools, has been adopted as the informal, yet de facto standard, vector format for the Web. Despite not having the formal support of the W3C, it manages to exist with enormous support from both users and developers. The SWF file format allows for easy mixing and delivery of both vector and bitmap graphics. The much talked about, but less implemented, SVG (**S**calable **V**ector **G**raphic) format is the other vector format for the Web. (The SVG and Flash formats are covered in more detail later in this chapter.)

LOSSLESS OR LOSSY?

What do all file formats for the Web have in common? Compression. Compression is the key that creates small graphics. Compression is not a necessary feature in other computer graphic file format specifications, which is why the file formats you'll find on the Web might be new to you. Web-based image file formats have to implement impressive compression schemes in order to transform large images to small file sizes. Unfortunately, at times, with compression comes loss of quality.

Before going too heavily into formats, it's necessary to define some terms. Lossless compression means that even though the file is compressed (enjoys a smaller file size than an uncompressed image), it will not lose any quality. A lossless image will contain identical data regardless of whether it is compressed or uncompressed. The popular file format GIF uses lossless compression.

Lossy compression is the opposite of lossless compression. Data is removed from the image in order to achieve compression. Often, this loss of data is not visible because the compression algorithm was designed to reduce data that wasn't essential. The popular JPEG file format uses lossy compression.

tip

GIF PRONUNCIATION

GIF is officially pronounced with a soft "G" as in "jiffy." Many people pronounce it with a hard "G." as well. I pronounce it both ways, depending on my mood. Because the word is an acronym for **G**raphics **I**nterchange **F**ormat, you would think it should have a hard "G." But it doesn't. Some people don't care and pronounce it the way it should be pronounced grammatically instead of the way it was pronounced back in its CompuServe days. Some people don't know it should have a soft "G" and pronounce it with a hard "G." Some people don't care either way.

GIF COMPRESSION

Unlike most other computer graphic file formats, GIF (**G**raphic **I**nterchange **F**ormat) was designed specifically for online delivery because it was originally developed for CompuServe in the late 1980s. GIF uses a compression scheme called LZW, which is based on work done by **L**empel-**Z**iv and **W**elch. The patent for LZW compression is owned by a company called Unisys, which charges developers such as Netscape and Adobe licensing and royalty fees for selling products that use the GIF file format.

Every so often, there is speculation that individual web publishers will be charged by Unisys for GIF files on their web sites. This is unlikely, as software vendors such as Microsoft, Adobe, Macromedia, Corel, Jasc, and others pay the licensing fees so that end users, such as you and me, can create GIFs using their products without any penalty. You would only have to worry about paying Unisys if you were writing software that allowed others to author GIF files.

GIFs are accepted by all graphical browsers for the Web, GIFs are small, and GIFs do things that many other file formats do not, such as animation, transparency, and interlacing. For now, the GIF format looks like it will continue to be a prevalent file format on all web pages.

The GIF file format, by definition, can contain only 256 colors (8-bit) or less. This is not the case with JPEGs, which can contain millions of colors (24-bit). Because GIFs are an indexed color file format (256 colors or less), it's extremely beneficial to have a thorough understanding of bit-depth settings and palette management when preparing GIF images. You will find more information about this in Chapter 11, *"Speedy Graphics."*

TRANSPARENCY IN THE GIF FILE FORMAT

There are two different flavors of GIF: **GIF87a** and **GIF89a**. GIF87a supports transparency and interlacing whereas GIF89a supports transparency, interlacing, and animation. As of this book's printing, the major browsers (Netscape and Internet Explorer) all support both GIF format specifications. You don't really have to refer to the names GIF89a or GIF87a unless you want to sound nerdy. Most of us simply call these files by the features used, be it a transparent GIF, animated GIF, or plain vanilla GIF.

GIF compression is lossless, meaning that the GIF compression algorithm will not cause any unwanted image degradation. The process of converting a 24-bit (millions of colors) image to 8-bit (256 colors) or fewer colors will cause image degradation on its own, however, so don't get too excited!

INTERLACED GIFS

If you've toured the Web much, you've encountered interlaced GIFs. They're images that start out blocky and appear less and less blocky until they come into full focus.

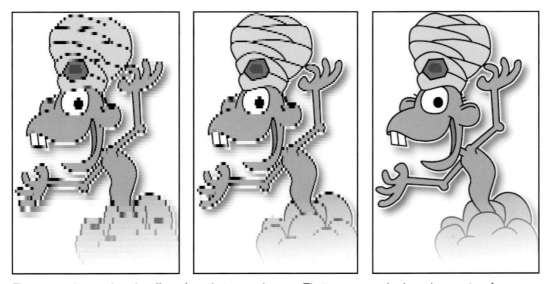

These examples simulate the effect of interlacing on a browser. The image starts chunky and comes into focus over time. This allows the end viewer to decide whether to wait for your graphic to finish or just click onward.

Interlacing doesn't affect the overall size or speed of a GIF. In theory, interlacing is supposed to make it possible for your end viewer to get a rough idea of your visuals and to make a decision whether to wait or click onward before the image finishes rendering. Again—in theory—this is supposed to save time. Unfortunately for the end viewer, being forced to wait for the entire image to finish coming into focus to read essential information is often a frustrating experience. In other words, interlaced images save time only if you don't have to wait for them to finish.

My recommendation is that you do not use interlaced GIFs for visual information that is critical to viewing your site. An imagemap or navigation icon, for example, must be seen in order to fulfill its function. Although interlaced GIFs serve their purpose on non-essential graphics, they only frustrate end users when used on essential graphics.

INTERLACED GIFS IN FIREWORKS & PHOTOSHOP

You create an interlaced GIF in an image editing program. It is important to note that you won't see the results in any software application except a browser.

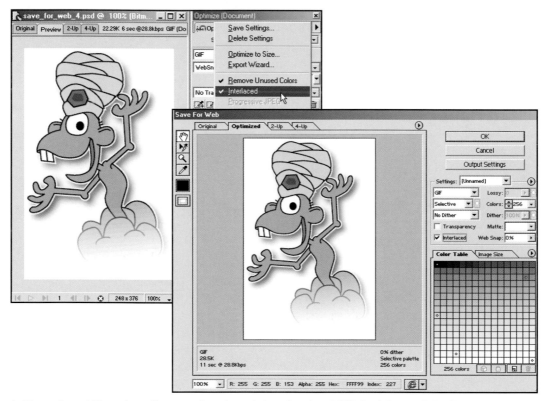

In Fireworks and Photoshop, all you need to do is click an Interlaced GIF check box, and the file is automatically written for you.

TRANSPARENT GIFS

Transparent GIFs are used to create the illusion of irregularly shaped artwork. All of the computer-made images end up in rectangular-shaped files; it's the nature of the medium. Certain file formats, such as GIF, can store masked regions, which create the illusion of shapes other than rectangles. This "masked region" appears to be transparent. Creating transparent GIFs is discussed in Chapter 16, *"Transparent GIFs."*

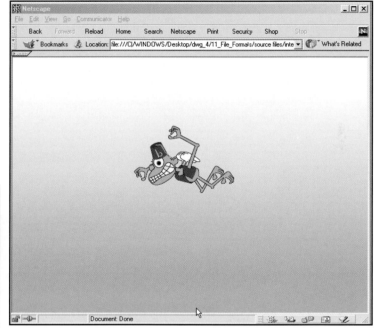

Here, the transparent artwork is shown in context.

Once the GIF transparency is recognized within browser software, the browser enables the rectangular artwork to appear irregularly shaped.

Animated GIFs

Animated GIFs are part of the GIF89a specification. They are often called multi-block GIFs because multiple images can be stored as separate blocks within a single GIF document. When the GIF document is viewed, the multiple images display, one at a time, and produce a slideshow effect. Once the animated GIF file has finished downloading, it can play very fast and look more like animation than a slideshow.

Animated GIFs can include custom palette information and be set to play at different speeds. They can also include interlacing and transparency settings. The beauty of animated GIFs is that they require no plug-ins, and the authoring tools to create them are often free and easy to learn. As well, major browsers (Netscape and Internet Explorer) support them, so you can include them in web pages without worrying about compatibility or accessibility. Specific instruction on how to create animated GIFs and apply custom palettes is available in Chapter 24, *"Animation & Audio."*

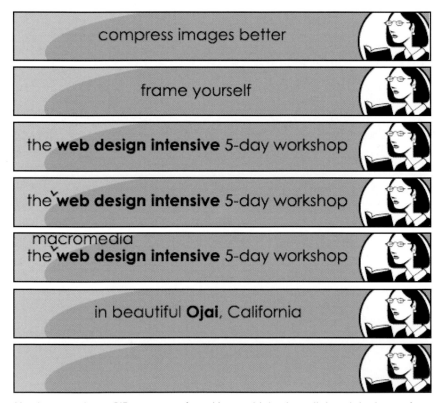

Here's a seven-frame GIF animation of an ad banner. It's hard to tell the subtle changes from frame to frame when viewed in sequence, but once the frames are played in motion over time, the text pops into place. It totals 6.82K in size. Why? There is very little information changing among the different frames of the animation.

JPEG COMPRESSION

The JPEG (pronounced jay-peg) file format offers a 24-bit (millions of colors) alternative to the 8-bit (256 colors) GIF file format. This is great for photographic content because 24-bit photographs will always look better than 8-bit photographs, since photographs require much more than 256 colors to create the range of continuous tones and gradients contained within them. One added advantage to dealing with JPEGs is that they don't need you to define the palette for them, unlike GIFs. Whenever an image format includes millions of colors (24-bit), color palette issues disappear. This is because enough colors are allowed to rely on the original image's color information, and substitute colors are no longer necessary. With the JPEG format, the only things you need to worry about are the quality of the image and the image's file size.

JPEG • 13.48K   **GIF • 62.88K**

JPEG • 41.0K   **GIF • 110.3K**

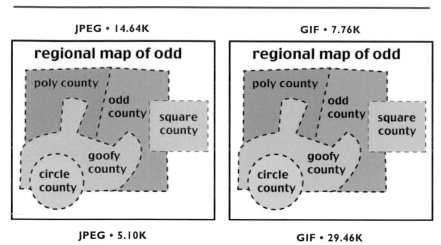

JPEG • 14.64K   GIF • 7.76K

JPEG • 5.10K   GIF • 29.46K

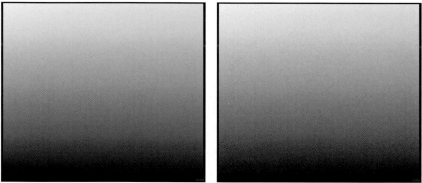

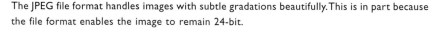

The JPEG file format handles images with subtle gradations beautifully. This is in part because the file format enables the image to remain 24-bit.

JPEG is a lossy compression algorithm, meaning that it removes information from your image and, therefore, causes a loss in quality. JPEG does a great job of doing this, so the difference in information data is often not visible or objectionable. It does introduce artifacts in some instances, especially where it encounters solid colors or the compression level is set to Low for the image. This is a by-product of its lossy compression methods.

Another difference between GIF and JPEG is the fact that you can save JPEGs in a variety of compression levels. This means that more or less compression can be applied to an image, depending on which looks best.

Unlike the GIF file format, JPEGs require both compression and decompression. This means that JPEG files need to decompress when they're viewed. Although a GIF and a JPEG might be identical sizes, or sometimes even when the JPEG is smaller, the JPEG may take longer to download or view from a web browser because of the added time required to decompress it.

PROGRESSIVE JPEGS VERSUS STANDARD JPEGS

Progressive JPEGs support interlacing (where the graphic starts chunky and comes into focus). They were initially introduced by Netscape and are now additionally supported by Internet Explorer. Most graphic applications like Macromedia Fireworks and Adobe Photoshop give you the option of creating standard or progressive JPEGs. If you are using an older version of Adobe Photoshop, you can download a plug-in, JPEGiT!, that will let you create progressive JPEGs at http://www.in-touch.com/pjpeg2.html#software.

Some of the really old browsers did not offer support for progressive JPEGs. In these cases, the progressive JPEG would appear with a broken image icon.

Low • 2.88K

Med • 4.65K

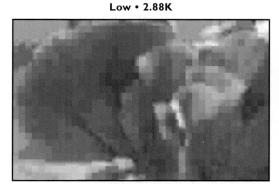

High • 9.69K

Max • 14.55K

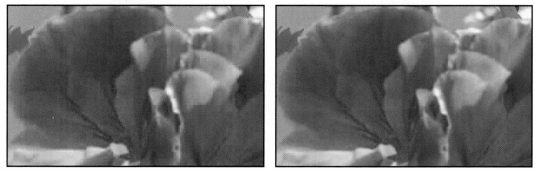

SELECTIVE JPEG COMPRESSION

Under normal JPEG compression, the entire image is compressed. In most cases, this is acceptable. However, there might come a time when you want to compress various parts of the JPEG independently. For example, you might want to compress blurred or unfocused areas of a photograph much more than you would want to compress a picture of someone's face. Selective JPEG compression is a way of allowing you to define and compress specific areas of a JPEG differently. Adobe Photoshop refers to this process as "Weighted Optimization," and Macromedia Fireworks calls it "Selective JPEG Compression."

PNG

PNG (**P**ortable **N**etwork **G**raphics, or more fondly known as "PNG Not GIF") holds some promise as a web file format. The W3C (**W**orld **W**ide **W**eb **C**onsortium at http://www.w3.org/pub/WWW/Press/PNG-PR.en.html) has made a formal endorsement of PNG, which has, in turn, caused Netscape and Explorer to partially support the format. You can read and download the entire PNG recommendation at the W3C web site (http://www.w3.org/Graphics/PNG/). The PNG format was partially developed by Thomas Boutell (http://www.boutell.com/boutell/png).

PNG uses a lossless compression method, meaning that no quality loss is incurred when it's applied to images. PNG is compressed using any number of pre-compression filters and is then decompressed when viewed—similar to the JPEG format, except the PNG format is lossless. This enables PNG to retain every original detail and pixel, with no loss of quality.

Unlike GIF or JPEG, PNG can be stored at many different bit depths using different storage methods. GIF, for example, can be stored only in 8-bit or lower bit depths. JPEGs must be stored in 24-bit and no lower. PNG can be stored in either 8-bit, 24-bit, or 32-bit. This makes PNG one of the most flexible formats available for web images and also one of the more difficult formats to program for developers. For this reason, PNG support for browsers and imaging software has been slow coming.

GAMMA CORRECTION

Gamma correction enables an image to display properly on different platforms without losing contrast or brightness in the translation. Differences in gamma among different platforms can make an image seem darker or lighter on a platform other than the one it was created on. PNG has the capacity to store a value that represents the gamma of the system on which the image was created. This value can then be used by the displaying system to correct for its gamma value, if known.

The only caveat for gamma correction to work is that both the creating and displaying systems must know their own gamma, and this is usually not the case in today's web world. Here's a case of a good idea with little to no browser or tool support.

ALPHA CHANNEL TRANSPARENCY

The PNG format has the capacity to store a variable transparency value known as alpha channel transparency. This allows your images to have up to 256 different levels of partial transparency (or translucency).

If you want to find out what browsers support the PNG format, and more specifically what features, be sure to visit http://www.libpng.org/pub/png/pngapbr.html. You can test your browser to see if it can view PNG files by browsing to http://www.w3.org/Graphics/PNG/Inline-img.html. If you can see the two images on this page, woo-hoo! Your browser is able to view PNG files.

PNG Transparency Comparison

GIF Features	PNG Features
Up to 256 colors	Up to 32-bit color
Progressive display capabilities	Up to 16-bit grayscale
Transparency	Full alpha channel support (for alpha masks)
100% lossless compression	Gamma correction
	Superior compression

PNG Browser Support
(not all features supported equally)

Macintosh	Windows
Internet Explorer 5.0 or later	Internet Explorer 4.01 or later
Netscape Navigator 4.04 or later	Netscape Navigator 4.04 or later

PNG RESOURCES

Thomas Boutell's PNG Page
http://www.boutell.com/boutell/png

The PNG Specification at W3C
http://www.w3.org/Graphics/PNG

My misconception about PNG images was that you had to use a 32-bit palette to use alpha channel transparency, which was not true. The PNG format allows any entry in any palette to represent any channel, either red, green, blue, or alpha (these palettes are called RGBA instead of RGB).

So, why isn't everyone using the PNG format then? Until recently, most browsers did not support the PNG format. Even today, the really cool features in the PNG format, such as alpha transparency and gamma correction, are still not supported in all browsers. Because PNG isn't supported in 3.0 browsers, larger sites cannot afford to use them due to the risk of alienating a significant part of their audience. It is still unclear if browser and developer support will increase to make PNG the true replacement to the GIF format. Here today, PNG tomorrow?

DIGITAL WATERMARKS

The term *watermark* is traditionally used to describe special printed paper that guarantees proof of authenticity and ownership. Dollar bills are a good example of watermarked currency, which has special information embedded in the paper stock to prevent counterfeiting.

Digital watermarks are a new technology that follow a similar principle, only the embedded copyright information is not visible until loaded into a computer that can read it. Watermarking technology can embed copyright notification, ownership, audience (adult or general interest material), and usage information (restricted or royalty free). The watermark signature can be read by Photoshop and Digimarc.

Digimarc (http://digimarc.com) offers a digital watermarking service that offers watermarking software and a database/retrieval service for professionals. Their fee structure is listed on their site.

The PictureMarc (http://www.digimarc.com/imaging/plugin.htm) plug-in for Photoshop is digital watermarking software that enables you to embed watermarks into digital documents for print- or web-based submission. When PictureMarc is invoked, you are given the opportunity to obtain your own "creator ID," which links your images to up-to-date contact information that is stored on the Digimarc site.

Every time an image is opened or scanned into Photoshop, PictureMarc performs a quick detection and adds a "©" to the image window's title bar. By clicking on the "©" symbol on the title bar, PictureMarc launches your web browser and displays detailed information about the image and lists whatever contact details you have provided.

This service supports CMYK, RGB, LAB, Grayscale, and Index Color color spaces, and it works with any file format type that Photoshop supports on 95/98/NT/2000/ME and Mac (PowerPC only) platforms. A minimum image size of 256×256 pixels is required, which makes its usefulness for the Web limited to larger images, thereby unfortunately excluding navigational graphics, buttons, bullets, and rules.

SVG

SVG is the first "formal" vector format for the Web that has the full endorsement and support of the W3C. SVG is a language that describes graphics in XML. This means it's marked up in text. This is remarkable because it means that graphics can be created from scratch using only simple text instructions. For example, if you wanted to draw a black square on your web page using SVG, the code would look something like this:

code

```
<SVG WIDTH="500" HEIGHT="500">
<RECT X="34" Y="69" WIDTH="293" HEIGHT="250" RX="0" RY="0"
STYLE="STROKE-MITERLIMIT:4;STROKE-LINEJOIN:MITER;
STROKE-WITDTH:1;STROKE-OPACITY:1;STROKE:RGB(0,0,0);
FILL-OPACITY:1;FILL:RGB(0,0,0);OPACITY:1"/>
</SVG>
```

That's going to download a lot faster than any GIF or JPEG for sure! And because it is created using XML (text), it can be easily searched, modified, updated dynamically, etc. If you are concerned that you will have to type this code in manually, don't worry—several SVG development tools already exist, including Adobe Illustrator 9 and later. I have included a list of SVG development tools at the end of this section. Now you know that SVG is created using XML and downloads fast, the following chart highlights many other important features:

SVG Features	Description
Vector Format	Objects are created using mathematical instructions, which can be easily scaled and zoomed without any loss of quality or increase in file size.
Text Object Model	Objects are created using simple text, which means that anyone with a text editor can create SVG graphics. This also means they can be easily searched and updated dynamically.
CSS Usage	SVG relies on CSS (Cascading Style Sheets) to achieve absolute positioning. Other CSS attributes, like z-index, are also supported.
Bitmap Support	Traditional bitmap graphics (GIF and JPEG) can be incorporated into SVG documents.
Text Support	Text can be easily added to SVG documents and can also be formatted using CSS.
Clipping Paths	SVG objects can be defined as clipping paths, which can be used to create special effects.
	continues...

SVG Features	Description
Mask Support	SVG objects can be specified as masks for compositing with the background.
Gradients & Patterns	Both linear and radial gradients are supported in the SVG format. Objects can be used as patterns to fill or stroke an SVG object.
Opacity Support	You can adjust the opacity value of any SVG object.
Transformations	SVG objects can be rotated, skewed, and scaled. This can be used to create powerful animations.
Filter Effects	Client-side filter effects are being developed to automate some commonly used special effects. Yes, just like Photoshop.
Animation	Using the SVG animation elements, it is possible to create motion paths, fade-in or fade-out effects, and objects that grow, shrink, spin, or change color.
Scripting	SVG has its own scripting element, which can help make your SVG objects respond to user actions, like clicking the mouse.

As you can probably tell by now, SVG has great promise. Remember, all of these features are possible without any graphic files. Instead, they are created using simple text, which will make downloads go quickly. Like any other new web format, it will take time to become adopted by developers and Internet users. As of this writing, there was only one plug-in available from Adobe that enables the viewing of SVG content in a browser; you can find it at http://www.adobe.com/svg/viewer/install/main.html.

SVG has the potential of becoming the standard for portable wireless devices. Its small size and vector capabilities make it ideal for wireless communications. Research is already being conducted in this area. You can see some really impressive examples of SVG being used on several different portable devices at http://research.bitflash.com/sdvg/SVGBDemoRep.html.

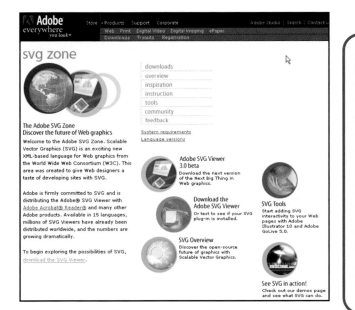

tip

SVG RESOURCES

If you are looking for information on SVG, visit the links below. They offer you more information than you could ever want. There are also some really cool examples of SVG in action.

W3C
http://www.w3.org/Graphics/SVG/Overview.htm8

Adobe SVG Zone
http://www.adobe.com/svg/main.html

Nokiko SVG Project
http://www.nokiko.com/svg

Adobe has devoted an entire section of its web site to SVG. You can download Adobe's SVG plug-in and see many examples of SVG at http://www.adobe.com/svg/main.html.

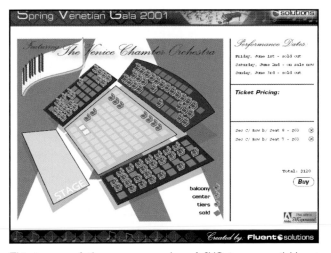

This is one of the many examples of SVG in use available at **Adobe.com**.

SWF

The SWF (**S**mall **W**eb **F**ile) format was developed by Macromedia and is supported by Flash, Director, and many Adobe authoring tools as well. It's difficult to be involved with web design and not be exposed to Flash in one way or another. One of the hottest and most used vector animation and interactivity tools on the Web, it has become the informal vector standard for the Web.

Macromedia Flash contains vector drawing tools, strong animation capabilities, and an extensible scripting architecture that makes it possible to create everything from animated banners to entire web sites to complete web applications. While Flash creates vector artwork natively, it also allows for easy inclusion of

bitmap graphics, such as GIF, JPEG, and PNG files. Flash allows for the scaling of both vector and bitmap artwork, which is a great benefit that other web formats do not offer. Using a system of reusable objects called symbols and instances, Flash is able to export SWF files that contain rich graphics and complex interactivity but are very small in size. Since Flash 4 MP3 audio compression has been added to further reduce file size. These capabilities have made Flash a popular choice among many web designers. In fact, a large community of Flash developers has developed around the software over the last few years. Note that the SWF format now can be created by many programs: Adobe LiveMotion, Corel, ePicture Pro, and others.

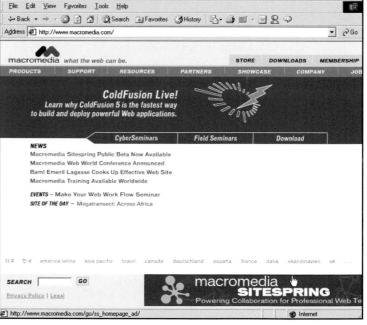

Because Flash uses vectors, all or just portions of a web site can be set to scale with the size of the browser window. In this illustration, notice how small the center of the site gets when the browser window is reduced.

As the browser window is expanded, the vector portions of the site scale proportionately. Notice how the center portion is much larger and easier to read.

If there is a drawback to the SWF format, it's the fact that it is not a native MIME type and therefore requires a plug-in, called the Flash Player, in order to be viewed in a browser. As of July 2002, Macromedia states that 97.8% of all internet users have a version of the Flash Player installed. This number is slightly deceptive because there are so many versions of the Flash Player in circulation, and the Macromedia statistics don't cite which version of the player these numbers relate to. You can check http://www.macromedia.com/software/player_census/flashplayer for more current statistics. Today, the good news is that the Flash Player comes pre-installed with the latest browsers and most operating systems.

SWF Features	Description
Vector Format	SWF supports vectors, which offer small file sizes with the ability to scale with the browser window.
Compression	Through a system of symbols, compression routines, and instances, SWF files can contain complex graphics, animation, and interactivity and still have a small file size.
Bitmap Support	Traditional bitmap graphics (GIF, JPEG, and PNG) can be included in SWF files.
Audio Support	SWF supports MP3 audio compression, an audio format that offers superior compression and quality.
Animation	SWF supports complex animation.
Scripting	SWF has its own scripting language (ActionScript), which can add interactivity to your projects or create entire web applications.

FLASH RESOURCES

Flash Training Products (http://www.lynda.com**)**
> Flash 5 Hands-On-Training
> Learning Flash 5
> Advanced Flash 5: Introduction to ActionScripting
> Optimizing Flash 5 Content
> Animation Principles with Flash 5
> Much, much more!

Flash Resource Sites
> Ultrashock
  http://www.ultrashock.com
> FlashForward2002
  http://www.flashforward2003.com
> FlashPlanet
  http://www.flashplanet.com
> Actionscript.org
  http://www.actionscript.org

Flash Inspirational Sites
> Janet Jackson
  http://janet-jackson.com
> Relevare
  http://www.relevare.com
> Second Story
  http://www.secondstory.com

WBMP

The WBMP (**W**ireless **B**itmap) is a new format designed to deliver graphics to wireless devices, such as cellular phones and PDAs (**P**ersonal **D**igital **A**ssistants). The WBMP format is black and white (1-bit) and is part of the WML (**W**ireless **M**arkup **L**anguage) specification. Just as many of us web designers thought we were free of the web-safe palette, some of us are being asked to create images that look good in black and white!

Before you continue, here are some important terms that relate to this section. You don't have to memorize them; just read through them to familiarize yourself with this new area of web development.

WBMP	Term Description
WAE	**W**ireless **A**pplication **E**nvironment. This refers to the overall structure for delivering wireless information. This would be similar to the World Wide Web structure for browsers.
WAP	**W**ireless **A**pplication **P**rotocol. The protocol used to deliver data to wireless devices. This is similar in function to the HTTP protocol, which is used to deliver web pages to browsers.
WML	**W**ireless **M**arkup **L**anguage. The code used to create WAP browser pages so they can be viewed through wireless devices. WML is actually a subset of XML, but let's not get too technical here. This is just like HTML, which is used to deliver content through web browsers.
WBMP	**W**ireless **B**itmap. Black-and-white (1-bit) graphic format used with WML to deliver graphics to wireless devices.

So what is a WBMP really? You already know that it is a black-and-white (1-bit) image. It is an uncompressed image format. Because it's only a 1-bit image, using a non-compressed image is reasonable for wireless connections. Now, converting existing images to the WBMP format will certainly result in a loss of quality—unless of course they are already black-and-white (1-bit) images. Hopefully, as this format continues to develop and wireless broadband increases, this format will begin to support more color. In addition to being limited to black and white, WBMP images are also limited in size, especially since cellular phones lack the capability to scroll sideways. As a general rule, most WBMP images should not exceed 90×24 pixels. Now, that is really tiny! The truth is, however, that most wireless devices have really tiny screens anyway. The file size of the WBMP should not exceed 1,461 bytes because of limitations on most of the current WAP-enabled phones.

There are some WBMP development tools available, and most of them are for Windows with just a few available on the Macintosh. Because this is a new file format, most of these development tools are pretty simple applications. In addition to these programs, there are some plug-ins available for Adobe Photoshop, Macromedia Fireworks, and PaintShop Pro that will let you convert existing artwork to the WBMP format. Here's a list of some web sites that offer WBMP development tools:

WAP Draw
http://www.hit-solutions.fi/wapdraw

WBMP Creator
http://www.wbmpcreator.com

WBMP Butterfly
http://www.wap-shareware.com/directory/wbmptools/wbmpbutt.shtml

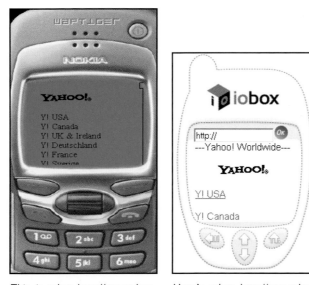

This is what http://wap.yahoo. com looks like through the Wap Tiger v1.6 WAP emulator. Notice the pretty black Yahoo! logo. ;-)

Here's what http://wap.yahoo. com looks like through the WAP emulator at iobox.com. Notice the slight differences in text spacing.

IMODE

Imode is another format used for wireless Internet delivery that is widespread in Japan. In fact, there are more than 27 million users of Imode there! To author for Imode delivery, you would use cHTML (compact HTML). There are some special imode-only tags as well as special characters, which are symbols for joy, kisses, love, sadness, hot spring baths, telephones, Shinkansen train, encircled numbers, etc.

WBMP RESOURCES

iobox (WAP emulator**)**
http://www.iobox.com

yospace (Emulators and WAP information**)**
http://www.yospace.com

Open Mobile Alliance (Formal WAP specification**)**
http://www.wapforum.org

SUMMARY

It's important to understand some of the basics of file formats so that you know which one to choose for web delivery. Each file format has strengths and weaknesses and is best suited for certain types of images or delivery. Here is a brief summary of each file type that was reviewed in this chapter:

> For line art, vectors are much smaller and faster to download than bitmaps. Unfortunately, the only vector format for the Web that has gained much acceptance (Flash) still relies on plug-ins for most browser versions.

> GIF uses a lossless compression scheme, and is limited to 256 colors or fewer (8-bit). It supports interlacing, transparency, and animation.

> JPEG uses lossy compression and is limited to 24-bit. It supports interlacing in its progressive format but does not support transparency or animation.

> PNG can use lossy or lossless compression, and it is capable of storing gamma and alpha channel information. Unfortunately, older browsers cannot render PNG images without a plug-in.

> SVG is a vector format that has great promise and is the first vector format supported by the W3C. SVG graphics are created using text (XML) and can easily incorporate bitmap graphics.

> SWF is the compressed file that is exported from Macromedia Flash and a number of other programs. It is currently considered by many to be the unofficial vector format for the Web. Offering animation, interactivity, and powerful scripting capabilities, it can be used to create banners, web sites, or entire web applications.

> WBMP is a 1-bit (black-and-white) graphic format designed to be delivered to wireless devices, such as cellular phones and PDAs.

10

Speedy Graphics

Introduction

If you look through a book or magazine and see a compelling picture, who cares if the file was 80 gazillion megabytes or one kilobyte? In the print world, there is no experiential penalty to viewing images with large file sizes. On the Web, the exact opposite is true, because large files can cause your audience to leave your site in frustration, regardless of how alluring your pictures promise to be.

It has never been the job of an artist to care about the file savings of a graphic. Although the process of optimizing graphics for the Web has been around now for a few years, it will be a new concept for some of you, especially print designers making the transition to web production. Fortunately, image creation and optimization software has improved and evolved to meet the demands and needs of web designers. With the current crop of tools, such as ImageReady, Fireworks, PaintShop Pro, etc., the job of optimizing images is much easier than ever before.

This chapter reviews the most popular file formats—GIF and JPEG—and shows you how to squeeze every kilobyte out of your graphics to ensure they're small, fast, and lookin' good. This is accomplished through understanding compression principles and how to use web image optimization tools.

If you read the last chapter, you should be familiar with the lossy versus lossless compression methods, and you now have the background needed to delve a little further into the nuances of file-size savings. This chapter reviews some of the most popular tools for image optimization, including Adobe ImageReady and Macromedia Fireworks.

11

CHECKING DOWNLOAD SPEEDS

Many of you will be developing web sites with direct access to DSL, T1, or better. This can make it impossible to test how fast your graphics will download over a 56k modem connection.

A company called **OptiView** (http://www.optiview.com) offers a free web-based service that will let you test your page on a 56k simulator. Sweet. This means you can keep the T1 and still test your pages on a 56k connection.

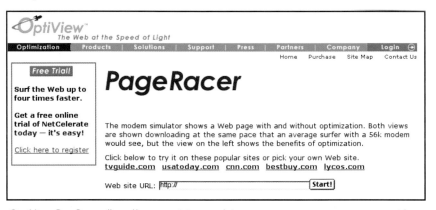

OptiView PageRacer (http://www.optiview.com) is a great way to test your pages without having to use a modem.

note

MORE TO DOWNLOADING SPEED

While our **lynda.com** web site has grown dramatically over the past few years, it still contains very small images in terms of file size. Unfortunately, there are times when it is still slow. This has nothing to do with the size of our images at all, but with the speed of our web server or the unforeseen bottlenecks of the Internet on any given day.

Many newcomers to web publishing subscribe to a large service, such as AOL, Earthlink, or GeoCities. These services often provide free web space (the exact amount varies), and it's easy to be attracted to them when you're thinking about posting your first web site. This can work out well for small sites, but for a large, professional site, it pays to go with a service that is dedicated to hosting web sites (a presence provider) as opposed to a service that also hosts Internet connections (an Internet Service Provider, or ISP).

Sometimes, there just isn't anything anyone can do about connection speeds. Even today, with all of the research and innovation that has gone into creating reliable, secure, and redundant network systems, things still go crazy and connection speeds can grind to a halt. Still, you do have control over a big part of the equation, which is to make your images as small as possible. If you do your part, then the Web will be a more tolerable place for all of us.

WHAT SIZE YOUR FILE REALLY IS

How can you tell how many kilobytes an image is? You would think to look to your hard drive, but even that can be deceptive.

Macs and PCs differ in terms of file size reporting. On a Mac, if you look at your hard drive for the file size of an image, you'll notice that the file size numbers are all nicely rounded figures: 11K, 33K, and 132K. Your computer rounds up the size of a file to the next largest number depending on how large your hard drive partition is. Have you ever had a file read two different file sizes on a hard drive and a floppy? That's because the computer rounds off the size of the file depending on what size storage medium it's on.

 radiopict.get info

Kind: Adobe Photoshop™ 3.0.4 document
Size: 44K on disk (36,152 bytes used)

On a Mac: The only way to get information about the true byte size of a file is to do a Get Info command. First, highlight the file you want to check in the Finder, go to the File menu, and then choose *Get Info*.

Location:	C:\WINDOWS\Desktop\icon folder
Size:	963 KB (986,667 bytes)
Size on disk:	976 KB (999,424 bytes)

On Windows: The file size shown in the Properties dialog box is different from the actual file size. The *Size* option refers to the actual size of the file, which in this case is **986,667** bytes. The *Size on disk* option refers to the actual amount of hard drive space the file takes up. It's the different file Size because of file clusters in the Windows operating system. Confusing? I know... Just pay attention to the Size information in parentheses, and you will be OK.

PHOTOSHOP ICONS & SPACE

Photoshop typically saves images with an icon. The icon is a small, visual representation of what the image looks like, which the file references. Photoshop icons take up a little extra room on your hard drive. This ultimately won't matter because, when you send the files to your server as part of your web site design, you'll transmit them as raw data, which will strip off the icon anyway. But if your goal is to get a more accurate reading of the true file size, you should set your preferences in Photoshop to not save an icon.

Whether you are using a Macintosh or a Windows machine, you will encounter this same problem with Photoshop. Personally, I like to leave my Photoshop icons turned on. I deal with so many images on my hard drive that it's very helpful to me to see the icons. I trust the file size increase to disappear once I post the images to a web site and enjoy the luxury of a visual representation of my images on my hard drive.

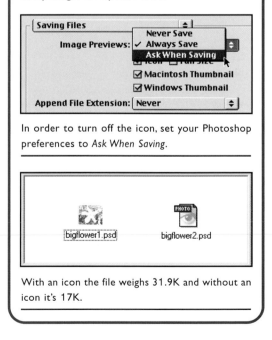

In order to turn off the icon, set your Photoshop preferences to *Ask When Saving*.

With an icon the file weighs 31.9K and without an icon it's 17K.

FILE SIZE IN FIREWORKS, IMAGEREADY, & PHOTOSHOP

Both Fireworks and ImageReady give better feedback about file size than Photoshop. These tools were developed as web graphics tools, as opposed to Photoshop, which was developed originally for print graphics. Now that Photoshop has the *Save for Web* feature, it is better suited for web graphics. Here are some examples of how to read the image size of files in both products.

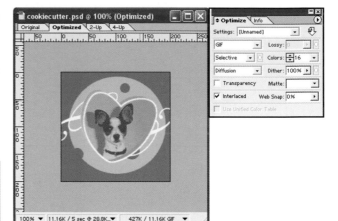

ImageReady lets you see the file size of an image right from the document window. Similar to Fireworks, clicking on the *Optimized* tab will reveal the image size based on the settings of the *Optimize* panel. You can compare image settings using the *2-Up* and *4-Up* tabs.

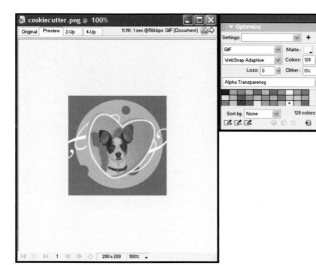

To see the file size of an image while working in **Fireworks**, you can click on the *Preview tab* at the top of the document window. The image appearance and file size are based on the settings you set in the *Optimize* panel. Right from the document window, you can even do compression comparisons by using the *2-Up* and *4-Up* tabs.

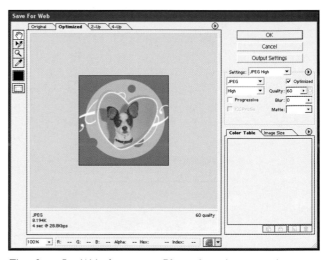

The *Save For Web* feature in **Photoshop** has everything you need for good image optimization. You can view the image size information and downloading speed, compare optimization settings, and much more.

EVALUATING THE STYLE OF YOUR IMAGE

Throughout this book, you'll notice that I reference different styles of images. Line art is the style that contains a lot of solid colors and lines, such as what you would find in a graphic, illustration, or logo. Continuous-tone art is the style that contains subtle gradations or tones, like those found in photographic content. Hybrid art is a combination of both styles.

Different compression types are designed for different styles of images. GIF compression works much better on line art than photographs. JPEG compression works much better on photographs. Hybrid imagery will work better with JPEG or GIF, depending on the image.

Identifying the style of the image in question will help you make the decision of where to start on your quest for compression. Note: The acronyms of GIF (**G**raphic **I**nterchange **F**ormat) and JPEG (**J**oint **P**hotographic **E**xpert **G**roup) describe what types of files these compression algorithms were designed for: GIFs for graphics and JPEGs for photographs.

Line art

Continuous-tone artwork

Hybrid artwork

tip

DON'T JPEG A JPEG

Don't apply JPEG compression to a file that already has it. Each time you add JPEG compression, the image will lose quality. The first time, it won't be noticeable, but multiple JPEG applications will degrade the image beyond repair. Save your files as Photoshop files or in other non-destructive formats, such as PICT, TIFF, EPS, BMP, or TGA, to ensure that saving the image as a JPEG is the last step.

note

OLDER BROWSER CONCERNS

I only use Optimized JPEG compression on my web site because Baseline Standard and Progressive JPEGs are not supported by older browsers. The penalty of using these other types of JPEGs will result in a broken image icon. That's too steep a penalty for me. If you are using browser detection (see Chapter 18, *"JavaScript: Rollovers & More"*) or some other method of distributing multiple sets of pages to your audience, then the advantages of Baseline Optimized and Progressive JPEGs might be attractive to you.

SAVING PHOTOGRAPHS AS GIFS—NONE DITHER METHOD

8-bit GIF • 26.7K

7-bit GIF • 21.0K

6-bit GIF • 15.7K

5-bit GIF • 11.6K

4-bit GIF • 8.23K

3bit GIF • 4.99K

2-bit GIF • 3.29K

1-bit GIF • 1.46K

SAVING PHOTOGRAPHS AS JPEGS

Max • 15.7K

High • 9.72K

Med • 4.87K

Low • 3.34K

SAVING PHOTOGRAPHS AS GIFS—DITHER METHOD

8-bit GIF • 27.9K

7-bit GIF • 22.4K

6-bit GIF • 17.0K

5-bit GIF • 12.9K

4-bit GIF • 10.1K

3-bit GIF • 7.01K

2-bit GIF • 4.80K

1-bit GIF • 2.91K

While some of the GIF files produced smaller file sizes, the quality was not as good as the smaller JPEG. This example demonstrates clearly that JPEG is the superior compression method for photographic content.

SAVING GRAPHICS AS GIFS—NONE DITHER METHOD

8-bit GIF • 9.72K

7-bit GIF • 8.13K

6-bit GIF • 6.78K

5-bit GIF • 5.34K

4-bit GIF • 4.49K

3-bit GIF • 3.34K

2-bit GIF • 2.27K

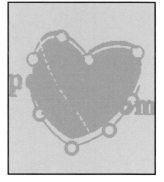

1-bit GIF • 1.20K

SAVING GRAPHICS AS JPEGS

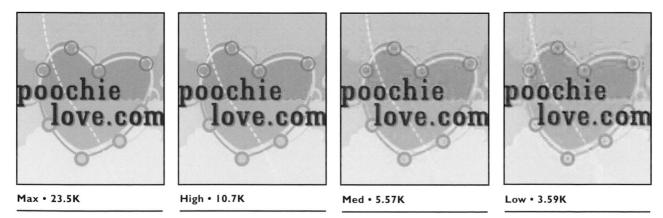

Max • 23.5K

High • 10.7K

Med • 5.57K

Low • 3.59K

saving graphics as gifs—dither method

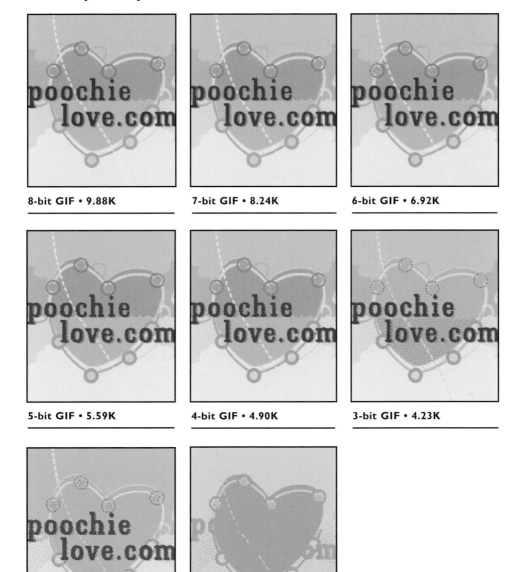

8-bit GIF • 9.88K

7-bit GIF • 8.24K

6-bit GIF • 6.92K

5-bit GIF • 5.59K

4-bit GIF • 4.90K

3-bit GIF • 4.23K

2-bit GIF • 3.30K

1-bit GIF • 1.74K

These examples demonstrate clearly that the GIF file format produces smaller files for graphic-based content.

MAKING SMALL JPEGS

The good news is that making small JPEGs is infinitely easier than making small GIFs. There are no palettes, dithering, indexing, or color-depth issues (which are described later in this chapter). It's fairly simple: JPEGs are best for photographs or continuous-tone images. JPEG compression is applied to an image when you save it and appears as a file format choice in Photoshop and other imaging applications that support web graphics.

JPEG files can be saved in RGB, CMYK, or grayscale. I have crashed my web browser when displaying CMYK-based JPEG files, so don't try that at home! All web files should be prepared in RGB or grayscale (see Chapter 12, *"Color Issues,"* for more details).

JPEG compression uses a lossy method, meaning it eliminates data. This means that the more compression you apply to an image, the lower the file size and the quality. It is your job to judge that fine line between a small file size and sufficient quality.

Photoshop implements three types of JPEG compression: Baseline Standard, Baseline Optimized, and Progressive. Here is a summary of each format:

Baseline Standard: JPEG compression can be set at different levels. The more compression you add on a scale from 1–12, the smaller the file will become. The scale applies to quality, so a setting of 12 would result in the highest quality, the least amount of compression, and the largest file size.

Baseline Optimized: Baseline Optimized JPEG compression can result in slightly smaller JPEG files.

Progressive: Progressive JPEG files might be slightly larger than those using Baseline Standard methods, but this format supports interlacing, meaning the image will appear chunky before it comes into full focus as it finishes downloading. The Progressive JPEG format is not supported by older browsers (those before Netscape 2.0 and IE 3.0). Progressive JPEG files will display as non-progressive JPEGs in older browsers.

JPEG EXAMPLES

A major difference between GIF and JPEG is the fact that you can save JPEGs in a variety of compression levels. This means that more or less compression can be applied to an image, depending on which looks best.

The examples on the following page were taken from Photoshop. Photoshop employs the JPEG compression settings of Max, High, Medium, and Low. In Photoshop, these terms relate to quality, not the amount of compression.

The test shows that there is not a whole lot of difference between low-quality and high-quality settings, except for images with a lot of line art or solid colors. As I've said, leave graphics for GIFs and photographs for JPEGs. Although there are good reasons for saving photographs in the GIF format (animation and transparency), there are no good reasons for saving graphics in the JPEG format unless the graphics are combined with photographs. With photographic content in general, don't be afraid to try low-quality settings. The file-size savings is usually substantial, and the quality penalties are not too steep.

Baseline Standard

Max • 15.7K

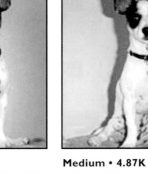

High • 9.27K

Medium • 4.87K

Low • 3.34K

Baseline Optimized

Max • 15.2K

High • 8.91K

Medium • 4.64K

Low • 3.10K

Progressive

Max • 14.8K

High • 9.0K

Medium • 4.72K

Low • 3.21K

MAKING SMALL GIFS

The GIF file-compression algorithm offers impressive file-size reduction, but the degree of file size savings has a lot to do with how you create your GIF images. Understanding how GIFs compress is the first step in this process.

GIFs use a compression scheme known as LZW compression, which seeks out patterns of data. Whenever it encounters areas in an image that do not have changes, it can implement much higher compression. This is similar to another type of compression called run-length compression (used in BMP, TIFF, and PCX formats), but LZW writes, stores, and retrieves its code a little differently. Similar to many types of run-length compression, however, GIF compression searches for changes along a horizontal axis, and whenever it finds a new color, adds to the file size.

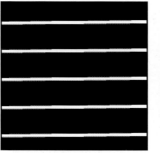  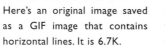

Here's an original image saved as a GIF image that contains horizontal lines. It is 6.7K.

Here's the identical image, only flipped on its side so that the lines are vertical. It is 72% bigger at 11.5K.

Try adding noise to the original. You'll be expanding the file size by more than eight times to 56K!

So what does the line test really teach? That artwork that has horizontal changes compresses better than artwork that doesn't. That anything with noise will more than quadruple your image's file size. That large areas of flat color compress well, and that complicated line art or dithering does not.

BIT DEPTH AFFECTS SIZE

Aside from the visual complexity of the image, there are two additional factors that affect file size: **bit depth** and **dithering methods**. With all GIFs, the fewer colors (lower bit depth), the smaller the resulting file. GIFs can be saved at any bit depth from 8 bits down to 1 bit. The bit depth refers to how many colors the image contains. Generally, the lower the bit depth, the smaller the GIF.

Your job when preparing a GIF is to take it down to its lowest bit-depth level and still maintain acceptable image quality. Depending on how important this image is, acceptable quality falls at 4-bit, which offers a 25% file-size reduction over the 8-bit version.

8-bit GIF • 9.72K

7-bit GIF • 8.13K

6-bit GIF • 6.78K

5-bit GIF • 5.34K

4-bit GIF • 4.49K

3-bit GIF • 3.34K

2-bit GIF • 2.27K

1-bit GIF • 1.20K

ANTI-ALIASING VERSUS ALIASING

Anti-aliasing can affect bit depth. If you work with aliased images instead, the file sizes will always be smaller. Aliased artwork doesn't always look good, so this is a decision you'll have to weigh depending on the imagery.

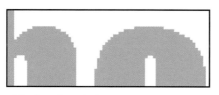

Here's an example of **aliased** text. It resulted in a file that totaled 5.78K when saved as a GIF.

Here's an example of **anti-aliased** text. It resulted in a file that's 7.5K when saved as a GIF. The anti-aliasing caused the file to be 23% larger!

Aliasing doesn't disguise the jaggy nature of pixel-based artwork.

Anti-aliasing creates a blended edge. This blending disguises the square, pixel-based nature of computer-based artwork.

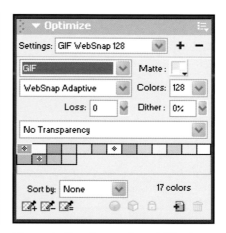

The **aliased** artwork used only 2 colors.

The **anti-aliased** artwork used 17 colors.

ALIASED ARTWORK

Most computer artists have never considered working with aliased artwork. It's assumed that artwork will always look better if it has anti-aliased edges. This is simply not true! Artists have never had to factor file size into their design considerations before. Having something load 23% faster is nothing to balk at. In many cases, aliased artwork looks just as good as anti-aliased artwork, and choosing between the two approaches is something that web designers should consider whenever possible.

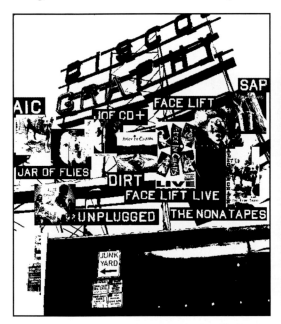

Part of the charm of this former **Alice in Chains** site (http://www.sonymusic.com/artists/AliceInChains/) was the fast download and rough graphics, which were aliased!

This background tile is aliased, and it looks great. To check out this, and other aliased background tiles, visit http://www.donbarnett.com/tilesets/set1.htm.

As well as considering whether to use aliased or anti-aliased graphics, you should also always work with browser-safe colors when creating illustration-based artwork for the Web. Examples of how browser-safe colors improve the quality of illustrations are demonstrated in Chapter 12, *"Color Issues."*

GIFS FOR LINE ART-BASED IMAGERY

GIFs work much better for graphics than photographs. By graphics, I am referring to line art, illustrations, cartoons, or logos. Such graphics typically use areas of solid color, and GIFs handle compression of solid color better than the varied colors found in photographs. Because the GIF file format is lossless, illustrations with limited colors (fewer than 256) won't lose any quality. Because JPEG is a lossy method, it actually introduces image artifacts into solid color.

GIF   **JPEG**

The left image, saved as a GIF file, weighs in at 6.06K. The right image, saved as a JPEG, weighs in at 7.95K. Not only does the JPEG look worse, but it's also bigger. Moral of the story? Use the GIF file format for line art.

GIF COLOR PALETTES

Color mapping refers to the colors that are assigned to a GIF image and can be taken from either the image or a predetermined palette of colors. Fireworks and ImageReady call palettes that are derived from existing colors' adaptive palettes. They enable you to apply external palettes (system or browser-safe are two examples) or make a best-guess palette (adaptive) based on the content of your image. While the number of colors in an image (bit depth) affect the size of the graphic, the palette additionally affects the quality of your image. Some images can endure fewer colors, while others cannot. If you understand how color affects size and quality, you will create better looking and faster loading web pages.

Adaptive palette

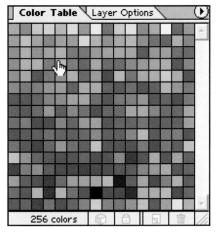

The adaptive palette looks the best because the colors are based on the content of the image. PaintShop Pro calls this type of palette a "nearest color palette." Fireworks and ImageReady call it an "adaptive palette."

Mac system palette

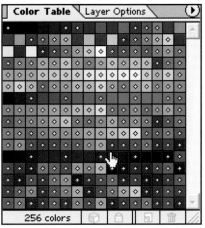

The system palette image looks much worse. Although it has the same number of colors as the adaptive palette, the colors are unrelated to the image and detract from the quality.

216 browser-safe palette

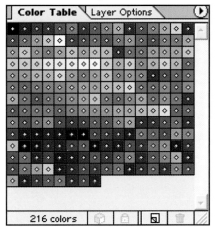

The browser-safe palette looks worst of all. Not only does it use fewer colors, but just like the system palette, the colors are unrelated to the image.

DITHERING & BANDING

When an image with millions of colors is converted to an image with 256 colors or fewer, image quality is lost. Basically, when colors are removed from the image, some sacrifices have to be made. This can take place in two forms: dithering or banding. Here are some definitions to remember:

Dithering is the positioning of different colored pixels within an image that uses a 256-color palette to simulate a color that does not exist in the palette. A dithered image often looks noisy or composed of scattered pixels.

An **adaptive palette** is used to convert the image to 256 colors based on existing colors within the image. Generally, adaptive dithering looks the best of all dithering methods.

Screen dithering is what happens when a 24-bit or 16-bit image is viewed on a computer with a 256-color video card. The image's color is reduced to 256 colors, and the dither looks uniform, as if a pattern was used.

Banding is a process of reducing colors to 256 or fewer without dithering. It produces areas of solid color and generates a posterized effect.

Understanding the terminology of dithering and banding is important because these are often effects that are undesirable. Bringing down the quality of images is necessary at times for speed considerations, but riding the line between low file size and good-enough quality means that you will often encounter unwanted results. These new terms help define the problems you'll encounter when creating web graphics and will be used throughout the rest of the book.

Screen dithering takes the form of a repeated pattern and creates a moiré appearance.

This is an example of image dithering. It rarely looks good, but is sometimes preferable to banding (see next example).

The banding in this image is extremely obvious. It resembles a posterization effect.

Here's a close-up of the banding. Instead of the dots you'll find in dithering methods, the computer takes the image and breaks it into regions of solid color.

ANIMATED GIF ISSUES

Just like other GIF files, the number of colors and amount of noise in the frames affects the overall file size. If you have a 100-frame animation with each frame totaling 5K, your animated GIF will be 500K. It simply multiplies in size according to how many frames you create and the file size of the individual frame of artwork. On the other hand, your end viewer is really waiting for only 5K servings at a time, so it's nothing like the painful waiting that a static 500K GIF would incur!

If you want to learn about controlling palettes for animated GIFs and/or techniques for optimization, turn to Chapter 24, *"Animation & Audio."*

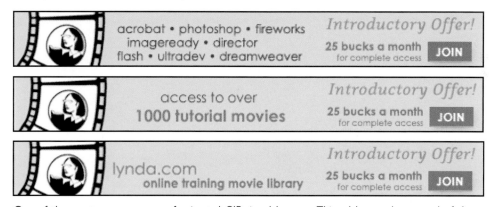

One of the most common uses of animated GIFs is ad banners. This ad banner has a total of three frames and is 12.8K. Each frame displays for 4.5 seconds and then moves on to display the next one.

FOUR RULES OF GIF COMPRESSION

There is never one pat answer for making the smallest possible GIFs. Choices between bit depth and dithering methods should always be based on the image's content. In general, images with subtle gradations will need to be dithered. Images with areas of solid color will look fine without dithering. Here are four rules to making smaller GIFs:

> Try to save the file at the lowest possible bit depth (fewest number of colors), while monitoring quality.

> Try to avoid dithering, if the image can withstand it.

> If possible, create images with lots of areas of solid color, and avoid noise, gradations, and/or photographic content.

> Avoid anti-aliasing, if the image can withstand it.

Hybrid images

As mentioned earlier, sometimes your image doesn't fall into the continuous-tone or the line art category, because it contains both. This is where choosing a compression method gets its trickiest. The only way to deal with an image like this is to try compressing it with GIF and JPEG to see which method produces a smaller file.

Many imaging programs support the ability to create GIF and JPEG files, but when you want to compare compression methods, it's great to have a dedicated image editor that is devoted to web tasks. Two such products are Macromedia Fireworks and Adobe ImageReady. Here is how you would compare compression methods in Fireworks and ImageReady:

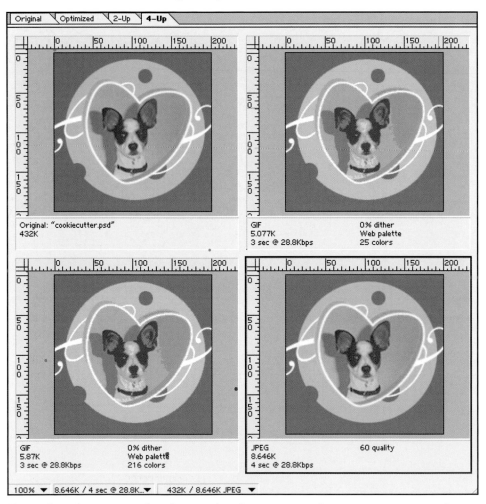

Most web graphics programs have features that allow you to see the same image compressed up to four different ways on the same screen. This is a great way to experiment with different optimization settings until you find the one that looks great and has a reasonable file size.

BATCH PROCESSING

Batch processing allows you to use a single setting over multiple files. Let's say you have a folder or directory filled with images that are in CMYK at 300 dpi. You want to use them for the Web, but you know they're in the wrong color mode and way too big. You could set up a script that would change the color mode to RGB, 72 dpi, and reduce the files to 50% of their original size. If you had 100 images, imagine doing this process 100 times. No way. This task is tailor made for batch processing.

Most popular web graphics programs support batch processing. Because versions of these products change frequently, it's best to learn the specifics of how to do batch processing by looking in the *Help* menu of these programs or by purchasing third-party books, videos, CD-ROMs, or online learning products.

From left to right are the options in Photoshop, ImageReady, and Fireworks.

speedy graphics

SUMMARY

An important part of web design is making sure images are small in file size so that they download more quickly. The tradeoff for speed is quality, so it's your job to evaluate where to draw the line. There are many tools to choose from for this process, but here are the principles to remember regardless of which tool you use:

> JPEG compression is best applied to photographic images or continuous-tone artwork.

> Quality settings in JPEGs affect file size. Find the lowest-quality setting that still looks good, so the file size will be as small as possible.

> Never apply JPEG compression to a file that has already been saved as a JPEG. The lossy compression method will degrade the image.

> GIF compression is best applied to graphics or images that contain line art.

> You can optimize the size of a GIF by reducing the number of colors it contains. Fewer colors translate to smaller file sizes.

> Dithering adds to the file size of a GIF, but should be used anyway for images that contain gradients or soft focus elements. If your image has a lot of solid colors, it will not require dithering and will be smaller if you don't use dithering methods in your file-saving procedure.

> With hybrid images (images that include line art and continuous-tone graphics) it's best to save as both GIF and JPEG and then compare the results.

11

COLOR ISSUES

INTRODUCTION

It would be so nice if, just like when you were a kid, you could pick from any color in your crayon box and start coloring web pages at whim. Things were so simple back then! The computer brings great freedom with far more color choices than even the fanciest crayon box ever offered, but at the same time introduces far more complexity than you might suspect. This chapter addresses the challenging color issues you will face.

Issues such as RGB versus CMYK, gamma, sRGB, hex, web safe, and ICC profiles are intense for anyone new to the Web. Even people who have been doing web design for a while have to check in with the latest specs and standards.

FROM PRINT TO THE WEB

Until the Web, most computer graphic artists created artwork for print, not for screen delivery. If you come to the Web from print, you might be familiar with the color space called CMYK. CMYK is a system developed for computer graphics, so the color on the screen can be accurately translated to printing inks. On the Web, your printing inks are composed of phosphors and pixels. This makes web developers vulnerable to all kinds of variables that do not exist in print, such as monitor calibration and gamma differences, which will be explained in detail soon, between platforms.

In many ways, working with screen-based color can be more fun than working with printed inks. There is no waiting for color proofs or working with CMYK values (which are much less vibrant than RGB), no high-resolution files, and no dot screens to deal with. Although working on the computer for computer delivery is a lot easier in some ways, don't be fooled into thinking that what you see on your screen is what other people will see on their screens. Just like its print-based counterpart, computer screen-based color has its own set of problems and solutions.

RGB VERSUS CMYK

The color of a pixel is made up of three projected colors of light that mix together optically. The projected light colors are red, green, and blue. Mixed together, these three colors create a color space called RGB. You might also hear about a CMYK color space, which is formed from cyan, magenta, yellow, and black. On a computer, the CMYK color space simulates printing inks and is used commonly by print designers. On the other hand, the work of web designers is screen based, so we have typically used RGB color space only.

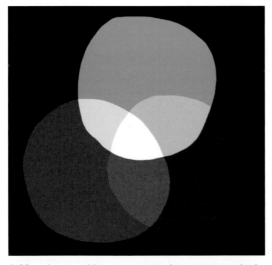

RGB color is additive, meaning that mixing multiple colors creates white. This color space was created for computer graphics to be viewed only onscreen.

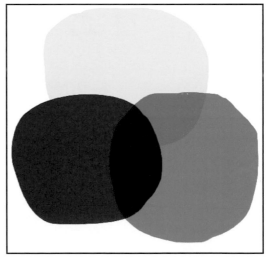

CMYK colors are subtractive meaning that mixing multiple colors creates black. This color space was created for computer graphics to be printed on paper using a four-color process.

CROSS-PLATFORM COLOR PROBLEMS: GAMMA & CALIBRATION

Have you ever looked at one image on two different computers and seen its color or contrast shift? This happens because there is no universal calibration model for screen-based color.

Calibration refers to how your monitor displays images. Have you ever been in a classroom or an office that has multiple computers where the same exact screen looks more blue or green on the different monitors? It's similar to what happens at home on different television monitors—they aren't calibrated to look identical.

There are three elements to calibrating a monitor:

> Phosphor color

> White point

> Gamma

Of the three, phosphor color is quite subtle in its effect (designers with highly tuned color sensibility will be able to see the difference, but typical users will not). The phosphor color is the only variable that is unchangeable, and that is because it has to do with hardware, not software. There is hardware that can measure the color phosphor of a monitor, but the only group of computer users likely to own this kind of hardware are digital photographers who are trying to match their monitors to their color photographic prints. Therefore, while it's possible to calibrate the phosphor color of monitors, it is unlikely that the majority of web visitors will have this capability.

The white point of your monitor can be set with software. Most average people, however, don't adjust their monitor settings. Again, the likelihood of having a standard white point across the majority of computer displays on the World Wide Web is highly unlikely.

Another issue with consistent color display has to do with gamma. Most Macintoshes are set to a gamma reading of 1.80, most SGIs are at 1.70, and most Windows systems are set to 2.2. This is why Macintosh images typically appear much darker on Windows systems. Gamma settings can be controlled through software, though it is doubtful once again that the average computer will bother doing so.

Still, web developers and software vendors have not given up on delivering more consistent color. You're about to read about two such delivery solutions: sRGB and ICC.

---

tip

LEARN MORE ABOUT CALIBRATION

"Why Do Images Appear Darker on Some Displays?"
Article by Robert W. Berger
http://www.bberger.net/gamma.html

ColorVision's Color Calibration Hardware
http://www.colorcal.com/cgi-bin/shop.cgi

RGB & ICC PROFILES

The problem of non-predictable color is currently being addressed by hardware and software manufacturers in a number of ways. There are two camps working on two different strategies. The first is **sRGB**, which proposes a more tightly defined color space that is tailored for onscreen delivery; the second involves **ICC** profiles, which travel along with a file and instruct the device (a printer or monitor) to display colors accurately.

The following sections cover these two approaches and describe how they will affect your web publishing color methodology.

WHAT IS SRGB?

On August 5th, 1996, Microsoft and Hewlett-Packard proposed a new color space standard called sRGB. This standard was accepted by the W3C and is going to find its way into many software and hardware packages in the future.

The proposal describes the problem that CRTs (**c**athode **r**ay **t**ubes, otherwise known as computer monitors) can be set to a nearly infinite combination of calibration settings. The core principle of sRGB is to produce a reliable and repeatable method of describing color that can be understood by CRTs and that would pick one calibration, based on an average monitor, to be used as a default for everyone.

Browsers and imaging software would benefit from a single description of RGB because they wouldn't have to support every possible flavor of RGB (like what we have today with no calibration standard). Because sRGB is based on an average monitor, many users won't have to recalibrate their settings.

For example, the Windows operating system is the most common operating system in the world today. If you use a Windows system, sRGB is the color space you're already using. The users most affected are non-Windows users, such as those creating graphics using Macs and UNIX systems (SUN, SGI, and Linux on Mac.)

Instead of relying on color profiles (which you'll learn more about in the next section) for accurate color management, sRGB represents a more tightly defined color space than RGB. In effect, sRGB defines the Windows operating system color and makes it a standard that other operating systems can emulate.

The idea is that imaging software would allow web designers to create artwork in an sRGB color space, and monitors and browsers would understand how to accurately display the results. Because the specifications of sRGB are more rigorous than RGB, the unpredictable color differences we see today would be eliminated.

One key component of sRGB is the fact that it calls for a standardized gamma setting of 2.20. Currently, RGB can be displayed at a variety of gamma settings. Because the majority of people who view the Web are using Windows, this setting made the most practical sense in that fewer people would see a change in the way their images appear.

The **sRGB proposal** listed a call for action, which will give you a good idea of what has to happen before sRGB is widely supported:

> OSs and all authoring tools must support sRGB calibration.

> Authoring tools should enable the use of the operating system color management tool to transform incoming images into sRGB.

> Authoring tools should enable users to view and edit text in sRGB.

> Web page creators should publish content in sRGB.

> Browser vendors should support style sheet extensions that use the OS color management tools.

> Organizations that create and support file formats should ensure that the file formats are capable of declaring their color space.

> Of course, it will take some time for this to really work well. It will take time, for example, for imaging programs to support sRGB (more on this later) and for hardware devices to recognize it.

The issues at the heart of **implementing sRGB**:

> The original image should be created in sRGB.

> The monitor should recognize sRGB.

> The browser software should display sRGB.

Here are some possible scenarios if the imaging software, browser, or CRT is **not aware of sRGB**:

> Image is not created in sRGB, and system doesn't recognize sRGB. This is the state of things today; colors vary wildly between platforms and monitors.

> Image is created in sRGB, but system does not recognize sRGB. On non-sRGB-compliant monitors, colors will most likely appear darker than they did in the original. (This is similar to creating an image on a Macintosh today and displaying it on a PC.)

> Image is created in sRGB, and system recognizes sRGB. The colors will display accurately on all devices that recognize sRGB.

My opinion about sRGB

When the sRGB standard was first proposed, I was not enthused. As a long-time Mac user, I didn't want my monitor to look like a Windows machine. I had accepted that everyone's color looked different, and didn't want a newer, more restrictive, color standard.

When I say "more restrictive," I mean that the colors on Windows machines are typically darker and have less range between lights and darks. As an imaging professional, I felt the sRGB standard was moving toward a worse standard. I was fine with letting everyone have their different settings—just as long as my better color was left alone!

Today, I've come to see the logic in sRGB, and I have softened my attitude. I still think it's a worse standard. Hey, VHS was worse than Beta, but it didn't stop VHS from becoming a standard, right? I used to own a Beta system, and I was grumpy about that change, too. Today, I have a DVD and don't even care about VHS vs. Beta. Things change—sometimes for the worse, and sometimes for the better. It's life.

Internet Explorer 5.2 for the Mac (which I currently use) displays all web pages in sRGB, just like its counterpart on Windows. Photoshop 6.0 defaults to an sRGB preview space, so my images look the same on Photoshop as they do on Internet Explorer. On the other hand, many Macintosh applications don't use sRGB yet (ie; Dreamweaver, Flash, Fireworks, GoLive, and ImageReady), so it's not perfect. I'd like to be able to create in any Macintosh application and have the color look identical regardless of where I viewed the artwork. Too bad for me. I suppose if all the software vendors that I use (Macromedia, Adobe, and Microsoft) implemented sRGB, however, I would be happier than if some of them did and some didn't.

The implementation of sRGB is in progress right now—it's not perfect and might never be perfect. There's no fighting it, so what you can't fight is better to understand. Because the sRGB standard is dependent on participation of software and hardware manufacturers, it will probably be many years before this solution is truly a solution.

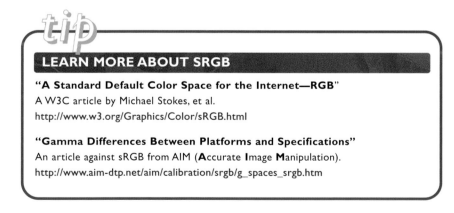

LEARN MORE ABOUT SRGB

"A Standard Default Color Space for the Internet—RGB"
A W3C article by Michael Stokes, et al.
http://www.w3.org/Graphics/Color/sRGB.html

"Gamma Differences Between Platforms and Specifications"
An article against sRGB from AIM (**A**ccurate **I**mage **M**anipulation).
http://www.aim-dtp.net/aim/calibration/srgb/g_spaces_srgb.htm

WHAT IS AN ICC COLOR PROFILE?

The ICC (**I**nternational **C**olor **C**onsortium) was founded by Adobe, Agfa, Apple, Kodak, Microsoft, SGI, and Sun, and has since grown to include more than 60 different software and hardware vendors. The purpose of the organization is to create and adhere to a device- and platform-independent color management system. If this sounds similar to the goals of sRGB, it is. The means of achieving the goal are different, however.

sRGB is a color space that exists exclusively for CRT and onscreen display. ICC device profiles are targeted more toward the printing industry but can be used by monitor devices as well. Ideally, you would create an image on your machine that would always look the same whether it was displayed on a computer monitor or printed on paper.

ICC color profiles are embedded into a file format as additional data that specifies the color characteristics of an image. For example, an RGB image profile specifies the gamma (lights and darks), white point (a "cool" or "warm" white), and phosphor colors (because monitors don't have perfectly pure lines of red, green, and blue). These measurements and settings remain with the file, and any device the image is ultimately viewed from can accurately interpret the data.

One of the problems with ICC CMS (**C**olor **M**anagement **S**ystems) is that it increases the file size of a document. This is not practical for web delivery because the color profile alone could take up to an unbelievable 750k for a full-blown profile, which is many times larger than an optimized web image.

```
None
Ask When Opening
✓ Monitor RGB

sRGB
Apple RGB
CIE RGB
ColorMatch RGB
NTSC (1953)
PAL/SECAM
SMPTE-240M
SMPTE-C
Wide Gamut RGB

Adobe Illustrator Monitor Default
Apple 12" RGB Standard
Apple 13" RGB Standard
Apple 16" RGB Page-White
Apple 16" RGB Standard
Apple 21" RGB Page-White
Apple 21" RGB Standard
Apple Multiple Scan 14
Apple Multiple Scan 15
Apple Multiple Scan 17 - 9300
Apple Multiple Scan 17 - D50
Apple Multiple Scan 17 - D65
Apple Multiple Scan 1705
Apple Multiple Scan 20 - 9300
Apple Multiple Scan 20 - D50
Apple Multiple Scan 20 - D65
Apple Performa Display
Apple Performa Plus Display
AppleVision - 9300
Color SW 1500 Pattern
Color SW 1500 Scatter
Color SW 2500 Pattern
Color SW 2500 Pattern Best 1
Color SW 2500 Pattern Best 2
Color SW 2500 Scatter
Color SW 2500 Scatter Best 1
Color SW 2500 Scatter Best 2
Color SW Automatic
ColorSync Display - 9300
```

The list of color profiles that ships with Photoshop is so long it scrolls right off the screen. The idea is, you should select the output device as you work on your image, so when you save it the correct color profile will be tied to that image.

MY OPINION ABOUT ICC

The good news is that the ICC color profiling method doesn't translate your original image into another color space; it simply adds a description of the color assumptions to the file. It is then up to other devices and software applications to read and compensate for the description.

However, browsers, for example, do not read color profiles. In addition, the Achilles heel of this approach is that color profiles significantly increase the file size—a kiss of death for web graphics.

I think, at best, ICC is good for print designers who want to tightly control how their images look on their screen and how those same images print to printers. For web designers, ICC has little relevance or use.

tip

LEARN MORE ABOUT ICC

ICC Color Profile Specification (in PDF)
http://www.color.org/ICC-1_1998-09.PDF

Color Management for the WWW
http://www.color.org/wpaper2.html

Adobe Glossary of Color Terms
http://www.adobe.com:80/support/techdocs/c9fe.htm

SRGB IN PHOTOSHOP

To my knowledge, Photoshop was one of the first imaging programs to use sRGB. In fact, it ships with sRGB as the default color space. Note: You may choose to turn off sRGB in Photoshop if you would prefer to. We have a movie on our web site that describes how to do this: http://www.lynda.com/tips/ps_profiles.html.

Here is a side-by-side comparison of the exact same image in Adobe Photoshop (left) and Adobe ImageReady (right). Photoshop ships with sRGB as the default color space, whereas ImageReady and other web applications use the old undefined flavor of RGB.

ACCURATE WEB SITE COLOR!

Certain web sites require accurate color, even at the expense of requesting visitors to load a plug-in. Let's say you have a clothing catalog web site or a car site where someone is choosing a color. It is mighty important in those types of situations that you can display dead-on correct color.

Pantone has a product called "Spyder" that ensures screen-to-screen and screen-to-print color accuracy. It requires a Pantone Color Reference card and the use of an ICC profile that describes the characteristics of your monitor. The profile is then used to ensure screen-to-screen and screen-to-printer color accuracy. To learn more about this tool, visit http://www.pantone.com/products/products.asp?idArea=2&bShowProducts=1.

Apple Computer is licensing a technology called "ColorSync," and many vendors such as Adobe and Kodak are integrating it into their software. ColorSync is a color calibration system that involves downloading a plug-in from Apple. For more information on this tool, visit http://www.apple.com/colorsync/ and http://www.adobe.com/products/golive/.

SUMMARY

sRGB, color profiles, and gamma settings make web life interesting to say the least. Ultimately, the proponents of ICC and sRGB will create standardized color calibration, but for the moment, these new standards are partially supported at best.

> sRGB is a proposed color space that will be adopted by image editors and CRT manufacturers in the future. This will benefit the industry when the support is widespread. So far, at the time this book was published, it is supported by current versions of Photoshop and Internet Explorer.

> ICC profiles ensure that images are displayed correctly on different devices. Unfortunately, the profiles are too large to be web savvy, so they aren't useful to web developers yet.

> On sites that require accurate color, you might need to turn to plug-in solutions, such as Pantone's Spyder. But be aware that these are based on the assumption that your site's visitors have accurately calibrated their screens.

browser–Safe Color

Introduction

You might have heard of the browser-safe palette, Netscape palette, 216 palette, web palette, and/or 6×6×6 color cube. All these terms refer to the same set of colors, which this chapter will describe in detail.

A lot of people credit me with the browser-safe palette, but it's a misplaced honor (if you can call it that!). I do have the distinction of being the first author to identify and publish the colors, but I can't take credit for creating them.

The browser-safe palette was developed by browser programmers, I assure you. The colors within the palette weren't carefully chosen by me, or any other designer. That's because, for a designer, the browser-safe color palette leaves a lot to be desired. Mostly, it contains far less light and dark colors than I wish it did, and it's heavy on highly saturated colors and low on muted, tinted, and toned colors.

INTRODUCTION CONTINUED

The only reason to use the browser-safe palette is if you have a concern that your web design work will be viewed from a 256-color (8-bit) computer system. When I published the browser-safe color chart in my first book, *Designing Web Graphics*, waaay back in 1996, the "majority" of computer users had 8-bit video cards. Today, the minority have them, so the justification for using the browser-safe palette has diminished greatly if you are developing your site for users who have current computer systems.

There may be a resurgence, however, in the need for the browser-safe palette when designing for alternative online publishing devices, such as cell phones and PDAs. Those systems are still in 1-bit (black-and-white) or 8-bit color. Right now, very few people are designing their web sites to work on those systems, so the need for the browser-safe color palette is definitely downgraded to a mere shadow of its former glory.

note

SO THEN, IS THE BROWSER-SAFE PALETTE DEAD?

Though this might seem blasphemous to older readers of this book, I believe it's safe to design without the palette. I believe this because so few computer users view the Web in 256 colors anymore.

Keep in mind, however, that many companies that hire designers and developers still feel it's a badge of web design honor to work with these colors, so you might want to know how to use them if you have to. At this point, the palette is built into Photoshop, PaintShop Pro, Illustrator, FreeHand, Fireworks, Dreamweaver, GoLive, and just about any professional web design/development tool, so using it is fairly easy.

Conversely, there's no harm in using the browser-safe palette either. It simply limits your choices to 216 colors. Most people do not have a lot of color picking confidence, and working with

limited color choices is easier. There's no right or wrong when it comes to which colors you pick, but it is more important to know how to combine colors in pleasing and effective ways.

Who would have thought that computers would mature as quickly as they have? In those early days of the Web, only the professional designer had a system that supported thousands or millions of colors. Today, any consumer with a Gateway or iMac is going to see all the colors you can throw their way. It's progress folks!

Those of us who had to learn to design for the Web in the old days developed a skill that is fast becoming obsolete. So much for moving forward—it's great liberation in my opinion!

WHAT IS THE BROWSER-SAFE PALETTE?

Let's say you've created images with millions of colors (JPEGs) or GIF images with custom colors of your choosing. What happens in a browser encounter on a system that is limited to 256 colors (8-bit)? It converts all your colors to its own fixed palette. On an 8-bit color system, even though your end user wants to see all the colors on your web page, they can't. It's both a hardware limitation and a browser software limitation.

The hardware limitation is based on your end user's video card. An 8-bit video card cannot display any more than 256 colors. The question is, which 256 colors will the video card display when it encounters an image with thousands or millions of colors? That's where the software comes in. The browser software makes a decision about which colors to display. Instead of pooling colors from the web image, it chooses colors from its own fixed palette. There is no way it can display a color outside of this fixed palette. Honest.

Fortunately, the two most popular browsers (Netscape and Internet Explorer) share the same fixed palette. It contains a core of 216 colors and allows 40 additional colors, which differ from platform to platform. Most prefer to work with these 216 common denominator colors when necessary. I refer to this palette as the browser-safe palette throughout this book. This means that if you stick to the 216 common colors, they will be honored universally across all browsers, operating systems, and computer platforms.

Notice how the browser-safe colors in the example on the right have no sense of organization? They are organized by math, not beauty.

On the next four pages, you will find the same 216 colors, organized in a more useful way: by color (hue) and value (lights to medium tones to darks).

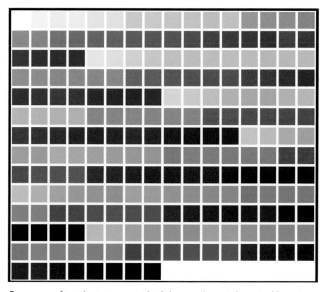

Browser-safe colors were picked by math, not beauty. Here is a version of the browser-safe palette, straight out of the computer.

The browser-safe palette is composed of mathematical color combinations, and if you are math-phobic like many people, you might think you have to memorize 216 different numeric combinations to understand it. You don't. There are really only six numbers to remember. In fact, this color system is sometimes referred to as the 6×6×6 color cube because it contains six possible values of red, green, and blue (RGB).

R	G	B
0	0	0
51	0	0
102	0	0
153	0	0
204	0	0
255	0	0

The six RGB values are 0, 51, 102, 153, 204, and 255, from dark to light; they are separated by 51 numbers.

BROWSER-SAFE COLOR CHARTS ORGANIZED by VALUE

FFFFFF R=255 G=255 B=255	FFFFCC R=255 G=255 B=204	FFFF99 R=255 G=255 B=153	CCFFFF R=204 G=255 B=255	FFFF66 R=255 G=255 B=102	CCFFCC R=204 G=255 B=204	FFFF33 R=255 G=255 B=051	CCFF99 R=204 G=255 B=153	
99FF99 R=153 G=255 B=153	CCFF00 R=204 G=255 B=000	CCCCFF R=204 G=204 B=255	66FFFF R=102 G=255 B=255	FFCC66 R=255 G=204 B=102	99FF66 R=153 G=255 B=102	CCCCCC R=204 G=204 B=204	66FFCC R=102 G=255 B=204	
33FFFF R=051 G=255 B=255	CCCC66 R=204 G=204 B=102	66FF66 R=102 G=255 B=102	FF99CC R=255 G=153 B=204	99CCCC R=153 G=204 D=204	33FFCC R=051 G=255 B=204	CCCC33 R=204 G=204 B=051	66FF33 R=102 G=255 B=051	
FF9966 R=255 G=153 B=102	99CC66 R=153 G=204 B=102	33FF66 R=051 G=255 B=102	CC99CC R=204 G=153 B=204	66CCCC R=102 G=204 B=204	00FFCC R=000 G=255 B=204	FF9933 R=255 G=153 B=051	99CC33 R=153 G=204 B=051	
9999FF R=153 G=153 B=255	33CCFF R=051 G=204 B=255	CC9966 R=204 G=153 B=102	66CC66 R=102 G=204 B=102	00FF66 R=000 G=255 B=102	FF66CC R=255 G=102 B=204	9999CC R=153 G=153 B=204	33CCCC R=051 G=204 B=204	
00FF00 R=000 G=255 B=000	CC66FF R=204 G=102 B=255	6699FF R=102 G=153 B=255	00CCFF R=000 G=204 B=255	FF6666 R=255 G=102 B=102	999966 R=153 G=153 B=102	33CC66 R=051 G=204 B=102	CC66CC R=204 G=102 B=204	
FF6600 R=255 G=102 B=000	999900 R=153 G=153 B=000	33CC00 R=051 G=204 B=000	FF33FF R=255 G=051 B=255	9966FF R=153 G=102 B=255	3399FF R=051 G=153 B=255	CC6666 R=204 G=102 B=102	669966 R=102 G=153 B=102	
996699 R=153 G=102 B=153	339999 R=051 G=153 B=153	CC6600 R=204 G=102 B=000	669900 R=102 G=153 B=000	00CC00 R=000 G=204 B=000	CC33FF R=204 G=051 B=255	6666FF R=102 G=102 B=255	0099FF R=000 G=153 B=255	
339933 R=051 G=153 B=051	CC3399 R=204 G=051 B=153	666699 R=102 G=102 B=153	009999 R=000 G=153 B=153	FF3300 R=255 G=051 B=000	996600 R=153 G=102 B=000	339900 R=051 G=153 B=000	FF00FF R=255 G=000 B=255	
CC3333 R=204 G=051 B=051	666633 R=102 G=102 B=051	009933 R=000 G=153 B=051	FF0099 R=255 G=000 B=153	993399 R=153 G=051 B=153	336699 R=051 G=102 B=153	CC3300 R=204 G=051 B=000	666600 R=102 G=102 B=000	
6633CC R=102 G=051 B=204	0066CC R=000 G=102 B=204	FF0033 R=255 G=000 B=051	993333 R=153 G=051 B=051	336633 R=051 G=102 B=051	CC0099 R=204 G=000 B=153	663399 R=102 G=051 B=153	006699 R=000 G=102 B=153	
9900CC R=153 G=000 B=204	3333CC R=051 G=051 B=204	CC0033 R=204 G=000 B=051	663333 R=102 G=051 B=051	006633 R=000 G=102 B=051	990099 R=153 G=000 B=153	333399 R=051 G=051 B=153	CC0000 R=204 G=000 B=000	
990033 R=153 G=000 B=051	333333 R=051 G=051 B=051	660099 R=102 G=000 B=153	003399 R=000 G=051 B=153	990000 R=153 G=000 B=000	333300 R=051 G=051 B=000	3300FF R=051 G=000 B=255	660066 R=102 G=000 B=102	
330066 R=051 G=000 B=102	0000CC R=000 G=000 B=204	330033 R=051 G=000 B=051	000099 R=000 G=000 B=153	330000 R=051 G=000 B=000	000066 R=000 G=000 B=102	000033 R=000 G=000 B=051	000000 R=000 G=000 B=000	

FFFF00 R=255 G=255 B=000	**FFCCFF** R=255 G=204 B=255
99FFFF R=153 G=255 B=255	**CCFF00** R=204 G=255 B=102
FFCCCC R=255 G=204 B=204	**99FFCC** R=153 G=255 B=204
CCFF33 R=204 G=255 B=051	**FFCC99** R=255 G=204 R=153

FFCC33 R=255 G=204 B=051	**99FF33** R=153 G=255 B=051
CCCC99 R=204 G=204 B=153	**66FF99** R=102 G=255 B=153
FFCC00 R=255 G=204 B=000	**99FF00** R=153 G=255 B=000
FF99FF R=255 G=153 B=255	**99CCFF** R=153 G=204 B=255

FF9999 R=255 G=153 B=153	**99CC99** R=153 G=204 B=153
33FF99 R=051 G=255 B=153	**CCCC00** R=204 G=204 B=000
66FF00 R=102 G=255 B=000	**CC99FF** R=204 G=153 B=255
66CCFF R=102 G=204 B=255	**00FFFF** R=000 G=255 B=255

33FF33 R=051 G=255 B=051	**CC9999** R=204 G=153 B=153
66CC99 R=102 G=204 B=153	**00FF99** R=000 G=255 B=153
FF9900 R=255 G=153 B=000	**99CC00** R=153 G=204 B=000
33FF00 R=051 G=255 B=000	**FF66FF** R=255 G=102 B=255

CC9933 R=204 G=153 B=051	**66CC33** R=102 G=204 B=051
00FF33 R=000 G=255 B=051	**FF6699** R=255 G=102 B=153
999999 R=153 G=153 B=153	**33CC99** R=051 G=204 B=153
CC9900 R=204 G=153 B=000	**66CC00** R=102 G=204 B=000

6699CC R=102 G=153 B=204	**00CCCC** R=000 G=204 B=204
FF6633 R=255 G=102 B=051	**999933** R=153 G=153 B=051
33CC33 R=051 G=204 B=051	**CC6699** R=204 G=102 B=153
669999 R=102 G=153 B=153	**00CC99** R=000 G=204 B=153

00CC66 R=000 G=204 B=102	**FF33CC** R=255 G=051 B=204
9966CC R=153 G=102 B=204	**3399CC** R=051 G=153 B=204
CC6633 R=204 G=102 B=051	**669933** R=102 G=153 B=051
00CC33 R=000 G=204 B=051	**FF3399** R=255 G=051 B=153

FF3366 R=255 G=051 B=102	**996666** R=153 G=102 B=102
339966 R=051 G=153 B=102	**CC33CC** R=204 G=051 B=204
6666CC R=102 G=102 B=204	**0099CC** R=000 G=153 B=204
FF3333 R=255 G=051 B=051	**996633** R=153 G=102 B=051

9933FF R=153 G=051 B=255	**3366FF** R=051 G=102 B=255
CC3366 R=204 G=051 B=102	**666666** R=102 G=102 B=102
009966 R=000 G=153 B=102	**FF00CC** R=255 G=000 B=204
9933CC R=153 G=051 B=204	**3366CC** R=051 G=102 B=204

009900 R=000 G=153 B=000	**CC00FF** R=204 G=000 B=255
6633FF R=102 G=051 B=255	**0066FF** R=000 G=102 B=255
FF0066 R=255 G=000 B=102	**993366** R=153 G=051 B=102
336666 R=051 G=102 B=102	**CC00CC** R=204 G=000 B=204

FF0000 R=255 G=000 B=000	**993300** R=153 G=051 B=000
336600 R=051 G=102 B=000	**9900FF** R=153 G=000 B=255
3333FF R=051 G=051 B=255	**CC0066** R=204 G=000 B=102
663366 R=102 G=051 B=102	**006666** R=000 G=102 B=102

663300 R=102 G=051 B=000	**006600** R=000 G=102 B=000
6600FF R=102 G=000 B=255	**0033FF** R=000 G=051 B=255
990066 R=153 G=000 B=102	**333366** R=051 G=051 B=102
6600CC R=102 G=000 B=204	**0033CC** R=000 G=051 B=204

003366 R=000 G=051 B=102	**3300CC** R=051 G=000 B=204
660033 R=102 G=000 B=051	**003333** R=000 G=051 B=051
330099 R=051 G=000 B=153	**660000** R=102 G=000 B=000
003300 R=000 G=051 B=000	**0000FF** R=000 G=000 B=255

BROWSER-SQFE COLOR CHQRTS ORQQNIZED by HUE

Hex	R	G	B

330000 R=051 G=000 B=000 | 660000 R=102 G=000 B=000 | 990000 R=153 G=000 B=000 | CC0000 R=204 G=000 B=000 | FF0000 R=255 G=000 B=000 | 663333 R=102 G=051 B=051 | 993333 R=153 G=051 B=051 | CC3333 R=204 G=051 B=051

CC0033 R=204 G=000 B=051 | FF3366 R=255 G=051 B=102 | 990033 R=153 G=000 B=051 | CC3366 R=204 G=051 B=102 | FF6699 R=255 G=102 B=153 | FF0066 R=255 G=000 B=102 | 660033 R=102 G=000 B=051 | CC0066 R=204 G=000 B=102

CC0099 R=204 G=000 B=153 | FF33CC R=255 G=51 B=204 | FF00CC R=255 G=000 B=204 | 330033 R=051 G=000 B=051 | 660066 R=102 G=000 B=102 | 990099 R=153 G=000 B=153 | CC00CC R=204 G=000 B=204 | FF00FF R=255 G=000 B=255

FF99FF R=255 G=153 B=255 | FFCCFF R=255 G=204 B=255 | CC00FF R=204 G=000 B=255 | 9900CC R=153 G=000 B=204 | CC33FF R=204 G=051 B=255 | 660099 R=102 G=000 B=153 | 9933CC R=153 G=051 B=204 | CC66FF R=204 G=102 B=255

330099 R=051 G=000 B=153 | 6633CC R=102 G=051 B=204 | 9966FF R=153 G=102 B=255 | 3300CC R=051 G=000 B=204 | 6633FF R=102 G=051 B=255 | 3300FF R=051 G=000 B=255 | 000000 R=000 G=000 B=000 | 000033 R=000 G=000 B=051

666699 R=102 G=102 B=153 | 6666CC R=102 G=102 B=204 | 6666FF R=102 G=102 B=255 | 9999CC R=153 G=153 B=204 | 9999FF R=153 G=153 B=255 | CCCCFF R=204 G=204 B=255 | 0033FF R=000 G=051 B=255 | 0033CC R=000 G=051 B=204

3399FF R=051 G=153 B=255 | 6699CC R=102 G=153 B=204 | 99CCFF R=153 G=204 B=255 | 0099FF R=000 G=153 B=255 | 006699 R=000 G=102 B=153 | 3399CC R=051 G=153 B=204 | 66CCFF R=102 G=204 B=255 | 0099CC R=000 G=153 B=204

00CCCC R=000 G=204 B=204 | 33CCCC R=051 G=204 B=204 | 66CCCC R=102 G=204 B=204 | 99CCCC R=153 G=204 B=204 | 00FFFF R=000 G=255 B=255 | 33FFFF R=051 G=255 B=255 | 66FFFF R=102 G=255 B=255 | 99FFFF R=153 G=255 B=255

006633 R=000 G=102 B=051 | 339966 R=051 G=153 B=102 | 00CC66 R=000 G=204 B=102 | 66CC99 R=102 G=204 B=153 | 33FF99 R=051 G=255 B=153 | 99FFCC R=153 G=255 B=204 | 00FF66 R=000 G=255 B=102 | 009933 R=000 G=153 B=051

009900 R=000 G=153 B=000 | 339933 R=051 G=153 B=051 | 669966 R=102 G=153 B=102 | 00CC00 R=000 G=204 B=000 | 33CC33 R=051 G=204 B=051 | 66CC66 R=102 G=204 B=102 | 99CC99 R=153 G=204 B=153 | 00FF00 R=000 G=255 B=000

66CC33 R=102 G=204 B=051 | 99FF66 R=153 G=255 B=102 | 66FF00 R=102 G=255 B=000 | 336600 R=051 G=102 B=000 | 669933 R=102 G=153 B=051 | 66CC00 R=102 G=204 B=000 | 99CC66 R=153 G=204 B=102 | 99FF33 R=153 G=255 B=051

333300 R=051 G=051 B=000 | 666600 R=102 G=102 B=000 | 666633 R=102 G=102 B=051 | 999900 R=153 G=153 B=000 | 999933 R=153 G=153 B=051 | 999966 R=153 G=153 B=102 | CCCC00 R=204 G=204 B=000 | CCCC33 R=204 G=204 B=051

CC9900 R=204 G=153 B=000 | FFCC33 R=255 G=204 B=051 | 996600 R=153 G=102 B=000 | CC9933 R=204 G=153 B=051 | FFCC66 R=255 G=204 B=102 | FF9900 R=255 G=153 B=000 | 663300 R=102 G=051 B=000 | 996633 R=153 G=102 B=051

CC3300 R=204 G=051 B=000 | FF6633 R=255 G=102 B=051 | FF3300 R=255 G=051 B=000 | 333333 R=051 G=051 B=051 | 666666 R=102 G=102 B=102 | 999999 R=153 G=153 B=153 | CCCCCC R=204 G=204 B=204 | FFFFFF R=255 G=255 B=255

FF3333 R=255 G=051 B=051	**996666** R=153 G=102 B=102	**CC6666** R=204 G=102 B=102	**FF6666** R=255 G=102 B=102	**CC9999** R=204 G=153 B=153	**FF9999** R=255 G=153 B=153	**FFCCCC** R=255 G=204 B=204	**FF0033** R=255 G=000 B=051
993366 R=153 G=051 B=102	**FF3399** R=255 G=051 B=153	**CC6699** R=204 G=102 B=153	**FF99CC** R=255 G=153 B=204	**FF0099** R=255 G=000 B=153	**990066** R=153 G=000 B=102	**CC3399** R=204 G=051 B=153	**FF66CC** R=255 G=102 B=204
663366 R=102 G=051 B=102	**993399** R=153 G=051 B=153	**CC33CC** R=204 G=051 B=204	**FF33FF** R=255 G=051 B=255	**996699** R=153 G=102 B=153	**CC66CC** R=204 G=102 B=204	**FF66FF** R=255 G=102 B=255	**CC99CC** R=204 G=153 B=204
9900FF R=153 G=000 B=255	**330066** R=051 G=000 B=102	**6600CC** R=102 G=000 B=204	**663399** R=102 G=051 B=153	**9933FF** R=153 G=051 B=255	**9966CC** R=153 G=102 B=204	**CC99FF** R=204 G=153 B=255	**6600FF** R=102 G=000 B=255
000066 R=000 G=000 B=102	**000099** R=000 G=000 B=153	**0000CC** R=000 G=000 B=204	**0000FF** R=000 G=000 B=255	**333366** R=051 G=051 B=102	**333399** R=051 G=051 B=153	**3333CC** R=051 G=051 B=204	**3333FF** R=051 G=051 B=255
3366FF R=051 G=102 B=255	**003399** R=000 G=051 B=153	**3366CC** R=051 G=102 B=204	**6699FF** R=102 G=153 B=255	**0066FF** R=000 G=102 B=255	**003366** R=000 G=051 B=102	**0066CC** R=000 G=102 B=204	**336699** R=051 G=102 B=153
33CCFF R=051 G=204 B=255	**00CCFF** R=000 G=204 B=255	**003333** R=000 G=051 B=051	**006666** R=000 G=102 B=102	**336666** R=051 G=102 B=102	**009999** R=000 G=153 B=153	**339999** R=051 G=153 B=153	**669999** R=102 G=153 B=153
CCFFFF R=204 G=255 B=255	**00FFCC** R=000 G=255 B=204	**00CC99** R=000 G=204 B=153	**33FFCC** R=051 G=255 B=204	**009966** R=000 G=153 B=102	**33CC99** R=051 G=204 B=153	**66FFCC** R=102 G=255 B=204	**00FF99** R=000 G=255 B=153
33CC66 R=051 G=204 B=102	**66FF99** R=102 G=255 B=153	**00CC33** R=000 G=204 B=051	**33FF66** R=051 G=255 B=102	**00FF33** R=000 G=255 B=051	**003300** R=000 G=051 B=000	**006600** R=000 G=102 B=000	**336633** R=051 G=102 B=051
33FF33 R=051 G=255 B=051	**66FF66** R=102 G=255 B=102	**99FF99** R=153 G=255 B=153	**CCFFCC** R=204 G=255 B=204	**33FF00** R=051 G=255 B=000	**33CC00** R=051 G=204 B=000	**66FF33** R=102 G=255 B=051	**339900** R=051 G=153 B=000
CCFF99 R=204 G=255 B=153	**99FF00** R=153 G=255 B=000	**669900** R=102 G=153 B=000	**99CC33** R=153 G=204 B=051	**CCFF66** R=204 G=255 B=102	**99CC00** R=153 G=204 B=000	**CCFF33** R=204 G=255 B=051	**CCFF00** R=204 G=255 B=000
CCCC66 R=204 G=204 B=102	**CCCC99** R=204 G=204 B=153	**FFFF00** R=255 G=255 B=000	**FFFF33** R=255 G=255 B=051	**FFFF66** R=255 G=255 B=102	**FFFF99** R=255 G=255 B=153	**FFFFCC** R=255 G=255 B=204	**FFCC00** R=255 G=204 B=000
CC6600 R=204 G=102 B=000	**CC9966** R=204 G=153 B=102	**FF9933** R=255 G=153 B=051	**FFCC99** R=255 G=204 B=153	**FF6600** R=255 G=102 B=000	**993300** R=153 G=051 B=000	**CC6633** R=204 G=102 B=051	**FF9966** R=255 G=153 B=102

WHY DOES THE BROWSER-SAFE PALETTE EXIST?

Why was the browser-safe palette developed by browser software manufacturers? First of all, because it can be generated by a mathematical equation. The palette is built by math, and math alone! As well, the easiest solution to the 8-bit hardware limitation is for the browser software to impose a fixed palette.

Those of you who have authored multimedia using Macromedia Director have been able to assign custom palettes to specific pieces of artwork using palette channels. HTML has no means with which to do this. There is no "change palette" HTML tag, and color lookup tables (CLUTs) are not of a MIME type recognized by browsers. Because of this, the browser has to deal with the issue instead of depending on your input.

If a browser created 256 color palettes based on the colors within images, it would quickly run out of colors anyway. Then it would have to map all the rest of the images to whatever palette it established based on the first few images. It's actually better that the browsers use a fixed palette, because at least you can identify it and work within its constraints.

HOW & WHEN TO USE THE BROWSER-SAFE COLOR PALETTE

The first decision related to using or not using browser-safe color is whether your audience will benefit from its use or not. While the majority of web users today have better systems than before, there is no harm in using the palette. The only harm is that it limits your color choices, which might not be something you want to do. If you do decide to use the palette, you might think that I advocate using the browser-safe palette at all times. I do not, and I am alarmed when I see the palette misused.

When should you use browser-safe colors? Let's take a look at the following chart.

Scenario	Browser-Safe Color
Hexadecimal Color	Yes.
Flat Color	Yes, (areas of solid color).
Continuous-Tone Images	No, never.
Hybrid Images	Yes, (areas of solid color).

To explain when to use this palette, I'll define the four possible scenarios that relate to browser-safe colors:

> **Hexadecimal-Based Color**
  Within the HTML code, when you specify colors for your background, text, links, visited links, or active links, you must use hexadecimal code.

> **Flat Color**
  Graphics that contain solid colors or lines.

> **Continuous-Tone Art**
  Graphics or photographs that contain blends, gradients, tones, and soft focus.

> **Hybrid Art**
  Art that combines continuous tone and flat color.

The following sections go into greater depth about when and how to use the browser-safe colors.

note

HEXADECIMAL CONVERSION

Most current web software applications convert RGB colors to hexadecimal notation for you automatically. In previous editions of this book, I recommended that you convert the numbers yourself. That is no longer necessary.

On an 8-bit system, the reason to use browser-safe hexadecimal colors is to avoid color shifting of your link colors. On a system that supports thousands or millions of colors, there is no reason to use browser-safe colors exclusively.

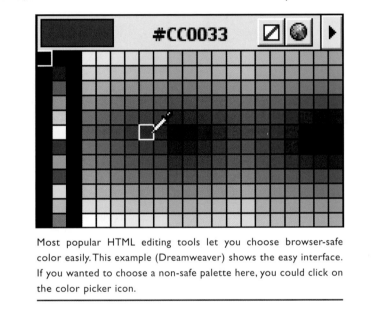

Most popular HTML editing tools let you choose browser-safe color easily. This example (Dreamweaver) shows the easy interface. If you wanted to choose a non-safe palette here, you could click on the color picker icon.

FLAT COLOR ARTWORK

Again, only abide by these rules if you are concerned that your audience will view your site with a system that is limited to 256 colors. In those cases, flat color artwork (such as some logos, cartoons, or drawings) will have problems. Instead of shifting the color, which is what happens with hexadecimal-based color, the browser-safe palette will cause the artwork to appear dithered. Here are some examples of the unwanted effects of dithering.

On a millions-of-color display, you might not notice any differences between these two illustrations. The one on the left was created using non-safe colors and the one on the right was created using browser-safe colors.

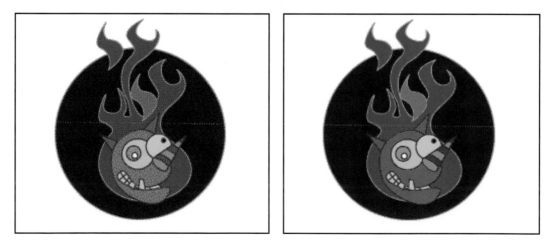

On an 8-bit display, look at what happens to the left version. It is filled with unwanted dots caused by dithering. Why? The colors in the right logo are browser safe, and the colors in the left are not.

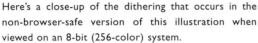

Here's a close-up of the dithering that occurs in the non-browser-safe version of this illustration when viewed on an 8-bit (256-color) system.

The close-up of the version created with browser-safe colors will not dither, regardless of which bit depth the end-viewer's system supports. Hint: Always create this type of artwork using browser-safe colors.

In popular imaging applications, it's just a matter of picking a color, and the program will convert the RGB values to hexadecimal code for you. In Photoshop, you can choose any color this way.

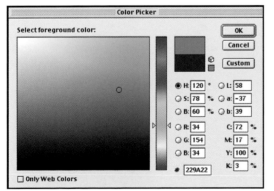

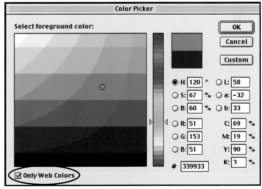

This image shows a non-safe green color, its RGB value, and its hexadecimal translation.

To change the color to a web-safe color, you simply check the *Only Web Colors* palette. Web color palettes are found in most professional web authoring tools, including Photoshop, ImageReady, Fireworks, Dreamweaver, Flash, and GoLive.

PHOTOGRAPH-BASED ARTWORK

Continuous-tone artwork (photographs) is the one type of image that really does not benefit from using browser-safe colors. The reason is that the browsers convert photographs, but do a great job of it, unlike the terrible job they do with hexadecimal-based color and illustration-based artwork.

It is not necessary to convert photographic-based images to the browser-safe palette or even an 8-bit palette. The browser does its dithering dirty work, regardless of how you prepare the image. It's best to leave the image in an adaptive palette or 24-bit file format because photographs look better in 24-bit browser environments. JPEGs will always produce the smallest file size for photographs, and JPEG is a 24-bit file format, unlike GIF, which cannot save images at higher bit-depths than 8-bit (256 colors). More information on how to save JPEG and GIF images with adaptive and web-safe palettes follows later.

JPEG • 24-bit	**Adaptive GIF • 24-bit**	**Web-safe GIF • 24-bit**

JPEG • 8-bit	**Adaptive GIF • 8-bit**	**Web-safe GIF • 8-bit**

Notice how every image in the 24-bit column looks better than the 8-bit column? People with better video cards see the Web in better color. Look carefully however, and notice that all the 8-bit images look the same, while the JPEG and adaptive GIF look much better. This shows that the browsers convert 8-bit images no better than you could convert them yourself. So why not let your more fortunate audience see your images with better fidelity? The moral of the story—don't use browser-safe colors on photographs!

JPEG ARTWORK CANNOT RETAIN BROWSER-SAFE COLORS

Unfortunately, files that are converted to JPEGs do not retain precise color information. The lossy compression method that's used throws away information and introduces compression artifacts, even though they are often not easily visible. Because of this, there is no way to accurately control color using the JPEG file format.

What this means is that you cannot accurately match foreground GIFs to background JPEGs or foreground JPEGs to background GIFs. Even if you prepare images in browser-safe colors, they will not remain browser safe when converted to JPEG—no matter what you do. JPEGs are not good for solid colors. This is one more reason not to use JPEGs when dealing with flat-style illustration, logos, cartoons, or any other graphical image that would not lend itself to having unwanted dithering.

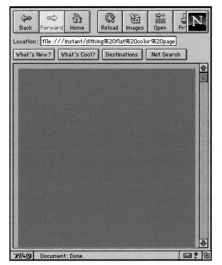

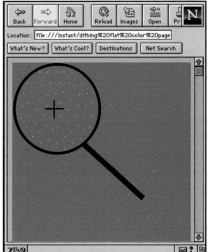

Here's an example of a solid browser-safe color (RGB values 51, 153, 153).

When saved as a GIF file, this color stayed browser safe.

When saved as a JPEG, the color shifted from 51, 153, 153 to 53, 153, 155. It is no longer browser safe, as is evident by the dither that appears when it's displayed in Netscape under 8-bit monitor conditions. Note: If you use the highest quality JPEGs, color inconsistency can be avoided, but you will have to deal with larger files sizes. Seems like if one thing doesn't get you, something else certainly will!

HYBRID IMAGE CHALLENGES

Like most things in life, there are exceptions to the rules. When you have an image that combines flat color and continuous-tone art, you have to combine browser-safe colors and non-safe colors. If you map the continuous-tone artwork to browser-safe colors, it will look terrible; and if you leave the solid colors in non-safe colors, they will dither. It is possible to combine techniques to achieve a hybrid image, but only in the GIF and PNG formats. There is no way to lock a browser-safe color in the JPEG format. Instructions for creating hybrid images as GIFs in browser-safe and non-safe colors follow.

HYBRID IMAGE AS GIF IN PHOTOSHOP

Whenever you deal with hybrid images that contain solid and continuous tones, it's best to save in an adaptive GIF palette instead of the web-safe palette. So what's the moral of the story? Use an adaptive GIF palette with hybrid images. It will usually (though not always) retain the browser-safe colors and will produce a much better-looking, continuous-tone image. On 8-bit systems, it will look the same as if you had forced it into the browser-safe system yourself.

There is one potential disadvantage to this technique. If you use adaptive palettes, you will often use more colors than if you stick to browser-safe colors. This sometimes results in larger file sizes. It's that "beauty versus size" thing again, and it all boils down to your own personal preferences.

Photoshop adaptive　　　**Photoshop web**

Photoshop adaptive　　　**Photoshop web**

These two images show the differences between saving with an adaptive palette (left) and a browser-safe palette (right). You can see that the adaptive palettes look better than the web palettes.

When viewed on an 8-bit system, these images look identical. The browser converts the adaptive palette to the browser-safe palette as expected.

BROWSER-SAFE COLOR PICKING

In order to create artwork with browser-safe colors, you must learn to select the correct colors, paint and fill with them, and shift existing documents to contain them. The first step is learning how to load the palette into your image editor, and the next step is learning to paint, fill, and shift to it. Unfortunately, there are so many image editors on the market that I don't have space to include all of them. You might want to check out the Tips section of the lynda.com site for movies that describe color picking features in many web authoring applications.

NON-SAFE IMAGES WITH SOLID COLORS

What about images that weren't created with browser-safe colors but should have been? ImageReady, Photoshop, and Fireworks all have a nifty feature that shifts colors toward the browser-safe colors when they encounter solid areas of color that are not safe.

note

CLUT FILES

CLUT is an acronym for **C**olor **L**ook**U**p **T**able. A CLUT is the file that assigns the specific colors to any 8-bit or lower bit-depth computer image. Photoshop and ImageReady use these files in two different ways. You can load a CLUT into the swatches palette for color picking, or you can assign colors to an image that uses it. In Photoshop, a CLUT file is also called a swatch, a palette, or a color table. Other imaging programs use CLUT files, too, but sometimes they have no way of viewing them or accessing them.

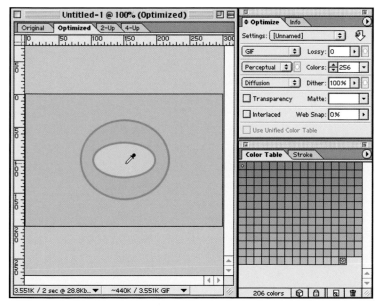

In ImageReady, Photoshop, and Fireworks, you can take a non-safe color and shift it to a browser-safe color. First, eyedrop on the color, and then press the cube icon. The cube icon in both programs stands for the browser-safe cube. The non-safe color that you selected with the eyedropper will be replaced with a browser-safe color.

BROWSER-SAFE MOUSEPADS

A few years ago, there was a flurry of browser-safe mousepads on the market. Here's your guide to finding them, should you want one! One caveat applies to these items (and the printed color charts in this book as well): It is impossible to re-create RGB colors with CMYK inks. For this reason, the truest color guides are found in electronic form instead of printed form (such as those found at http://www.lynda.com/files). Nevertheless, having the chart in print can save a lot of time, even if the chart isn't 100% accurate.

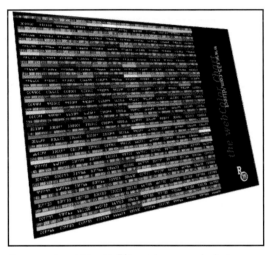

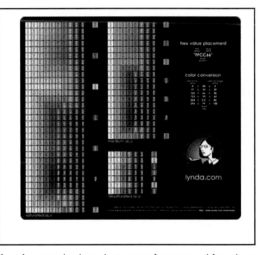

Raymond and **Dante Pirouz** have a web design supply company at http://www.r35.com. You can order a mousepad or poster showing the browser-safe palette from them if you'd like to keep a handy printed reference near your computer.

Lynda.com also has a browser-safe mousepad for sale at http://store.lynda.com/store/comersus_listcategories andproducts.asp?idCategory=44.

PANTONE'S BROWSER-SAFE SOLUTIONS

Pantone has come to the browser-safe rescue with a product called ColorWeb Pro (http://www.pantone.com). This product includes an Internet-safe color picking system that consists of a printed swatch set and a System Color Picker that displays the 216 safe colors in the Apple Color Picker dialog box.

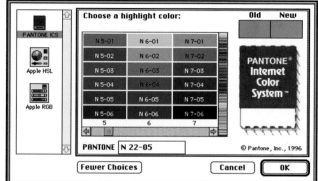

The Pantone Internet Color Guide looks like a typical Pantone color swatch book, except that it has a web-color spin. It profiles and organizes the 216 browser-safe colors in chromatic order and lists the values for RGB, CMYK, hexadecimal, and Hexachrome (their proprietary color format for picking printing ink colors).

If you install Pantone's ColorWeb software, it will add another entry, called Pantone ICS, into the Apple Color Picker choices. Pantone ICS will enable you to pick from the 216 browser-safe colors.

note

WARNING: CMYK CONVERSION TO RGB

It should be noted that there is no perfectly accurate way to convert CMYK values to RGB. The numbers that the Pantone Internet Color Guide cites for CMYK Internet-safe values are ballpark approximations and do not yield browser-safe colors when converted to RGB. The two color spaces (RGB and CMYK) do not share common colors consistently. Some RGB colors are outside of the CMYK color gamut, and nothing can be adjusted to create a reliable conversion method.

ColorWeb Pro adds an additional color picker that displays 1,024 Pantone colors and allows you to locate the closest browser-safe color to it. It also ships with a printed fan book that contains all 1,024 colors. This book is a beautiful and useful tool, even if you aren't a print designer! Pricing and order information for ColorWeb Pro is available at the Pantone web site.

browser-safe color

summary

Browser-safe color is a huge subject, with lots of variables and different implementations. This chapter covered the what, why, where, and how of browser-safe color, outlining the specs and software tools for producing safe graphics and safe HTML code. Here's a summary of the main points in this chapter:

> Always use browser-safe color with HTML-based schemes, such as your background, text, links, visited link, and active link colors.

> Always use browser-safe color for graphics that include areas of solid color.

> Don't use browser-safe colors on photographs.

> Save photographs in the JPEG format when possible.

> If you have a hybrid image that has areas of solid color and continuous-tone imagery, use the GIF format with an adaptive palette.

> It is possible to shift solid color artwork to browser-safe colors using Fireworks, Photoshop or ImageReady.

> Never save browser-safe colors as JPEGs.

HTML COLOR TAGS

INTRODUCTION

When you work with color on the Web, you have two choices: to create colored artwork or to specify color in your HTML or CSS. Other chapters have focused on graphics; this one concentrates on the tags that produce colored backgrounds, text, and table cells.

Adding color via HTML really is the easy part. It's understanding the aesthetic principles of color design and cross-platform differences that makes color on the Web a complex subject.

Many of you will be using HTML editors that support color design without making you write the code by hand. That's totally acceptable, but this chapter will give you that "under-the-hood" understanding of what the HTML editors are doing for you. Others might discover that your HTML editor doesn't support every color attribute you want. It's always possible to begin a page in a WYSIWYG editor and then later edit the source code in a text editor in order to add additional color attributes.

For those who write code in text editors, this should provide a handy guide for referencing that specific tag or attribute you knew existed but couldn't remember!

HEXADECIMAL-BASED COLORS

If you want to add colors on your site—such as colored text, colored links, colored backgrounds, and colored borders—describing them by their hexadecimal values is the only way HTML lets you do it.

#	0	1	2	3	4	5	6	7	8	9	10	11	12	13	14	15
HEX	0	1	2	3	4	5	6	7	8	9	A	B	C	D	E	F

What on earth are hexadecimal values, you may well wonder? Hexadecimal values are based on base-16 mathematics. Here's a little table that shows how hexadecimal numbers translate from our standard base-ten counting system.

RGB	0	51	102	153	204	255
HEX	00	33	66	99	CC	FF

Here's a very handy chart that shows how to convert browser-safe RGB values to hexadecimal values. Notice that the hex values never exceed two digits, unlike the RGB values, some of which are three digits long. This makes hexadecimal code a more uniform system than RGB numerics.

DEFAULT COLORS

If you don't specify any color attributes in your HTML, the page will display in default colors:

In order to change these default colors, you must learn a bit about color attributes that are allowed within HTML tags. The following sections will show examples of how to code color changes this way.

COLOR ATTRIBUTES

If you want to change the colors in HTML, you will want to know which tags can be affected by color attributes. The following sections will go through the **BODY**, **FONT**, and **TABLE** tags and show how you can modify colors with HTML.

Tag	Attribute(s)	Description
BODY	BGCOLOR, TEXT, LINK, VLINK, ALINK	Sets colors for the document background, text, links, visited links, and active links, respectively.
FONT	COLOR	Sets the color of the font.
TABLE	BGCOLOR	Sets the background color for the entire table.
TR	BGCOLOR	Sets the background color for the table row.
TD	BGCOLOR	Sets the background color for the table cell.
TH	BGCOLOR	Sets the background color for the table heading.

THE BODY TAG

The **BODY** tag of your document affects the background, text, links, visited links, and active links. If you add a color attribute to this tag, it is possible to alter the color scheme of your HTML page.

```
╔══════════════ Netscape: color attributes ═══════════╗
║                                                       ║
║  This shows colored background, text, link, vlink and ║
║  active link colors:                                  ║
║                                                       ║
║  background is #FFFFFF                                 ║
║                                                       ║
║  text is #006699                                      ║
║                                                       ║
║  links are #009966                                    ║
║                                                       ║
║  visited links are #006600                            ║
║                                                       ║
║  active links are #996633                             ║
║                                                       ║
╚═══════════════════════════════════════════════════════╝
```

code

```
<body background="#FFFFFF" text="#006699" link="#009966"
vlink="#006600" alink="#996633"></body>
```

Here's a list of possible attributes that can be modified using color within the **BODY** tag.

Attribute	Modification
BGCOLOR	Color of the background of the web page
TEXT	Color of the text
LINK	Color of the link
VLINK	Color of the link after it's been visited
ALINK	Color of the active link while the mouse is pressed down

LINK COLORS

Link color can affect the border color around linked images or the color of linked text. Here's an example of how to set this up in an HTML document:

code

```
<html>
<head>
<title>Adding Color to My Page</title>
</head>
1  <body bgcolor="#000000"
text="#CCCCFF" link="#CCFF00">

<h1>Here's an example of a
<a href="http://www.monkeyland.com">
text-based hyperlink</a>. </h1>
<br>
<h1>Here's an example of a linked graphic
with a fat, colored border: </h1>

<p><a href="http://www.monkeyland.com">
2  <img src="monkeyland.jpg" BORDER="10"></a></p>

</body>
</html>
```

code deconstruction

I   The **LINK** attribute within the **BODY** tag establishes the color for the linked text or graphic. The **<A HREF></A>** tag produces linked text.

2   The **IMG** tag inserts an image, and the **BORDER** attribute enables you to set a width for the border, measured in pixels. Note: If you don't want a border, you can set this to **BORDER="0"**.

Here's an example of creating colored links. The border around the graphic was made wider with the **BORDER** attribute.

USING COLOR NAMES INSTEAD OF HEX

You don't have to use hexadecimal numbers inside the color attribute tags; you can use words, too. Here's a list of color names that will work in Netscape.

aliceblue	chartreuse	darkolivegreen	firebrick	
antiquewhite	chocolate	darkorange	floralwhite	ivory
aqua	coral	darkorchid	forestgreen	khaki
aquamarine	cornflowerblue	darkred	fuchsia	lavender
azure	cornsilk	darksalmon	gainsboro	lavenderblush
beige	crimson	darkseagreen	ghostwhite	lawngreen
bisque	cyan	darkslateblue	gold	lemonchiffon
		darkslategray	goldenrod	lightblue
blanchedalmond	darkcyan	darkturquoise	gray	lightcoral
	darkgoldenrod	darkviolet	green	lightcyan
blueviolet	darkgrey	deeppink	greenyellow	lightgoldenrodyellow
brown	darkgreen	deepskyblue	honeydew	lightgreen
burlywood	darkkhaki	dimgray	hotpink	lightgrey
cadetblue	darkmagenta	dodgerblue	indianred	lightpink

lightsalmon	mediumseagreen	orange	red	
lightseagreen	mediumslateblue	orangered	rosybrown	steelblue
lightskyblue	mediumspringgreen	orchid	royalblue	tan
lightslategray	mediumturquoise	palegoldenrod	saddlebrown	teal
lightsteelblue	mediumvioletred	palegreen	salmon	thistle
lightyellow		paleturquoise	sandybrown	tomato
lime	mintcream	palevioletred	seagreen	turquoise
limegreen	mistyrose	papayawhip	seashell	violet
linen	moccasin	peachpuff	sienna	wheat
magenta	navajowhite	peru	silver	white
		pink	skyblue	whitesmoke
mediumaquamarine	oldlace	plum	slateblue	yellow
mediumorchid	olive	powderblue	snow	yellowgreen
mediumpurple	olivedrab	purple	springgreen	

note

COLOR NAMES ARE RARELY BROWSER SAFE

Out of all the possible color names, only ten of them are browser safe!

Aqua	Black	Blue	Cyan	Fuchsia	Lime	Magenta	Red	White	Yellow
0000FF	000000	0000FF	00FFFF	FF00FF	00FF00	FF00FF	FF0000	FFFFFF	FFFF00

COLOR NAME ATTRIBUTE

You don't have to use hexadecimal numbers inside the color attribute tags; you can use words, too.

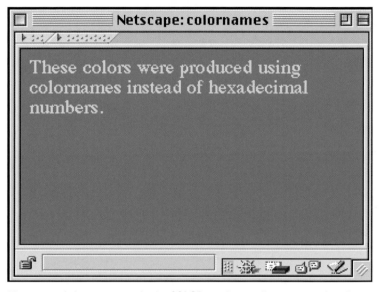

Using any of the names inside the **COLOR** attribute will generate colored text in Netscape.

code

```
<html>
<head>
<title>colornames</title>
</head>
I <body bgcolor="darkgreen" text="lightblue">
<h1>These colors were produced using colornames
instead of hexadecimal numbers.
</h1>
</body>
</html>
```

code deconstruction

I   You don't have to use hexadecimal numbers to define color—certain color names work as well. Here's an example of using **"darkgreen"** and **"lightblue"** as color names within the **BODY** tag.

THE FONT TAG

You can also assign specific colors to individual lines of text by using the **FONT** tag.

Here's an example of using the **FONT** tag to insert color attributes so that individual words or letters can be colored.

code

```
<html>
<head>
<title>Adding Color to My Page</title>
</head>
<body bgcolor="#FFFFFF">
<h1>This page is where I
<font color="#99FFFF">will </font>
<font color="#CCFF99">play </font>
<font color="#CC99CC">with </font>
<font color="#CC0000">color </font>
using all the nifty color tags I can learn
the font tag.
</h1>
</body>
</html>
```

code deconstruction

I The **FONT** tag can contain a color attribute, which can be specified by using color names or hex numbers. It must be closed with a **</FONT>** tag each time you want the specific colored-text attribute to end.

THE TABLE TAG

The **BGCOLOR** attribute works in table cells as well as the body of the HTML document.

code

```
   <html>
   <head>
   <title>tables</title>
   </head>
   <body bgcolor="#660099"
   text="#CCCCFF">
1  <center>
2  <table border="1">
3  <tr><th bgcolor="#003366" height="200"
   width="200">Hello</th>
   <th bgcolor="#990033" height="200"
   width="200">Hola!</th></tr>
   <tr><td bgcolor="#666600" height="200" width="200"
   align="center">You</td>
   <td bgcolor="#996666" height="200" width="200"
   align="center">Me</td></tr>
   </table>
   </center>
   </body>
   </html>
```

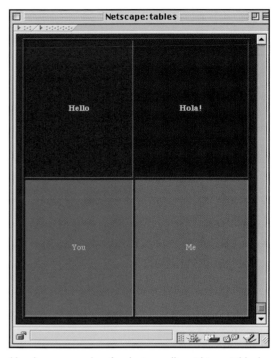

Here's an example of coloring cells within a table by using the **BGCOLOR** attribute within the **TABLE** tag.

code deconstruction

1 The **CENTER** tag instructs the table to be centered in the page.

2 The **TABLE** tag establishes the beginning of the table command. The **BORDER** attribute assigns an embossed border to the table. In this example, the border is set to 1 pixel, but you could turn it off using a value of 0, or increase its size by specifying a larger number.

3 **TR** initiates a table row. **TH** stands for table header. Everything within the **TH** tag will automatically be bold and centered. The **BGCOLOR** attribute allows a color to be established within the table cell and can be specified by using hexadecimal color or color names. The **HEIGHT** and **WIDTH** attributes assign dimensions to the table cells by using pixel-based measurements. The **ALIGN="CENTER"** attribute centers the text within the table cells.

HTML COLOR TAGS

SUMMARY

Fortunately, HTML allows you to change colors so we aren't stuck with the boring defaults. The HTML is fairly simple; here's a little review of this chapter:

> You can change the default colors of your page using the **BODY** tag attributes: **BGCOLOR**, **TEXT**, **LINK**, **ALINK**, and **VLINK**.

> You can change the text color in the body of your HTML text using the **FONT** tag along with the **COLOR** attribute and hex or name value.

> You can change your tables to contain color using the **TABLE BGCOLOR** attribute.

14

background TILES

INTRODUCTION

Sometimes the most simple enhancements to a web site can make all the difference between an average design and exceptional one. The power of background tiles in web design is often underestimated. This chapter will show compelling examples of how tiles can create richly layered pages that take up much less bandwidth than you might expect.

Perhaps you think it would take way too long to download an image that fills a viewer's browser screen and that it would be irresponsible to prepare images of this size for web graphics. Making full-screen, wall-to-wall graphics on the Web would seem to be an impossible feat given the slow modems and phone lines that some of us squeeze connections through—not to mention the fact that full-screen graphics can mean one thing to a compact portable computer web user and another to someone with a 21" monitor!

Repeated, tiled background patterns are the solution to many of these issues. This chapter covers an **HTML** tag called **<BODY>** and the attribute **BACKGROUND**, which allows a single small image to be repeated endlessly so that it fills an entire web page, regardless of size. These single small images will be referred to in this chapter as background tiles. They have the advantage of being small, so they load fast and are able to repeat over the size of whatever web screen they appear on. Because small graphics load faster than big ones, this technique works well for covering a lot of web page real estate without incurring a lot of overhead in downloading time.

TILEð bⲁckgRounds

The **BODY** tag and **BACKGROUND** attribute enables the browser to repeat a small graphic and turn it into a full-screen graphic. It accomplishes this effect by taking a single image and tiling it, creating a repeating image that will fill any size screen regardless of computer platform and browser area. The browser needs to load only a single source file for the pattern, and once it's downloaded, it fills the entire web page. This saves time because the wait time is for a single, small image even though the result is that the entire screen fills with an image. Repeated tiles are a great solution for creating full-screen graphics for low-bandwidth delivery systems such as the Web.

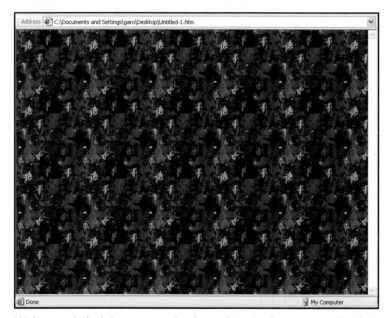

This is the source artwork for the tile.

With artwork that's been prepared to have a "seamless" appearance, the tile is repeated in a browser window, and you can't really see the source tile anymore.

Bandwidth limitations aren't the only problem that tiled background patterns solve. One of the great frustrations most web designers share is HTML's inability to allow for images to be layered. If you consider that layering is a main feature of programs such as Photoshop, QuarkXPress, and PageMaker, you will understand why this feature in HTML is sorely missed. Cascading Style Sheets are the answer to some designer's layering needs (see Chapter 23, *"Cascading Style Sheets"*), but using tiled background patterns is still a much easier and more backward-compatible method for layering multiple images.

HTML allows text, links, and images to go on top of tiled backgrounds, making it an extremely useful and economical design element. The HTML code for this tiling effect is quite simple. The real challenge is making the art look good and controlling whether the seams of each repeated image are obvious or invisible.

DETERMINING TILED PATTERN SIZES

One of the first questions that comes to mind is how big the tiled image should be. HTML puts no restrictions on the size of a source for a background tile. The image has to be in a square or rectangle, however, because that's the native shape of all computer files.

The size of the image is entirely up to you. You should realize that the size of a tile is going to dictate how many times it repeats. If a viewer's monitor is 640✕480 pixels and your tile is 320✕240, it will repeat four times. If it were 20✕20 pixels, it would repeat 32 times.

If your tile has images that repeat on each side, it will not show visible seams, and the viewer will not know how many times it repeats. If the image has an obvious border around it, the border will accentuate the fact that the image is being tiled. The size of your tile is up to you and the effect you are striving for.

Be aware, however, that file size restrictions must still be honored. If you create a tile that takes up a lot of memory, it will take the same amount of time to load as any other kind of huge graphic you put on the Web. If need be, refer back to Chapter 11, *"Speedy Graphics,"* for methods of minimizing file sizes.

If you use an image source that has large dimensions, it will not repeat as often. If it is large enough, it will not repeat at all. In that event, the speed advantages of having a small image load once and automatically repeat without incurring any additional download time would not exist. On the other hand, if you could make a large graphic in dimensions and not file size, loading it in as a background image instead of a regular graphic could have its merits.

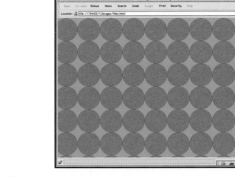

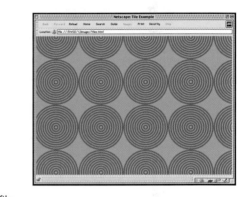

Small source file.

Medium source file.

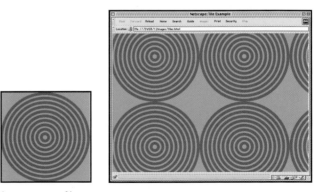

Large source file.

FULL-SCREEN BODY BACKGROUNDS

Why would you use an image with large pixel dimensions as a tiled background, since it seems to defeat the point? Because it could go behind other images and text, making a full-screen backdrop to other images on your page. HTML doesn't easily let you put text or images over regular images. The easiest way around this restriction is to use a background tile.

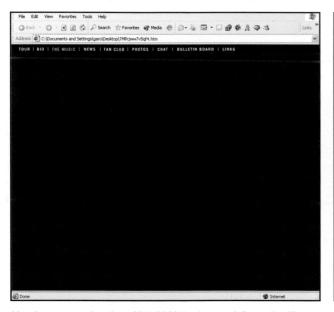

Here's an example of an 896×1000 background from the **Kenny Lattimore** site (http://www.kennylattimore.com), which is only 18K. Because it only has two colors and has a lot of areas of solid color, it compressed extremely well as a GIF even though the image was so large.

Combined with HTML text, this page looks rich and layered, and it is not too large to download.

The background tile for the center frame of the **Frank Lloyd Wright** site (http://www.pbs.org/flw) uses a photographic background JPEG that measures 1014×600, and weighs 13.7K.

By adding HTML and graphical type, the design is finished with just a few simple additions.

Here is the source file for http://www.flowerbud.com. It utilizes a simple graphic background. It is 1000×700 and weighs 11.3K.

The graphic background completes the design by filling in some of the white space along the left side of the page design.

FILE FORMATS FOR PATTERNED TILES

GIFs and JPEGs are standard file formats for the Web, and tiled patterns are no exception. Just remember to follow the kilobyte rule. Every kilobyte of file size represents one second of download time for your viewers who have a 56K modem connection. This may be a conservative and unscientific "rule," but it's easy to remember, and anyone who has a slow, dial-up connection will be grateful that you err on the conservative side of judgment. The full size of the background pattern gets added to the download! If you have a background that's 60K and two images that are 10K each, the total file size of your page will be 80K. You would have just added a minute of download time to your page. Therefore, tiled backgrounds that take up a lot of memory are extra annoying to your audience during download. Remember, not everyone has broadband!

Be careful if you are trying to match foreground and background tile images. They must both be the same file format—GIF and GIF or JPEG and JPEG—if you want the colors to match perfectly.

As usual, always save your file names in lowercase and use the extensions **.jpg** or **.gif** to let the HTML code know what kind of image it has to load. I usually put the word "pat" somewhere in a pattern file name, just for my own reference. That way I know what I intended to use the file for when I search for it in a text list, such as my server directory!

It is simple to include a patterned background in an HTML document (shown on the following page). Here's the minimum code required:

code

```
   <html>
 | <body background="pat.gif">
   </body>
   </html>
```

code deconstructed

| The **BODY BACKGROUND** attribute enables you to add a background tile to the page. The "**pat.gif**" is the name of the image being tiled in this example.

If you wanted to have an image lay over a background (shown on the following page), the code would look like this:

code

```
   <html>
   <body background="pat.gif">
 | <img src="wwjungle.gif">
   </body>
   </html>
```

code deconstructed

| The **IMG** tag enables you to include an image that will lay over the background tile image.

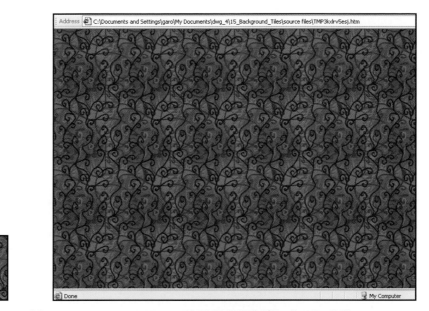

Here's the **pat.gif** image and the result of using **BODY BACKGROUND ="pat.gif"**.

The finished web page using the **<IMG SRC="wwjungle.gif">** code.

DIRECTIONAL TILES

It's possible to make skinny and tall tiles, or fat and short tiles, for directional tile effects. A tile in a horizontal shape will fill the browser window from top to bottom, and a tile in a vertical shape will fill the browser from left to right.

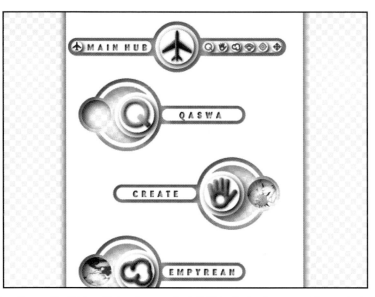

I'm sure you've seen tiles all over the Web with borders on the left. This tile by **Ammon Haggerty** is a nice twist on that technique and creates a right and left border with soft edges. The finished effect is more impressive than the lone tile!

National Design Museum's designer **Elizabeth Roxby** developed this tall tile, which fills the screen in a horizontal motion as it loads. The effect is spectacular once other images and typography are laid over the simple tile.

AESTHETICS OF BACKGROUNDS

Always pay attention to contrast and value (lights and darks) when creating background tiles. If you have a light background, use dark type. If you have a dark background, use light type. If you aren't going to change your browser's default colors for text, links, visited links and active links, use a light background (one that is about the same value as the default light gray you see as the background color of most browsers). The light background will ensure that the default colors of black, blue, and purple text will read against your custom background.

When making art for pattern tiles, try to use either all dark values or all light values. If you have both darks and lights in a background, neither light nor dark type will work consistently against them. This is a basic rule to follow, and your site will avoid the pitfalls of poor background tile aesthetics. Using either all dark values or all light values seems like common sense, but tour the Web a bit and you'll soon see rainbow-colored backgrounds with unreadable black type everywhere.

Make sure your images read. I don't mean your tiles should go to school to learn phonetics or anything; instead, I'm talking about readability of image versus background.

When the background has high contrast, HTML text will not read well on top of it.

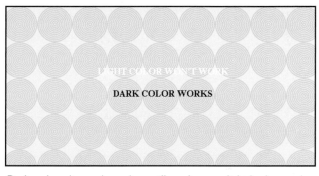

Dark and medium value colors will read over a light background.

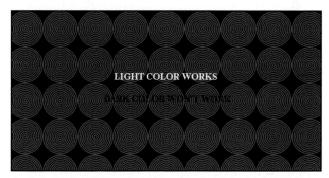

With a dark background, the reverse is true. It's not enough to make a cool-looking background tile. Always check to ensure your type reads over it as well! If it doesn't read, make the necessary adjustments to the color or contrast of the background image.

background TILES

SUMMARY

I hope this chapter inspired you to think about background tiles as an important element in your web graphics repertoire. Tiles can offer a big effect for low overhead. Here's a review of the principles described in this chapter:

> There is no "correct" size for a background tile. The size will affect the visual effect, however, in terms of how many times the tile repeats before it fills the browser screen.

> Full-screen backgrounds can add a lot of visual interest to a boring page.

> Pay attention to contrast and readability. It's easy to get carried away with complicated, high-contrast backgrounds that result in unreadable web pages.

> You can control the direction in which the background tile loads if you make a thin, horizontal tile or a fat, vertical tile.

Transparent gIFs

introduction

Most of us don't think about the fact that computer images are always stored in square or rectangular files. It doesn't matter if you make a graphic on a transparent layer in Photoshop, ImageReady, Fireworks, or any other image editor; if you save and reopen it in another program, it will be in a rectangle. What's wrong with rectangles? Nothing, really, except that they can become mighty boring and predictable after a while.

The Web especially suffers from an abundance of rectangular shapes. The browser window is in a rectangle, frames are in rectangles, and buttons and graphics are often in rectangles, too. I call this problem "rectangle-itis." Too many rectangles on a page can make your visitors feel boxed in and claustrophobic.

The solution to the rectangle problem is to learn about transparency on the Web. Transparent graphics include masks with which you can obscure or reveal parts of an image, creating the illusion of an irregular shape.

There are a few different methods for implementing transparency on a site. You can fake it with any file format (my favorite method) or you can create a transparent GIF file, the most widely supported file format that supports transparency. This chapter covers all these methods (of course!) and discusses some of the tools and techniques.

WHAT IS TRANSPARENCY?

Transparency is the term used for masked images on the Web. Creating transparent images is a tricky business because the standard masking procedures for print or imaging applications don't apply to web images. Of the two most popular web image formats, GIF and JPEG, only GIF supports transparency features. Therefore, in order to make irregularly shaped web images, you must either make GIF images or learn to fake transparency with the GIF or JPEG format.

The web page on the left with lots of rectangular images looks boxy and unsophisticated. Even though this page still contains three images, it looks much better on the right when they don't appear inside rectangular shapes (http://www.lynda.com/jodi).

FAKING TRANSPARENCY

There are two types of transparency: One involves masking, and the other involves trickery. The easiest one to use is the latter, which is pretty easy to explain.

MASKING

Let's say you want a shape to appear to be free-floating even though it must be stored in a rectangular computer file. Simply make the background behind the shape the same color as your web page. If you put the two together, there should be no obvious rectangular border. Sound simple? It is.

Image with matching background color

Image alone

You can easily create the illusion of an irregularly shaped image by making the foreground artwork include the same color as the target background on your web page.

TRICKERY

There are two ways to achieve the fake transparency technique. You can use the **BODY BACKGROUND** or the **BGCOLOR** tag and attribute.

The **BODY BGCOLOR** attribute involves making another small graphic with the same solid color as the background color of the shape.

HTML code

```
<HTML>
<HEAD>
<TITLE>transparency</TITLE>
</HEAD>
<BODY BACKGROUND=bluebg.gif>
<CENTER>
<IMG SRC=circle.gif>
</CENTER></BODY></HTML>
```

XHTML code

```
<html xmlns=
"http://www.w3.org/1999/xhtml">
<head>
<title>transparency</title>
</head>
<body background="bluebg.gif">
<center><img src="circle.gif"
alt=""/>
</center>
</body>
</html>
```

To use the **BGCOLOR** attribute, select the same color as the background, find its hexadecimal equivalent, and insert that code into your HTML.

HTML code

```
<HTML>
<HEAD>
<TITLE>transparency</TITLE>
</HEAD>
<BODY BGCOLOR=#C9F0DE>
<CENTER>
<IMG SRC=circle.gif>
</CENTER></BODY></HTML>
```

XHTML code

```
<html xmlns=
"http://www.w3.org/1999/xhtml">
<head>
<title>transparency</title>
</head>
<body bgcolor="#C9F0DE">
<center><img src="circle.gif"
alt=""/>
</center>
</body>
</html>
```

note

WARNING: BROWSER PREFERENCES

It is important to be aware that if your visitor has changed his or her browser settings to override the colors you've chosen, the illusion you create will be automatically broken.

Although web designers count on background colors they pick to achieve the illusion of irregularly shaped images, end viewers can uncheck *Allow page to specify colors*, which will override the specified color choices! To view sites as the designers intended them, make sure this option is checked in your browser's preferences. This is the default for most browsers, so you and your end user only need to worry about the problem if preferences are changed.

Page & Link
Text: ▮
Background: ▮
Read Links: ▮
Unread Links: ▮
☑ Underline links

Page Content
☑ Show pictures
☑ Animate GIFs
  └ ☑ Allow Looping
☑ Show style sheets
  └ ☐ Use my style sheet
    └ Select Style Sheet...
☑ Play sounds
☑ Show frames
☐ Use ColorSync(TM)
☑ Allow page to specify fonts
☑ Allow page to specify colors
(No style sheet selected)

In order to view sites the way the designer intended, always check *Allow page to specify colors*.

THERE'S NO FAKING PATTERNED TILES

The method you just learned works beautifully if you have a solid background color. The minute you put a pattern behind the image, however, the illusion is ruined.

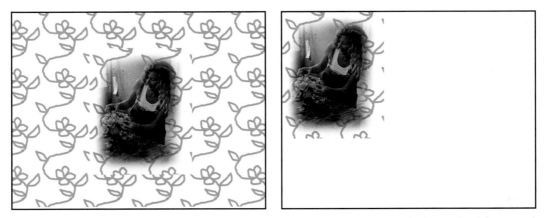

Notice the mis-registration between the foreground graphic and the background tile? Background and foreground images experience an offset that's difficult to control in HTML. This is one of the hazards of "faking" transparency with a pattern background tile.

Even if you apply the same pattern to the foreground image document, it won't line up with your HTML background tile. Why? There's a different offset in the way foreground images and background images are aligned. Two potential solutions to this will be discussed later in this book (in Chapter 22, *"Frames,"* and Chapter 23, *"Cascading Style Sheets"*). Meanwhile, the simple solution is to use true transparency instead of faking it.

GIF TRANSPARENCY

The GIF file format supports transparency (masking). GIF transparency is challenging because the file format is limited to 1-bit masking (whereas Photoshop transparency supports 8-bit masking). What this means in plain English is that you are restricted to creating a mask with a single value: on or off. Photoshop, on the other hand, allows you to use up to 256 values of on or off, which is why you can easily layer images with feathered edges, glows, and drop shadows. In a 1-bit GIF transparency world, such subtlety is not possible.

It's important to understand the 1-bit masking limitation, because if you aren't careful, the results of your transparency efforts can easily go awry, and you'll end up producing images with unwanted halos and edges. GIF is able to store a 1-bit mask, and the mask is not visible until it's loaded into a web browser.

This foreground image was originally created against white. When the color white is instructed to become transparent in the GIF file format, the white will disappear. This is only visible once the graphic is placed on top of a different color or pattern.

Here's the transparent GIF in the browser window. If you look closely at the edges, you will see an unwanted, lighter-colored halo. This was caused by anti-aliasing against the original background color (white), which is described in the next section.

This is a close-up of the anti-aliased edge of the type. Because it is against a white background, the burgundy type gradually fades to white around the edges. This makes the type look smooth at 1:1. It's quite obvious here because the image has been enlarged.

Here is a close-up view of the anti-aliased type against white, set to GIF transparency, and then placed on top of a background image of a different color. The white halo is residual from the fact that the image was originally anti-aliased against white.

The anti-aliased blended edge is precisely what causes fringing problems when the graphic is converted to a transparent GIF. Because transparent GIFs drop only one color out of your image, you will see all the remaining colors along the blended edges of anti-aliased artwork—even when what you really desire is for all of them to disappear. There is no way to avoid this because the GIF file format does not support masking for more than one color. A solution for eliminating these unwanted fringes is covered in the next section.

GLOWS, SOFT EDGES, & DROP SHADOWS

Because of the problems anti-aliasing introduces in GIFs, artwork with glows, soft edges, and drop shadows can look awful as transparent GIFs. One popular solution is to build your artwork against the same color background it will be seen against in the web browser. The artwork will look terrible when you make it, but it will look fine when it's displayed against the final background in a web browser.

One popular solution is to build artwork against the same color background that is predominant within the pattern.

If you prepare an image this way, you will correct the image's predisposition to favor any other color, which will eliminate unwanted fringes, halos, and matte lines.

This technique works well with drop shadows.

It also works well with glows.

TOOLS & TECHNIQUES FOR GIF TRANSPARENCY

So far, the principles of transparency have been covered. This next section will describe methods for producing transparent GIF graphics. Because there are so many graphic tools on the market and because versions change so often, I am going to generalize a bit, using Photoshop as the primary tool of reference. Other tools that work well for creating transparent images include: Macromedia Fireworks, Adobe ImageReady, Corel PhotoPaint, and PaintShop Pro.

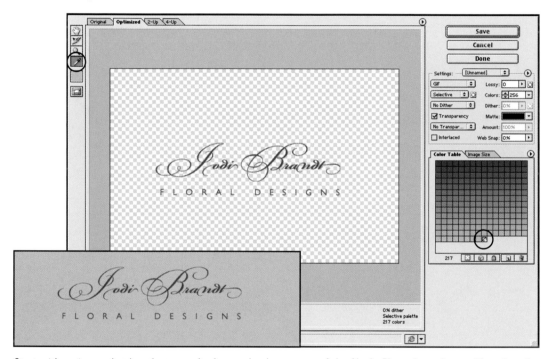

Start with an image that has the target background color as part of the file. In Photoshop, choose *File > Save For Web*. In the Save For Web interface of Photoshop, you can use the eyedropper to knock a color away. Click with the *eyedropper*, and then click the *Transparency button* in the Color Table. The color will appear with a diagonal line through it, and it will disappear on the screen. When you click *Save*, the file will be stored with an invisible transparency mask, which will show up when it is placed over a background image in an HTML document.

The other method is to begin with a document that is against a transparent background (indicated in Photoshop by a checkerboard pattern). In this example, there is a background color layer, but it's been turned off. Do this before you choose *File > Save For Web*. By choosing a *Matte color* that matches the target background image color, Photoshop automatically inserts that color underneath the anti-aliased edge of any graphic.

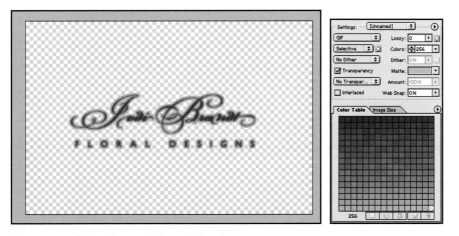

This even works for glows and drop shadows!

TRANSPARENT GIFS

SUMMARY

Adding transparent graphics to your site will undoubtedly result in a more visually appealing page. The trick is to know how to avoid the unwanted halos and edges that can easily result from anti-aliasing. Here's a summary of the key points in this chapter:

> If you are creating an irregularly shaped graphic against a solid background color in your HTML, don't bother with GIF transparency at all. Use the faking method described earlier; just be sure to match file formats (such as GIF on top of GIF or JPEG on top of JPEG).

> Using aliased edges on your artwork will eliminate the possibility of unwanted halos and edges.

> For glows, drop shadows and soft-edged artwork, make sure you anti-alias to the target background color.

> If you are going to use a pattern background, anti-alias to the predominant color within the pattern.

Rules & Bullets

Introduction

This chapter covers how to make rules and bullets with standard HTML/XHTML tags and/or custom graphics. The point of making these types of graphics and HTML tags is to create order, hierarchy, and visual cues for navigation.

You will find rules and bullets in print design, but the techniques for creating them are different for the Web. In print, you can easily highlight information using multiple colored inks, or a splash of color behind some text. This is possible on the Web, too, but might involve code instead of picture boxes and text effects.

The area of rules and bullets offers a creative playing field—you can use just about any style graphic for these types of effects. Imaging tools such as Photoshop, Fireworks, or PaintShop Pro are great resources for building graphics of these types.

HORIZONTAL RULES

A horizontal rule that serves as a page divider is something you'll rarely see in print design. These divider rules are commonly observed across web sites the world over, however, because they are part of the current XHTML, and former HTML, specification. Some are embossed, some are thick, some are thin, and some are colored or have different shapes. The web term for these lines is *horizontal rule*, and they are used for many things:

> Defining a page break

> Completing an idea

> Beginning a list

> Separating one picture from another

Web pages have no set length like printed pages. The visual techniques and metaphors available to print designers—such as using a block of color behind text or images, changing the text color in an isolated paragraph or sidebar, or using a different screened-back image or picture frame to separate an idea or theme—are possible on the Web, but not nearly so easy as a simple HTML/XHTML rule.

If you want to add horizontal rules to your pages, you have some choices. You can use XHTML/HTML code, or you can insert your own artwork to make custom horizontal rules, and vertical rules, too. When all else fails, there are also libraries of horizontal rule clip art.

HORIZONTAL RULES, THE HTML & XHTML WAY

Because XHTML has been formally recommended by the W3C, the governing body of web standards, I felt it was important to show you the code for creating horizontal rules in both HTML and XHTML. Their syntax is very similar, but there are some important differences. Which one should you use? At this point, it doesn't really matter because current browsers support both syntaxes. Feel free to work with the newer standard or to use the older techniques with HTML. You don't take a big risk either way.

The basic HTML standard horizontal rule tag looks like this: **<HR>**.

html syntax

```
<HTML>
<BODY>
Some Text
<HR>
Some More Text
</BODY>
</HTML>
```

Some Text
Some More Text

This will put an embossed, double-pixel line horizontally through your page at whatever point you insert it into an HTML document. If you stretch your browser window wider, the horizontal rule will get wider; vice versa if you narrow your window. Horizontal rules have no set width, except to fill the horizontal distance of your browser screen.

The basic XHTML standard horizontal rule tag can actually be written one of two ways. So, which one do you use? If you use the syntax shown below you will ensure that this works well in older browsers. As you can see, the XHTML tag is written in lowercase, which is required by XHTML but not HTML. It also includes a single space and contains a forward slash, which indicates the closing point of the horizontal rule. Here is an example:

xhtml syntax

```
<html>
<body>
Some Text
<hr />
Some More Text
</body>
</html>
```

Some Text
Some More Text

Notice that the visual results are the same. This code will work in older browsers, so there's no harm in adopting this new syntax. For a more detailed explanation of XHTML, check out Chapter 9, *"HTML & XHTML."*

Sometimes you might want to add some breathing room because the horizontal rule will butt up underneath whatever text or image that was in the HTML code before it. The following HTML and XHTML code examples add a row of empty space above and beneath the rule:

html syntax

```
<HTML>
<BODY>
Some Text
<BR><BR>
<HR>
<BR><BR>
Some More Text
</BODY>
</HTML>
```

xhtml syntax

```
<html>
<body>
Some Text
<br /><br />
<hr />
<br /><br />
Some More Text
</body>
</html>
```

Some Text
Some More Text

Adding the **
** tag above and beneath the horizontal rule is a good way to add some space between the objects above and beneath it.

advanced HORIZONTAL RULE-making

> Change the rule's width.

> Change the rule's weight (thickness).

> Change both the rule's width and weight.

> Left-align the rule.

> Eliminate fake emboss shading.

> Make the rule vertical.

The following code changes the width of the line:

code	xhtml syntax
`<HR WIDTH="25">`	`<hr width="25" />`

Using a **WIDTH** attribute adjusts the length of the line. Notice that if you define a width, the resulting horizontal rule is automatically centered. Any value you put after the = (equals) sign tells the rule how wide to be in pixels.

The following code changes the weight, or thickness, of the line. Notice that this rule stretches the length of a page:

html syntax	xhtml syntax
`<HR SIZE="10">`	`<hr size="10" />`

By changing the **SIZE** attribute, the entire line gets thicker.

The following code changes the thickness and width at the same time. Here's an example that shows the results of code specifying the rule to be a square (equal height and width):

html syntax	xhtml syntax
`<HR SIZE="25" WIDTH="25">`	`<hr size="25" width="25" />`

By changing the **SIZE** and **WIDTH** together, you can make other rectilinear shapes like this square.

The following code aligns the square left and sizes it at 10 pixels high and 10 pixels wide:

html syntax

```
<HR ALIGN="LEFT" SIZE="10" WIDTH="10">
```

xhtml syntax

```
<hr align="left" size="10" width="10" />
```

You can use alignment tags on horizontal rules, too.

The following code eliminates the fake emboss shading:

html syntax

```
<HR NOSHADE>
```

xhtml syntax

```
<hr noshade="noshade" />
```

The **NOSHADE** attribute creates a black line.

The following code changes the size and width to make a horizontal rule look vertical:

html syntax

```
<HR WIDTH="10" SIZE="200">
```

xhtml syntax

```
<hr width="10" size="200" />
```

Horizontal rules don't have to be horizontal; just adjust the **HR WIDTH** and **SIZE** attribute.

note

EDITING SOFTWARE FOR CUSTOM RULES

It's possible to make custom horizontal rules using an image-editing software package, such as Photoshop, Fireworks, or PaintShop Pro. Simply make the artwork look like a horizontal rule, and make sure you save it as a GIF or a JPEG, depending on which format offers the best compression for the custom art you created. To revisit instructions on compression techniques, read Chapter 11, *"Speedy Graphics."*

HORIZONTAL RULES & BACKGROUND TILES

If you include a background tile on your web page and insert horizontal rules, the rules will appear to have an embossed effect.

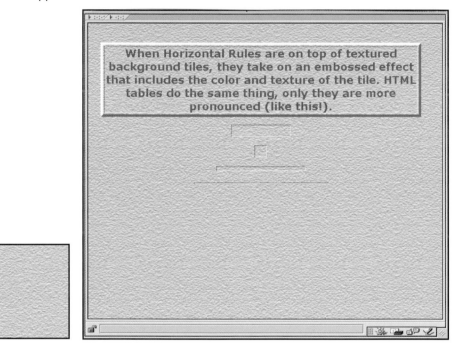

This example shows the source tile and the HTML page in which it was used, along with horizontal rules and tables.

DO-IT-YOURSELF HORIZONTAL RULES

Anything gets old when you see it too often, and horizontal rules are no exception. If you want to be a little more creative, here are some tips for creating custom artwork to design your own rules. When you create your own horizontal rule art, your artwork dictates the length, width, and height of the rule. It's a graphic like any other graphic. It can be aliased, anti-aliased, a GIF, a JPEG, interlaced, transparent, blurred, 2D, 3D—you name it. If you know how to make it, it can be a horizontal rule.

To include a graphic as a horizontal rule, the HTML/XHTML code would be:

html syntax

```
<IMG SRC="your_horizontal_rule_art_here.gif">
```

xhtml syntax

```
<img src="your_horizontal_rule_here.gif" />
```

VERTICAL RULES

Creating vertical rules is not an easy task in the land of web graphics. Making the custom artwork is identical to making any other custom artwork in this chapter; that is not the problem. The placement of the artwork is what poses a challenge, as it involves other programming techniques using tables or CSS.

Vertical lines can be aligned with HTML/XHTML tables, or you can make a background tile with a single stripe down the left side.

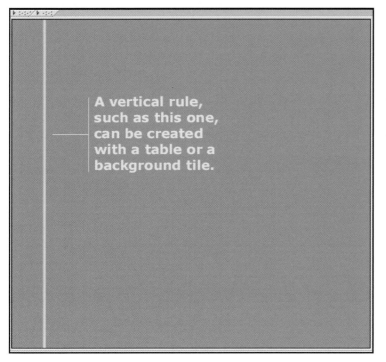

A vertical rule, such as this one, can be created with a table or a background tile.

How do you get vertical lines aligned to a web page? There is no easy way to assign vertical columns using HTML! Check out the lesson on how to position vertical ruled lines in Chapter 21 *"Alignment & Tables."*

CLIP ART RULES

Many individuals create and distribute free clip art, and it can also be found from commercial sources. Clip art is a wondrous thing in a pinch, and with tools like Photoshop (and other image editors), there's no end to the cool ways you can personalize clip art files. Make sure that the images are royalty free in the respective licensing agreements if you are going to modify them. Some authors have stipulations that must be honored. Read the readmes! Here are some popular clip art collections:

Art & Other Essentials
Jay Boersma's prolific image collection.
http://www.ecn.bgu.edu/users/gas52r0/Jay/art.html

Yahoo! Search for Clip Art
The best and latest clip art listings.
http://www.yahoo.com/Computers_and_Internet/Graphics/Clip_Art

BULLETS

Lists of one type or another are pretty popular in all forms of publishing, including web publishing. Bullets are often used to emphasize list items. On the Web, bullets can look standardized, with solid circles in front of text (much like those generated by a word processor), or they can include custom artwork that looks more typical of a CD-ROM or magazine page layout. Creating custom bullets is similar to creating custom horizontal rules. Basically, any artwork that you're capable of creating is a candidate for bullet art.

When designing bulleted lists for the Web, you can choose from either HTML bullets or image-based bullets. HTML bullets are created by using code tags that identify the type of list you are creating; such bullets appear as basic circles or squares. Image-based bullets are those you generate from clip art or your own artwork, and they can be used to enhance a list or provide added functionality, such as links.

note

WARNING: GRAPHICS VERSUS MARKUP

Keep in mind, however, that HTML/XHTML-generated bullets maintain the "structure of the markup," meaning the list will be treated as a list if read by a speech reader for a visually impaired person or translated into another language by a translation script. By using a graphic instead of code, you are forfeiting the structure of your list.

CODE-BASED BULLETED LISTS

Using code-based bullets is certainly less work than creating your own custom artwork. Simple and clean design often looks best without a lot of custom artwork on a page. There will be many instances where an HTML-based bullet or indent will do the job more effectively than custom bullet artwork.

To create a list with solid circle bullets, use the **UL** tag, (**U**nordered **L**ist). To create such a bulleted list within text items, use the **UL** tag along with the **LI** (**L**ist **I**tem) tag, as shown in the following code:

html syntax

```
<UL>
<LI> The first thinga-dingy
<LI> The second thinga-dingy
<LI> The third thinga-dingy
</UL>
```

xhtml syntax

```
<ul>
<li> The first thinga-dingy</li>
<li> The second thinga-dingy</li>
<li> The third thinga-dingy</li>
</ul>
```

Using the "unordered" list tags , and "list item" tags produces this result:

- The first thinga-dingy
- The second thinga-dingy
- The third thinga-dingy

The results of using the HTML **<UL>** tag.

Lists can be nested by inserting a new tag where you want the list to indent or move to another level. The following code uses an additional **UL** element to create a bulleted list nested within another bulleted list:

html syntax

```
<UL>
<LI> The first thinga-dingy
<LI> The second thinga-dingy
<LI> The third thinga-dingy
   <UL>
   <LI> More types of thinga-dingies
   <LI> Yet More types of thinga-dingies
   </UL>
</UL>
```

xhtml syntax

```
<ul>
<li> The first thinga-dingy</li>
<li> The second thinga-dingy</li>
<li> The third thinga-dingy</li>
   <ul>
   <li> More types of thinga-dingies</li>
   <li> Yet More types of thinga-dingies</li>
   <li> Even More types of thinga-
        dingies</li>
   </ul>
</ul>
```

You can nest lists within lists, by repeating the "ordered" or "unordered" list tags. The results look like this:

- The first thinga-dingy
- The second thinga-dingy
- The third thinga-dingy
  - More types of thinga-dingies
  - Yet More types of thinga-dingies
  - Even more types of thinga-dingies

You can nest bulleted points by adding multiple **UL** elements.

You can have the items in your list be links to other pages or sites by using the **<A HREF></A>** element within an ordered list or an ordered list. The following code shows how to use link tags to include links within a bulleted list:

html syntax

```
<UL>
<LI> <A HREF="http://www.domain.com">
     The first thinga-dingy</A>
<LI> <A HREF="http://www.domain.com">
     The second thinga-dingy</A>
<LI> <A HREF="http://www.domain.com">
     The third thinga-dingy</A>
</UL>
```

xhtml syntax

```
<ul>
<li> <a href="http://www.domain.com">
     The first thinga-dingy</a></li>
<li> <a href="http://www.domain.com">
     The second thinga-dingy</a></li>
<li> <a href="http://www.domain.com">
     The third thinga-dingy</a></li>
</ul>
```

Including links within a list is a matter of using link tags within lists. The results look like this:

- The first thinga-dingy
- The second thinga-dingy
- The third thinga-dingy

The items in your list can be straight text or hypertext by changing a few tags.

CREATING ORDERED & DEFINITION LISTS

At times, you might not want your lists to be preceded with bullets. When creating a list of steps to be followed in order, for example, using numbers rather than bullets will help get your point across. Such numbered lists are called ordered lists. Likewise, lists such as glossaries can appear with indents rather than bullets or numbers. These lists are known as definition lists.

To make a list that automatically generates numbers in front of its items, use the **OL** (**O**rdered **L**ist) element. The following code lines show how to use the **OL** element to produce a numbered list:

html syntax

```
<OL>
<LI> The first thinga-dingy
<LI> The second thinga-dingy
<LI> The third thinga-dingy
</OL>
```

xhtml syntax

```
<ol>
<li> The first thinga-dingy</li>
<li> The second thinga-dingy</li>
<li> The third thinga-dingy</li>
</ol>
```

> Using the "ordered list" would automatically generate numbers, instead of bullets in front of each "list item":
>
> 1. The first thinga-dingy
> 2. The second thinga-dingy
> 3. The third thinga-dingy

The **OL** tag generates ordered (numbered) lists.

If you want to change the shape of the automatically generated bullets, you can use the special tags, as shown in the following code:

html syntax

```
<UL>
<LI TYPE=circle>Circle-shaped Bullet
<LI TYPE=square>Square-shaped Bullet
</UL>
```

xhtml syntax

```
<ul>
<li type="circle">
    Circle-shaped Bullet</li>
<li type="square">
    Square-shaped Bullet</li>
</ul>
```

> Thingy Dingies
>
> The first thinga-dingy
> The second thinga-dingy
> The second thinga-dingy

Using the **DL** definition list tags creates indented lists.

> ● Circle-shaped Bullet
> □ Square-shaped Bullet

Using the **TYPE** attribute, you can change the shape of HTML-generated bullets.

You can also set up organized lists by using alphabetic and Roman numeric criteria by adding the variations shown in the following table:

Tag	Type	Example
TYPE=1	Numbers	1, 2, 3
TYPE=A	Uppercase letters	A, B, C
TYPE=a	Lowercase letters	a, b, c
TYPE=I	Uppercase Roman numerals	I, II, III
TYPE=i	Lowercase Roman numerals	i, ii, iii

The following code shows variations of the HTML **TYPE** tag, which produces these results:

html syntax

```
<OL>
<LI TYPE="1"> Thingy One
<LI TYPE="1"> Thingy Two
<LI TYPE="1"> Thingy Three
<BR><BR>
<LI TYPE="A"> Thingy One
<LI TYPE="A"> Thingy Two
<LI TYPE="A"> Thingy Three
<BR><BR>
<LI TYPE="a"> Thingy One
<LI TYPE="a"> Thingy Two
<LI TYPE="a"> Thingy Three
<BR><BR>
<LI TYPE="I"> Thingy One
<LI TYPE="I"> Thingy Two
<LI TYPE="I"> Thingy Three
<BR><BR>
<LI TYPE="i"> Thingy One
<LI TYPE="i"> Thingy Two
<LI TYPE="i"> Thingy Three
<OL>
```

An example of all the different types of HTML-generated bullets.

CREATING CUSTOM BULLETS

If you want to use bullets that show more creativity than the basic square or circle, or if you need added linking functionality, you can create your own custom-made bullets. Custom-made bullets can be ornamental, where their sole purpose is to decorate the beginning of a list item. Or they can be functional, where they serve as icons that link you to another page or site.

If you plan to make your own artwork or use clip art for buttons, you'll need to use different HTML tags to make the art behave as you want. For visual enhancement only, use the **IMG** tag to include image-based bullets at the front of a list, as shown in the following code example. You won't use the **OL** or the **UL** tags because the image itself is what is creating both the bullet and the indent. Note that you do have to put a **BR** tag at the end of each list item to tell the browser to jump to a new line for the next entry in the list. This wasn't necessary when working with the HTML tags because it's a built-in part of the list functionality. I've also used an alignment tag (see Chapter 21, *"Alignment & Tables"*) to flow the type properly next to the artwork. Here's the code:

html syntax

```
<IMG SRC="rarrow.gif"
ALIGN="middle"> Important Item One<BR>
<IMG SRC="rarrow.gif"
ALIGN="middle"> Important Item Two<BR>
<IMG SRC="rarrow.gif"
ALIGN="middle"> Important Item Three<BR>
<IMG SRC="rarrow.gif">
```

xhtml syntax

```
<img src="rarrow.gif" align="middle"
alt="bullet" />Important Item One<br />
<img src="rarrow.gif" align="middle"
alt="bullet" />Important Item Two<br />
<img src="rarrow.gif" align="middle"
alt="bullet" />Important Item Three<br />
<img src="rarrow.gif" align="middle"
alt="bullet" />Important Item Four<br />
```

Here's a list that uses custom images for bullets.

- Important Item One
- Important Item Two
- Important Item Three
- Important Item Four

This example shows the result of using **IMG SRC** instead of HTML-generated bullets. The red arrow (`rarrow.gif`) is a separate piece of art that's been used multiple times on this page.

If you want to use the bullets as icons to link to another site or page, use the **<A HREF></A>** tag, as shown in the following code example. Because linked images typically have a blue border around them, you'll want to use the **BORDER="0"** tag inside the **IMG** tag. Note the hand-shaped cursor on the snake in the following image. Your viewer's cursor will change to this when gliding over a linked image to let the viewer know the image is a link.

html syntax

```
<A HREF><IMG SRC="lynda.gif"
ALIGN="middle" BORDER="0"></A> Lynda<BR>
<A HREF><IMG SRC="jamie.gif"
ALIGN="middle" BORDER="0"></A> Jamie<BR>
<A HREF><IMG SRC="stinky.gif"
ALIGN="middle" BORDER="0"></A>Stinky<BR>
<A HREF><IMG SRC="elmers.gif"
ALIGN="middle" BORDER="0"></A> Elmers<BR>
<A HREF><IMG SRC="jasonjr.gif"
ALIGN="middle" BORDER="0"></A> Jason Jr.<BR>
<A HREF><IMG SRC="climber.gif"
ALIGN="middle" BORDER="0"></A>Climber<BR>
<A HREF><IMG SRC="sam.gif"
ALIGN="middle" BORDER="0">
</A>Sam (whose tail is growing back)<BR>
```

xhtml syntax

```
<a href=""><img src="lynda.gif" align=
"middle" border="0" alt="Lynda" /></a>
Lynda<br />
<a href=""><img src="jamie.gif" align=
"middle" border="0" alt="Jamie" /></a>
Jamie<br />
<a href=""><img src="stinky.gif" align=
"middle" border="0" alt="Stinky" /></a>
Stinky<br />
<a href=""><img src="elmers.gif" align=
"middle" border="0" alt="Elmers" /></a>
Elmers<br />
<a href=""><img src="jasonjr.gif" align=
"middle" border="0" alt="Jason Jr." /></a>
Jason Jr.<br />
<a href=""><img src="climber.gif" align=
"middle" border="0" alt="Climber" /></a>
Climber<br />
<a href=""><img src="sam.gif" align=
"middle" border="0" alt="Sam" /></a>
Sam (whose tail is growing back)<br />
```

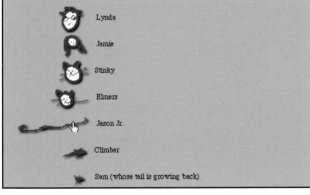

This example shows using **IMG SRC**, but changing the artwork inside each tag.

CREATING CUSTOM BULLET ART

Any paint program provides a good experimentation ground for making custom bullet artwork. There are no specific guidelines except to keep in mind the scale of the type the bullets will precede. It's very difficult to design anything with much detail that is small enough to match the scale of 12-point type, such as those typically generated by HTML. If you want to make larger icons for custom bullets, be sure to enlarge

the type in the list as well. More info on controlling type size is available in Chapter 20, "HTML Type."

The following bullet examples were created using the *Layer: Layer Style* menu and the *Layer Style* dialog box in Photoshop. By changing the Style, Direction, and other settings, you can see the possibilities for many variations on a theme.

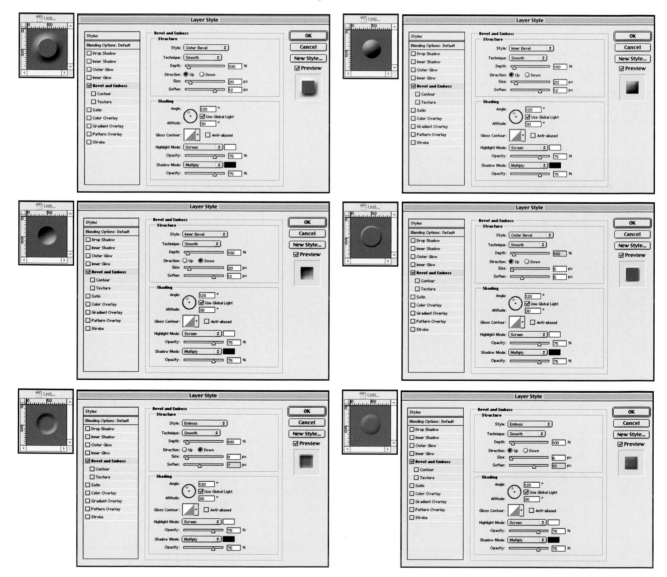

CLIP ART BULLETS

You'll find clip art for bullets all over the World Wide Web. Clip art bullets follow the same rules for custom bullet art; use the **IMG** element if you want the artwork for decoration only and the **<A HREF=""><IMG SRC="" BORDER="0"></A>** code if you want it to contain a link. Clip art typically already exists in web file formats GIF or JPEG, and if not, you can use Photoshop or other image editors to convert them.

Bullets can be abstract, such as dots and cubes, or they can be icons that actually mean something. **Michael Herrick**, of http://www.matterform.com, has invented something called **QBullets**, after "cue-bullet," or bullets that cue you to their hint or function. These buttons are part of a proposed interface standard that his site discusses in detail. I agree with the principle of his idea, but I prefer to let people explore their own artwork than rally around the standard of someone else's.

Basically, the idea is that QBullets act as visual metaphors to let your audience know the subject of your list. The email button is a miniature envelope, the download button looks like a floppy disk, a new item has the word "new item," and so on. Herrick's opinion is that bullets should inform your reader about what is at the other end of the link: large download, outside web site, FTP, telnet, form, and so on.

Here's a sample image and close-up that shows part of the Legend page from the **QBullet**s site. QBullets can be used free of charge in exchange for a credit and a link to Herrick's page (http://www.matterform.com).

RULES &
BULLETS

SUMMARY

As you can see from this chapter, there are many ways to design rules, bullets, and buttons on the Web. Techniques covered here included:

> There are many different settings in HTML/XHTML for customizing horizontal rules by adjusting the **SIZE** and **WIDTH** attributes.

> If you use a background tile on your web page and there is a horizontal rule, the tile will show through the emboss of the rule.

> You can use any kind of artwork for custom horizontal rules or bullets; just insert the artwork into your page using the **IMG** element.

> HTML/XHTML bulleted lists can include numbered, indented, or bullet symbols, depending on whether you use ordered lists, definition lists, or line item lists.

> Realize that if you do choose to use artwork instead of code, you could be compromising the structural markup of your document.

17

JavaScript: Rollovers & More

Introduction

If you've been surfing the Web for any length of time, I am sure you've encountered pages that contained JavaScript, even if you weren't aware of it. JavaScript comes in many forms; it can be used to perform a number of different tasks on a web page, such as rollovers, open new browser windows, and perform complex browser detection. A rollover is an image that changes to another image when the mouse is moved over it. This visual cue has been used so often that most web surfers are trained to look for rollovers to identify links on a web page. If rollovers are used effectively, they can enhance the user's experience and help establish a logical navigation system; if they are used gratuitously, they can ruin even the best-designed web pages.

Before I dive into the nooks and crannies of this chapter, let me first touch on the subject of JavaScript. JavaScript is a scripting language that extends the capabilities of HTML, enabling many features never before possible. There are many different programming languages to enhance HTML/XHTML, such as the widely used Perl, XML, VBScript, AppleScript, and/or Java. The absolute beauty of JavaScript, however, is that you can view, copy, and paste the source code to teach yourself how to use it, just like you can with HTML/XHTML. Not only that, but some popular HTML editors, and image editors, write JavaScript so that you don't have to know how to program the language yourself. Phew!

INTRODUCTION CONTINUED

This chapter focuses on how to use JavaScript for rollover buttons, browser detection, and window resizing. I am not a JavaScript programmer, so I will be highlighting many tools that allow the automatic generation of JavaScript. The emphasis here will be on the practical implementations of using JavaScript to enhance your web pages, not on teaching you the language. There are many fine resources for that, which will be noted throughout the chapter.

THE SHORT HISTORY OF JOVOSCRIPT

The term "JavaScript" has nothing to do with the popular programming language that Sun Micro-systems developed called Java. Originally, in fact, JavaScript was slated to be called "LiveScript." The name was changed for marketing reasons because it was believed at the time that anything with the word "Java" in it would be embraced by the web development community with ease. Ironically, Java's promise of cross-platform compatibility and widespread use for the Web has fallen flat, but JavaScript's promise of extended functionality to HTML/XHTML has far exceeded many people's expectations.

JavaScript, in its most simple sense, is a scripting language that can be used to extend and enhance HTML/XHTML. A simple comparison between HTML and JavaScript might deem HTML as the "static" medium and JavaScript as the "dynamic" medium. That's because JavaScript can do many things that HTML cannot, such as sequencing and moving images (animation), responding to interaction (multimedia), and triggering other extensions, such as ActiveX, Java, and plug-ins.

Unlike other popular programming languages, such as Perl, JavaScript is client-sided, which in this case means that JavaScript is built into the browser and

requires no additional compiling. In simple terms, this means that JavaScript can co-exist inside basic HTML/XHTML pages and can be studied, copied, and pasted just like HTML/XHTML. Other programming languages get "compiled," which is a post-processing technique that renders the code usable by computers. By the time you see the compiled code, you can no longer break it apart or deconstruct it. One of the great advantages to JavaScript is that browsers understand it without the need for this extra compiling step.

While it is possible to study, copy, and paste other people's JavaScript code into your own, it is widely accepted that you credit other people's JavaScripts if you use them. Comments are different in JavaScript than they are in standard HTML/XHTML because JavaScript comments are introduced with a pair of slashes (//). Everything following the pair of slashes to the end of the line is ignored by the browser, such as // **Bill Weinman's Common JavaScript Rollover Engine**. If the next line of code does not have the pair of slashes (//), it is no longer treated as a comment by the browser. If you copy someone's code and they have credited themselves or someone else, leave these comments intact.

LEARNING JAVASCRIPT

Like HTML/XHTML, many people wonder if they have to learn it. While I strongly urge you to learn the basics of HTML/XHTML, in this chapter I use Dreamweaver to write my JavaScript code. That's because I do not know how to write it from scratch.

Is it better to know how than not to? Probably! Those people who write their own JavaScript look at the code from WYSIWYG editors such as Dreamweaver and consider it to be "verbose." By that, I mean that it's longer than and not as streamlined as it could be. My feeling is, if it works and spares me the effort of learning a new language, I'm all for it. But I'm an artist, not a programmer! It's probably the equivalent of using "clip art" in graphics (which I would rarely consider doing!).

tip

JAVASCRIPT REFERENCES

Here are some of my favorite resources for learning JavaScript:

URLs
http://webdeveloper.earthweb.com/webjs
http://www.webreference.com/js
http://www.w3schools.com/js/

HTML & JavaScript for Visual Learners
Chris Charuhas
Visibooks, LLC
ISBN: 0970747926
$24.50

Designing with JavaScript
Nick Heinle
O'Reilly
ISBN: 156592360X
$34.95

ROLLOVERS

In my opinion, no other method is as successful for indicating that a graphic is linked than rollovers. Rollover is a term used for graphics that change when the mouse rolls over them—hence the word "rollover." They are also sometimes referred to as "mouseovers," which is a JavaScript syntax term, or "image swaps," which is the type of JavaScript event invoked for rollovers. For simplicity's sake (and who doesn't need more simplicity in their lives these days?), I'm gonna call 'em rollovers in this chapter.

Making the artwork for a rollover is a different process than coding it. Successful rollovers require two parts: the correct artwork and the correct code. I'm going to focus on a variety of tools and techniques for creating rollovers and code. First, let's look at making the artwork.

CREATING ROLLOVER ARTWORK

There are many types of rollovers, but I am going to identify four styles for the purposes of this chapter: replacement, pointing, multiple, and pop-up menus. **Replacement** is the simplest type of rollover, where the original artwork is replaced by new artwork when the mouse rolls over it. **Pointing** is the term I'll use for leaving the original artwork the same but making an additional piece of artwork appear to its side, such as a dot or an arrow. A **multiple** rollover is when the mouse rolls over one piece of artwork, triggering its replacement of new artwork and additional artwork somewhere else on the page. If this description is confusing, please see the images below.

Pop-up menus have to be one of the most requested techniques my students ask to be taught. Pop-up menus are similar to rollovers because the main image changes when you move the mouse over it. However,

pop-up menus will also reveal a submenu of images at the same time. As you can imagine, this can make working with large and complex navigations much easier and more presentable. Pop-up menus are also one of the most difficult things to create because of the complex code needed for them to work properly in multiple browsers. The good news is that Fireworks makes creating pop-up menus a cinch. You will learn about this feature later in this chapter.

When creating artwork for JavaScript-based rollover buttons, it's essential that the artwork is the same size, even when it appears different. For the examples below, the artwork on the following page was used. There are many software applications that will create images for rollovers. The following sections will cover ImageReady and Fireworks. Later, this chapter will cover how to create the JavaScript code using Dreamweaver.

Replacement: Where the rollover artwork is replaced with other artwork.

Pointing: Where another graphic (a dot) appears to follow your mouse.

Multiple: Upon the rollover, additional artwork appears somewhere else onscreen.

Replacement Example

The replacement example requires two pieces of artwork, identically sized.

When the mouse rolls over the word "rollover," this new artwork replaces it.

Pointing Example

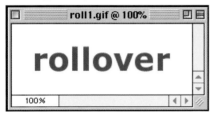

The pointing example require three pieces of art. First we have the the word "rollover."

Before the mouse rolls over the word, a second piece of art—a blank image (placeholder for red dot)—is showing. When the mouse rolls over the word *"rollover,"* the third piece of art—a red dot—appears and replaces the blank placeholder.

Multiple Example

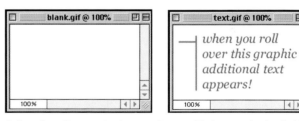

The multiple example requires four pieces of artwork. The word "rollover" in blue is what shows before the mouse rolls over it. When the mouse rolls over the word "rollover" in blue, it is replaced with the word "rollover" in green.

Before the rollover, a third piece of art—a blank image (a placeholder) is showing. When the mouse rolls over the word "rollover" in green, the fourth piece of art, the description text, appears and replaces the blank placeholder.

USING LAYERS FOR ROLLOVERS

Rollovers require a minimum of two different images: an image for the unclicked state and another for the clicked state. Many programs such as Photoshop, ImageReady, Fireworks, and PaintShop Pro use layers. The great thing about layers is that they easily allow you to create different versions of the same artwork and help you maintain registration between states of the rollover.

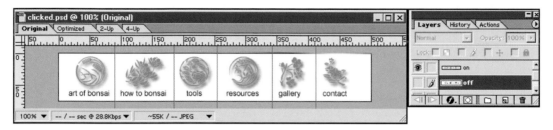

This example in Photoshop shows a single image with two layers. By clicking the eye icon in the left column of the Layers palette, you can pre-visualize the effect of the rollover.

CUTTING THE ROLLOVERS APART

Some programs have a rulers and guides feature that allows you to drag grid lines onto your screen for cutting apart images. This is useful for rollovers and other web graphics (such as cutting apart a large image to later rebuild inside an HTML table). Once you have set up rule lines, the selection tool will snap to the grid lines. These grids are very useful in helping you select the same size icon for both the on and off layers.

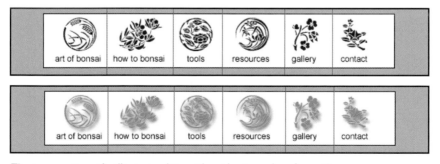

The two versions of rollover graphics with guides turned on for cutting purposes.

The image can be a GIF or a JPEG, depending on what source art you use for the rollover. A good rule of thumb is to name the files with a suffix of "on" or "off." For example, if you select the tools icon, name it **toolson.gif**. The rollover files you create can now be accessed by scripting languages or other authoring tools.

SLICING & OPTIMIZATION

Slicing allows you to create multiple graphics and ensure that different rollover graphics are the identical size. As well, slicing allows you to optimize graphics (using GIF or JPEG) depending on what compression type is best for your imagery. All of the graphic applications we've mentioned so far (ImageReady, PaintShop Pro, and Fireworks) actually do the slicing for you, as well as write the HTML code for the resulting table.

Using a slice tool, you can slice the image into sections to create the rollover and optimize each section differently.

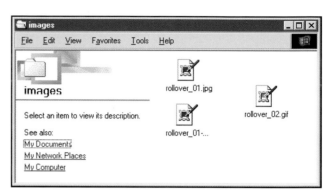

ImageReady (shown here), as well as all the other graphic applications I've mentioned, give you the option to save the HTML and images. The HTML file that is exported will contain all the necessary HTML and JavaScript for your rollover. Whatever name you assign the HTML file will be reflected in the resulting image filenames.

Inside the images folder, you can see the graphic files exported by ImageReady. The **rollover_01.jpg** and **rollover_01-over.jpg** were exported for the rollover, and the **rollover_02.gif** image was exported for the text.

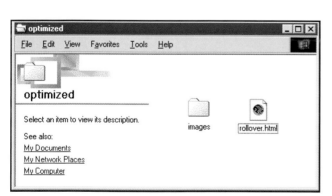

The graphics application wrote the HTML file and placed all the necessary graphics inside a folder called images. The HTML file can now be opened in an HTML editor, like GoLive or Dreamweaver, and can easily be inserted into a new or existing page.

This is the **rollover.html** file that ImageReady wrote automatically. Notice that it wrote all the necessary HTML and JavaScript and that you don't have to code a thing yourself. Life is sweet!

THE ROLE OF TABLES WITH ROLLOVERS

Fireworks, ImageReady, and PaintShop Pro not only write the JavaScript code and images for rollovers, but these programs also place images inside fixed tables to ensure precise alignment.

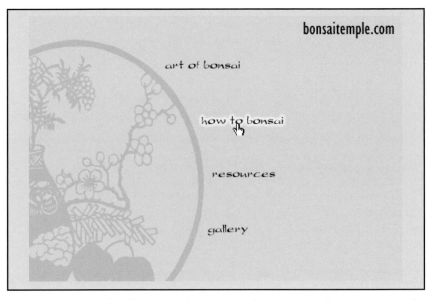

This example, created in Fireworks, shows that both static and rollover images can be generated within the same document.

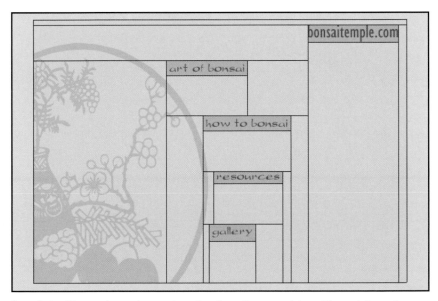

I used the Slice tool to select regions for the rollovers and logo. The red lines give you a preview of the HTML table that will be generated when this file is exported.

HTML EDITOR ROLLOVERS

As described earlier, you can use a graphics application such as ImageReady, Fireworks, or PaintShop Pro to create the artwork and HTML, and those tools will even write the JavaScript for your rollovers. This approach is really helpful when you are starting from scratch. However, there will come times when you already have artwork and all you need is the HTML and JavaScript. Have no fear—the WYSIWYG HTML editors, such as Dreamweaver and GoLive, make the process of creating rollovers a cinch.

REPLACEMENT ROLLOVERS

Replacement rollovers are by far the easiest kind of rollover to create in an HTML editor. The rollover code on the following page was generated by Dreamweaver. You don't have to know how to write this yourself when you use a tool like Dreamweaver or GoLive.

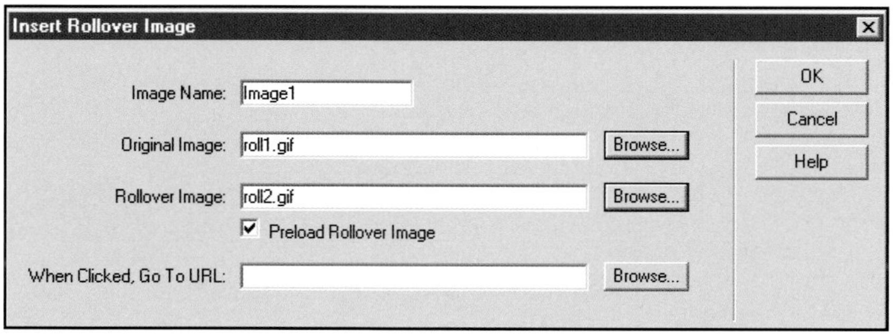

Most HTML editors (Dreamweaver MX is shown here) allow you to use a *Browse* button to locate the rollover artwork for the original *(up)* state and then browse for the rollover *(over)* state. Once you enter the artwork into a dialog box like this, the program will write the JavaScript for you.

replacement rollover code

```
<!DOCTYPE html PUBLIC "-//W3C//DTD HTML 4.01 Transitional//EN">
<html>
<head>
<title>Untitled Document</title>
<meta http-equiv="Content-Type" content="text/html; charset=iso-8859-1">
<script language="JavaScript" type="text/JavaScript">
<!--
function MM_preloadImages() { //v3.0
var d=document; if(d.images){ if(!d.MM_p) d.MM_p=new Array();
var i,j=d.MM_p.length,a=MM_preloadImages.arguments; for(i=0; i<a.length;
i++)
if (a[i].indexOf("#")!=0){ d.MM_p[j]=new Image; d.MM_p[j++].src=a[i];}}
}

function MM_swapImgRestore() { //v3.0
var i,x,a=document.MM_sr; for(i=0;a&&i<a.length&&(x=a[i])&&x.oSrc;i++)
x.src=x.oSrc;
}

function MM_findObj(n, d) { //v4.01
var p,i,x; if(!d) d=document; if((p=n.indexOf("?"))>0&&parent.frames.length)
{
d=parent.frames[n.substring(p+1)].document; n=n.substring(0,p);}
if(!(x=d[n])&&d.all) x=d.all[n]; for (i=0;!x&&i<d.forms.length;i++)
x=d.forms[i][n];
for(i=0;!x&&d.layers&&i<d.layers.length;i++)
x=MM_findObj(n,d.layers[i].document);
if(!x && d.getElementById) x=d.getElementById(n); return x;
}

function MM_swapImage() { //v3.0
var i,j=0,x,a=MM_swapImage.arguments; document.MM_sr=new Array;
for(i=0;i<(a.length-2);i+=3)
if ((x=MM_findObj(a[i]))!=null){document.MM_sr[j++]=x; if(!x.oSrc)
x.oSrc=x.src; x.src=a[i+2];}
}
//-->
</script>
</head>

<body onLoad="MM_preloadImages('on.gif')">
<a href="javascript:;" onMouseOver="MM_swapImage('roll1','','on.gif',1)"
onMouseOut="MM_swapImgRestore()"><img src="off.gif" name="roll1" width="36"
height="16" border="0" id="roll1"></a>
</body>
</html>
```

THE POINTING ROLLOVER

The pointing rollover is more complex than simply switching out two pieces of art, like the first replacement example. In the example below, I created the following artwork in Fireworks. The rollover code on the following page was generated by Dreamweaver.

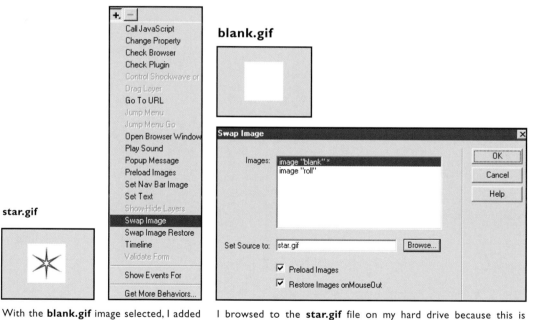

roll.gif

I created a *two*-column, *one*-row table and assigned it to have a *0* Border so the borders wouldn't show. Next, I inserted the artwork **blank.gif** into the *left* cell and **roll.gif** into the right cell.

blank.gif

star.gif

With the **blank.gif** image selected, I added the Behavior Swap Image by clicking on the *plus sign* inside the Behaviors palette and then choosing *Swap Image*.

I browsed to the **star.gif** file on my hard drive because this is the file I wanted to replace the **blank.gif**. Once I clicked *OK*, Dreamweaver wrote all the necessary code.

pointing rollover code

```html
<!DOCTYPE html PUBLIC "-//W3C//DTD HTML 4.01 Transitional//EN">
<html>
<head>
<title>Untitled Document</title>
<meta http-equiv="Content-Type" content="text/html; charset=iso-8859-1">
<script language="JavaScript" type="text/JavaScript">
<!--
function MM_preloadImages() { //v3.0
var d=document; if(d.images){ if(!d.MM_p) d.MM_p=new Array();
var i,j=d.MM_p.length,a=MM_preloadImages.arguments; for(i=0; i<a.length; i++)
if (a[i].indexOf("#")!=0){ d.MM_p[j]=new Image; d.MM_p[j++].src=a[i];}}
}

function MM_swapImgRestore() { //v3.0
var i,x,a=document.MM_sr; for(i=0;a&&i<a.length&&(x=a[i])&&x.oSrc;i++)
x.src=x.oSrc;
}

function MM_findObj(n, d) { //v4.01
var p,i,x; if(!d) d=document; if((p=n.indexOf("?"))>0&&parent.frames.length)
{
d=parent.frames[n.substring(p+1)].document; n=n.substring(0,p);}
if(!(x=d[n])&&d.all) x=d.all[n]; for (i=0;!x&&i<d.forms.length;i++)
x=d.forms[i][n];
for(i=0;!x&&d.layers&&i<d.layers.length;i++)
x=MM_findObj(n,d.layers[i].document);
if(!x && d.getElementById) x=d.getElementById(n); return x;
}

function MM_swapImage() { //v3.0
var i,j=0,x,a=MM_swapImage.arguments; document.MM_sr=new Array;
for(i=0;i<(a.length-2);i+=3)
if ((x=MM_findObj(a[i]))!=null){document.MM_sr[j++]=x; if(!x.oSrc)
x.oSrc=x.src;
x.src=a[i+2];}
}
//-->
</script>
</head>

<body onLoad="MM_preloadImages('star.gif')">
<table width="200" border="0">
<tr>
<td><img src="blank.gif" name="blank" width="36" height="16" id="blank"></td>
<td><a href="javascript:;"
onMouseOver="MM_swapImage('blank','','star.gif',1)"
onMouseOut="MM_swapImgRestore()"><img src="roll.gif" name="roll" width="36"
height="16" border="0" id="roll"></a></td>
</tr>
</table>
</body>
</html>
```

THE MULTIPLE ROLLOVER

Programming the multiple rollover took a bit more work than the other two examples. It's helpful to once again see the different pieces of art involved, and their names, so you can reference what was done. The rollover code that follows was generated by Dreamweaver.

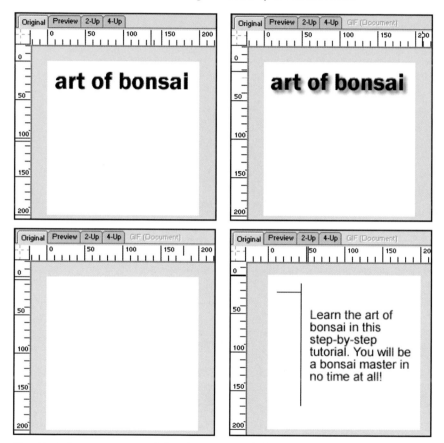

The blank image was created for the *up* state (before the rollover occurs), and the description text on the right was created to show once the rollover was triggered. Note that these graphics are different, but the dimensions of them are identical. It is critical that the size of your rollover graphics be the size dimensions in all the variations, regardless of whether they contain images or not.

Next, I created a table using *two columns* and *one row*, with borders set to *0*.

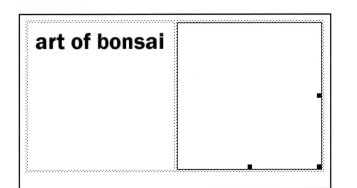

I inserted the **startroll** image into the first table cell and the blank image into the next.

I named the rollover image by selecting it and entering the name **roll** into the Property Inspector panel. I named the blank image **blank** by highlighting it and entering it also. I selected **startroll.gif** and clicked on the *Behaviors* button to launch the Behaviors panel. I chose to make this *4.0 browser compatible* and clicked on the *plus sign* to select *Swap Image*.

I selected the image **roll** and browsed to find the replacement artwork **endroll.gif**. Next, I selected the image **blank** and browsed to select the file called **text.gif**.

multiple rollover code

```
<!DOCTYPE html PUBLIC "-//W3C//DTD HTML 4.01 Transitional//EN">
<html>
<head>
<title>Untitled Document</title>
<meta http-equiv="Content-Type" content="text/html; charset=iso-8859-1">
<script language="JavaScript" type="text/JavaScript">
<!--
function MM_preloadImages() { //v3.0
var d=document; if(d.images){ if(!d.MM_p) d.MM_p=new Array();
var i,j=d.MM_p.length,a=MM_preloadImages.arguments; for(i=0; i<a.length; i++)
if (a[i].indexOf("#")!=0){ d.MM_p[j]=new Image; d.MM_p[j++].src=a[i];}}
}

function MM_swapImgRestore() { //v3.0
var i,x,a=document.MM_sr; for(i=0;a&&i<a.length&&(x=a[i])&&x.oSrc;i++)
x.src=x.oSrc;
}

function MM_findObj(n, d) { //v4.01
var p,i,x; if(!d) d=document; if((p=n.indexOf("?"))>0&&parent.frames.length)
{
d=parent.frames[n.substring(p+1)].document; n=n.substring(0,p);}
if(!(x=d[n])&&d.all) x=d.all[n]; for (i=0;!x&&i<d.forms.length;i++)
x=d.forms[i][n];
for(i=0;!x&&d.layers&&i<d.layers.length;i++)
x=MM_findObj(n,d.layers[i].document);
if(!x && d.getElementById) x=d.getElementById(n); return x;
}

function MM_swapImage() { //v3.0
var i,j=0,x,a=MM_swapImage.arguments; document.MM_sr=new Array;
for(i=0;i<(a.length-2);i+=3)
if ((x=MM_findObj(a[i]))!=null){document.MM_sr[j++]=x; if(!x.oSrc)
x.oSrc=x.src;
x.src=a[i+2];}
}
//-->
</script>
</head>

<body onLoad="MM_preloadImages('endroll.gif','text.gif')">
<table width="200" border="0">
<tr>
<td><a href="javascript:;"
onMouseOver="MM_swapImage('startroll','','endroll.gif','blank','','text.gif',
1)"
onMouseOut="MM_swapImgRestore()"><img src="startroll.gif" name="startroll"
width="36" height="16" border="0" id="startroll"></a></td>
<td><img src="blank.gif" name="blank" width="36" height="16" id="blank"></td>
</tr>
</table>
</body>
</html>
```

POP-UP MENUS IN FIREWORKS

One of the most remarkable features in Fireworks MX is the Insert Popup Menu feature. With just a few clicks, you can create a complex navigation system that would have otherwise taken an extensive knowledge of JavaScript to create, not to mention countless hours of testing. A pop-up menu is similar to a rollover with the exception that a pop-up menu has a submenu of options when you roll over it. The submenu can contain rollovers as well.

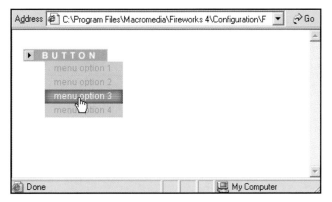

This is an example of a pop-up menu, created using Fireworks MX.

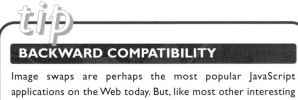

BACKWARD COMPATIBILITY

Image swaps are perhaps the most popular JavaScript applications on the Web today. But, like most other interesting scripts, image swaps aren't possible in older browsers and attempts to use them can produce JavaScript errors.

Using Dreamweaver or GoLive to create image-swapping rollovers will ensure compatibility with older browsers because you are given a choice whether to target 4.0 or lower browsers. If you're going to write the rollover script yourself, however, you will need to test it in older browsers to see if your code works.

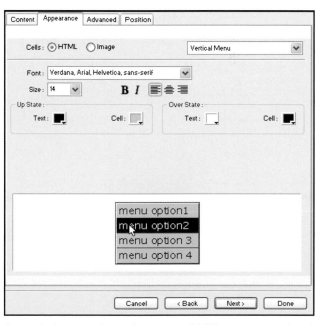

Fireworks provides you with a sort of pop-up menu wizard that will walk you through the process of creating the pop-up menu. This is a very cool feature!

Fireworks lets you choose between an HTML- or an image-based pop-up menu.

BROWSER DETECTION

There are times when you might want to serve two different pages to your audience, and Dreamweaver and GoLive have built-in JavaScript scripts to help you detect which browser is viewing your page. The giant caveat to this is that in order for this method to work successfully, your end user must have a Java-enabled browser. Some people have older browsers (before 3.0) or have turned JavaScript off in their browser preferences. Even though this method works, it is not foolproof because of JavaScript being turned off.

Here's the code that Dreamweaver writes. GoLive writes an automatic browser detection script as well.

code

```
<!DOCTYPE html PUBLIC "-//W3C//DTD HTML 4.01 Transitional//EN">
<html>
<head>
<title>Untitled Document</title>
<meta http-equiv="Content-Type" content="text/html; charset=iso-8859-1">
<script language="JavaScript" type="text/JavaScript">
<!--
function
MM_checkBrowser
(NSvers,NSpass,NSnoPass,IEvers,IEpass,IEnoPass,OBpass,URL,altURL)
{ //v4.0
var newURL='', verStr=navigator.appVersion, app=navigator.appName,
version =
parseFloat(verStr);
if (app.indexOf('Netscape') != -1) {
if (version >= NSvers) {if (NSpass>0) newURL=(NSpass==1)?URL:altURL;}
else {if (NSnoPass>0) newURL=(NSnoPass==1)?URL:altURL;}
} else if (app.indexOf('Microsoft') != -1) {
if (version >= IEvers || verStr.indexOf(IEvers) != -1)
{if (IEpass>0) newURL=(IEpass==1)?URL:altURL;}
else {if (IEnoPass>0) newURL=(IEnoPass==1)?URL:altURL;}
} else if (OBpass>0) newURL=(OBpass==1)?URL:altURL;
if (newURL) { window.location=unescape(newURL);
document.MM_returnValue=false;
}
}
//-->
</script>
</head>

<body
onLoad=
"MM_checkBrowser(4.0,1,2,4.0,1,2,2,'version4.htm','version3.htm')
;return
document.MM_returnValue">
</body>
</html>
```

LAUNCHING ANOTHER WINDOW

You might have come to some sites that trigger a smaller browser window with no controls on the top. This is done using JavaScript. I'm not sure I personally like this trend, since I prefer the comfort of seeing a Back button and familiar navigation symbols, but if it's something you want to do, it's easy using Dreamweaver or GoLive.

Open a document that contains a link that you want to open a new browser window. Select the *link* and access the Behaviors panel (in Dreamweaver) or the Actions interface (in GoLive). These interfaces offer ready-made scripts that will launch a new browser window from clicking the link you selected.

Open Browser Window ✕

URL to Display: policy.html   Browse...   OK

Window Width: 350   Window Height: 400   Cancel

Attributes: ☐ Navigation Toolbar   ☐ Menu Bar   Help

☐ Location Toolbar   ☐ Scrollbars as Needed

☐ Status Bar   ☐ Resize Handles

Window Name:

This is the interface in Dreamweaver MX that lets you launch another window. The URL field is where you can type an address to an external web site or use the Browse button to locate a page on your hard drive. Whichever attributes you select will appear when the new browser window is opened. If you want to have a navigation toolbar, for example, you could check that checkbox and Dreamweaver would write the code to leave that in.

code

```
<html>
<head>
<title>new browser window</title>
<meta http-equiv="Content-Type" content="text/html; charset=iso-8859-1">
<script language="JavaScript">
<!--
function MM_openBrWindow(theURL,winName,features) { //v2.0
  window.open(theURL,winName,features);
}
//-->
</script>
</head>

<body bgcolor="#CCCC99" background="images/reserve_bg.gif"
text="#000033" link="#333300" vlink="#666600">
<table width="550" border="0" height="348">
  <tr>
    <td colspan="2" width="588">
<img src="images/reservetitle.gif" width="200" height="50"></td>
  </tr>
  <tr valign="top">
    <td height="36" colspan="2" width="588">
<font face="Verdana, Arial, Helvetica, sans-serif" size="2">
You may make a reservation by telephone at (805) 646-6635 or complete the
form below, and we will contact you within 24 hours with a confirmation.
Please review our
<a href="#"
onClick="MM_openBrWindow('policy.html','','width=350,height=400')">
reservation policy and information</a>.</font></td>
  </tr>
```

actual code continues (not shown)

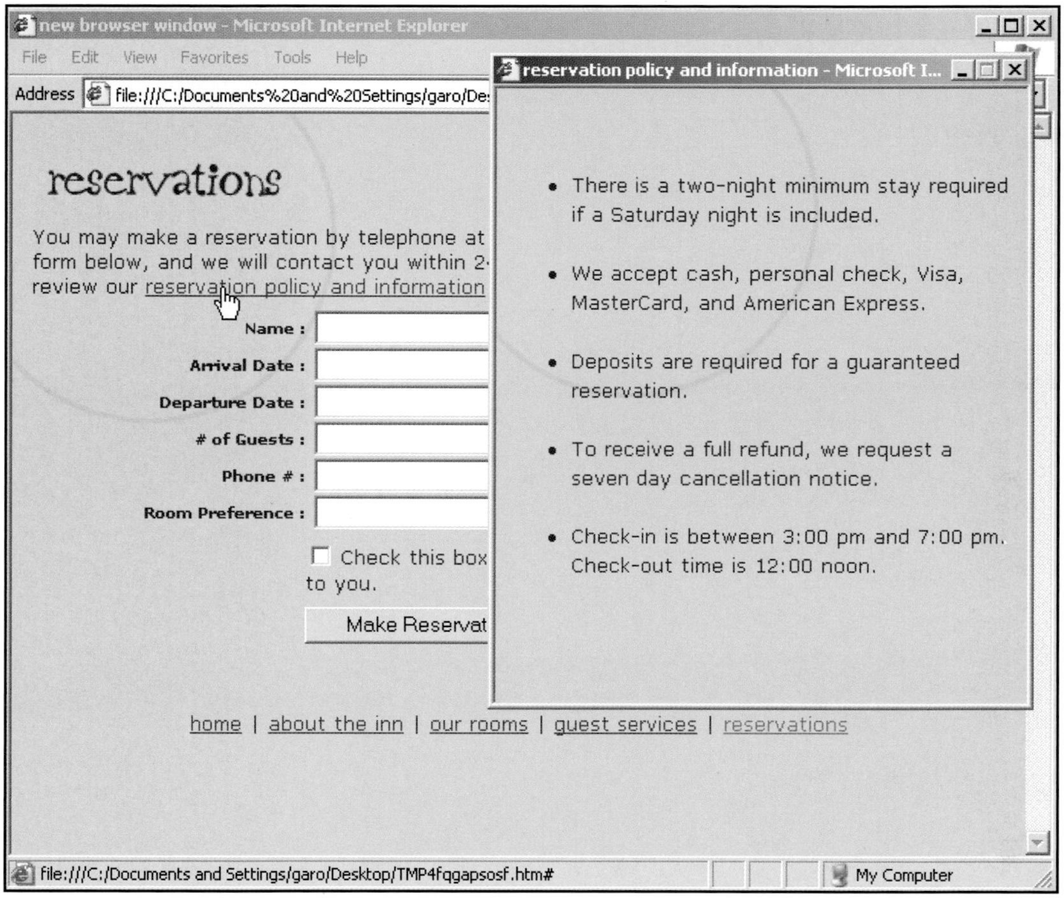

Here's the little browser window it launched for me.

JavaScript: Rollovers & More

summary

JavaScript is useful for extending the capabilities of HTML. This chapter focused on three things that JavaScript makes possible: rollovers, browser detection, and launching presized browser windows. Here's a brief recap of the key issues:

> Rollover graphics are great devices for indicating that a graphic is linked. It is necessary to make correct artwork and code for rollovers to work.

> Whenever you make artwork for rollover graphics, it's important to remember that the on and off states must be exactly the same dimensions; otherwise, registration will be problematic.

> Making complex rollovers involves giving your artwork a name that JavaScript can reference. You can trigger multiple events with a rollover by using the Name attribute.

> Many JavaScript functions are available in tools like Dreamweaver and GoLive. This makes it possible to add features such as predetermined sized browser windows and browser detection without having to write the JavaScript code yourself.

Imagemaps

INTRODUCTION

The graphics we've discussed so far in this book have been of two varieties: linked or static. An imagemap (also called a hotspot) is a linked graphic that contains multiple links instead of one. There are two kinds of imagemaps: client-side and server-side. Both types of imagemaps are defined by coordinates that define the area of the image that will be clickable. For a client-side imagemap, the coordinates are contained inside the HTML document. For a server-side imagemap, the coordinates are stored in a separate file on a server.

You will often see a list of underlined text links on a page. This is simply a list of multiple URLs assigned to multiple text objects. Instead of using multiple text links, however, the designer could have attached the list of URLs to a single image by creating an imagemap.

An imagemap is a method for creating multiple links from a single graphic. It takes a bit longer to download than normal text links because of the added time required to download the graphic file. Most of the time, it's worth the wait because imagemaps are a more convenient and visual way to present multiple links to your audience. They can also be a great way to save space on a page.

This chapter covers a variety of methods for making imagemaps, assigning the map coordinates, and including the coordinates in your HTML.

SERVER-SIDE Imagemaps

To be truthful, very few web developers program server-side imagemaps any longer. For this reason, authoring techniques for this type of imagemap are not covered in this chapter.

Server-side imagemaps are no longer used because they require extra scripting, and the coordinate information must reside on the server instead of inside the document. This can add extra bandwidth demand to a server if you have a lot of users accessing the imagemap at the same time.

As well, server-side imagemaps do not offer accessibility to people who access the Web via search engines or screen readers. You'll learn more about accessibility in Chapter 8, *"Accessibility Issues."* If you do want to learn how to program a server-side imagemap, you can visit http://hoohoo. ncsa.uiuc.edu/docs/tutorials/imagemapping.html.

CLIENT-SIDE Imagemaps

Client-side imagemaps are the most common type of imagemaps used today. Server-sides are used less frequently, and are frowned upon by the accessibility and web standards communities. An added bonus for client-side imagemaps is that they are easier to make than server-side maps, and they are also easier for the browser to execute. Anytime you hear the term "client-side," it means that the information is contained within your code and the browser does not have to access the server to deliver the file to the end user. This puts much less stress on the server, which means your client-side imagemap will be more responsive and faster to download.

In general, it's more complicated to create an imagemap than it is to code single linked images using the **<A HREF><IMG SRC></A>** method. Imagemaps are complicated on a number of fronts. You must determine and document each region's coordinates in pixels. The regions have to be put into a document in a specific manner, and if a comma, space, or coordinate is wrong, the map won't work properly. On the following page is the code for a client-side imagemap.

```
<HTML>
<HEAD>
<TITLE>client-side imagemaps</TITLE>
<META HTTP-EQUIV="Content-Type" CONTENT="text/html; charset=iso-8859-1">
</HEAD>
<BODY BGCOLOR=#FFFFFF>
<IMG SRC="navbar1.png" WIDTH="378" HEIGHT="36" BORDER="0" USEMAP="#navbar1_Map">
<MAP NAME="navbar1_Map">
<AREA SHAPE="rect" ALT="" COORDS="250,4,372,31" HREF="products.htm">
<AREA SHAPE="rect" ALT="" COORDS="127,4,248,32" HREF="about.htm">
<AREA SHAPE="rect" ALT="" COORDS="4,4,126,32" HREF="home.htm">
</MAP>
</BODY>
</HTML>
```

Client-side imagemap data is always located inside your HTML. You can tell that this code is for a client-side imagemap because it uses the attribute **USEMAP**. The numbers separated by commas indicate coordinates that define the regions of the imagemap.

```
<HTML>
<HEAD>
<TITLE>server-side imagemap</TITLE>
<META HTTP-EQUIV="Content-Type" CONTENT="text/html; charset=iso-8859-1">
</HEAD>
<BODY BGCOLOR=#FFFFFF>
<A HREF="navbar1.map">
  <IMG SRC="navbar1.png" WIDTH="378" HEIGHT="36" BORDER="0" ISMAP></A>
</BODY>
</HTML>
```

Notice that there aren't any coordinates in this HTML. Server-side map coordinates are stored in a map definition file, not in the HTML. Note the **ISMAP** attribute; it signifies a server-side imagemap, whereas **USEMAP** signifies a client-side imagemap. In this example, the file **navbar1.map** is the definition file, and the file **navbar1.png** is the image.

http://www.cgibook.com/links.html

Here's an example of the left hand side of a client-side imagemap reading on the bottom navigation bar of Netscape.

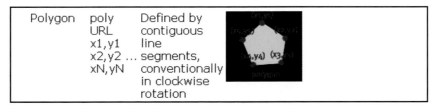

| Polygon | poly
URL
x1,y1
x2,y2 ...
xN,yN | Defined by
contiguous
line
segments,
conventionally
in clockwise
rotation | |

This graphic shows the coordinate locations on this example of a polygon. This image is taken from **WebMonkey's** excellent article about imagemaps, written by Patrick Corcoran, which you can read at http://hotwired.lycos.com/webmonkey/96/39/index2a.html.

CLIENT-SIDE IMAGEMAP CODE

Creating client-side imagemaps (and server-side imagemaps) involves documenting the regions of the map and creating a list of coordinates. This type of code is typically created in either an imaging program or an HTML editor. Later in this chapter, you'll learn about creating imagemaps with Fireworks and ImageReady. For the moment, it's first useful to understand the code that is required for an imagemap. In this client-side imagemap example, the coordinates are stored in the HTML, which is not the case in a server-side imagemap file.

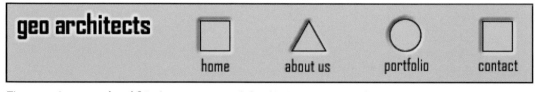

The artwork **geoarch.gif** is the source artwork for this imagemap example.

code

```
I   <img src="geoarch.gif"
    width="500" height="75" border="0"
2   usemap="#geoarch_Map"
3   alt="navbar">
4   <map name="geoarch_Map">
5   <area shape="rect"
    alt="" coords="445,11,489,65"
    href="contact.htm">
    <area shape="circle"
    alt="" coords="380,37,26"
    href="portfolio.htm">
6   <area shape="poly" alt=""
    coords="257,63, 286,10, 316,64"
    href="about.htm">
7   <area shape="rect"
    alt="" coords="180,10,216,66"
    href="home.htm">
8   </map>
```

code deconstruction

I   **IMG** defines the artwork for the imagemap.

2   The **usemap="#geoarch_Map"** indicates that the map name **_geoarch** is being used.

3   **ALT** is the **ALT** attribute for the imagemap image (**geoarch.gif**). If users have their images turned off, they won't be able to see the imagemap, but they will be warned it's there!

4   The **MAP NAME** is first requested in the **USEMAP** attribute, but it is defined here in the **MAP NAME** element. It's a good idea to use a file name that corresponds to your image. In this example, the image **geoarch.gif** uses the map name **geoarch_Map**.

5   **AREA SHAPE** describes which shape is being used by the imagemap. In this example, it is a rectangle. The **COORDS** show how the polygon is defined, starting from the top-left coordinate.

6   Notice that this **AREA SHAPE** is a **"poly"**.

7   This **AREA SHAPE** is a **"rect"**.

8   As is true of many HTML elements, the closing tag is required for **MAP**.

imagemaps & XHTML

The syntax for creating XHTML imagemaps is almost identical to the HTML syntax. In XHTML, you must properly close the area tag with a trailing slash. In addition, you will notice that **id="geoarch_Map"** has been added as part of the **<map>** tag. This is what the XHTML code for a client-side imagemap would look like:

code

```
       <?xml version"1.0"?>
       <!DOCTYPE html PUBLIC
       "-//W3C//DTD XHTML 1.0 Transitional//EN"
       "http://www.w3.org/TR/xhtml1/DTD/xhtml1-transitional.dtd">
       <html xmlns="http://www.w3.org/1999/xhtml">
       <head>
       <title>geoarch</title>
   I   <meta http-equiv="Content-Type" content="text/html;
       charset=iso-8859-1" />
       </head>
       <body bgcolor="#FFFFFF">
   2   <img src="geoarch.gif" width="500" height="75"
       border="0" usemap="#geoarch_Map" alt="navbar" />
   3   <map id="geoarch_Map" name="geoarch_Map">
   4   <area shape="rect" alt="" coords="445,11,489,65"
       href="contact.htm" />
       <area shape="circle" alt="" coords="380,37,26"
       href="portfolio.htm" />
       <area shape="poly" alt="" coords="257,63, 286,10, 316,64"
       href="about.htm" />
       <area shape="rect" alt="" coords="180,10,216,66"
       href="home.htm" />
       </map>
       </body>
       </html>
```

code deconstruction

I   Notice the inclusion of a trailing slash here. This is part of the XML syntax guidelines and is a requirement of XHTML.

2   Note that the **usemap** attribute is present. This indicates the beginning of a client-side imagemap. The **alt** attribute text will be displayed if users are viewing the pages with images turned off.

3   Notice the addition of the **id="geoarch_Map"** to the **<map>** tag. The "**id**" attribute is an XHTML attribute used to name elements.

4   Notice the trailing slash at the end of each "**area**" tag. This is a syntax requirement for XHTML.

importance of the alt attribute

The **ALT** attribute provides alternative information to images that can be read by text-based browsers. Some users might visit your site using browser software that does not recognize imagemaps, or maybe they've turned off their images because they're in a hurry or because they have a disability and can't see them. Adding one simple **ALT** attribute to your HTML can accommodate all these situations. Here's where the attribute would be included:

code

```
<a href="http://www.geoarch.com/cgi-bin/geoarch.map">
<img src="inavbar.gif" alt="navigation bar"
border="0" ismap>
```

importance of width & height attributes

By adding **WIDTH** and **HEIGHT** attributes to image tags within HTML and XHTML, you give the browser information about the size of your graphic. This is good for a couple of reasons. First of all, the browser doesn't have to calculate the image size because you've supplied it with the information, which saves time. It also allows the text to load before the images, which can be a good thing with large images—audiences have something to look at while they're waiting! So then, here's the way to implement the **WIDTH** and **HEIGHT** attributes:

code

```
   <a href="http://www.geoarch.com/cgi-bin/geoarch.map">
   <img src="inavbar.gif"
I  width="500" height="75"
   alt="navigation bar"
   border="0"
   ismap>
```

code deconstruction

I   The values you put inside the **WIDTH** and **HEIGHT** attributes reflect how large the image is, in pixels. You can even resize an image if you enter values that are larger or smaller than the image! Basically, the browser uses your information for the image size instead of looking to the image itself for size information.

do you really need an imagemap?

It's always important to carefully analyze whether you really need an imagemap or whether there's some other way to accomplish the same goal. For example, if your image is composed of rectangles or can be seamed together by using rectangular shapes (for more on transparent irregular shapes, see Chapters 16, *"Transparent GIFs,"* and 21, *"Alignment & Tables"*), it might be easier for you to load multiple single graphics with independent links than to load one graphic with multiple links.

You will see examples of imagemaps used all over the Web on opening menu screens. Sometimes an imagemap is used even when the menu bar is composed of rectangular shapes. Some sites do this because the one image loads faster than multiple images would. This is a valid reason to use an imagemap, but even so, the difficulty of creating and maintaining one—links do change, ya know!—might outweigh the performance increase.

If you have images, such as those shown at http://www.donbarnett.com/tiles which don't have obvious rectangular regions that you can cut apart as individual images, an imagemap is your only choice.

IMAGEMAPS USING IMAGE EDITORS

I think it's great to use an image editor for creating imagemaps. That's probably because I am an artist—not a coder—by nature. What's nice is that you can create the imagemap from an imaging program, and you never have to write a line of code! The first step, of course, is to create the artwork. The examples below were done in Fireworks MX.

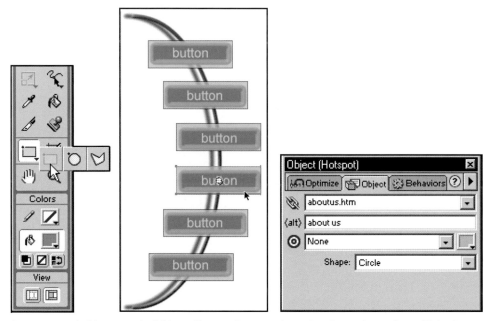

Imagemap tools (shown to the left) usually come in rectangle, oval, or free polygon shapes. To begin, use the tools to select a *shape* and define each imagemap area. Next, select the individual hotspot area (shown in the middle) and specify the **URL** and **ALT** information in the imagemap regions area (shown to the right).

```
     Title: fw_navbar
 1 <html>
 2 <head>
 3 <title>fw_navbar</title>
 4 <meta http-equiv="Content-Type" content="text/html;">
 5 <!-- Fireworks 4.0  Dreamweaver 4.0 target.  Created Thu Sep 27 13:11:48
   GMT-0700 (Pacific Daylight Time) 2001-->
 6 </head>
 7 <body bgcolor="#ffffff">
 8 <img name="fw_navbar" src="images/fw_navbar.gif" width="500" height="115"
   border="0" usemap="#m_fw_navbar"><!-- fwtable fwsrc="fw_navbar.png"
   fwbase="fw_navbar" fwstyle="Dreamweaver" fwdocid = "742308039" fwnested="0"
   -->
 9 <map name="m_fw_navbar">
10 <area shape="circle" coords="437,44, 34" href="contact.htm" title="contact
   us" alt="contact us" >
11 <area shape="circle" coords="349,46, 36" href="clients.htm" title="our
   clients" alt="our clients" >
12 <area shape="circle" coords="264,44, 36" href="portfolio.htm" title="our
   portfolio" alt="our portfolio" >
13 <area shape="circle" coords="170,44, 35" href="aboutus.htm" title="about us"
   alt="about us" >
14 </map>
15 </body>
16 </html>
17
```

Once you create all the shapes and define all your information, you export the graphic and HTML, and the image editor creates everything you need. You won't have to type a single line of code!

IMAGEMAP SOFTWARE TOOLS

MapEdit (Windows/PC/Mac/UNIX**)**
http://www.boutell.com/mapedit

CuteMap (Windows**)**
http://www.globalscape.com/products/cutemap/index.asp

Glenn Fleishman's
Server-Side to Client-Side Online Converter
http://www.popco.com/popco/convertmaps.html

OTHER IMAGEMAP RESOURCES

There are many software utilities available that write image-maps. Most HTML editors include imagemap functionality as well. Here's a short list of additional imagemap resources.

Tutorial URLs
http://hotwired.lycos.com/webmonkey/96/39/index2a.html
http://webdeveloper.internet.com/html/html_image_mapping.html
http://www.htmlgoodies.com/tutors/im.html

imagemaps

summary

Imagemaps enable you to assign multiple URLs to a single image. Making an imagemap is not terribly complicated, but here are some things to keep in mind:

> Before you begin, decide whether you need a client-side or server-side imagemap. Client-side imagemaps are much more widely supported and endorsed by accessibility and standards groups.

> To tell which type of imagemap someone's HTML code contains, just look for the **USEMAP** and **ISMAP** attributes. If you find **USEMAP**, you're looking at a client-side imagemap; if you find **ISMAP**, it's a server-side imagemap. If it contains both, you have both!

> Some graphics are well suited to be cut apart, but others require the use of imagemaps. It's important to assess whether an imagemap is the appropriate technique for the job at hand. Sometimes it's easier to create multiple images and link them individually than to create an imagemap.

19

HTML Type

INTRODUCTION

Written words are one of the most important communication vehicles of our culture. Type, therefore, is one feature that most web sites must have, yet the challenging issues surrounding web-based type are not obvious at first glance.

Many designers do not think of type as text; instead they use fonts and typefaces as devices and vehicles to communicate visually. Most of us look at type as an aesthetic medium and take for granted that type's purpose is also to represent text-based data. HTML-based text is used for search engines, data analysis, email transmissions, automated language translations, and text readers for the visually impaired. Unfortunately, the Web has many facets to it, and what is design to one person can easily become unusable to another.

Visual design is about control. Typography is an incredibly powerful visual design medium, but good typography requires much more control than HTML currently affords. HTML is about display flexibility and cross-platform distribution of information. The tension between these two contradictory missions is discussed throughout this book.

This chapter focuses on the HTML code used to create web type, and it examines HTML-based type. (A focus on the aesthetics of typography is located in Chapter 2, *"Web Aesthetics."* Information about CSS and its relation to typography can be found in Chapter 23, *"Cascading Style Sheets."*)

HTML-BASED TYPOGRAPHY

The advantages of using HTML for most body type is that the memory and download time required for using native text is much lower than that used for graphics. Many sites are text-intensive, and HTML-based type is the only choice for presenting large quantities of written information in a timely and efficient manner. As well, HTML-based type is searchable by search engines, which is important for getting your site listed and cross-referenced by other sites.

The controversy about HTML-based type is that with CSS, so many more typographic options are available. CSS, however, can't be used for all audiences. Nevertheless, the trend in web page design today is to not use the HTML code presented in this chapter, but instead to code your type using CSS, which you will learn about in Chapter 23, *"Cascading Style Sheets."*

The reality is that a lot of older sites formatted their type using HTML techniques, so you will be able to deconstruct those sites by reading this chapter. As well, even if you do format your type using CSS, you will still find that a lot of the methods used are borrowed from HTML, which you will learn about in this chapter. Therefore, it's important to have a foundation in HTML type before you move on to CSS-based type, which you will learn about in Chapter 23, *"Cascading Style Sheets."*

HTML-BASED TAGS

The following examples and code demonstrate how to use HTML type tags.

Headings

Headings are created using the **H** and /**H** tags. The tags always have to be in the **BODY** part of an HTML file.

> **Welcome to this Site!**
>
> **Welcome to this Site!**
>
> **Welcome to this Site!**

code

```
<html>
<body>
<h3>Welcome to this Site!</h3>
<h4>Welcome to this Site!</h4>
<h5>Welcome to this Site!</h5>
</body>
</html>
```

Blinking Text

Use with caution! Many find this tag annoying. This tag is not supported/rendered in some newer browsers (IE 5.0 or higher and Netscape 6.x or higher).

code

```
<blink>flash news!</blink>
```

Bold

> Talk **LOUD!**
>
> Talk **LOUD!**

code

```
<html>
<body>
<p>Talk
<b>LOUD!</b><br><br>
Talk
<strong>LOUD!</strong></p>
</body>
</html>
```

HTML FONT CHOICES

Italic

Are you *ever going to shut up?*

Are you *ever going to shut up?*

code
```
<html>
<body>
<p>Are you <i>ever going to shut up?</i></p>
<p>Are you <em>ever going to shut up?</em></p>
</body>
</html>
```

Preformatted

PRE tag text shows up in Courier or monospace type.

```
When are you   g   o   i   n   g   to be QUIET?
```

code
```
<html>
<body>
<pre> When are you     g     o     i     n     g     to
be QUIET?</pre>
</body>
</html>
```

Changing Font Sizes

Use the **FONT** tag and **SIZE** attribute to change size.

Do you ever **listen** to direction anymore?

code
```
<html>
<body>
Do you ever <font size="5">listen</font> to
direction anymore?
</body>
</html>
```

Centering Text

You center text by using the **CENTER** tag.

I'm in the middle...

code
```
<html>
<body>
<center>
I'm in the middle...
</center>
</body>
</html>
```

Chances are, the person looking at your web page is using the default settings for whatever browser he or she is viewing the page from. Most browsers use a Times Roman font by default. I've seen sites that include instructions to the viewer to change the default font to some other typeface. Good luck! I know very few web visitors who would take the time to change their settings to see one single page. If you want your HTML type to be something other than Times Roman, don't count on asking your viewer to change his or her web browser settings as a foolproof method. In fact, I imagine an extremely low percentage of viewers would actually act on the suggestion.

The **FONT TAG** is used to describe attributes of text, such as the typeface, size, color, and justification. If you do specify a **FONT FACE**, request a font that is most likely to be found on the majority of end-users' machines. A list of common fonts is in Chapter 2, *"Web Aesthetics."*

note

THE FONT TAG IS DEPRECATED

Most HTML typographic control is based on the **FONT** tag. The **FONT** tag has been deprecated from HTML and XHTML. This doesn't mean that you can't use it in transitional HTML 4 and XHTML 1—you can do so and still have valid documents that conform to standards. Deprecation means that a better technology is available to address the concern, and it is preferable to use that technology. That technology is, of course, CSS. You'll learn how to work with CSS in Chapter 23, *"Cascading Style Sheets."*

FACE ATTRIBUTE OF THE FONT TAG

The **FONT** element enables you to specify which font your page will be displayed in. The main caveat about using this is that your end user must have the font you request installed, or the tag will not work.

Here is code using the **FACE** attribute of the **FONT** tag.

code

```
<html>
<body>
<font face="helvetica, arial"> TESTING,
</font> one, two, three.
</body>
</html>
```

TESTING, one, two, three.

To add size variation, add the **SIZE** attribute to the tag.

code

```
<html>
<body>
<font face="helvetica, arial" size="5">
TESTING,
</font> one, two, three.
</body>
</html>
```

TESTING, one, two, three.

To change the color, add the **COLOR** attribute to the tag.

code

```
<html>
<body>
<font face="helvetica, arial" size="5"
color="#CC3366">TESTING,
</font> one, two, three.
</body>
</html>
```

TESTING, one, two, three.

HTML FOR TEXT GRAPHICS

The most basic way to insert a graphic on a page is to use the **IMG** tag.

Here's how to insert the drop shadow artwork, (created earlier), on a page.

code

```
<html>
<body>
<img src="dropshad.jpg">
</body>
</html>
```

If you want to link the drop shadow image to another source, combine the **IMG** tag with an **<A HREF>**.

code

```
<html>
<body>
<a href="http://www.domain.com">
<img src="dropshad.jpg"></a>
</body>
</html>
```

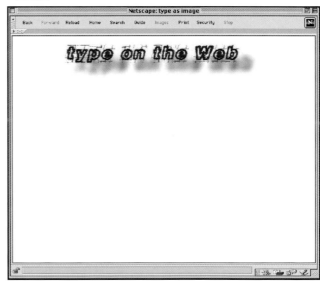

This page uses a text graphic inserted with HTML.

WHAT ABOUT PDF?

PDF stands for **P**ortable **D**ocument **F**ormat. It was developed long before the Web existed as a means of transporting documents to end users who didn't own the software applications the documents were created in. If, for example, I wanted to send a client a QuarkXPress document, and he or she didn't own QuarkXPress, my client could still see my layout with all the correct fonts and images intact.

PDFs are great if you have forms or documentation that need to uphold formatting. The IRS uses PDF forms to make tax reporting forms available online. We use PDF for the our FlashForward conference as a courtesy to our attendees who want a nicely printed version of the web site. PDF is a great solution for transferring, but it's not a substitute for HTML or online delivery. For more information, visit http://www.adobe.com/prodindex/acrobat/adobepdf.html.

If you want to learn how to use Acrobat, my company **lynda.com** has an online training module, a book, and a CD-ROM that can help you.

lynda.com Online Movie Library
$25 per month (or $250 per year)
http://movielibrary.lynda.com

Acrobat 5 Hands-On Training
Garrick Chow
(Developed by Lynda Weinman)
Peachpit Press
ISBN: 0-321-11275-X

Learning Acrobat 5 with Garrick Chow
CD-ROM
http://www.lynda.com/products/videos/acro5cd

HTML Type

SUMMARY

Typography is one of the most exciting design mediums at our disposal, yet the Web has been weak to support much typographic control using straight HTML. You probably shouldn't use HTML for type on your site. Ideally, you'll use CSS instead. To summarize this chapter:

> The **FONT** tag has been deprecated from the formal HTML standard. Use CSS instead. If you do use the **FONT** tag, be aware that your site might not retain the typographic formatting on future browsers.

> The attributes of the **FONT** tag allow you to specify faces, size, color, and justification. Just be careful that your end user has the font you request.

> PDF is useful if you have online documentation or forms that require exact positioning and fonts. It should not be used as an HTML substitute.

Alignment & Tables

Introduction

In most layout software for print applications, such as QuarkXPress and PageMaker, you simply place an image or text block where you want it, and there it stays. Unfortunately, in HTML, things aren't so nice and easy. Alignment is one of the trickiest web design challenges of all.

Part of the problem is that unlike paper, a web page has no fixed size. Some browsers have predefined sizes that the viewing window fits to; others let you size the screen to fill your monitor. Some members of your audience will see your page through tiny portable computer screens. Others will have 21" monitors. In addition, some of your viewers will change the font size defaults, which will make everything line up differently than you planned. The list of variables goes on and on and on! It's no wonder alignment is hard, given all these possibilities.

This chapter looks at various alignment options within basic HTML/XHTML, including the use of tables, spacers, and images. (It's also possible to establish alignment using Cascading Style Sheets, as discussed in Chapter 23, *"Cascading Style Sheets."*) Unfortunately, HTML/XHTML was never intended to be a page layout description language. In fact, XHTML is a significant move backward in favor of a more structured language and strongly emphasizes the use of style sheets to describe the appearance of data. This should come as no big surprise with the number of devices that are now capable of accessing the Web.

HOW BIG IS a web page?

Because you can scroll a web page vertically or horizontally, there is no set length or width restriction on a web document. The amount of text and artwork you choose to place on any given page dictates its size. If you position artwork that is so wide it spans horizontally or so tall it spans vertically, the page will fit to the size of your artwork. Scrollbars appear in most browsers automatically when the artwork is oversized in either direction.

Your first page creates the most important impression because that is where most of your visitors will make the decision to either enter your site or wander elsewhere. If you want your opening graphic to be visible on most computer monitors, you will probably want to know what size to make your artwork.

It's a difficult question to answer because computer monitor sizes and resolutions vary. Most portable computer screens today are at a resolution of 1024×768 or 800×600, though older models are still as small as 640×480.

I've personally settled on 695×420 pixels as a good width and height for an opening graphic or splash screen if you are targeting a resolution of 800×600. This not only takes into account the resolution at which the end user is viewing, but it also takes "browser chrome" into account. Browser chrome is the space the browser interface takes up with things like back buttons, scroll bars, URL fields, etc. This size is not cast in stone, and I realize it will seem far too conservative for many of your web sites. I have based this size preference on the many possible conditions my site might be viewed from.

Some artists choose to make their screens wider than my conservative estimate of 695 pixels. There are lots of clever ways to tell your audience how wide to open the browser window, as shown by the next example. After you establish the size of your pages, move on to the following sections, which will examine techniques for lining up artwork within them.

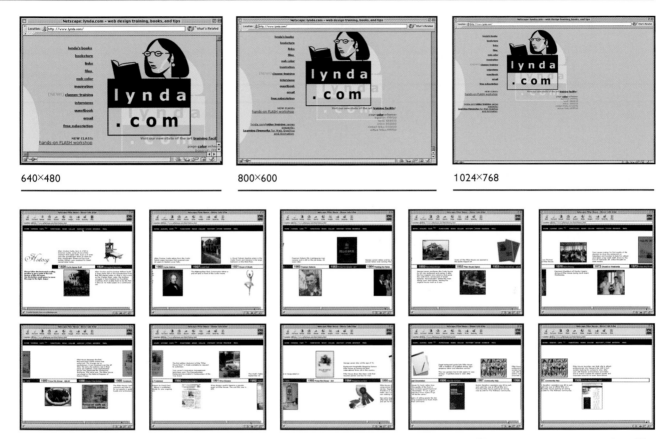

640×480

800×600

1024×768

At http://www.pillarhouse.com, the history section uses a horizontal scrolling method that takes 12 browser screens to complete. This page was made wide by writing the HTML code to place a lot of images to the right, thus making the page open wide to display all the images.

USING HTML/XHTML FOR ALIGNMENT

If you hang around this industry long enough, you'll soon realize that many HTML purists don't take kindly to using HTML for layout. In fact, you'll encounter hostility from some authorities in this subject because they believe that developers who use HTML to "design" pages are ruining the founding principles of HTML. You might not realize that HTML was intentionally designed to be customized by the end user to provide changeable font sizes, colors, and window sizes, and that precise layout interferes with this feature. That is why Netscape and Internet Explorer—instead of the W3C Standards committee—initiated most of the alignment tags and attributes that are in vogue today.

With the introduction of XHTML, we have seen a significant move to separate structure from format. Because XHTML follows the strict guidelines and rules of XML, the variances between browsers should lessen. XHTML was purposely designed to separate the structure of an HTML document (i.e., headers, body text, lists, etc.) from the formatting characteristics (such as whether the text is centered or colored or the size of a font).

With the growing support for XHTML it looks like Cascading Style Sheets (see Chapter 23, *"Cascading Style Sheets"*) will become more widely used for specifying the formatting of HTML documents and that HTML will return to its earliest roots of a structure-only language. This is really a good thing, especially since CSS affords more precise control than many of the solutions this chapter covers.

You'll find information about CSS formatting in Chapter 23, *"Cascading Style Sheets."* The following section reviews some of the HTML alignment methods.

TEXT ALIGNMENT TAGS & ATTRIBUTES

These tags relate to text elements. The following is an example of how they look on a web page.

Paragraph breaks: Insert the tag **<P>** where you want spaces between paragraphs. Notice that the HTML and XHTML syntax vary slightly. Although the the **</P>** is optional and works in HTML, it's required with XTHML:

```
<p>this is a line of text separated by a paragraph break.
<p>this is a line of text separated by a paragraph break.
```

HTML Syntax

```
<p>this is a line of text separated by a paragraph break.</p>
<p>this is a line of text separated by a paragraph break.</p>
```

XHTML Syntax

```
this is a line of text separated by a paragraph break.

this is a line of text separated by a paragraph break.
```

Output

Line breaks: Put the tag **
** where you want the text to wrap to the next line but not create any extra space:

```
This is a line of text separated by a line break.<br>
This is a link of text separated by a line break.<br>
```

HTML Syntax

```
This is a line of text separated by a line break.<br />
This is a link of text separated by a line break.<br />
```

XHTML Syntax

```
This is a line of text separated by a line break.
This is a link of text separated by a line break.
```

Output

Centering text: Use the tag **<CENTER>** before you center text and/or images and use the closed tag when you want text and images below it to return to left-justified formatting:

```
<center>this is some<br>
text that has been<br>
centered on the page.<br>
</center>
```

HTML Syntax

```
<center>this is some<br />
text that has been<br />
centered on the page.<br />
</center>
```

XHTML Syntax

```
      this is some
   text that has been
centered on the page.
```

Output

Preformatted text: Preformatted text typically uses a different font, such as the typewriter-style Courier, instead of the default Times Roman. The **<PRE>** tag lets you set the spacing and indents of your type. (For more examples of the **<PRE>** tag, check out Chapter 20, "HTML Type," and Chapter 9, "HTML & XHTML."

```
<pre> anything y o u  type    between
     t h e pre  t a g s   will use w h a t e v e r<br />
 sp a ces you    t  y  p  e  !
</pre>
```

XHTML Syntax

```
<pre> anything y o u  type    between
     t h e pre  t a g s   will use w h a t e v e r<br>
 sp a ces you    t  y  p  e  !
</pre>
```

HTML Syntax

```
anything y o u  type    between
    t h e pre  t a g s   will use w h a t e v e r

sp a ces you    t  y  p  e  !
```

Output

No break: Use the tag **<NOBR>** if you want to force a line of text to not wrap with the width of the browser window. The closed tag **<NOBR/>** signifies when you want the no break formatting to end. Note that that the **<NOBR>** tag is not part of HTML standards, and there is no XHTML syntax for it.

```
<nobr>
This tag will force
all of the text to
appear on one line!
</nobr>
```

HTML Syntax

```
This tag will force all of the text to appear on one line!
```

Output

note

LEADING WITH HTML

Leading is a typographic term for the amount of space between multiple lines of text. Creating extra space between lines of type in HTML isn't obvious unless you know about a couple of workarounds. If you add multiple **P** tags, for example, you will only get a single line of space between carriage returns because HTML recognizes only one **P** tag at a time. For multiple lines of space, there are two techniques: using the **P** tag or using the **PRE** tag with the entities element ** **. The ** ** element stands for "no break space." If you want more precise control over leading, you need to use CSS, which is described in Chapter 23, *"Cascading Style Sheets."*

The technique below allows you to insert extra **P** tags because it recognizes the string ** ** as invisible content and inserts a paragraph break after it anyway. The **&** entity displays an ampersand in the browser.

An alternative method would use the **PRE** tag. In the instance below, space is created between lines of type by inserting multiple carriage returns while typing. These carriage returns create the extra leading.

```
you can use the paragraph tag



to insert extra paragraph spaces



but you must add the non-breaking space entity!
```

```
you can use the pre tag

to also insert extra paragraph spaces

and it will honor the spacing you type

              with the keyboard!
```

P tag code

```
<p>you can use the paragraph tag

<p> 

<p> 

<p>to insert extra paragraph spaces

<p> 

<p>but you must add the non-breaking
    space entity!
```

PRE tag code

Here's the code for the above example using **PRE**:

```
<pre>you can use the pre tag

to also insert extra paragraph spaces

and it will honor the spacing you type

              with the keyboard!

</pre>
```

IMAGE ALIGNMENT TAGS

These tags cause text to align in relationship to the images it's next to. Note that the **ALIGN** attribute is associated with the **P** tag, not the text.

`align="top"` Aligns text to the top of your image:

code

```
<p align="left">
<img src="a-tonneke.jpg" width="200"
height="202" align="top">
E-Flowers, Inc. is a florist that specializes
in exotic and hard to find flowers. We pride
ourselves in our wide range of exotic and
hard to find flowers that you just cannot
find elsewhere. Our low prices and excellent
selections have made us one of the best
floral companies in the nation. If we do not
have the flower you are looking for, we will
do everything we can to locate it for you,
at no extra cost! At E-Flowers, we believe
that a little extra effort goes a long way.
With more than 200 retail locations across
the United States we are sure to have a
location near you. So, next time you are
looking for that hard to find flower; be
sure to check out E-Flowers and let us
bring some happiness into your life!</p>
```

`align="middle"` Aligns text to the middle:

code

```
<p align="left">
<img src="a-tonneke.jpg" width="200"
height="202" align="middle">
E-Flowers, Inc. is a florist that specializes
in exotic and hard to find flowers. We pride
ourselves in our wide range of exotic and
hard to find flowers that you just cannot
find elsewhere. Our low prices and excellent
selections have made us one of the best
floral companies in the nation. If we do not
have the flower you are looking for, we will
do everything we can to locate it for you,
at no extra cost! At E-Flowers, we believe
that a little extra effort goes a long way.
With more than 200 retail locations across
the United States we are sure to have a
location near you. So, next time you are
looking for that hard to find flower; be
sure to check out E-Flowers and let us
bring some happiness into your life!</p>
```

Pretty Flowers

About E-Flowers, Inc.

E-Flowers, Inc. is a florist that specializes in exotic and hard to find flowers. We pride ourselves in our wide range of exotic and hard to find flowers that you just cannot find elsewhere. Our low prices and excellent selections have made us one of the best floral companies in the nation. If we do not have the flower you are looking for, we will do everything we can to locate it for you, at no extra cost! At E-Flowers, we believe that a little extra effort goes a long way. With more than 200 retail locations across the United States we are sure to have a location near you. So, next time you are looking for that hard to find flower, be sure to check out E-Flowers and let us bring some happiness into your life!

Pretty Flowers

About E-Flowers, Inc.

E-Flowers, Inc. is a florist that specializes in exotic and hard to find flowers. We pride ourselves in our wide range of exotic and hard to find flowers that you just cannot find elsewhere. Our low prices and excellent selections have made us one of the best floral companies in the nation. If we do not have the flower you are looking for, we will do everything we can to locate it for you, at no extra cost! At E-Flowers, we believe that a little extra effort goes a long way. With more than 200 retail locations across the United States we are sure to have a location near you. So, next time you are looking for that hard to find flower; be sure to check out E-Flowers and let us bring some happiness into your life!

`align="bottom"` Aligns text to the bottom:

code

```
<img align="left">
<img src="a-tonneke.jpg" width="200"
height="202" align="bottom">
E-Flowers, Inc. is a florist that specializes
in exotic and hard to find flowers. We pride
ourselves in our wide range of exotic and
hard to find flowers that you just cannot
find elsewhere. Our low prices and excellent
selections have made us one of the best
floral companies in the nation. If we do not
have the flower you are looking for, we will
do everything we can to locate it for you,
at no extra cost! At E-Flowers, we believe
that a little extra effort goes a long way.
With more than 200 retail locations across
the United States we are sure to have a
location near you. So, next time you are
looking for that hard to find flower; be
sure to check out E-Flowers and let us
bring some happiness into your life!</p>
```

`align="left"` Aligns text to the left side:

code

```
<img align="left">
<img src="a-tonneke.jpg" width="200"
height="202" align="left">
E-Flowers, Inc. is a florist that specializes
in exotic and hard to find flowers. We pride
ourselves in our wide range of exotic and
hard to find flowers that you just cannot
find elsewhere. Our low prices and excellent
selections have made us one of the best
floral companies in the nation. If we do not
have the flower you are looking for, we will
do everything we can to locate it for you,
at no extra cost! At E-Flowers, we believe
that a little extra effort goes a long way.
With more than 200 retail locations across
the United States we are sure to have a
location near you. So, next time you are
looking for that hard to find flower; be
sure to check out E-Flowers and let us
bring some happiness into your life!</p>
```

Pretty Flowers

About E-Flowers, Inc.

E-Flowers, Inc. is a florist that specializes in exotic and hard to find flowers. We pride ourselves in our wide range of exotic and hard to find flowers that you just cannot find elsewhere. Our low prices and excellent selections have made us one of the best floral companies in the nation. If we do not have the flower you are looking for, we will do everything we can to locate it for you, at no extra cost! At E-Flowers, we believe that a little extra effort goes a long way. With more than 200 retail locations across the United States we are sure to have a location near you. So, next time you are looking for that hard to find flower; be sure to check out E-Flowers and let us bring some happiness into your life!

`align="right"` Aligns text to the right side:

code

```
<p align="left">
<img src="a-tonneke.jpg" width="200"
height="202" align="right">
E-Flowers, Inc. is a florist that specializes
in exotic and hard to find flowers. We pride
ourselves in our wide range of exotic and
hard to find flowers that you just cannot
find elsewhere. Our low prices and excellent
selections have made us one of the best
floral companies in the nation. If we do not
have the flower you are looking for, we will
do everything we can to locate it for you,
at no extra cost! At E-Flowers, we believe
that a little extra effort goes a long way.
With more than 200 retail locations across
the United States we are sure to have a
location near you. So, next time you are
looking for that hard to find flower; be
sure to check out E-Flowers and let us
bring some happiness into your life!</p>
```

HORIZONTAL & VERTICAL SPACE TAGS

The horizontal and vertical space tags allow you to insert empty space around a graphic, creating breathing room.

HSPACE & VSPACE: The **HSPACE** and **VSPACE** attributes position the image with breathing room around the type. In this case, a value of 40 pixels was used, leaving 20 pixel spaces on the right and left sides and at the top and bottom of the image. This process always puts equal numbers of pixels on the left/right/top/bottom. It is not possible, without using style sheets—to only add 20 pixels to the right and of the image, for example.

Pretty Flowers

About E-Flowers, Inc.

E-Flowers, Inc. is a florist that specializes in exotic and hard to find flowers. We pride ourselves in our wide range of exotic and hard to find flowers that you just cannot find elsewhere. Our low prices and excellent selections have made us one of the best floral companies in the nation. If we do not have the flower you are looking for, we will do everything we can to locate it for you, at no extra cost! At E-Flowers, we believe that a little extra effort goes a long way. With more than 200 retail locations across the United States we are sure to have a location near you. So, next time you are looking for that hard to find flower; be sure to check out E-Flowers and let us bring some happiness into your life!

code

```
<p align="left">
<img src="a-tonneke.jpg" width="200"
height="202" align="left" vspace="60"
hspace="60">
E-Flowers, Inc. is a florist that specializes
in exotic and hard to find flowers. We pride
ourselves in our wide range of exotic and
hard to find flowers that you just cannot
find elsewhere. Our low prices and excellent
selections have made us one of the best
floral companies in the nation. If we do not
have the flower you are looking for, we will
do everything we can to locate it for you,
at no extra cost! At E-Flowers, we believe
that a little extra effort goes a long way.
With more than 200 retail locations across
the United States we are sure to have a
location near you. So, next time you are
looking for that hard to find flower; be
sure to check out E-Flowers and let us
bring some happiness into your life!</p>
```

WIDTH & HEIGHT ATTRIBUTES

These attributes work by allowing you to specify the width and height values (in pixels) of a graphic. This can accomplish two things: It causes the text on the page to load before the graphic, and it makes space for the graphic to come into the proper location. Using width and height attributes within HTML is very important for downloading speed, and many plug-in **EMBED** tags require that you include width and height information.

There's a lesser known feature of **WIDTH** and **HEIGHT**, however. If you put in values that are larger or smaller than the physical dimensions of your original image, they will actually enlarge or shrink your image. In the following example, the actual dimension of the flower image is 200×202 pixels. By entering a value of 300×175, I scaled it larger. By entering a width of 116 and height of 85, I shrunk the image. This doesn't always look good, but it is nevertheless used from time to time as a visual effect. The following images illustrate these alignment tags.

code

```
<img src="a-tonneke.jpg"
width="300" height="175" align="left"
<IMG SRC="a-tonneke.jpg"
width="116" height="85" align="left">
```

It is also possible to put percentages into the **WIDTH** and **HEIGHT** attributes.

code

```
<img src="a-tonneke.jpg"
width="100%" height="100%" align="left">
```

Using percentages with the **HEIGHT** and **WIDTH** will distort the image, but it will also cause it to respond to the shape of the browser window instead of the image's native size. In this example, the image stretches to 100% of the browser size and changes depending on how wide your browser is opened.

If you use the actual size of the image for the **HEIGHT** and **WIDTH** values, your page will load faster because the browser doesn't have to assess the size on its own. It is recommended that you always put the desired **HEIGHT** and **WIDTH** values into your HTML, unless you are going after a visual effect of scaling or shrinking. Most of the WYSIWYG HTML editors automatically insert the **HEIGHT** and **WIDTH** values for you.

Next, we move on to alignment techniques that do not use HTML code—they involve making custom artwork that serves to align images.

ALTERNATIVES TO HTML USING ARTWORK

Using images for custom alignment involves creating spacer art. This art exists on the web page for the sole purpose of making spaces between text and images. For the spacer art to be invisible, you have two options: to make the spacer art the same color as your background or to make the spacer artwork a transparent GIF that contains only one color (making the entire graphic transparent).

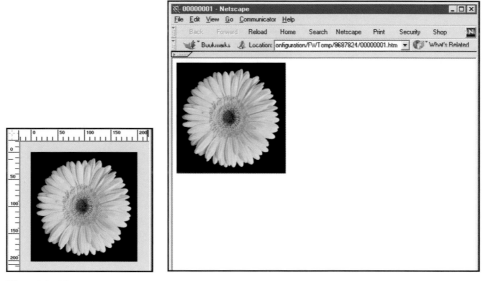

The original image.

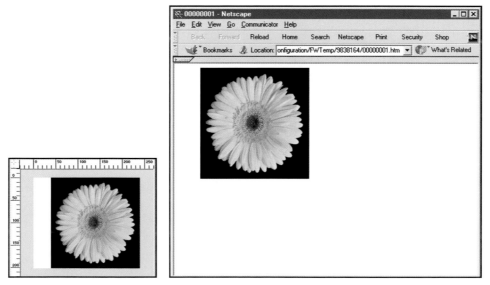

Here is the image with 40 pixels of white space inserted to the left.

TABLES FOR ALIGNMENT

Tables for the Web were originally conceived to produce columns of text or numbers in individual cells, much like a spreadsheet or chart. Even though tables were invented to support text and numbers, you can put graphics and anything else supported by HTML inside table cells, too. All the graphic tags I've described so far work within the table tags. Because of this, I've made a distinction in this chapter between data tables and graphic tables.

A web designer who knows how to use tables for page layout control will be a much happier camper than one who doesn't. Learning to write the code for tables will offer lots of formatting options that HTML doesn't directly support.

DATA TABLES

Data-based tables are precisely what the HTML working group (http://www.w3.org) had in mind when they published the code. These are the typical kinds of tables you see on most sites. They contain text and numbers, links, and occasionally graphics. They often have telltale borders around the cells, which look slightly dimensional, and are created by employing embossed lines of varying width to divide individual chart sections.

Data tables often use embossed lines to divide up all the cells and sections.

If you use a pattern background or solid color background, the embossing shows through and looks as if it's a lighting effect.

Table borders are similar to horizontal rules on steroids: The HTML code magically manufactures vertical and horizontal lines of different widths and thicknesses with a few choice strokes of code and tags. They seem complicated by appearance, but you will probably be surprised at how easy they are to create and use.

THE <FRAME> & <RULES> ATTRIBUTES

There are two HTML attributes that can give you more precise control when you are formatting your HTML table borders, but only if you are using Internet Explorer 5.0 or a later browser. Neither of these attributes will display correctly, if at all, in Netscape Navigator. The <FRAME> and <RULES> attributes give you an additional amount of design control when it comes to formatting the interior and outer HTML table borders.

The <FRAME> attribute sets which of the table's outer borders will be rendered and has nine possible values, which are listed in the chart below:

Value	Description
void	No frame appears (default).
above	Border appears on top side.
below	Border appears on bottom side.
hsides	Border appears on top and bottom sides.
vsides	Border appears on right and left sides.
lhs	Border appears on left side only.
rhs	Border appears on right side only.
box	Border appears on all four sides.
border	Border appears on all four sides.

This table has been formatted with the <FRAME> attribute using the "hsides" value and is being previewed in Internet Explorer 6.0 for Windows.

code

```
<table width="600" frame="hsides"
bordercolor="#000000">
```

The <RULES> attribute sets which of the table's inner borders will be rendered and has five possible values, which are listed in the chart below:

Value	Description
all	Border appears around each cell.
cols	Border appears between columns only.
groups	Border appears between cell groups.
none	Hides all interior borders.
rows	Border appears between rows only.

Address	C:\WINDOWS\Desktop\TMPofabkngzz.htm	

Today's Forecast		
Location	High	Low
Los Angeles	75	60
Denver	79	62
Kansas City	77	55
Chicago	74	54
Miami	84	68

Done   My Computer

This table has been formatted with the <RULES> attribute using the "rows" value and is being previewed in Internet Explorer 6.0 for Windows.

code

```
<table width="600" rules="rows"
bordercolor="#000000">
```

HTML TABLE TAGS

When creating data or graphics tables for the Web, you work with the same HTML tags. The table tags allow you to put information inside individual cells. Understanding the tag structure for data tables enables you to work with the graphic tables later in this chapter.

You always begin a table with **TABLE** and end it with the /**TABLE** tag. The **TR** and /**TR** tags indicate the start and end of a new row. The **TD** and /**TD** tags mark the content of each data cell. The XHTML code for this example would be identical, but in lower case.

```
upper left   upper right
bottom left bottom right
```

code
```
<table>
<tr>
<td>upper left</td>
<td>upper right</td>
</tr>
<tr>
<td>bottom left</td>
<td>bottom right</td>
</tr>
</table>
```

By adding the **TH** (**T**able **H**eader) attribute, you can add header information to tables, which is displayed in most browsers as bold headlines.

```
upper left upper right
bottom left bottom right
```

code
```
<table>
<tr>
<th>upper left</th>
<th>upper right</th>
</tr>
<tr>
<td>bottom left</td>
<td>bottom right</td>
</tr>
</table>
```

The **BORDER** attribute gives the table an embossed look and feel. Here's an example of such code, with the HTML below:

```
upper left  upper right
bottom left bottom right
```

code
```
<table border="2">
<tr>
<th>upper left</th>
<th>upper right</th>
</tr>
<tr>
<td>bottom left</td>
<td>bottom right</td>
</tr>
</table>
```

The **COLSPAN** attribute allows one row to fill more than one column. Here's an example of such code, with the HTML below:

```
Longer Text on One Line
upper left  upper right
bottom left bottom right
```

code
```
<table border="2">
<tr>
<td colspan="2">
Longer Text on One Line</td>
</tr>
<tr>
<th>upper left</th>
<th>upper right</th>
</tr>
<tr>
<td>bottom left</td>
<td>bottom right</td>
</tr>
</table>
```

The **ROWSPAN** attribute takes up columns and rows. It is not any specific size or shape; the dimensions are dictated by the content you insert. Here's an example of such code, with the HTML below:

| Tall Cell | Upper Left | Upper Right |
| | Bottom Left | Bottom Right |

code

```
<table border="2">
<tr>
<td rowspan="2">
Tall Cell</td>
<td>Upper Left</td>
<td>Upper Right</td>
</tr>
<tr>
<td>Bottom Left</td>
<td>Bottom Right</td>
</tr>
</table>
```

WIDTH and **HEIGHT** attributes can include pixel-based or percentage-based values. The two images below show the same code in two different browser windows. When the browser is dragged out to be larger, the **WIDTH** attribute, which is using percentage values, stretches with it. Here's an example of such code, with the HTML in the next column:

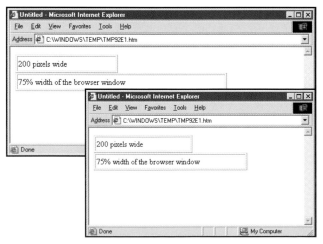

code

```
<table border="2" width="200" height="35">
<tr>
<td>200 pixels wide</td>
</tr>
</table>
<table width="75%" height="35">
<tr>
<td>75% width of the browser window</td>
</tr>
</table>
```

The code **<TABLE WIDTH=# of pixels>** and **<TABLE HEIGHT=# of pixels>** let you dictate the shape of the table by pixels (or percentages, shown next). Here's an example of such code, with the HTML below:

| Upper Left | Upper Right |
| Bottom Left | Bottom Right |

code

```
<table border="2" width="200" height="100">
<tr>
<td>Upper Left</td>
<td>Upper Right</td>
</tr>
<tr>
<td>Bottom Left</td>
<td>Bottom Right</td>
</tr>
</table>
```

The code **<TABLE CELLPADDING=# of pixels>** puts a uniform space inside the cells, governed by the number of pixels entered after the = (equal) sign. Here's an example, with the HTML on the next page:

| Upper Left | Upper Right |
| Bottom Left | Bottom Right |

code

```
<table border="1" cellpadding="10">
<tr>
<td>Upper Left</td>
<td>Upper Right</td>
</tr>
<tr>
<td>Bottom Left</td>
<td>Bottom Right</td>
</tr>
</table>
```

The code **CELLSPACING=# of pixels>** puts a thicker line weight around the cells. Here's an example of such code, with the HTML below:

code

```
<table border="2" CELLSPACING="10">
<tr>
<td>Upper Left</td>
<td>Upper Right</td>
</tr>
<tr>
<td>Bottom Left</td>
<td>Bottom Right</td>
</tr>
</table>
```

You can adjust the alignment of data inside cells by using the **VALIGN** attribute, which allows you to specify top, middle, bottom, and baseline. Here's an example of such code, with the HTML in the next column:

code

```
<table border="2" height="100">
<tr>
<td valign="bottom">Upper Left</td>
<td valign="middle">Upper Center</td>
<td valign="top">Upper Right</td>
</tr>
<tr>
<td valign="top">Bottom Left</td>
<td valign="middle">Bottom Center</td>
<td valign="bottom">Bottom Right</td>
</tr>
</table>
```

You can also specify, right, left, and middle alignment values within the **TR**, **TH**, and **TD** tags by using the **ALIGN** attribute. Here's an example of such code, with the HTML below:

code

```
<table border="1" height="100">
<tr valign="top">
<td>Upper Left</td>
<td>Upper Center</td>
<td>Upper Right</td>
</tr>
<tr valign="bottom">
<td>Bottom Left</td>
<td>Bottom Center</td>
<td>Bottom Right</td>
</tr>
</table>
```

You can also put graphics inside tables by using the `IMG SRC="name.gif"` tag instead of text or values. Here's an example of such code, with the HTML below:

code
```
<table border="1">
<tr>
<td><img src="arts.jpg"
width="287" height="239"></td>
</tr>
</table>
```

The following example shows how you can mix text and graphics inside cells of a table:

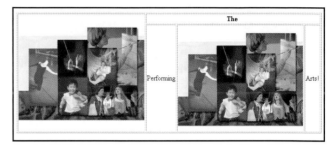

code
```
<table border="2">
<tr>
<td rowspan="2"><img src="arts.jpg"></td>
<th colspan="3">The</th>
</tr>
<tr>
<td>Performing</td>
<td><IMG SRC="arts.jpg"></td>
<td>Arts!</td>
</tr>
</table>
```

This last example showed how to insert graphics into your tables by using the `IMG` tag. The following section explains how you can work with graphics more seamlessly, eliminating the telltale border around table cells.

GRAPHIC TABLES FOR PAGE LAYOUT

Table support was the first real hook designers had for being able to control layout of page design. If you use tables to create a design grid, all the things that basic HTML has kept you from doing are suddenly possible. You want a vertical row of linked type in the middle of your page or a vertical rule graphic? No problem! You want your graphics aligned left or right to a specific grid defined by pixels? No problem! You want to define the size of your page and not let the browser do that for you? No problem! Basically, if you're used to working with PageMaker or Quark-XPress, you're used to working with design grids. Tables take more effort, but if you do some planning, you can use them much the same way.

PERCENTAGES VERSUS PIXELS

One of the key principles of using tables for alignment is understanding the differences and power of using percentages and/or pixels. Tables based on percentages scale to the size of your browser, and tables based on pixels are fixed in size.

PERCENTAGE-BASED TABLES

One of my favorite tricks is to center a graphic or text using tables so it remains centered regardless of the size of the browser. You do this with percentages and alignment attributes. Here's the code and the effect it produces:

code

```
<table width="100%"
border="1" height="100%">
<tr>
<td align="center">
<img width="226" height="226"
src="peppergrill.gif"></td>
</tr>
</table>
```

This code established that the table was 100 percent of the browser size, and the image contained within was centered on the horizontal and vertical axes.

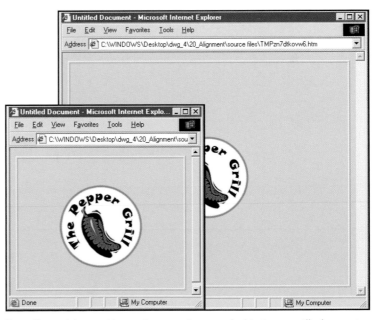

Regardless of how wide my browser is opened, this image will always stay centered because of the table trick I'm using.

PIXEL-BASED TABLES

Pixel-based tables are useful for creating large graphics, cutting them apart, and reassembling them with a table. This is done for a few reasons. First, you could create a large graphic that contained artwork that was soft and hard edged. By slicing the image up and reassembling it into tables, you could compress various regions differently. You could also include animation or roll-overs inside some of the table regions.

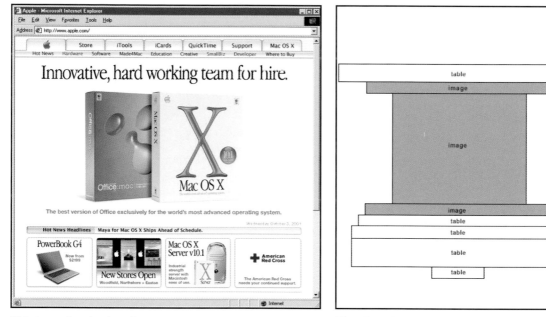

This image, found at http://www.apple.com, is actually composed of lots of individual images that have been reassembled seamlessly using several HTML tables.

This allowed the designers to combine JPEG, GIF, and animated GIF elements into their design. It also allowed for the site's content to be easily changed.

You can achieve a table of fixed pixel widths (like the example shown below) by knowing the exact size of each graphic and reassembling it using tables. In our book *Creative HTML Design.2*, my brother and I show the following example:

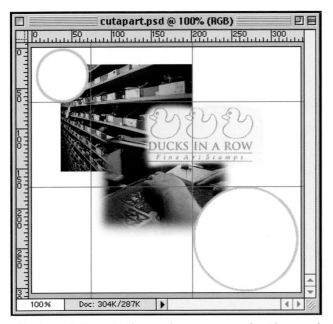

This shows the image inside a graphics program, with guides turned on. The guides show where the images were cut apart. Using the info palette, with Preferences set to measure in pixels, not inches, I was able to get the exact dimension for each region of the table in order to piece this back together again. Animated GIF files were used for the two circle regions, and the rest of the images were saved as GIF files.

Here's the code to piece the graphics together again.

code

```
<table border="0"
cellspacing="0"
cellpadding="0">
<tr>
<td><img src="cutapart1.gif"></td>
<td><img src="cutapart2.gif"></td>
<td><img src="cutapart3.gif"></td>
<tr>
<td><img src="cutapart4.gif"></td>
<td><img src="cutapart5.gif"></td>
<td><img src="cutapart6.gif"></td>
<tr>
<td><img src="cutapart7.gif"></td>
<td><img src="cutapart8.gif"></td>
<td><img src="cutapart9.gif"></td>
</table>
```

note

TERMINATE YOUR TABLES!

A problem that many encounter when they make tables for the purpose of assembling images is either forgetting to terminate their tables (close the **TD** tag) or putting the close tag on a separate line. Here are two bad examples, both of which leave spaces between the images and break the illusion of this technique.

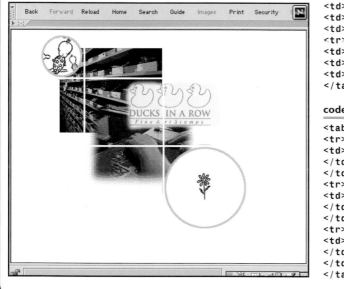

code for no termination

```
<table border="0" cellspacing="0" cellpadding="0">
<tr>
<td><img src="cutapart1.gif">
<td><img src="cutapart2.gif">
<td><img src="cutapart3.gif">
<tr>
<td><img src="cutapart4.gif">
<td><img src="cutapart5.gif">
<td><img src="cutapart6.gif">
<tr>
<td><img src="cutapart7.gif">
<td><img src="cutapart8.gif">
<td><img src="cutapart9.gif">
</table>
```

code with termination in the wrong place

```
<table border="0" cellspacing="0" cellpadding="0">
<tr>
<td><img src="cutapart1.gif">
</td><td><img src="cutapart2.gif">
</td><td><img src="cutapart3.gif">
<tr>
<td><img src="cutapart4.gif">
</td><td><img src="cutapart5.gif">
</td><td><img src="cutapart6.gif">
<tr>
<td><img src="cutapart7.gif">
</td><td><img src="cutapart8.gif">
</td><td><img src="cutapart9.gif">
</table>
```

INDENTS USING TABLES

If you ever want to create some space in your layout that creates an indent, use a table. Here is the example and the code:

code

```
<table width="443" border="0">
<tr>
<td width="100"></td>
<td width="339">
This is an example of creating an indent with a table. This is an example of creating an indent with a table. This is an example of creating an indent with a table. This is an example of creating an indent with a table. This is an example of creating an indent with a table. This is an example of creating an indent with a table. This is an example of creating an indent with a table. This is an example of creating an indent with a table. This is an example of creating an indent with a table. This is an example of creating an indent with a table. This is an example of creating an indent with a table. This is an example of creating an indent with a table. This is an example of creating an indent with a table. This is an example of creating an indent with a table. This is an example of creating an indent with a table. This is an example of creating an indent with a table. This is an example of creating an indent with a table.  This is an example of creating an indent with a table. This is an example of creating an indent with a table. This is an example of creating an indent with a table. This is an example of creating an indent with a table. This is an example of creating an indent with a table. This is an example of creating an indent with a table. This is an example of creating an indent with a table. This is an example of creating an indent with a table. This is an example of creating an indent with a table. This is an example of creating an indent with a table. This is an example of creating an indent with a table. This is an example of creating an indent with a table. This is an example of creating an indent with a table.
</td>
</tr>
</table>
```

WYSIWYG TABLES

It should be noted that all WYSIWYG HTML editors let you create tables without programming the code. It's so much easier to use them—instead of hand coding—that it's really worth your time to invest in one of them. It's important to understand how tables in HTML work, however, because it's still necessary from time to time to edit the automatic code WYSIWYG editors generate.

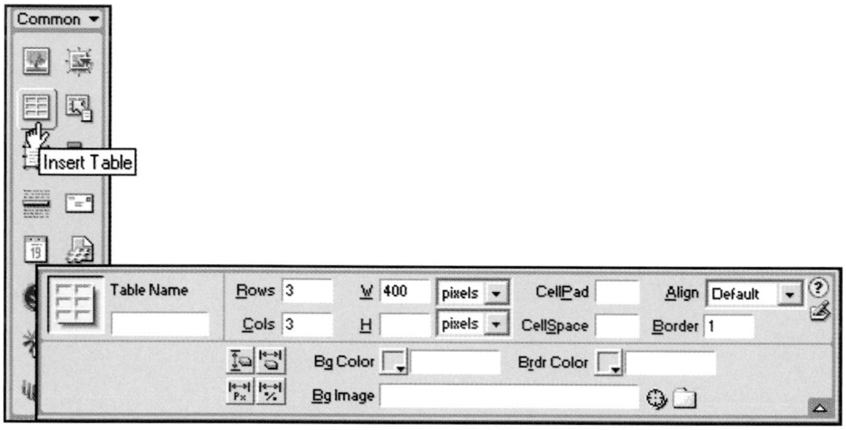

It's possible to create tables easily with the help of WYSIWYG editors. Shown above is Dreamweaver, which will generate or edit a table based on the values entered into helpful inspector palettes.

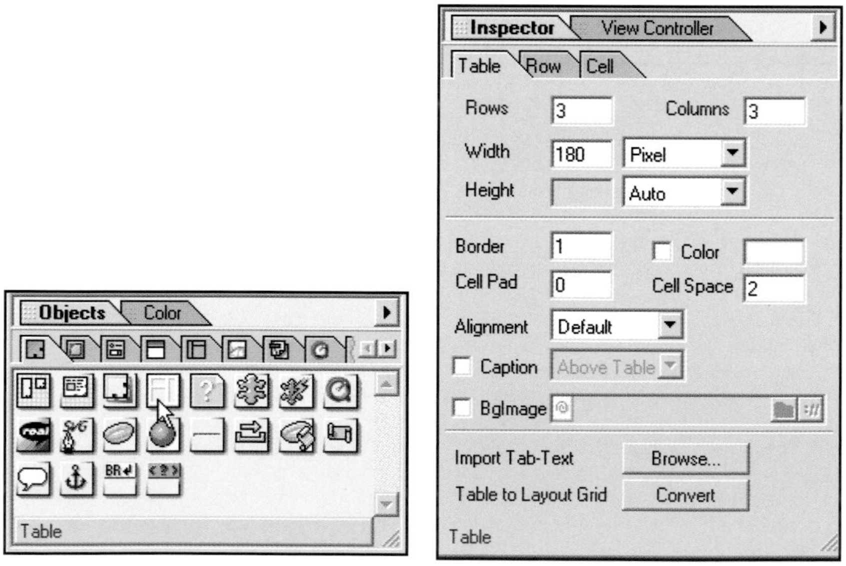

Adobe GoLive is another WYSIWYG HTML editor, which will also generate a table based on the values entered into these palettes.

IMAGING SOFTWARE TABLES

Many of the imaging software packages have the ability to generate table code. This ability lets you create your graphics and design your page layouts all in one single application. Of the tools available to do this today, Macromedia Fireworks and Adobe ImageReady are my favorites.

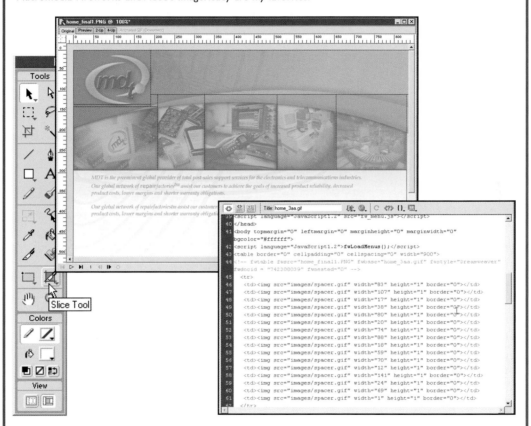

The Slice tool is available in the toolbar in Macromedia Fireworks. It is also found in other imaging applications, such as Photoshop, ImageReady, and PaintShop Pro.

When you drag out a slice, the slice regions are shown in green. Each slice can be independently named and compressed. In Fireworks, you can set up the links, the type of image (rollover or still image), the compression settings, and the name of the slice all from the Object Properties palette.

The thin red lines give you a preview of the HTML table that will be created for this specific layout. In the example above, Fireworks wrote the HTML table without me ever writing a line of code or entering an HTML editor. Many image editors and page-layout applications now give you the ability to export HTML tables. This is great because it can save you a lot of production time.

TABLE TIPS & TRICKS

As you work with tables, you will discover that things can get a bit complex and sometimes down right frustrating. To help you navigate through some of the more common problems, I have included some HTML table tips and tricks in this section. They may not solve all of your problems, but they can certainly make your life a bit easier and save you from a headache or two! ;-)

Basic Table Gotchas: There are some basic principles you should be aware of as you begin using tables to control the alignment of text and graphics on your pages. The short exercises in this section will help you understand how to work around some of the problems you might encounter in the different browsers.

PERCENTAGE TABLES

Create a table with *2* columns and *1* row. Set the width to *100%* and the border to *1*. In the first column cell, set the **BGCOLOR** to *blue*. Do not set the column widths. Before you add any content, preview your table in both browsers.

Both browsers display this consistently. Hooray!

In the second column, type this: *Netscape just cannot get tables to behave!* Preview in both browsers again.

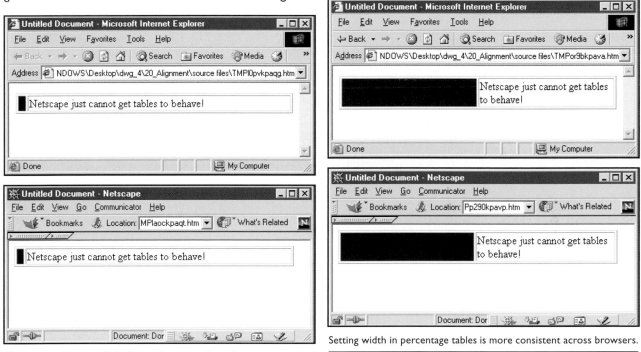

Now set the first cell's width to *50%*.

Unfortunately, you still don't get the desired results.

Setting width in percentage tables is more consistent across browsers.

The HTML code for the corrected table looks like this:

code

```
<table width="100%" border="1">
<tr>
<td bgcolor="#0000FF"
width="50%"> </td>
<td>Netscape just cannot get tables to
behave!</td>
</tr>
</table>
```

FIXED-PIXEL TABLES

Create a table that has *1* row, *2* columns at *400*px wide and a border of *1*. Save your page as **fixed.html**. In the first column cell, set its background color to *blue*. Set the width of this cell to *200*px, which should be half the table's width. In the second column cell, type this: "Netscape and Internet Explorer implement tables differently!" Preview your page in both browsers. What happens? Look at the example:

Now set the second column's width to *200*px. Save and test in both browsers.

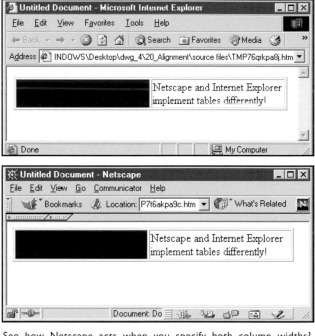

Netscape (top) doesn't display the table divided in half whereas IE (bottom) does.

See how Netscape acts when you specify both column widths? Netscape requires all column widths to be set to display the layout properly. Just setting one won't do the trick if one cell has content and the other doesn't.

The HTML code for the corrected table looks like this:

code

```
<TABLE WIDTH="400" BORDER="1">
<TR>
<TD BGCOLOR="#0000FF" WIDTH="200"> </TD>
<TD WIDTH="200">Netscape and Internet
Explorer implement tables differently!</TD>
</TR>
</TABLE>
```

TABLE BORDER TRICK

Create a table with a single cell. Use no border, spacing, or padding. The width of the table is irrelevant although it should be the desired setting you want for your finished table. For this exercise, I used a 400px width, but this would work as well with any setting. Set the **BGCOLOR** of the table to whatever color you like. This is the color you want for the table border.

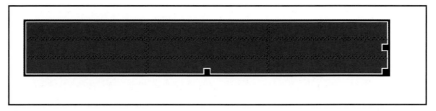

Add a new table inside the first table, with a width of 400px with the desired number of rows and columns. Set cellspacing to 1px. This will create a nested table, one table inside another table. Set the cell color of each cell to white.

![Untitled Document - Microsoft Internet Explorer window showing a nested table with three rows and three columns]

A beautiful and consistent table border.

ALIGNMENT & TABLES

SUMMARY

Alignment in HTML is very challenging. This chapter should serve as a reference when you want to program specific types of alignment of text or images. Here's a summary of this chapter:

> Alignment tags and attributes enable you to align text and images by specifying center, left, right, top, bottom, and middle alignment.

> For some audiences, it's still recommended that you use tables to align artwork and text because they offer much greater control than alignment tags and elements. CSS will be used for alignment as the support for it between the browsers increases.

> Tables can contain absolute pixel dimensions or percentages. This chapter shows good examples of both types of tables.

> You can slice and reassemble images to create optimization settings for each graphic or to include dynamic media such as rollovers or animations.

> WYSIWYG and image editors are making table creation less about math and more about design.

> Certain versions of Internet Explorer and Netscape Navigator render tables differently so be sure you test your pages in both browsers on the Mac and Windows platforms.

Frames

Introduction

Since their beginning, frames have existed in a love-hate relationship with the web design community. Frames offer many pros and cons that you need to carefully consider before implementing them on your site. This chapter will address these pros and cons as well as the technical aspects of frames. It's my intention to educate you on these nuances so you can make an educated decision about frames when you are designing your sites.

To this day when I lecture, I often poll my audience to see who "hates frames." To this day, many hands still raise, and frames are still a subject of heated controversy and disagreement. What's the deal? What's good about frames, and what's bad? What are they, and how do you make them? How do you offer alternate content for those who don't like framed sites, and how do you avoid the serious pitfalls? By the end of this chapter, you should have a good handle on how to make frames and whether or not you want to bother with them.

WHAT ARE FRAMES?

When we teach workshops, my husband, Bruce, likes to use a silly analogy for frames. He has our students imagine TV dinner trays as the frameset, and uses peas, corn, the entrée, and dessert tray as the metaphors for the frame content. While it usually produces a few chuckles, I mention it here because I think it actually helps describe the simple (yet complex!) nature of frames.

You see, frames contain multiple HTML pages. The main frame container is called the frameset, because it holds all the other HTML pages. It is, in Bruce's terms, the TV dinner tray for the HTML courses.

When you're programming frames, it can get very confusing, because you are dealing with multiple HTML documents. Each document contains all the various features we've described so far—background colors, tiles, images, imagemaps, type, tables, etc. It's one thing to manage these items on a single page, and quite another to manage multiples of them on a single page. Not to mention that you can "target" areas on a framed site and targets are used less frequently on single pages.

Before we get into how you make frames and targets, you might understandably wonder why anyone would use frames to begin with. Frames enable regions of a page to stay stationary, while allowing other regions of a page to change.

This is useful for navigation, because it allows you to set up navigation links that will be present on every page of your site without substituting the entire page, which is what would happen if you tried to program navigation on standard non-frame pages. Consistent navigation is something CD-ROM multi-media developers have always taken for granted, but it has proven much more difficult in web development.

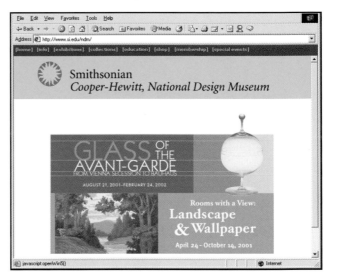

This example illustrates the two frame regions of the **Cooper-Hewitt National Design Museum** (http://www.si.edu/ndm). By dividing this screen into two separate pages, the middle stage" can change, while the top navigation area is anchored and locked. By clicking on an item in the "navigation" region, the "content" is updated through a method called "targets." In practice, any region of a framed site can be made to lock or substitute content.

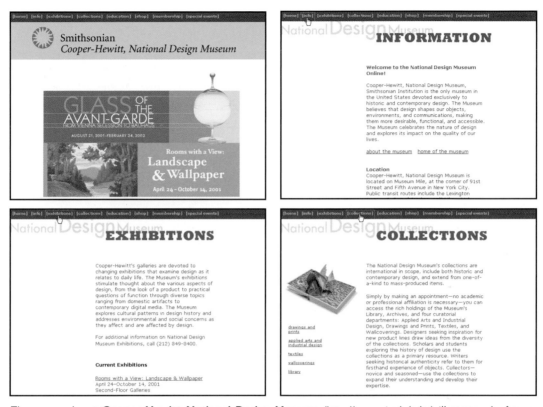

These examples at **Cooper-Hewitt National Design Museum** (http://www.si.edu/ndm) illustrate why frames are useful and why many web developers choose to use them. If you click on the top navigation bar of this site, the middle of the screen changes, but the navigation area remains the same. This is the result of frames. This example shows frames with no borders, which gives the page a more connected design.

FRAMES PROS & CONS

So, why are frames so controversial? The function of a frames-based site is very practical, but the implementation is often plagued with problems. In other words, an unsuspecting and inexperienced web developer can seriously abuse frames without an understanding of the pitfalls.

To backtrack a moment, when frames were introduced in 1997 by Netscape, they were implemented poorly. There was no way to turn off borders of frame regions, leaving ugly scrollbars and lines all over anyone's site who programmed them. It was impossible to print or bookmark a frame, and the Back button would usually take you to the last site you visited rather than the last frame you visited.

Given that a web page is already a small amount of real estate to work with, dividing it up with lots of lines and scrollbars can understandably annoy your end user. That is one reason frames have a bad reputation—if you don't hide all the lines and scrollbars, it can actually present a more confusing presentation than not. Therefore, the very thing that a frames-based site should be good at (navigation) is actually something it can royally mess up if handled poorly.

Frames can be modified to appear transparent—if you know all the tricks (which, of course, you'll be learning in this chapter)! Most of the early complaints are unfounded, but there are still a few gotchas you need to know about.

If it's critical that your audience print one of your pages, you might still shy away from frames. The frame will print if your end user last clicked within it (making it active), but if not, the browser might print another region. The Windows version of Internet Explorer offers great printing support for frames because it lets you choose what part of the frameset you want to print. As a safeguard, it is good to include a PDF file and/or a page that removes itself from the frameset (again, you'll learn how in this current chapter). Bookmarking a framed site is still problematic because the bookmark will refer to the frameset (remember that TV dinner tray?) and not the specific page or frame region that one might expect.

My company, **lynda.com**, at one point had a problem with a secure ordering page for electronic commerce inside a frames-based site. Although that page was indeed secure, the telltale sign of a secure server (the little lock icon in the bottom-left corner) was not showing. We received numerous complaints that our server was not secure (which it was) and that we should fix it. Our solution? We took the secure ordering page out of the frameset. You'll see how to do this later in the chapter, when I describe target practices.

So, after reading all this, you might wonder if you should use frames at all. I used to avoid them like the plague, but with the capability to turn off borders and make them transparent under most conditions (if printing, security, and bookmarking are not an issue to you), then you might grow to like using them.

FRAMES BASICS

I've explained the TV dinner metaphor; now, let's put it to action. Frames require multiple HTML documents. Each HTML document is like any other HTML document in that it must contain the proper basic structure—with an **HTML**, **HEAD**, and **BODY** elements. The frameset that was used on the Pyramid Flowers site (http://www. pyramidflowers.com) site contained five HTML documents: a container that holds them all together, a top navigation, a side navigation, a bottom navigation area, and a content area.

When you view the source of a frames-based site, you will likely be viewing the source code for the outer container. It is more complicated to view the source of each interior frame, so it's difficult to teach yourself how to program frames by viewing the source of framed sites that you like.

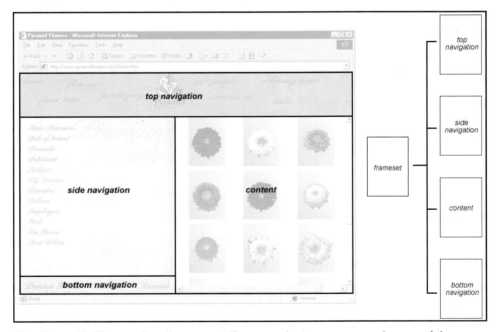

The Pyramid Flowers (http://www.pyramidflowers.com) site uses a complex set of frames to display a large amount of information. This example illustrates the relationship between a finished frames-based page and what is behind the scenes. The frameset HTML document holds the other four HTML documents in this example.

LEARNING FRAMES

Rather than work further with the **Pyramid Flowers** site, which offers a relatively complex example of frames, I believe it would be best to start with a simple two-frame screen (which you might guess by now means that there would need to be three HTML documents). The figure below shows a simple frameset. The code for the frameset follows.

code for a frameset

```
<html>
<head>
<title>Learning Frames</title>
</head>
<frameset cols="129,468">
<frame src="Left.html">
<frame src="Right.html">
</frameset>
</body>
</html>
```

The XHTML is almost identical, except it requires a correct DOCTYPE declaration, each frameset and frame tag would be in lowercase, and would have a trailing slash. For example, **<frame src="Left.html"/>** would be the correct XHTML syntax for the frame element.

Notice that the **FRAMESET** and **FRAME** tags are inside this main document. The following two documents don't require any frame tags—they are just standard HTML documents nested inside the container frameset.

code for the left frame

```
<html>
<Head>
<title>LEFT FRAME</title>
</head>
<body bgcolor="#FFFFFF">
<h1>LEFT</h1>
</body>
</html>
```

code for the right frame

```
<html>
<head>
<title>RIGHT FRAME</title>
</head>
<body bgcolor="#FFFFFF">
<h1>RIGHT</h1>
</body>
</html>
```

In this example, the borders default to "on," and they can be resized by the end user. Let's proceed through examples which show how to change the frame borders.

This figure below shows the result of increasing the size of the frame border.

code for increasing the border size

```
<frameset cols="129,468"
frameborder="yes" border="20"
framespacing="20">
<frame src="Left.html">
<frame src="Right.html">
</frameset>
```

This figure shows you the result of putting a *0* value inside the frame border element.

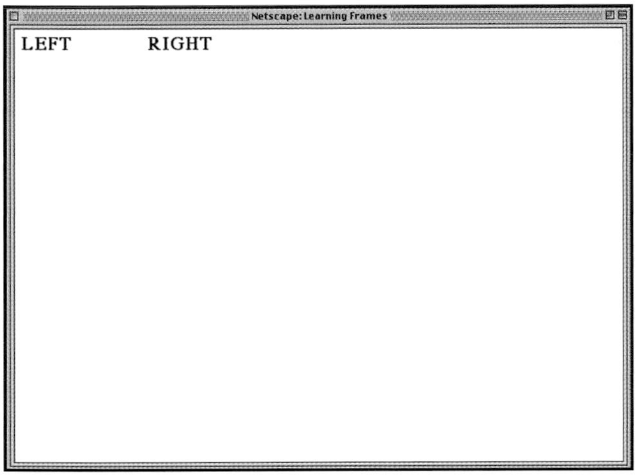

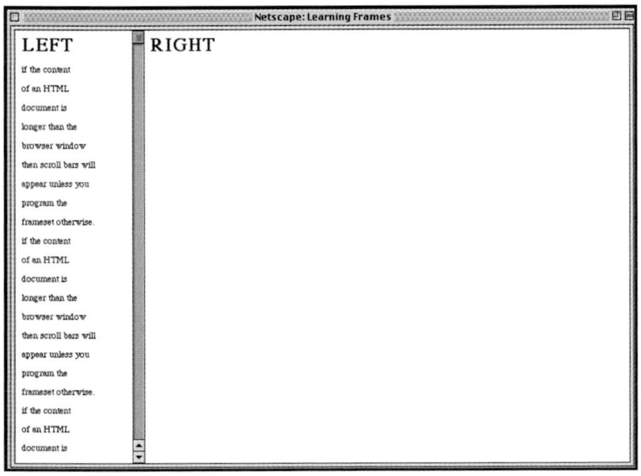

You can clip the content that extends beyond the size of the browser with the **SCROLLING** element.

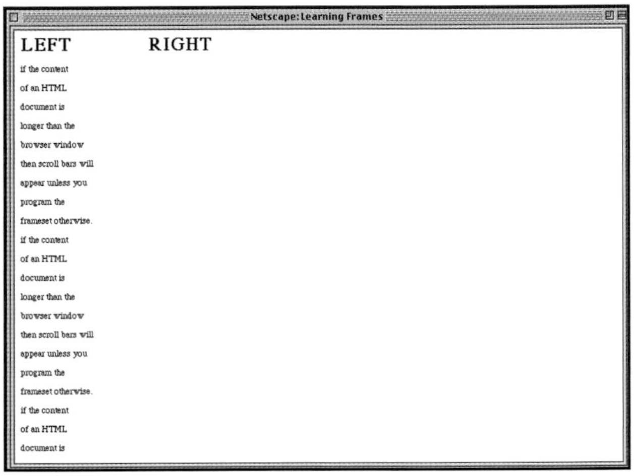

code for zero border

```
<frameset cols="129,468"
frameborder="yes" border="0"
framespacing="0">
<frame src="Left.html">
<frame src="Right.html">
</frameset>
```

code for clipping the content

```
<frameset cols="129,468"
frameborder="no" border="0"
framespacing="0">
<frame src="Left.html" scrolling="no">
<frame src="Right.html">
</frameset>
```

Note: The identical code will result in a scrollbar if the content of one of the frames extends farther than the size of the browser window.

It's also possible to use relative positioning (as opposed to absolute positioning with pixels). If you want to set one part of your frameset to be fixed (left side) but allow the right side to be sized to whatever size the end user's browser is set, use the asterisk (*) symbol to signify a wild card. For example, **<FRAMESET COLS="129,*">** would instruct the browser to keep the left side fixed at 129 pixels but scale the right side to whatever size the window scales to. The example below shows setting the size with percentages instead of pixels. Regardless of how wide or big I open my browser in this condition, the frame regions will always be **25%:75%** of my screen.

You can also nest framesets inside each other. Notice in the HTML code that there are two sets of opening and closing **FRAMESET** tags. This is required when you nest frames for complex framesets.

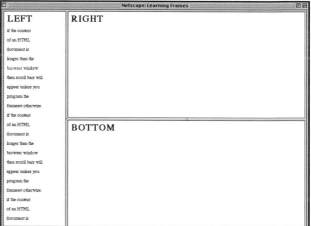

code for nested frames

```
<frameset cols="129,468"
frameborder="yes">
<frame src="Left.html"
name="" scrolling="no">
<frameset rows="229,229">
<frame src="Right.html">
<frame src="Bottom.html">
</frameset>
</frameset>
```

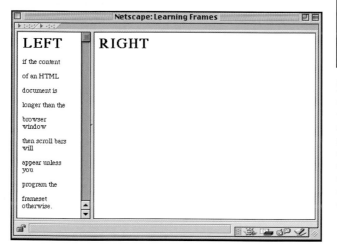

code for relative positioning

```
<frameset cols="25%,75%">
<frame src="Left.html">
<frame src="Right.html">
</frameset>
```

TARGET PRACTICE

Once you've learned how to program frames, the next step is to learn to program targets. Targets enable additional links or HTML pages to load into specific regions of your frameset. The following examples will demonstrate how to use targeting in your framesets.

The first step to using targets is to name your frames. You can name them Fred, Wilma, or even Bozo—but it's better to name them something that is meaningful. In our example I've chosen the boring, but useful names "Left" and "Right." I am going to work with linking in the following examples.

If all I do is insert a link to my site in the **Left.html** document, once I click on that link, the browser thinks I want to put my site into the same HTML document that contained the link.

If, instead, I wanted to have my document load into the right frame, I would need to name my frame so I could use it as a target.

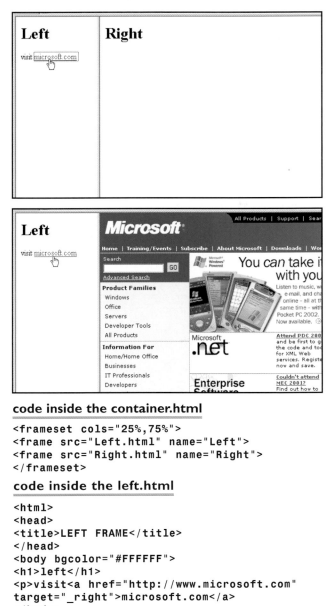

code inside the container.html

```
<frameset cols="25%,75%">
<frame src="Left.html" name="Left">
<frame src="Right.html" name="Right">
</frameset>
```

code inside the left.html

```
<html>
<head>
<title>LEFT FRAME</title>
</head>
<body bgcolor="#FFFFFF">
<h1>left</h1>
<p>visit<a href="http://www.microsoft.com"
target="_right">microsoft.com</a>
</body>
</html>
```

If I wanted to have my document load in a new window outside of the frameset, I would set the target to "**_blank**". This would cause the link to appear in a new browser window.

code for using new window as a target

```
<html>
<head>
<title>LEFT FRAME</title>
</head>
<body bgcolor="#FFFFFF">
<h1>Left</h1>
<p>visit<a href="http://www.microsoft.com"
target="_blank">microsoft.com</a>
</body>
</html>
```

If I wanted to load my site and replace the entire frameset with my site by itself, I would program **TARGET="_parent"**. The identical effect would be achieved by choosing **TARGET="_top"**.

code for replacing the frameset

```
<html>
<head>
<title>LEFT FRAME</title>
</head>
<body bgcolor="#FFFFFF">
<h1>Left</h1>
<p>visit<a href="http://www.microsoft.com"
target="_parent">microsoft.com</a>
</body>
</html>
```

Target	Description
_self	Loads the HTML into the same frame as the link
_blank	Launches a new browser window
_parent	Replaces the frameset with the HTML that was linked to
_top	Loads the HTML into the full window that is open

FUN WITH FRAMES

Now that a lot of the technical barriers of frames have been solved, such as the capability to print a specific frame from a browser and navigate between frames with the Back button, I've seen a lot more acceptance and creative uses of frames. I'd like to share some of the cool techniques I've seen used for frames in this section.

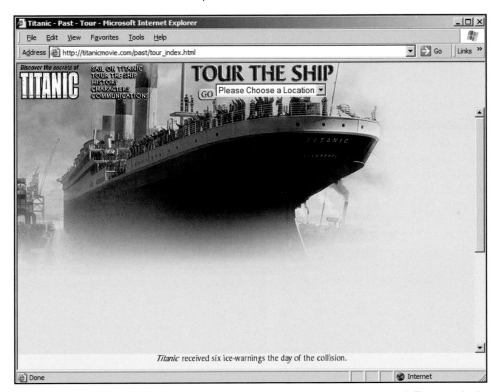

Here is an example of using background tiles in frames (http://www.titanicmovie.com). The same background is used in different regions, and matches up by setting the frame regions to perfectly line up to the artwork. The next few examples will show you how this was accomplished.

note

WARNING: FRAMES & NETSCAPE

If you are working with frames and trying to get a background image to match across multiple frames, there is a little glitch in Netscape that you need to be aware of. Unfortunately, Netscape Navigator doesn't support frames as well as Internet Explorer. This problem is resolved in Netscape Navigator 6.0 and above. As the browser window is resized, in some sizes your background image may not match perfectly. There is no quick fix for this, your best bet is to design your background images so this little offset does not ruin the design.

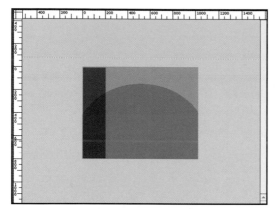

Want to try this yourself? Cut it into two slices, and note the exact size of each region. In this example, I've made the left side 200 pixels wide. I used ImageReady's slicing capabilities to make two images: one that was 200 pixels wide and the other that was 824 pixels wide. These images were named **left.gif** and **right.gif**.

The **left.html** document looked like this.

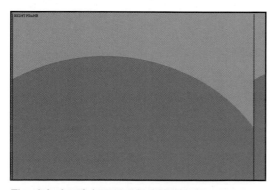

The **right.html** document looked like this.

code inside the left.html

```
<body bgcolor="#FFFFFF"
background="right.gif">
RIGHT FRAME
</body>
```

code inside the right.html

```
<body bgcolor="#FFFFFF"
background="right.gif">
RIGHT FRAME
</body>
```

code inside the container.html

```
<frameset cols="200,*"
border="0" framespacing="0">
<frame src="left.html">
<frame src="right.html">
</frameset>
```

Note: The **COLS** attribute is set to 200 fixed pixels and uses a wild card (*), which puts the right side of the frameset into percentages.

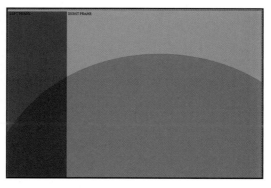

Here's the finished result of reassembling the background tiles into a frameset. The code for this is called **container.html**.

My brother, Bill Weinman, programmed this interesting frameset based on a design by Don Barnett for his site **WebMonster Networks** at http://www.webmonster.net. The code for his site on the following page.

Left   **Top**   **Middle**   **Right**   **Bottom**

It contains six frames: the outer container, four separate sets for the borders, and one interior set for the central content. The striped borders are actually tiny frame regions that contain a striped background tile. Here's how the pages look separated.

code for webmonster's frameset

```
<HEAD>
<TITLE>WebMonster Networks</TITLE>
</HEAD>
<FRAMESET COLS="*,616,*" BORDER=0 FRAMEBORDER=0 FRAMESPACING=0>
  <FRAME SRC="/frames/black.html" SCROLLING=no MARGINHEIGHT=0 MARGINWIDTH=0>
  <FRAMESET ROWS="*,416,*" BORDER=0 FRAMEBORDER=0 FRAMESPACING=0>
    <FRAME SRC="/frames/black.html" SCROLLING=no MARGINHEIGHT=0 MARGINWIDTH=0>

    <FRAMESET COLS="8,*,8" BORDER=0 FRAMEBORDER=0 FRAMESPACING=0>
      <FRAME SRC="/frames/vert.html" SCROLLING=no MARGINHEIGHT=0 MARGINWIDTH=0>
      <FRAMESET ROWS="8,*,8" BORDER=0 FRAMEBORDER=0 FRAMESPACING=0>
        <FRAME SRC="/frames/top.html" SCROLLING=no MARGINHEIGHT=0 MARGINWIDTH=0 NAME=content>

        <!-- content goes here -->
        <FRAME SRC="/front/front.html" SCROLLING=no MARGINHEIGHT=0 MARGINWIDTH=0>

      <FRAME SRC="/frames/horiz.html" SCROLLING=no MARGINHEIGHT=0 MARGINWIDTH=0>
      </FRAMESET>
      <FRAME SRC="/frames/vert.html" SCROLLING=no MARGINHEIGHT=0 MARGINWIDTH=0>
    </FRAMESET>
    <FRAME SRC="/frames/black.html" SCROLLING=no MARGINHEIGHT=0 MARGINWIDTH=0>
  </FRAMESET>
</FRAME SRC="/frames/black.html" SCROLLING=no MARGINHEIGHT=0 MARGINWIDTH=0>
</FRAMESET>
```

NO FRAMES

I highly recommend that you create alternative content for those who visit your site with older browsers that cannot see frames. Whatever you place into the **BODY** of the **NOFRAMES** content will appear to those people who are not able to view frames.

code

```
<html>
<head>
<title>Learning Frames</title>
</head>
<frameset cols="25%,75%">
<frame src="left.html" name="left">
<frame src="right.html" name="right">
</frameset>
<noframes><body bgcolor="#FFFFFF">
(Insert your "no frames" content here.)

</body></noframes>
</html>
```

CREATING A "BLEED" BORDER

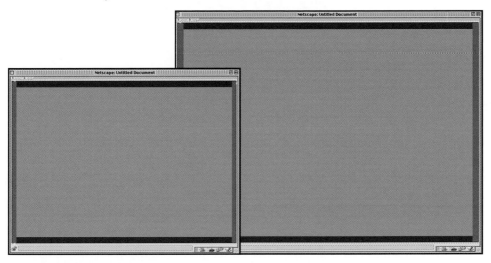

Here's an example of what my brother did, using solid background colors, not artwork. No matter how small or large this page is sized within the browser, it will always have edges that bleed to the sides.

code for a frameset using solid background colors

```
<FRAMESET COLS="20,*,20" ROWS="*" BORDER="0" FRAMESPACING="0"
FRAMEBORDER="NO">
  <FRAME SRC="left.html">
  <FRAMESET ROWS="*,20" COLS="*" FRAMEBORDER="NO" BORDER="0"
  FRAMESPACING="0">
    <FRAMESET ROWS="20,*" COLS="*">
      <FRAME SRC="top.html" SCROLLING="NO">
      <FRAME SRC="inside.html" SCROLLING="NO">
    </FRAMESET>
    <FRAME SRC="bottom.html" SCROLLING="NO">
  </FRAMESET>
  <FRAME SRC="right.html" SCROLLING="NO">
</FRAMESET>
```

Note: The main trick to this technique is to combine absolute pixel values (in this case, 20-pixel borders) with the wild card (*) for whatever percentage is left to fill.

FRAMES

SUMMARY

This concludes the chapter on frames. As I've stated, frames are something most people either love or hate. I happen to have personally shifted from hating them in Netscape 2.0 to loving them in 4.0 and later browsers. Most of the problems of frames have been worked out by the browsers; now it's just a matter of knowing how to handle frames so you don't fall prey to the pitfalls. Here's a summary of what to do:

> Use frames when you want to use a consistent navigation device throughout your site. Frames allow that region to remain stationary, while allowing other content to change around it.

> If possible, turn off the borders and scrollbars of your frames. There is already a limited amount of real estate on a web page, and too many frames can create confusing navigation and a boxed-in aesthetic.

> Use **TARGET** to control where linked content appears within your frames.

> You can create interesting special effects with background tiles and fills using frames. Combining fixed pixel dimensions and percentage dimensions allows some regions to stay fixed, while others scale with the size of the browser window.

Cascading Style Sheets

Introduction

CSS (**C**ascading **S**tyle **S**heets) offers a means to separate "style" from "structure." What exactly does that mean? At its inception, HTML was only intended to be a structural markup language. Structure is independent of the way something looks. Structure defines whether text on the page is a headline or body copy, whether a list should be alphabetized or numeric, and so on. Structure is very important when it comes to accessibility issues (when someone who is visually impaired uses an audio reader, for example) or when a web page is shown on a device other than a browser. Because HTML originally offered no means to style a document (change the font, the color, or format text and pictures precisely), many tags were introduced over time that dealt with the appearance of document. Many times, these tags that dealt with style interfered with structure.

To give an example of this interference between style and structure, imagine a headline on a web page. The HTML code could instruct this text to be a headline by virtue of an **H** tag. The **H1** tag will cause the type to be set in a large, bold, black, generic Times Roman font. Instead of using the **H1** tag, designers who didn't want their headline to look so generic might use the **FONT** tag instead. Through this tag, they could tell the text to be large, bold, and to be any font or color they chose. While both techniques produced something that I looked to the end user like a headline, the **H1** approach kept the structure intact, while the **FONT** tag changed the appearance and didn't identify what the structure was.

Enter style sheets to the rescue. Style sheets can change the appearance of your web pages without affecting the structure. In other words, you can have your headline maintain its structure and have its style, too.

IMPLEMENTATION VERSUS STANDARDS

While the **W**orld **W**ide **W**eb **C**onsortium (W3C) strongly advocates that you use style sheets, and offers a great deal of documentation and support, there is a problem with using them. The problem is that browsers "implement" style sheets with varying degrees of success. By this, I mean not all browsers interpret style sheets the same way. There are still major implementation differences between Netscape and Explorer, not to mention that different (especially older) versions of the same browser support style sheets differently.

The promise that style sheets hold is a designer's best dream. Designers want pixel-precise control, better layout options, and more consistent and robust typographic control. HTML was designed to separate the structure of a document from the presentation so that HTML pages could be accessed by anyone, by any device, or on any browser. While this was started out as a goodwill theory, the passing of Section 508, which is described in detail in Chapter 8, *"Accessibility Issues,"* makes CSS a mandatory practice for many sites.

Sadly, until the browsers support style sheets in a uniform manner, that promise will not be totally met. While using style sheets is always better than using no style sheets, backward compatibility can pose a strong deterrent for some.

This is the site for **alistapart.com**, shown in a browser that properly supports Cascading Style Sheets.

Here is the same site shown in an older version of the browser that doesn't support style sheets. All the information is still here, but it doesn't look very good.

What this means is that you need to make a decision as to whether style sheets are appropriate for your site. If you know that your audience is likely to be using a specific browser, testing style sheet implementation is easy. If you think your audience will be viewing your site from older browsers, you might have to do a considerable amount of testing to ensure that you're getting the desired results from your code.

Be sure to check out WaSP (**W**eb **S**tandards **P**roject) at http://www.webstandards.org. You'll find numerous articles on the benefits of using style sheets, as well as compelling arguments in their favor. The only reason style sheets pose any controversy at all is their lack of consistent implementation by browsers.

Another fantastic resource is found at http://www.alistapart.com. Here you'll find numerous articles about style sheets, accessibility, and design with lots of practical code examples, and great ideas.

Cascading Style Sheets will be described in this chapter from a practical perspective in terms of what is supported and what is promised. However, in the end, choosing to use CSS on your pages will be a decision that you will have to make based upon your intended audience and the browsers you expect them to be using.

READ THE SPECS!

The W3C has released two recommendations for Cascading Style Sheets: CSS1 and CSS2. The CSS1 recommendation was formalized on December 17, 1996 and revised on January 11, 1999. The CSS1 recommendation contains about **50** properties. The CSS2 recommendation was formalized on May 12, 1998. The CSS2 recommendation contains about **120** properties, including those of the CSS1 recommendation. In this chapter I will refer to them collectively as CSS unless there is a reason to make a distinction between the recommendations.

If you want to read about the recommendations, you will find them at:

W3C's CSS Recommendations
http://www.w3.org/TR/REC-CSS1
http://www.w3.org/TR/REC-CSS2

ANATOMY OF A STYLE SHEET

The anatomy of a style sheet includes some terminology that is likely new to you, such as declarations and selectors. Here are some examples of how these terms relate to style sheet programming.

RULES

At the very core of CSS are rules. To the left is an example of a simple CSS rule and to the right is an example of a CSS declaration.

```
h1 { color: green; }
```

```
{ color: green; }
```

Rules consist of two parts

The selector and the declaration. In the example above, the **H1** tag is the selector (the object being modified), and the color is the declaration (what part—color—and how—to green—the selector is being changed).

The declaration has two parts

The property and the value. In the example above, property is the color of the **H1** tag that is being modified. The value is set to green, which specifies how the property is being modified.

note

HTML 101: WHAT IS AN ELEMENT?

In case you haven't read the HTML chapter or have forgotten what an "element" is, I thought it would be a good idea to revisit that term here before moving on to the details of Cascading Style Sheets: it's the tag or tagset plus content. `<table border="1">` is the opening tag plus an attribute of the element **TABLE**.

note

CSS & ACCESSIBILITY

This chapter will show how Cascading Style Sheets play a critical role in making your web pages accessible. In Chapter 8, *"Accessibility Issues,"* the role of CSS and accessibility are covered more fully. Make sure you review that section to learn more about this important issue facing web designers.

ADDING CSS TO HTML

Defining your CSS rules is only a part of adding CSS to your pages. Once you have defined your rules, you need to add the CSS rule to your HTML document so it is rendered properly by the browsers. This is done by simply adding a small bit of code within the **<head>** tag of your HTML document. This code will serve as a container for all the CSS within your document.

This is an example of a simple page that contains CSS:

code

```
    <html>
    <head>
    <title>Untitled</title>
1   <style type="text/css">
2   <!--
3   h1 {color: green;}
4   -->
5   </style>
    </head>
    <body>
6   <h1>The Art of Bonsai</h1>
    </body>
    </html>
```

code deconstruction

1   The **STYLE** element is a container that goes in the **HEAD** section of your HTML document. The **TYPE** attribute specifies the type of style sheet being used, which in this case is **text/css**. The **STYLE** element can contain any number of different styles.

2   This is the opening tag of an HTML comment. By placing your styles within an **HTML** comment, users with older browsers not capable of viewing CSS will ignore the code instead of seeing the code displayed in error in their browser.

3   This style element contains one style, which applies to the **H1** tag, changing its color to green. **H1** is the selector, **color** is the property, and **green** is the value.

4   Closing HTML comment tag.

5   Closing style tag.

6   This line contains some text formatted with the **H1** tag, which has been redefined using the CSS code above.

GROUPING SELECTORS

As you add more and more styles to your pages, you might find yourself making the same stylistic change to multiple HTML elements. In these cases, you might consider grouping your CSS selectors. This can shorten the amount of code and make for a quicker download. As you will see, grouped selectors must be separated by a comma in order to function properly.

For example, if you had these CSS selectors in your document:

code

```
h1 {color: blue; font-family: verdana}
h2 {color: blue; font-family: verdana}
h3 {color: blue; font-family: verdana}
```

they could be optimized and grouped like this:

code

```
h1, h2, h3 {color: blue;
font-family: verdana }
```

code deconstruction

This rule specifies that all text within **h1**, **h2**, and **h3** tags will display in the Verdana font with a blue color.

CLASS SELECTORS

In the preceding examples, you learned how to create styles based on HTML elements using selectors. Selectors are related to HTML elements. If you wanted to apply a style to something that wasn't a tag (let's say there was a certain sentence in your document that you wanted to be bold, but it wasn't anything other than text from a structural definition), this kind of situation is where Class selectors are of value.

Another situation in which a Class selector comes in handy is when you want to style the appearance of HTML tags differently. Earlier you learned how to redefine the appearance of an HTML element (the **H1** tag). Suppose you don't want to format every **H1** tag the same way? This is a perfect place to consider creating a Class selector. Consider the code on the following page:

This is some text formatted with a class!

This text has not been formatted with a class.

code

```
  <head>
  <style type="text/css">
  <!--
1 .text1 {font-family: Verdana;}
  -->
  </style>
  </head>
  <body>
2 <h1 class="text1">This is some text
  formatted with a class!</h1>
3 <h1>This text has not been formatted
  with a class.</h1>
  </body>
```

code deconstruction

1 Class selectors are written in this syntax: always beginning with a dot (**.**) and a unique name. The rest of the syntax will follow the conventions you learned earlier.

2 The Class selector is applied to the HTML element using the class attribute and the name you assigned to the class. In this example I gave the class a name of "**text1**". Notice that the dot (**.**) is not included in the class attribute!

3 For comparison, this line has not been formatted using the Class selector.

By creating a Class selector, I could now apply this formatting anywhere in my document independent of the HTML element. It will apply this format only where it encounters this class, not across every instance of an HTML element like previously shown.

Here is an example of a Class selector being applied only to a specific portion of a paragraph:

There are five basic styles of bonsai.

code

```
  <head>
  <style type="text/css">
  <!--
1 .text1 {font-family: verdana;
  font-weight: bold;}
  -->
  </style>
  </head>
  <body>
2 <p>There are <SPAN CLASS="text1">five
  basic styles</SPAN> of bonsai.</p>
  </body>
```

code deconstruction

1 The Class selector syntax is displayed on this line with the **font-family** and the **font-weight** properties applied.

2 The **<SPAN>** tag is used to designate the area of text that is to be formatted using the Class selector. Notice that there is a closing **</SPAN>** tag to end the formatting.

BLOCK-LEVEL & INLINE-LEVEL ELEMENTS

Throughout this chapter and book, you will find many references to block-level and inline content, so it is important to understand what these terms mean.

Block-level elements act like boxes that start at the margin of one line of text and end so that the content after the closing element is forced to start on a new line of text. The content of a block-level element can be, and typically is, several lines long. Basically, block-level elements start and end a line of text. For example, the paragraph **<P>** element is a block-level element. It starts at one margin and anything that comes after the closing **</P>** element is forced to appear on a new line. Any formatting applied to a block-level element will affect everything within it. You cannot place one block-level element inside another block-level element. To do that, you would use an inline element, which I explain below. Let's consider the following example and code:

```
Mary Had a Little Lamb

Mary had a little lamb, its fleece
was white as snow.
```

code

```
<head>
<style type="text/css">
<!--
.body {font-family: Verdana, Arial,
Helvetica, sans-serif; font-size: 10px}
.lamb {color: #FF0000}
-->
</style>
</head>
<body bgcolor="#FFFFFF" text="#000000">
<div class="body">
<p>Mary Had a Little Lamb</p>
<p>Mary had a little lamb, its fleece<br>
was white as snow.</p>
</div>
</body>
```

code deconstruction

A **<DIV>** element is used to create a range, or invisible box if you will, around the two **<P>** elements. The body **CLASS** is attached to the **<DIV>** element, which causes both paragraphs to be formatted with the body **CLASS**. So, instead of applying the body **CLASS** to both paragraph elements, it was applied once to the **<DIV>** element. This results in less code, which is a good thing.

There are a bunch of block elements within HTML. I have listed some of them in the chart below.

Block Element	Definition
BLOCKQUOTE	Blockquote
BODY	Body
BR	Line break
DD	Definition description
DL	Definition list
DIV	Division
DT	Definition term
H1-H6	Heading levels
HR	Horizontal rule
HTML	Well … ;-)
LI	List item
OBJECT	Object
OL	Ordered list
P	Paragraph
PRE	Preformatted
UL	Unordered list

Inline elements: As described, inline-elements act like boxes as well, except they are used within block-level elements. This is the difference between the two. For example, if you have a **<DIV>** element that is formatting a paragraph of text with a style sheet and you want to format a single word within that **<DIV>** element, you would use the inline element **<SPAN>**. For example, consider the example and code below:

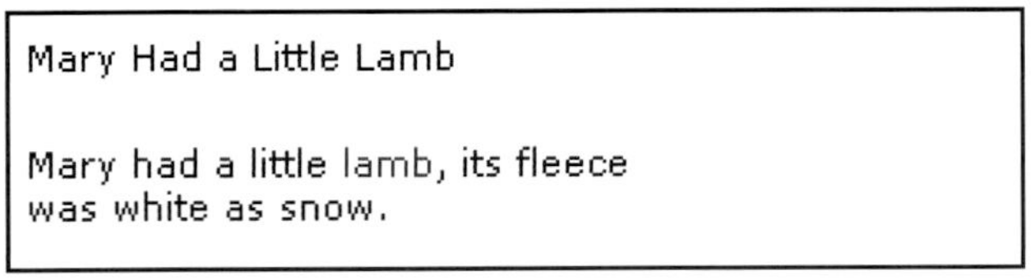

There are also a bunch of inline elements within HTML. I have listed some of them in the chart below.

Inline Element	Definition
A	Anchor
EM	Emphasis
I	Italic
IMG	Image
SPAN	Span
STRONG	Strong
TT	Teletype

Mary Had a Little Lamb

Mary had a little lamb, its fleece
was white as snow.

code

```
<head>
<style type="text/css">
<!--
.body {font-family: Verdana, Arial,
Helvetica, sans-serif; font-size: 10px}
.lamb {color: #FF0000}
-->
</style>
</head>
<body bgcolor="#FFFFFF" text="#000000">
<div class="body">
<p>Mary Had a Little Lamb</p>
<p>Mary had a little
<span class="lamb">lamb</span>,
its fleece<br>
was white as snow.</p>
</div>
</body>
```

code deconstruction

As you can see above, I used the **<SPAN>** element and lamb class to format the word lamb, which is within the **<DIV>** element. This is a good example of how the **<SPAN>** element is used.

PSEUDO-CLASSES

So far, you have learned about selectors, classes, and IDs. Things are about to get more interesting with pseudo-classes. These are class selectors that let the designer apply styles to elements that don't exist within the document. If you are scratching your head, don't worry. I had the same reaction when I was learning these. Thank goodness it wasn't dandruff. ;-)

Pseudo-classes let you apply styles to elements that you know will exist, but you just don't know when. For example, users are likely to move their cursor over a link at some point. The anchor tag is probably the most common pseudo-class. Let's look at a pseudo-class in context in the following code.

Click here to visit Macromedia.com

Here you can see an active link, being viewed in Netscape Navigator 4.77 for Windows, that has the line removed using a pseudo-class.

code

```
<head>
<style type="text/css">
1 a:link {text-decoration:none;}
</style>
</head>
<body>
2 <a href="http://www.macromedia.com">
Click here to visit Macromedia.com</a>
</body>
```

code deconstruction

1   This is the proper syntax to create a pseudo-class for the anchor tag. Because the decoration attribute has been set to none, there will not be an underline beneath this text link.

2   The pseudo-class is automatically applied to every anchor tag in the document. You do not have to add any additional code in the `<BODY>` portion of the document.

The following chart identifies the pseudo-classes available in the CSS2 recommendation. Note that pseudo-class selectors and links must be in a specific order to work properly (shown here).

Pseudo-Class	Definition
`:link`	Adds style to unvisited links.
`:visited`	Adds style to visited links.
`:hover`	Adds style to link when the mouse is over it.
`:active`	Adds style to link when it is clicked on.
`:first-child`	Adds style to an element that is the first child of another element.*
`:lang`	Can specify a language for an element.*

*   Using the `:first-child` and `:lang` pseudo-classes is really advanced. If you are interested in learning more about them, you should consider purchasing the following handy books:

Eric Meyer On CSS
Eric Meyer
New Riders Publishing
0-7357-1245-X

Designing CSS Web Pages
Christopher Schmitt
New Riders Publishing
0-7357-1263-8

note

COOL STUFF WITH PSEUDO-CLASSES

There are some neat things you can do with pseudo-classes, among them is the capability to remove or create text link effects. For example, you can use them to change the color of text when users move their mouse over the text link. You can also use them to remove the underline under text links altogether! Let's take a look at the code for some of these cool tricks.

```
a:link {   text-decoration: none}
```

This pseudo-class will remove the underline from all links on the page.

```
a:hover {   color: #FF0000; text-decoration: underline}
```

This pseudo-class will cause all text links on the page to turn red and underlined when the users move their mouse over the link.

Have fun and experiment with these pseudo-classes to see what kinds of effects you can come up with.

tip

BOOKS ON CSS

Cascading Style Sheets: Designing for the Web
Hakon Wium Lie and Bert Bos.
Addison-Wesley
ISBN: 0201596253

Eric Meyer on CSS
Eric Meyer
New Riders Publishing
ISBN: 0-7357-1245-X

Designing CSS Web Pages
Christopher Schmitt
New Riders Publishing
ISBN: 0-7357-1263-8

PSEUDO-ELEMENTS

Pseudo-elements are pretty similar to pseudo-classes, except they do not affect the anchor tag of a document. Instead, pseudo-elements can be used to control the first letter or line of text. In the CSS1 recommendation, there are two pseudo-elements: first-letter and first-line. These are used to format the first letter and line of text respectively. It is important to note that pseudo-elements can only be applied to block elements, such as the **<P>** tag.

A pseudo-element has a general form of:

```
p.dropcap:first-letter { font-size: 200% }
```

The first character in this paragraph has been formatted using the first-letter pseudo-element. As you can see, this is an easy way to add a drop-cap to your paragraphs of text. Cascading Style Sheets can really make things look better!

Here you can see a drop-cap that has been added to this paragraph using the first-letter pseudo-element. That was quick and easy. ;-)

code

```
<head>
<style>
p.dropcap:first-letter {font-size: 200%;
float: left}
</style>
</head>
<body>
<p class="dropcap"> The first character
in this paragraph has been formatted
using the first-letter pseudo-element.
As you can see, this is an easy way
to add a drop-cap to your paragraphs
of text. Cascading Style Sheets can
really make things look better!</p>
</body>
```

code deconstruction

I   This is what the code looks like for this pseudo-element. In this example, the font size was increased, floated to the left, applied to the **<P>** block element, and called "**dropcap**".

2   The pseudo-element is applied to the paragraph tag, one of the many block tags.

Next, let's take a look at the first-line pseudo-element. As you will see, the code for the two pseudo-elements is very similar:

```
p:first-line { font-variant: small-caps }
```

THE FIRST LINE OF THIS PARAGRAPH HAS BEEN formatted using the first-line pseudo-element. As you can see, this is an easy way to add a style to your paragraphs of text. Cascading Style Sheets can really make things look better!

Here you can see that the entire first line of the paragraph has been formatted differently from the rest of the text.

The code for the first-line pseudo-element does not look a whole lot different from the first-letter pseudo-element:

code

```
<head>
<style>
p:first-line { font-variant: small-caps }
</style>
</head>
<body>
<p>The first line of this paragraph has
been formatted using the first-line pseudo-
element. As you can see, this is an easy
way to add a style to your paragraphs of
text. Cascading Style Sheets can really
make things look better!</p>
</body>
```

Here is a chart that identifies the pseudo-elements available in the CSS2 recommendation.

Pseudo-Element	Definition
:first-letter	Adds style to the first letter of a text line.
:first-line	Adds style to the first line of text block.
:before	Inserts the content before an element.
:after	Inserts the content after an element.

HIDING STYLES FROM OLDER BROWSERS

If you enclose your style sheets inside HTML comments, browsers that don't understand the **STYLE** tag will be prevented from seeing it. Those browsers that do understand the style sheet will ignore the comment tag and apply the style sheet to the page.

code

```
<head>
<title>CSS Examples</title>
<style type="text/css">
<!--
h1 {font-family: Verdana}
-->
</style>
</head>
```

Note: Remember just because the style sheet itself is enclosed in HTML comments in the code above, browsers that don't understand the **STYLE** tag are prevented from displaying the style sheet in the browser window (that's one of the rules of HTML—ignore the tags you don't understand). Browsers that do understand the style sheet will ignore the comment tags and apply the style sheet to the page.

H1 font-family: Verdana

Working with Ducks in a Row Rubber Stamps

Because the style of art throughout the catalog is consistent, any of the designs may be used together side by side, or superimposed, making the possibilities for personal expression boundless.

You will find designs in our catalog which cover a vast array of categories, from floral images to humor, holiday stamps, border designs and decorative imagery, for all around use. You, as the stamping artist will be the one to create original art works from these designs, and nothing pleasures us more than to see the beautiful and original ways in which our designs are being used.

Throughout the catalog you will find some helpful hints on some of the uses and techniques to enjoy your stamps, but we're sure that you as the stamping artist can teach us a thing or two! One thing for certain, the possibilities are endless!

Here is an example in Netscape 3 showing a style sheet that was not hidden within any comment tags.

TYPES OF STYLE SHEETS

There are three popular types of style sheets: internal (embedded), external, and inline. The following sections provide you with an example and description of each. Knowing the different types and when to use them should make you feel much more comfortable working with style sheets. Here is a brief description of the three types of Cascading Style Sheets:

> **Internal style sheets** are the most common type of style sheet used. These are constructed using the **<STYLE>** element and are part of the HTML document, which means all the formatting information is contained within the **<HEAD>** portion of the HTML document. These types of style sheets are easy to create and are useful for creating consistent styles within a single page.

> **External style sheets** are the most powerful of the three. These style sheets exist as separate documents from the HTML page. This allows them to apply to multiple pages using the **<LINK>** element. With one change to the style sheet document, you can update hundreds or even thousands of pages! These types of style sheets are great for bringing design consistency to a large number of pages and can make updating multiple pages more efficient.

> **Inline style sheets** exist within the **<HEAD>** element of the HTML page and are created using the **<STYLE>** element. These styles are useful for applying a style to a document that contains styles from an internal or external style sheet. The inline style will override the styles defined by the internal or external style sheet.

INTERNAL

This is a code example of an "internal" style sheet. Notice the **<STYLE>** element is used inside the **<HEAD>** portion of the page. All of the formatting information is contained within the HTML page. These types of style sheets will only affect the appearance of this single page. They can be effective for creating design consistency within a single page. When would you use an internal style sheet? These are useful when you want the style to only apply to a single HTML page.

code

```
<html>                                  </style>
<head>                                  </head>
<title>Internal Style Sheet            <body>
Example</title>                         <h1>Internal Style Sheets are cool!
<style type="text/css">                 Woo-hoo!</h1>
<--                                     </body>
h1 {font-family: Verdana}               </html>
-->
```

EXTERNAL

Here's an example of an "external" style sheet. Notice the **<LINK>** element is using the **<HREF>** attribute to point to the **"external.css"** file. The **external.css** file is the document that contains all the formatting information for this HTML page. Because the formatting information exists independent of the HTML page, it can easily be applied to several HTML pages and updated more efficiently.

code

```
<html>
<head>
<title>External Style Sheet
Example</title>
<link rel="stylesheet" href="external.css"
type="text/css">
</head>
<body>
<h1>Check it Out!</h1>
<p>My style is cool, daddy-o</p>
</body>
</html>
```

code deconstruction

The file this document references is called **external.css**. You can give your style sheet any file name you want; just be sure to save it in text-only mode (just like HTML), upload it to the same directory as your HTML (or set the link to whichever directory in which it lives), and give it a **.css** extension. You don't have to put an external style sheet inside a comment tag because no style information is stored within the HTML code.

Your **external.css** document could look like this:

code

```
h1 {color: FFCC33; font-family: sans-serif}
p {background: black; font-family: verdana}
```

code deconstruction

The external style sheet document should not contain any HTML whatsoever—just CSS rules.

INLINE

An "inline" style sheet only applies to the parts of an HTML document that are specified and will override any style settings being applied by an external or internal style sheet.

code

```
<html>
<head>
<title>Inline Style Sheet Example</title>
<style type="text/css">
<!--
h1 {font-family: Verdana}
-->
</style>
</head>
<body>
<h1 style="font-family: Times New
Roman">Wow - Inline Style Sheets are
really powerful!</h1>
</body>
</html>
```

code deconstruction

In the example above, even though the "internal" style sheet formats all **H1** tags with Verdana font, the "inline" style will override that setting and format the text using Times New Roman.

When would you use an inline style sheet? Whenever you want a style to affect only a portion of an HTML page and/or you want to override the settings of an external or internal style sheet.

The disadvantage to this method is that you have to add the inline style code every single time you want to use it. The next **H1** text after this one would revert back to the default browser display unless you added yet another **STYLE** attribute or have an external style applied that defines the appearance of the **H1** element.

MEASUREMENT UNITS FOR TYPE

In order to work with style sheets, it's important to understand the types of measurement units that can be specified. Measurement units in electronic type are tricky, because when you specify a "twelve-point" typeface, it probably won't mean the same thing across computer platforms. Anyone who has ever looked at type on the same web page inside a Windows and Macintosh browser can attest that the same code does not produce the same results across platforms. Type size can even change between the browsers on the same computer!

With that in mind, let's look at some measuring units. Below, you'll see a list with the English name, the CSS name, and a short description for each measurement unit. I have also identified which are absolute and relative units, which is an important thing to know as you choose which unit to use with your designs. Here is a chart that identifies CSS length units.

English	Type	CSS	Description
Pixel	Relative	Px	In CSS, a pixel is the distance from one grid unit on a computer screen.
Point	Absolute	Pt	A point is 1/72 inch. How many pixels that is depends on the resolution of your screen, but it is 1 pixel on 72 dpi systems.
Pica	Absolute	Pc	6 picas equal 1 inch.
Em	Relative	Em	The size of the text is relative to the size of the parent element. A 2em type size applied to a body of text with a size of 12pt would be 24pt, or twice as large as the parent element.
Ex	Relative	Ex	1/2 em. The height of a lowercase "x."
Inch	Absolute	in	Same as the good, old ruler on your desk. ;-) 72 points equal 1 inch.
Centimeter	Absolute	cm	2.54 cm equal 1 inch.
Millimeter	Absolute	mm	25.4 mm equal 1 inch.

Most web-based graphics are a fixed number of pixels wide and a fixed number of pixels high, making their sizes consistent between operating systems. Text is not consistent between operating systems; therefore, I recommend that you use "pixels" as the measurements for your text. That way, the text will have a relative size to other text on the page.

WORKING WITH TYPOGRAPHY

CSS defines a number of different properties for working with text. The **font-family** property, for example, lets you specify a particular font family, either by name (like Verdana) or by generic type (like sans-serif).

Property: font-family
    Values: Name of the font family, for example, Verdana or Georgia, or one of the following generic names:
- serif
- sans-serif
- cursive
- fantasy
- monospace

You can also give a list of values for font-family:

```
H1 {font-family: Verdana, Helvetica, sans-serif}
```

In that case, the system would try to use Verdana, or if that's not available, Helvetica. Otherwise, it will use whatever sans-serif font "is" available.

Another useful text-related property is **line-height**. This property affects the space between lines, also referred to as "leading" in the print world, after the strips of lead used to provide the spaces between lines of metal type.

Property: line-height
    Values: number
            default
            Sets the amount of space between lines of text

The **line-height** is measured from the baseline of one line to the baseline of the next. The amount of space above and below the text is the same. For example, a **line-height** of 12pt would add 6pt of space above the text and 6pt of space below the text.

```
P {
  font-family: Georgia;
  font-size: 12px;
  line-height: 1.5em;
  }
```

This will set the **line-height** to **1.5 em**. (1em is the same as the font-size, so 1.5 em is one-and-a-half times the body size of the type, which would be 18px in this example). This would add 3px to space above and below (a total of 6px, or the difference between the **font-size** and the **font-height**) the text.

Absolute Positioning

Designers have long complained that it's not possible to absolutely position a graphic on a page using HTML. CSS offers a solution for this complaint, allowing designers the first real ability to position objects accurately inside the web browser window.

Absolute positioning can be achieved using either a Class selector or ID selector. Most web designers prefer to use an ID selector because an ID selector can only be used once. It is, however, possible and technically correct to use a Class selector—either will work just fine. If you were asking me, I would recommend that you use an ID selector in most cases.

In the example below, I created an ID selector to position the selected element in the uppermost left corner of the browser window.

code

```
1  #absolute {
2  position: absolute;
3  left: 0px;
4  top: 0px;
5  z-index: 1;
   }
```

code deconstruction

1   The ID selector always begins with a hash mark (#) and must be unique within the document. That means that you can only define it once, and you can only use it once. It works almost like the class selector (.), but is usually used for absolute positioning of objects on a page, where only one object will have any single position.

2   The **position** property can be either **absolute** or **relative**. Use **absolute** for objects that you want to have at a specific position on the page and **relative** for objects that you want to position relative to wherever they would have otherwise fallen. Absolute positioning was used in this example to position the graphic at a specific point on the page. An example of relative will be given a little later.

3
4   The **left** and **top** properties are used to position the object. These measurements are absolute measurements from the top-left corner of the screen, leaving no padding between the graphic and the edge of the screen. This style will place the graphic in the absolute upper-left corner of the screen.

5   Objects that are put on the screen with absolute positioning can be laid on top of each other. The **z-index** property tells the browser which objects should be on top of (or under) which other objects. Higher-numbered objects will overlay lower-numbered objects.

Here's a page that uses the absolute positioning I just defined in the code to your left.

code

```
<html>
<head>
<title>Buddah Gallery</title>
<style type="text/css">
<!--
#absolute {  position: absolute; left:
0px; top: 0px; }
-->
</style>
</head>
<body bgcolor="#FFFFFF" text="#000000"
background="buddha3.jpg">
<img src="buddha2.jpg" width="200"
height="267" id="absolute">
</body>
</html>
```

code deconstruction

I   Notice the **ID** attribute at the end of the **IMG SRC** line. This tells the browser to use the **"absolute"** ID selector to format this element. In this example, I have set the position of that selector to 0, 0, which will place the selected element in the upper-left corner of the browser window.

note

ID VERSUS CLASS

At this point, you might be wondering about the difference between a Class and ID selector. Functionally, it doesn't really matter because they both accomplish the same thing. However, there are a few nuances that make them different.

For starters, IDs start with a # symbol instead of a dot (.). Also, it is considered an error to use the same ID selector more than once. In fact, IDs should be used only once within a given document, and they should always have a unique name different from other IDs in the document. This makes them great for absolute positioning, where they would only want to use them once. Validation engines—and some future browsers—may flag errors on duplicate ID selectors. Classes are great for formatting text because they can be used multiple times on a web page. Because of this, you will find yourself probably using Classes most of the time.

DIV & ABSOLUTE POSITIONING

In the previous section, I set the absolute position of an image by formatting it using an ID selector. There are other ways to format the elements in your web pages. The **<DIV>** tag is an important part of positioning with cascading style sheets. The **<DIV>** tag acts like a container to hold other elements, much like a box would hold a pair of shoes.

The **<DIV>** element can be used to set up entire page layouts that would normally require HTML tables to achieve. In fact, the CSS **<DIV>** tag is what is intended to replace the HTML **<TABLE>** tag. It can take some time getting used to the **<DIV>** tag and how to manipulate it to get the page layouts you want. However, by using the **<DIV>** tag, you are making a significant separation between the structure and the formatting of your page, which is the goal of style sheets in the first place!

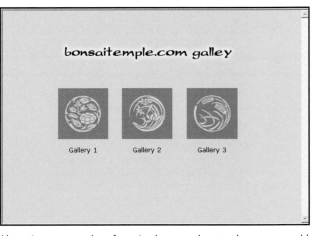

Here is an example of a simple page layout that you would normally create using tables, but instead was created using the **<DIV>** tag and classes.

In this example, you can't tell whether the layout was created using tables or absolute positioning with CSS. However, the code on the following page reveals this secret.

code

```
  <html>
  <head>
  <title>Buddah Gallery</title>
  <style type="text/css">
  <!--
1 .text {font-family: Verdana, Arial,
  Helvetica, sans-serif; font-size: 10px}
  -->
  </style>
  </head>
  <body bgcolor="#CCCC99" text="#000000">
2 <div id="gallery1"
  style="position:absolute; left:111px;
  top:154px; width:100px; height:100px;
  z-index:1"><img src="icon1.gif"
  width="100" height="100">
  </div>
3 <div id="gallery2"
  style="position:absolute; left:238px;
  top:154px; width:100px; height:100px;
  z-index:2"><img src="ico2.gif"
  width="100" height="100">
  </div>
4 <div id="gallery3"
  style="position:absolute; left:366px;
  top:154px; width:100px; height:100;
  z-index:3"><IMG SRC="icon3.gif"
  width="100" height="100">
  </div>
5 <div id="pagetitle"
  style="position:absolute; left:109px;
  top:56px; width:360; height:50;
  z-index:4"><IMG SRC="title.gif"
  width="360" height="50">
  </div>
6 <div id="text1" style="position:absolute;
  left:111px; top:267px; width:100px;
  height:20px; z-index:5" class="text">
  <p align="center">Gallery 1</p>
  </div>
7 <div id="text2" style="position:absolute;
  left:238px; top:267px; width:100;
  height:20; z-index:6" class="text">
  <p align="center">Gallery 2</p>
  </div>
8 <div id="text3" style="position:absolute;
  left:366px; top:267px; width:100;
  height:20; z-index:7" class="text">
  <p align="center">Gallery 3</p>
  </div>
  </body>
  </html>
```

code deconstruction

1 This is an internal class selector used to format the HTML text in this document. I used pixels for my text size to make sure it's viewed properly between the Mac and Windows operating systems.

2 This **<DIV>** tag is holding the first of the three gallery icons on the page. Notice that the position has been set to *absolute*, and the *top* and *left* values are defined to set its exact location within the browser window.

3 This **<DIV>** tag is holding the second gallery image and is defined the same as the first **<DIV>** tag.

4 This **<DIV>** tag is holding the third gallery image and is formatted like the others.

5 This **<DIV>** tag is holding the page title image. Notice that this code appears beneath the three images, but the actual image appears above the gallery images on the page. This occurs because the page title's location is defined in the absolute positioning properties, not by its position in the HTML code!

6 This **<DIV>** tag is holding the first block of text. Notice that this block of text has been formatted using the *text* class selector.

7 This **<DIV>** tag is holding the second block of text.

8 This **<DIV>** tag is holding the third block of text.

While this code might seem a bit complex and hard to navigate, it is the way of the future and knowing how to work with it will be essential to your success as a web designer. Don't panic—most of the WYSIWYG HTML editors will let you work in a visual environment and automatically create the code behind the scenes. Phew!

WYSIWYG EDITORS

You have the choice to author CSS from scratch or use an HTML editor such as Dreamweaver or GoLive. These editors make using CSS much easier, and the code they write is updated and current to support the most current CSS recommendations. If you do decide to use an HTML editor to write your CSS, make sure you are using a current version of Dreamweaver or GoLive. The current versions are most certain to write the best CSS code.

Whether you choose to use Dreamweaver or GoLive, you still have to know what you are doing, however, because there is no way for the HTML editor to decide for you whether to choose between an ID or a CLASS, pixels or inches. CSS is another challenge in the web publishing curve. Just when you thought HTML was finally manageable!

This chapter should familiarize you with CSS so that you can make these decisions within HTML browsers. Here are some other helpful references for CSS:

A List Apart's CSS Articles
http://www.alistapart.com/stories/indexCSS.html

WebReview's Style Sheet Reference Guide
http://www.webreview.com/style/index.shtml

TopStyle WYSIWYG CSS Editor
http://www.bradsoft.com/topstyle/index.asp

StyleMaster WYSIWYG CSS Editor
http://www.westciv.com/style_master/index.html

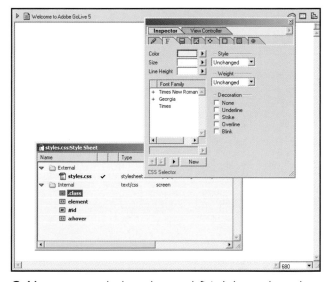

GoLive supports style sheets, but you definitely have to have a base knowledge of how they work to use it.

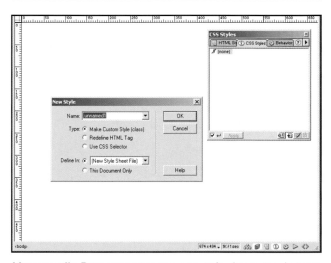

Macromedia Dreamweaver supports style sheets, too, but you must know what you are doing to use the WYSIWYG capabilities.

cascading STYLE SHEETS

summary

CSS style sheets are a powerful mechanism for enhancing the presentation quality of web text. Though not appropriate for all audiences due to browser compatibility (especially Netscape 4.x), all recent popular web browsers have excellent CSS support. Depending on your audience, CSS is now—and most certainly will become—an extremely useful method of designing web pages.

> Using CSS, you will be able to format your text in manners much closer to that of the printed page, and expect your layouts to work consistently—within certain limits—across platforms, browsers, and differing sizes and resolutions of displays. This chapter covered the basic principles of style sheets, so that you can use them now or wait until they are supported more widely.

> Internal style sheets are used within a single HTML document.

> External style sheets are used by multiple HTML documents.

> Inline style sheets only apply to part of an HTML document.

> It's best to use pixel measurements for specifying type, since they will produce the most reliable results.

> Be sure to put your style sheet rules within comment tags, so browsers that don't support CSS will ignore the code.

> While WYSIWYG editors support style sheets, you still need to understand what to specify within the various choices.

Animation & Audio

INTRODUCTION

This chapter covers a variety of ways to add animation and audio to a web page, using HTML, the GIF file format, the Macromedia SWF file format, and QuickTime. There are lots of different animation tools and technologies, but what about the animation content itself? If you've never made animation before, you might be asking what exactly constitutes animation, per se?

Animation creates the illusion of motion. It's really composed of a series of still images—shown in quick succession—the process of which tricks our minds into thinking that stationary artwork is truly moving. It's all fake! Making artwork for animation is an exercise in understanding how to fake motion through presenting changing artwork over time.

You can make animation without a dedicated animation program. If you use an image editor, such as Photoshop, try running a filter in incremental amounts over a still image. Try drawing the same artwork three times, and it will appear to jitter subtly—or not so subtly depending on how much each version changes. Try changing the opacity over multiple images, and you'll create artwork that appears to "fade up."

If you want to get ideas for animation, start by looking at existing animation on a VCR and single-framing through it, or try loading other people's animated GIFs into animating GIF programs to reverse-engineer what you like. Just be sure to realize that reverse-engineering doesn't mean stealing. The same copyright laws that apply to images apply to movies.

COMMON ANIMATION TERMINOLOGY

If you are new to animation, you might find many unfamiliar terms. Here is a short list of terms and their meanings:

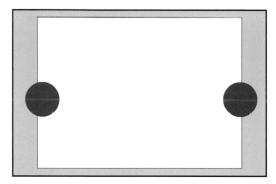

Keyframe: A keyframe is an extreme point of motion. If you were to make an animation enter on screen left and exit on screen right, the keyframes would identify the start and stop positions.

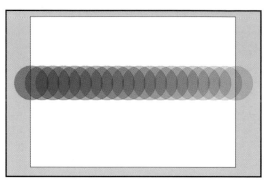

Inbetween or tween: Many programs that use keyframes also produce inbetweens or tweens. In this case, there are 20 inbetween frames between the two keyframes shown earlier. They are all shown at once on this page because a feature called *onion skinning*, which shows all the frames at once, has been turned on. In reality, each position of each circle is on an individual frame that would play back one at a time. In character animation, like what you see in *Snow White* or *Rugrats*, drawings are inbetweened by hand drawing each frame of artwork.

Timeline: A timeline usually keeps track of frames. In this example, there are two keyframes; one on Frame 1, and the other on Frame 20.

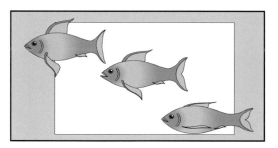

Frame-by-frame animation: Artwork that changes every single frame. Here's an example of frame-by-frame animation, with three frames showing at once.

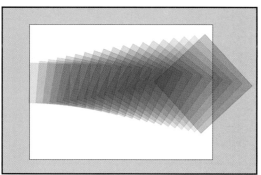

Motion graphics: Motion graphics involves taking artwork and moving its position, scale, or rotation, or changing its opacity, over time.

ANIMATED GIF FORMAT

This chapter uses the term "animated GIF," but the technical term for this type of file is GIF89a. The animated GIF format has been in existence since the late 1980s, but it wasn't supported by early web browsers. All the major web browsers support this spec, making it possible to include these types of files in web pages without worry of excluding any potential end viewers.

The GIF89a file format allows for multiple images to be stored inside a single GIF document. When displayed within browser software that recognizes the multiple images, the artwork streams in to the web page in a predetermined sequence, creating a slide-show style animation. The file format supports looping (the capability to repeat multiple images indefinitely) and timing delays between frames of artwork. The GIF file format also supports limited masking, meaning that GIF animations can use the same type of transparency supported by static GIF images.

Animated GIFs require no plug-ins and no programming, and they don't even require a live web connection, making them perfect for intranets and testing locally on your machine. Animated GIFs are simple to make, easy to include in HTML, and effortless for your web-viewing audience to see. They are one of the most elegant solutions for adding web animation and lack only in that they cannot include interactivity or sound. For an animated logo or button, however, animated GIFs are a pretty smart option. To include animated GIFs on web pages, you'll use the **IMG** element. A simple example of the code would look like this:

code

```
<IMG SRC="my_animation.gif">
```

GIF RESOURCES

Here are some recommended resources for learning how to create and code animated GIFs:

Webmonkey Animation Tutorial
http://www.hotwired.com/webmonkey/multimedia/tutorials/tutorial1.html?tw=multimedia

Optimizing Animated GIFs
http://www.webreference.com/dev/gifanim

Photoshop 7/ImageReady for the Web Hands-On Training
By Lynda Weinman and Jan Kabili
lynda.com/books and Peachpit Press
ISBN: 0-321-11276-8

Learning Macromedia Fireworks MX CD-ROM
By Donna Casey
lynda.com

ANIMATED GIF TECH NOTES

As you create animated GIF files, you'll discover that there are many terms that might be unfamiliar to you. Here's a short glossary:

Looping: Looping is the process of repeating an animation over and over and over. If the animation is 10 frames long and is looped three times, the end user will see 30 frames of the animation, with three repeats. The animation itself would still be 10 frames; however, it would contain a setting that would tell it to play the same animation three times. Tip: Be careful of unlimited looping animations as they can annoy your audience.

You can set the timing of an animated GIF, which is most commonly measured in units of 100, which approximately equals one second depending on processor speed. In this example (again from Fireworks), frame 3 has the value of 300, meaning it will hold for approximately three seconds while the other frames will play back at 1/5th of a second.

Frame delays: Frame delays can be used to alter the timing of animations. The common unit of measuring the timing is 100. In a loose way, 100 is supposed to equal one second of play time. The problem is that faster processors will play animated GIFs more quickly than slower processors; the Web is not like film or video, which have a set playback rate. Loosely, a good guide to follow is that 100 will equal one second. If you want your first frame to last five seconds, your next three to last one second each, and the last frame to last 15 seconds, your frame delays would look something like this:

> Frame 01=500
> Frame 02=100
> Frame 03=100
> Frame 04=100
> Frame 05=1500

Download speeds: The initial download time of the animated GIF will depend on your end user's connection speed, but once the animation has fully downloaded, playback speed will depend on the processor speed of his or her computer. This can make for wildly different frame delay timings on different systems, regardless of what frame delays you program. Almost all GIF animation software packages support frame delays.

Optimization: Animated GIFs can be optimized, just like regular GIFs. The same rules that applied to file size savings in Chapter 11, *"Speedy Graphics"* apply here. Like other GIFs, you want to make sure that you use as few colors as needed and try to avoid dithering or noise in your image.

Transparency & disposal methods: Disposal methods are a scary sounding term for how the animation is displayed in terms of its transparency. With a static GIF image, this is a non-issue. A transparent static image shows through to its background, and that's the end of the story.

With a multiple-frame GIF, however, this presents a bigger issue. Let's say I have an animated ball that's bouncing. If I make the ball transparent, and the image before it has already loaded, the transparency might show part or all of the frame before. Instead of the illusion of motion, the result would be the non-illusion resulting in each frame of my ball bouncing animation being visible at the same time. That's where the disposal method becomes important, which you'll learn about next.

Disposal method: The disposal method is what instructs the GIF animation on how to display preceding frames of the animation. Disposal methods are set within whatever GIF animation authoring software package you're using.

> *Unspecified:* Use this disposal method when you aren't using transparency. It will simply present each frame in its entirety and will not yield any added optimization to the file. If I had an animation that changed images every single frame, such as a slide show of changing visuals, I would use this disposal method.

> *Do not dispose:* This disposal method would reveal each preceding frame of an animation. Let's say I wanted to create an animation of my name hand-writing itself on the screen. If I left the "L" to draw itself only once and then used the subsequent frame to draw the "Y", I would be creating a smaller file size. Use this method when you want the prior frames to show through and you want file savings with no penalty to image quality.

> *Restore to background:* Instead of displaying the previous frame, the animation is set to show the background color or tile image of your web page.

> *Restore to previous:* This function is almost the same as Do Not Dispose except the first frame always stays visible underneath the rest of the animation. Netscape has known problems with supporting this disposal method.

Palettes: Most GIF animation software allows you to specify bit-depth values. Lower bit-depth settings will result in smaller, faster animated GIFs. One problem palette management issues in animated GIFs suffer from is that often the software or browser defaults to accepting a different palette for each frame, which causes palette flashing (a psychedelic feast for the eyes, to be sure)—most likely not the effect you were wishing to see.

The best way to avoid GIF animation palette problems is to map each frame of your animation to a common palette. Some programs do this automatically, and others require that you load a palette to achieve this result. This technique is called creating a "super" or "global" palette Creating a super or global palette is handled automatically by the tools reviewed in later sections of this chapter.

Interlacing: Interlaced GIFs were discussed in Chapter 10, *"Web File Formats."* Adding the interlace feature to a single or multiple GIF image will cause it to look blocky until it comes into focus. Personally, I dislike the effect, and especially dislike the effect in the context of animation. It sort of breaks the illusion of motion to see each individual frame come into full focus, don't you think?

GIF ANIMATION TOOLS

I can't cover every tool in this chapter due to space limitations and the fact that I don't use all of these different products regularly to give them justice here. I would like, however, to mention some of the noteworthy animation tools to check out:

Adobe ImageReady

ImageReady ships as part of Photoshop. It uses an interface identical to Photoshop, but has extended web-focused features, including a superb animated GIF editor.

http://www.adobe.com

Macromedia Fireworks

Macromedia Fireworks has a very strong web graphics focus, and has a superb animated GIF editor.

http://www.macromedia.com/software/fireworks

Ulead GIFAnimator (Windows)

Ulead GIF Animator includes the ability to create optimized animations, global palette building, support for Photoshop compatible plug-ins, automated moving sprites, and integrated transitions.

http://www.webutilities.com/ga/ga_main.htm

Totally Hip's WebPainter (Mac/Windows)

A standalone application that writes animated GIFs and QuickTime movies, this program works with vector and bitmap artwork, contains auto-transitions, uses multiple layers, and comes with Photoshop (Mac only). WebPainter also includes a "cel" animation interface that lets you use onion skinning (the computer equivalent of tracing paper), multiple cel editing, and foreground/background drawing cels. It saves the files as PICs, QuickTime movies, GIF89a's, and sequential GIF files. The product lacks sophisticated animation features found in more high-end packages, but it is useful for anyone wanting to learn how to create cel-style character animation. Because the product saves animation in so many formats, it is not hindered by any plug-in constraints. At the time this chapter was written, a free trial version was available from the Totally Hip web site.

http://www.totallyhip.com/lo/products/wp/index.html

BoxTop Software's GIFmation

This Photoshop plug-in includes the capability to optimize and check browser compatibility. It also provides support for onion skinning, coordinate image positioning, automatic image alignment, image editing and palette creation tools, and scale, crop, and flip features. GIFmation has excellent preview options, and many formats are supported for import.
http://www.boxtopsoft.com/gifmation.html

PhotoDisc Animation Series (Mac/Windows)

Animation clip art is usually pretty mundane. The folks at PhotoDisc, Inc. (a leading digital stock photo agency), however, went many steps ahead of the competition and published the work of renowned designer **Clement Mok** (http://www.sapient.com) to create some superb clip animation sequences. The two series, Metaphorically Blinking and EveryDay Objects Live, include photo-realistic animations of such things as chattering teeth toys and shaking alarm clocks. This product comes in two varieties: the basic version, with animations saved out as Animated GIFs and Shockwave documents with rollover and sound built-in, and the Pro Versions, which include the necessary Director files to allow end users to customize and edit the animations. The price is a little high for some, but the quality is worth it. The fact that the professional version lets you edit the Director files is a great bonus.
http://creative.gettyimages.com/photodisc

MACROMEDIA FLASH & SHOCKWAVE

Macromedia has been a long-time advocate for developing rich web experiences similar to that of a movie or a CD-ROM. They have pushed hard to create alternatives to the limitations of HTML and have two flagship products that achieve this goal: Macromedia Flash and Macromedia Director.

This chapter focuses on the two authoring tools and plug-in technologies related to Flash and Shockwave. Plug-ins allow browsers to extend the basic HTML capabilities, and they must be installed in the browser in order to show alternative content. Some plug-ins such as QuickTime, Real One Player, Shockwave, and Flash are preinstalled in newer browsers. In the case of Flash and Shockwave, the file format is now part of the newest Mac and Windows operating systems, which means that for these products, the user base is extremely large and you don't have to worry as much as you used to if you want to publish content that implements these technologies.

Flash and Shockwave offer unparalleled amounts of interactivity and dynamic content. While this kind of content is exciting, it can have a dark side. Many end users resent having to wait for movies or sounds to load in order to get to their content. As with anything on the Web, one must carefully weigh the benefits and disadvantages of choosing the rich multimedia path versus the standard HTML path.

MACROMEDIA FLASH FILE FORMAT

Flash was the first vector file format for the Web. As you learned in Chapter 10, *"Web File Formats,"* vectors often offer much smaller file sizes than their bitmap counterparts. Because the vector format of Flash was developed specifically for online delivery, a Flash document can contain movement, interactivity, and sound, as well as static images, and can still be smaller than if you put this same material into standard HTML web pages. You would set up the HTML for Flash content to scale to the browser with this HTML code:

code

```
<embed src="xxx.swf" width="100%"
height="100%">
```

The percentages tell the browser to display the content at 100% of its size, and the vector artwork renders out at whatever size the browser window appears. Alternatively, you can set the dimensions to match the height and width in pixels, and the content will not scale when the browser size is changed.

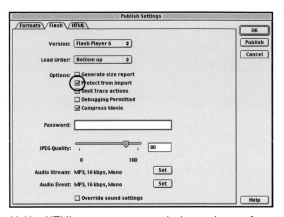

Unlike HTML content, you can lock people out from viewing the source files of your Macromedia Flash movies. When you're exporting Macromedia Flash content, you can check *Protect from import*, and Flash will be unable to reopen the `.SWF` file.

EMBED VERSUS OBJECT

The **EMBED** element isn't part of HTML or XHTML. The correct element to use according to standards is **OBJECT**. Because newer browsers have no trouble supporting **OBJECT**, the hope is that as older browsers are phased out, people will be able to use **OBJECT**.

LEARNING FLASH

Learning Flash can be challenging (it was for me!). But once you know it, like anything you know in life, it becomes a lot easier to use. I'll share a few of the basics with you in this chapter, but the best way to learn is to download the product and dive right in.

The file format for a Flash project is **.FLA**, and the file format for a Flash web movie is **.SWF**. If you view the source of a page and see that it includes a **SRC="xxx.swf"** file, you will know it's Flash content instead of HTML content.

In the following column are some recommended resources for learning Flash:

Learning Flash MX CD-ROM
(10 hours of movies, plus source files)
By Shane Rebenscheid
lynda.com

Flash MX Hands-On Training
By Kymberlee Weil
lynda.com/books and Peachpit Press
ISBN: 0-321-11272-5

Macromedia
http://www.macromedia.com/software/flash/
productinfo/tutorials/gettingstarted

Flash Kit
http://www.flashkit.com

We're Here
http://www.were-here.com

SENDING VISITORS TO PLUG-IN PAGES

If your end users don't have the necessary plug-in, you can write HTML code that will send them to the appropriate page when they click on the broken plug-in icon.

code for Flash

```
<embed src="xxx.swf"
pluginspace="http://www.macromedia.com/go/getflashplayer/"
type="application/x-shockwave-flash" width="xx" height="xx">
</embed>
```

code for Shockwave

```
<embed src="xxx.dcr"
pluginspace="http://www.macromedia.com/shockwave/download/"
type="application/x-director"
width="xx" height="xx">
</embed>
```

SHOCKWAVE CONTENT

Macromedia Director has been around almost as long as personal computers have. Among professionals, it's considered the premier authoring tool for multimedia content, and it boasts more than 300,000 registered users. Shockwave was established as a means of distributing Director movies over the Web.

Director is a very deep program that contains its own scripting language called Lingo. Director's Lingo engine is much faster and more powerful than the Flash Payer. Also, Director has advanced 3D modeling and scripting, which Flash does not have. Again, like Flash, Director has a high learning curve. This does not mean it's bad or something to be avoided; it just means that you wouldn't necessarily make a casual decision to use it on your site.

The thing about multimedia is that what looks simple to the end user is generally very difficult to create. It's one of the great ironies in this type of work. Although it's totally possible to program small interactive pieces in Director, most large projects are developed by teams of people.

SAVING SHOCKWAVE FILES

You can save Director content for web delivery by exporting it as a Shockwave movie. When I saved a simple animation created in Director, it automatically created the following:

code

```
codebase="http://download.macromedia.com/pub/shockwave/cabs/director/
sw.cab#
version=8,5,1,0"
ID=testMove width=320 height=240>
<param name=src value="testMove.dcr">
<param name=swRemote value="swSaveEnabled='true' swVolume='true'
swRestart='true' swPausePlay='true' swFastForward='true'
swContextMenu='true' ">
<param name=swStretchStyle value=none>
<PARAM NAME=bgColor VALUE=#FFFFFF>
<embed src="testMove.dcr" bgColor=#FFFFFF  width=320 height=240
swRemote="swSaveEnabled='true' swVolume='true' swRestart='true'
swPausePlay='true' swFastForward='true' swContextMenu='true' "
swStretchStyle=none
type="application/x-director"
pluginspage="http://www.macromedia.com/shockwave/download/"></embed>
</object>
```

MACROMEDIA DIRECTOR

Macromedia Director's initial focus was multimedia for disk-based delivery. Eventually, when CD-ROMs came of age, Director became the premiere authoring tool for interactive content.

Macromedia Director is based on a variety of interface elements that all work together. As the program has matured, so have its capabilities. This product is now one of the richest multimedia applications in the world. The interface is described in the next section, which shows how the different areas work together.

Over the years, the emphasis on CD-ROM delivery has shifted towards online delivery, yet Macromedia Director is still capable of creating CD-ROM and DVD titles as well.

FLASH VERSUS DIRECTOR

It's sometimes hard to decide whether to learn and use Macromedia Flash or Macromedia Director, but here's a chart to help you through the decision process:

	Flash	Director
Lower price	X	
Lower learning curve	X	
Most web publishing features	X	
Most CD-ROM publishing features		X
Long-form video		X
Short-form video	X	
Scripting for games & standalone apps	X	X
3D		X
Largest installed user base	X	
Build multi-user communities		X

QUICKTIME OVERVIEW

Although there are other streaming media formats, such as AVI and Real, QuickTime is the best movie format that there is—for web or professional DV authoring. It was the first computer video format and remains the best.

I remember the first time I saw a QuickTime movie played back on a computer. It was postage-stamp size, sputtering and skipping along at a snail's pace, with really bad sound and even worse sync. Everyone around me was really excited about it, but frankly, I thought they were nuts. I didn't "get" that the movie format I was looking at would someday change the history of filmmaking, multimedia, and now the Web.

Today, QuickTime movies are on almost every CD-ROM in existence because of pioneering advancements in digital movie and sound compression, sound sync, and impressive data rate speeds. Once QuickTime conquered the CD-ROM market, it took the film and video market by storm. That postage-stamp size movie capacity grew to support 4,000×4,000 pixel resolution, which matches the resolution of feature film quality film recorders. In the broadcast video world, QuickTime applications began outperforming systems that cost hundreds of thousands of dollars. Through the wonders of QuickTime, individuals on personal computers with the right equipment and software could actually produce feature films, music videos, industrials, and television commercials. QuickTime single-handedly created the desktop video explosion, which is still sending shock waves through video/film post houses and high-end equipment supply houses.

QUICKTIME BASICS

What exactly is a QuickTime movie? Just like animated GIF files, QuickTime movies can contain multiple frames. The content can be cartoons, vectors, or live action.

How do you make a QuickTime movie? There are numerous ways. If you have a copy of QuickTime player, you can open the following file formats and instantly convert them to QuickTime movies: MPEG audio and video; AVI video; AIFF, AU, WAV, and MIDI audio; GIF animations; and GIF, JPEG, SGI, Photoshop (PSD), BMP, MacPaint, PNG, Targa, and FLC images. It's recommended that you download QuickTime Pro (http://www.apple.com/quicktime/upgrade) if you plan to do serious QuickTime web authoring. It offers many extra features.

There are also many QuickTime movie creation tools. Some of those include Adobe's After Effects and Premiere, Macromedia Director, Discreet's Cleaner, and Totally Hip's WebPainter. After you make a QuickTime movie, here's how you embed it into your web page:

code

```
<embed src="placeholder.mov"
height="176" width="136">
```

Replace the name **"placeholder.mov"** with the name of your movie, and replace the values for **height** and **width** of the movie with your movie dimensions (add 16 to the height of the movie for the default movie controller unless you plan to turn it off with a **CONTROLLER=FALSE** command).

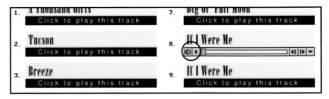

The QuickTime controller can be hidden or visible, with the **CONTROLLER=FALSE** or **TRUE** command. Check out this example at http://www.apple.com/quicktime/authoring/embed2.html. The song listings shown are using static images as "Poster" movies, which are described later in this chapter.

QUICKTIME WEB FEATURES

The web features list for QuickTime is long and impressive. In order to view the results of QuickTime, the end user must have the latest QuickTime plug-in installed. To install it on your system, go to http://www.apple.com/quicktime/download. To learn more about QuickTime authoring, visit http://www.apple.com/quicktime/tools_tips/tutorials.

QUICKTIME TRACKS

QuickTime is track-based, which means that different aspects of the format are controlled by different tracks. For example, there are movie tracks, audio tracks, text tracks, sprite tracks, video tracks, Flash tracks, music tracks, chapter tracks, and 3D tracks. Tutorials for working with others are at http://www.apple.com/quicktime/tools_tips/tutorials.

Using **QuickTime Pro**, you can view and edit all of the tracks for any movie.

MULTIPLE DATA RATE SAMPLES

The QuickTime plug-in recognizes what connection speed your end user is using. If you author and post multiple movies at different sizes, the browser can detect which one to display. This means that you could provide a large movie with a high data rate for end users with T1 lines and a smaller movie for 14.4 modem visitors. There is also an override feature that enables someone on a slower connection to choose to view or download the bigger movie.

Also look to outside developers, such as Adobe (Premiere and After Effects) and Discreet (Cleaner), for tools that render multiple movies at different sizes. This is a nice solution. If only web images could easily take this same approach!

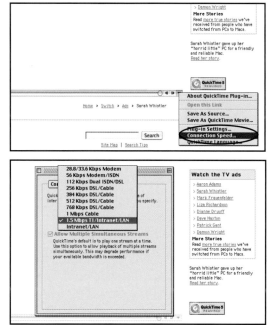

A free utility called **MakeRefMovie** (Mac/Windows) helps you easily author movies for multiple downloading speeds. Download this from http://www.apple.com/quicktime/developers/tools.html. This shows the authoring tool and how it handles the creation of three different-sized reference movies.

If you click on the *bottom right arrow* of a QuickTime movie in your browser (shown in the top image), you can get the plug-in settings information. The next window prompts you to select a connection speed. Which size movie is presented depends on your responses to these two dialog boxes (shown in the bottom image).

common quicktime codecs

QuickTime is able to achieve faster downloading time through three newly supported codecs:

Sorenson Video is considered to be the best compression format for web-based video. A sample on the QT site showed a 6.7 second movie that was only 11k (although it had a lot of compression artifacts that weren't that attractive, IMHO). For more information, visit http://www.sorenson.com.

QDMC (**QD**esign **M**usic **C**odec) provides high-fidelity audio at greatly reduced bit rates, giving web publishers access to a level of audio compression for music unavailable anywhere else. I heard it at MacWorld, and it ruled (as I drooled). You can hear a sample at http://www.qdesign.com.

QUALCOMM's PureVoice™ enables web authors to publish voice-based content suitable for any modem connection speed. PureVoice compresses the spoken word, such as a newscast, to a compact digital format, yet delivers an extremely high, voice quality experience for listeners. Look out RealAudio—this format sounds way better for voice-overs and narration sound tracks. You can visit http://www.cdmatech.com/solutions/products/purevoice.html for more information.

Command	QuickTime Description
HEIGHT	Specifies the size of the movie in web pages.
WIDTH	Specifies the size of the movie in web pages.
HIDDEN	Allows sound-only movies to play in the background without affecting the look of a web page.
AUTOPLAY	Starts the movie playing automatically.
LOOP	Loops movie playback automatically.
CONTROLLER	Specifies whether or not to display the QuickTime movie controller bar.
HREF	Indicates which URL to link to when the movie is clicked.
TARGET	Provides a frame target for the URL, specified in an **HREF** tag.
CACHE	Indicates whether the movie should be cached (Netscape Navigator 3.0).
BGCOLOR	Sets a background color for the movie display.
SCALE	Scales the movie display automatically.

DIGITAL VIDEO TERMINOLOGY

If you're new to digital video and sound terminology, you might need this handy glossary:

Codec: Software that translates video or audio between its uncompressed form and the compressed form in which it is stored. Two common video codecs are "Cinepak" and "Indeo". A codec of great interest to web developers is Sorenson, which results in much smaller file sizes than Cinepak or Indeo.

Data rates: Amount of information per second used to represent a movie. A single-speed CD-ROM movie would be created at a data rate of 100 Kilobytes per second (Kbps), whereas a movie for broadcast television would be created at 27 Megabytes per second (Mbps). The data rate is established when the movie is captured or recompressed.

DVD-ROM: A DVD-based alternative to the CD-ROM, which will hold up to 10 times the amount of current CD-ROM content.

Flattening: A post-processing pass that "flattens" the Mac resource fork of a QuickTime movie and makes the file cross-platform.

Frames differencing: Frames that contain only changes from the previous frames. Some compression algorithms rely on frames differencing to achieve smaller file size.

Keyframes: If you author a QuickTime movie, you will set "keyframes." The keyframes could be considered the fixed, non-changing points if the movie had to drop certain frames in order to play quickly enough. If you put in too many keyframes for the computer processor or Internet connection to handle, the movie will play slowly and will not look smooth or fluid.

kHz: Kilohertz is the measure of audio samples per second (the equivalent of "data rate" for video). Higher sample rates yield better sound quality and larger file sizes.

Sample rate: The number of samples per second for audio. The higher the sample rate, the larger the sound file.

Sample size: Audio sample sizes are generally 8-bit or 16-bit. The higher the bit depth, the better the sound and larger the file.

Sprite: A QuickTime track that is made up of small graphic elements, which are assigned position and time information. A bouncing ball could be used as a sprite: Only the ball graphic and its location would be stored over time, instead of a series of full-frame images.

Streaming: Movie or audio data that is visible in real time while it is downloading.

Tracks: Different media types that compose a movie. A movie can include an audio and video track, or text tracks, sprite tracks, or midi tracks (and more varieties that are yet to come).

Transcode: Transferring one file format to another without recompressing the data. If you wanted to change an AVI movie into a Cinepak movie, you could transcode the data so it wouldn't have to be recompressed.

sound on the web

Because the Web has effectively created the ultimate convergence of any and all mediums, it's possible to add sound to your web design bag o' tricks! Sound can be added to set a mood or ambience; it can be used to make buttons pop or to add narration to an instructional area of your site. Whatever your reason, it's possible to program your site to provide background ambient noise, real-time audio on demand, or sound that can be downloaded and played on external sound players. This section examines these options and other issues related to sound.

sound aesthetics

Just because you can add sound to your site doesn't mean you should. Keep in mind that people have very strong musical tastes, and while you might love Balinese gamelan music as much as I do, your end viewer might prefer Martin Denny.

My suggestion is that you be careful about looping sounds. In the event that your end viewer can't stand your choice of music or sound effect, you are effectively driving them away.

My point is, sound can be a wonderful thing to one person and an annoyance to another. You might think you are adding an enhancement to your site by including automatic sound, but it's my job to tell you that others might not agree.

working with sound files

Adding sound to your web page can be a risky proposition. Many people don't like musical accompaniment as they're perusing the Web, so if you do add sound to your pages it's best to include a sound off button too! This section of this chapter focuses on sound from a variety of perspectives. First, we'll take a look at common practices with sound files on the Web. Next, what authoring tools, file formats, and programming are used. Last, what resources are available to learn more about sound. This subject is large enough to fill volumes of books, so it's impossible to cover everything here.

COMMON PRACTICES WITH SOUND FILES

At the Flash-based site **Boarding.com**, a background sound is used. Sound can be used in a variety of creative ways and almost always contains a sound *on* or *off* button as a courtesy to visitors.

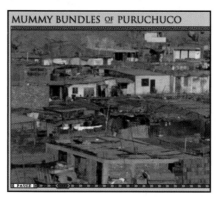

Macromedia Flash also allows you to add sounds to button states. This is something that you could not do in HTML without using JavaScript or DHTML.

Many sites provide links to listen to audio files over the Web. **Vitaminic.com** is one such site, but there are literally zillions to pick from. To find sites like this, visit **Google. com** and search for music downloads.

NationalGeographic.com has many different areas that present web-based documentaries complete with music and narration. Most of these presentations are created in Macromedia Flash or Director.

The **Survivor** TV show uses Real Audio to showcase scenes with video and sound. You have to download a player from http://www. real.com to see this content.

HOW TO GET SOUND SOURCE FILES INTO YOUR COMPUTER

Just like images have to be scanned or created directly in the computer, sounds have to be scanned or digitized or created from scratch as well. This is a complex or easy undertaking, depending on whether you're attempting to achieve professional-level sound or willing to accept a few snap, crackle, and pops. Below are some ideas for obtaining sound file sources:

Capture sound from CDs.

Most sound-capture software enables you to capture sound from audio CDs. Tips for capturing from CD sources are listed later in this chapter. Be careful about copyrights and other rights—it is not legal to take sound from your favorite band and stick it on your web site or otherwise use it. For more information about copyright laws and music, check out:

> "The Use of Music on a Multimedia Web Site: The Legal Issues"
> http://home.earthlink.net/~ivanlove/music.html

Use sound-editing software.

There are dedicated sound-editing packages, just like there are dedicated image editing "software packages. Sound editing software can cut or mix together disparate clips of sound, create transitions such as fades and dissolves, and process the sound with effects like echo, reverb, and playing in reverse. You might try reading the computer and sound trades to find hardware and software that fit your needs and budget. Or check out some suggested URLs:

> CNET Sound and Audio Reviews
> http://www.cnet.com/software/search/0,11066,
> 0-3227898-1202-0,00.html

> Freshmeat Sound Editing Software Reviews
> http://freshmeat.net/articles/view/354/

> Electronic Music Software Reviews
> http://www.electronicmusic.com/features/reviews/
> software

Use the microphone with your computer.

Many Macs and PCs ship with a microphone and simple sound editing software which you can use to record your voice for narration, greetings, or sound effects. This is a great way to add a personal greeting, to your site. I have wonderful sound bytes of my daughter singing songs and saying silly things as she was growing up that were all captured this way. Be aware, however, that professional sound designers would cringe at this recommendation! If you are planning to do professional-quality sound, use professionals! They have all kinds of equipment you won't begin to understand, which does things such as normalizing, equalizing, removing noise, mixing, dithering, resampling, and more. For a little tour around some professional sound sites, try:

> The MIDI Farm
> http://www.midifarm.com/info

> Professional Sound Corporation
> http://www.professionalsound.com

> Audio Engineering Society
> http://www.aes.org

DIGITAL AUDIO TERMINOLOGY

Sample rates: Sample rates are measured in kilohertz (kHz). The sample rate affects the "range" of digitized sound, which describes its highs and lows. Sound editing software is where the initial sample rate settings are established. Standard sample rates range from 11.025 KHz, 22.050 KHz, 44.10 KHz, to 48 kHz. The higher the sample rate, the better the quality.

Bit depth or sampling resolution: Sampling resolution affects quality of sound, just like dpi resolution affects the quality of images. Standard sampling resolutions are 8-bit mono, 8-bit stereo, 16-bit mono, and 16-bit stereo.

μ-law: μ-law used to be the only file format you'd find on the Web because it is generated by Unix platforms. Now that Macs and Windows are the predominant platforms of the Web, μ-law files are not seen as much. The sound quality is generally much lower than other sound formats, but the files are much smaller, too. μ-law files always have the file-name extension .au.

AIFC: AIFC is a new spec for the older **A**udio **I**nterchange **F**ile **F**ormat (AIFF). Both AIFF and AIFF-C files can be read by this format. AIFF and AIFC files are commonly used on SGI and Macintosh computers. Only 16-bit sound data can be recorded using this format.

MPEG: MPEG audio is well respected as a high-quality, excellent audio compression file format. MPEG audio has the advantage of a good compression scheme that doesn't sacrifice too much fidelity for the amount of bandwidth it saves. MPEG files tend to be small and sound good. On the IUMA site, there are two sizes of MPEG files: stereo and mono. MPEG audio layer 2 files always have the filename extensions .mpg or .mp2.

MP3: MPEG audio layer 3 files have an .mp3 extension. This has become the most compact and best-sounding file format for audio, and it has spawned the exchange of music files over the Web at unprecedented rates.

Making Small Audio Files

Audio on the Web has most of the same limitations as images—many files are too large to hear as inline components of a page. In this event, your audience will be required to download audio files in order to listen to them, and it's your job to choose a file format and compression rate. You will base these decisions on the platform you're authoring sounds from and then work to reduce your file size while keeping sound quality as high as possible. Let's take a look at the various audio standards and ways to reduce the size of audio files.

Rates & Bits

There are two components of an audio file that make it sound good (and take up space): the *sampling rate* and the *bit depth*, which is referred to as the sample resolution.

Generally when you first digitally record or "sample" a sound, you want to record it at 16-bit resolution at the 44.1 kHz sampling rate. Just like an image scan, it's always best to start with the most information and reduce down. Later, after processing the sound to your satisfaction with digital audio editing applications, you would resample the final file down to 8-bit, 22.05 kHz.

Sample rates are measured in kilohertz (kHz). The sample rate affects the range of a digitized sound, which defines its highs and lows. Higher sample rates result in larger file sizes. The sampling rate is set when the sound is digitized (captured) into the computer. Sound editing software is where the initial sample rate settings are established, and it should be set according to the type of sound being sampled. Some types of sounds can deal with lower sampling rates better. Narration, for example, doesn't depend on high and low ranges to sound good. Here are some sampling rates:

> 8 KHz
> 11 KHz
> 22.050 KHz
> 44.1 KHz
> 48 KHz

Sampling resolution dictates how much range the sound has in highs and lows. Higher kilohertz settings result in a bigger file size. The sampling resolution is also set when the sound is digitized (captured) into the computer. Sound editing software allows users to dictate which sample resolution the sound is captured at. Because noise is introduced at lower sample rates, it's necessary to evaluate individual sound elements to see how far down the sampling resolution can be set without introducing unacceptable noise. You can create digital sound at the following resolutions:

> 8-bit mono
> 8-bit stereo
> 16-bit mono
> 16-bit stereo

AUDIO FILE FORMATS

Many types of audio files are found and used on the Web. Choosing which one to use is often determined by what kind of computer system and software you're authoring sounds from. Here's a breakdown of the various formats:

AIFF (**A**udio **I**nterchange **F**ile **F**ormat) was developed by Apple and is used on Macintoshes and SGIs. It can store digital audio at all the sample rates and resolutions possible. You'll also hear about MACE (**M**acintosh **A**udio **C**ompression/**E**xpansion), which is the built-in compression standard for AIFF files. Just like in video, the type of compression you use is invisible to the end listener. It does dictate the size and quality of your end result, however. If you are going to author AIFF files, they should be saved with an .aif extension.

WAVE was developed by Microsoft and IBM and is the native sound file format to Windows platforms. Like AIFF, it can store digital audio at all the sample rates and resolutions possible. Basically, WAVE and AIFF files are considered equals in terms of quality and compression, and are easier to use depending on which platform you are authoring from. If you are going to author WAVE files, they should be saved with a .wav extension.

MPEG audio is well respected as a high-quality, excellent audio compression file format. Because MPEG files aren't native to any specific platform, your audience will need to download a helper application to hear them. If you are going to author MPEG sound files, they should be saved with the .mpg extension.

RealAudio was the first example of streaming audio on the Web. Streamed audio files come over the phone lines in small chunks, so the entire file doesn't have to be downloaded before it can be heard. The file can be up to one hour long because the data is coming in as you're hearing it—not first downloading fully to your hard drive. The sound quality is often compared to that of an AM radio station. Because of quality limits, it's best used for narration and not for music or other sounds. You must have the Real One player installed on your system to hear sounds play as soon as you click on a link that supplies real audio source material. You can author RealAudio content by using the RealAudio encoder, which can be obtained from http://www.real.com. You won't be able to offer RealAudio files from your web site unless your provider has paid RealAudio a server licensing fee. Contact RealAudio for more information.

HTML FOR DOWNLOADING SOUND FILES

A sound file gets the **<A HREF></A>** tag, just like its video and image-based counterparts. But unlike video, where there might be an associated thumbnail image, sounds are usually indicated by a sound icon or hypertext. Here are a few variations and the code you would use to produce them. Here's the code to link your audience to a sound and let them know what file size and format it is:

code

```
<a href="snd1.mp3">
Click here to download this sound!</a>
```

Or if you want to add an icon, too:

code

```
<a href="snd1.aif>
<img src="ear.gif">
Click here to download this sound!</a>
```

BGSOUND

The **BGSOUND** element is a Microsoft Internet Explorer 2.0 enhancement. **SRC** specifies the URL of the audio file to be played. The **LOOP** attribute specifies how many times the sound will be played while the HTML document is displayed, and it can either be a number or the string "infinite." The default for **LOOP** is 1 time. As mentioned earlier in the aesthetics section, considerable opposition to the use of this element has been expressed on the Web, especially the use of **LOOP=infinite** because users currently have no way to disable the audio.

code

```
   <bgsound src="...">
```

code deconstruction

The **BGSOUND** element causes an audio file to play automatically as an inline sound element. You can insert either **.wav** or **.midi** files. To make the sound loop, insert your file using the **BGSOUND** element and the **LOOP** attribute. The default loop value is **1** time, unless specified.

ANIMATION & AUDIO

SUMMARY

This chapter covered a tremendous amount of information. Here is a short summary:

If you want to use animation on your site, you have the option of using the animated GIF file format, the Macromedia SWF file format, or the Apple QuickTime format. Other technologies exist, such as Real and Windows Media, but this author does not think they're quality or cross-platform compatibility is as good.

Some animation authoring platforms require plug-ins, such as Macromedia Flash, Macromedia Director, and QuickTime. Be sure that the benefits outweigh the disadvantages of requiring a plug-in barrier between you and your audience.

Beware of endless animations or sounds that can annoy your audience.

Sound can be added to your site via HTML or plug-ins (Macromedia SWF, Real, or Quick-Time. Make sure that you learn about audio compression and choose a technology that is appropriate for your content.

CREATING COMMUNITY

INTRODUCTION

I have always suspected that a huge part of the success of the Internet is the fact that it serves a couple of essential human needs: the need to share as well as the need to listen. This is unlike other publishing mediums, which have historically been one-way vehicles for broadcasting information. Many sites publish information that is useful, but there is something about letting your audience have a voice and forum for participation that adds an entirely different dimension to the web publishing medium. Not every web site takes advantage of this distinction, but it's my belief that the ones that do offer opportunities for community are better liked and trafficked than those that don't.

Some web sites focus entirely on community, as they are composed of discussion forums or other methods of publishing a participant's words, images, sounds, or all of the above. Other web sites are commercial or informational, yet they have a community component that allows end users to participate.

New ways of creating communities are popping up every day: blogs, polls, chats, forums, and many variations thereof! This chapter will cover these and more. Every-one who participates in an online community, even passively as in the case of the readers of a newsletter, feels a sense of belonging. This often results in increased brand loyalty to your web site or products. Community has its pros and cons, as well as many faces, all of which will be discussed here, of course!

WHAT IS COMMUNITY?

From the Latin "*communis*," a community is a unified group of people or a group of people with a common interest. In the context of the Internet, a community is a group of people who participate in an online group of activities around a common interest. The common interest can be very specific, such as a community centered around collecting PEZ dispensers. Or it can be very broad, as in an auction site where everyone is there to auction, but the products being sold are as diverse as PEZ dispensers, automobiles, and real estate.

In the context of this chapter, community is regarded as a means to publish your audience or treat them as part of a special group. This can be achieved in many ways and to many different degrees. How deeply you rely on community on your site is a decision this chapter might help you make.

PROS & CONS OF COMMUNITY

While the notion of publishing your audience reaps all kinds of benefits, there is risk. It takes guts for Amazon.com, as a commercial store, to allow its end users to review their products. If a product gets bad reviews, it will hurt sales for that product, thereby hurting Amazon.com's ability to earn money. On its face value, allowing customers to post reviews is a questionable business decision on Amazon.com's part.

On the other hand, the positive side is that reviews are something you can't easily find in a physical bookstore. You can't poll the people standing next to you to ask them what they collectively thought about a book, or even if they've ever read it before. As well, readers on Amazon can even create recommended reading lists. Many people have developed loyalty to Amazon as a result of these community practices.

I have run listservs (more on these later) that turned into ugly places where participants have gotten into screaming matches (aka: flame wars) and made it unpleasant for everyone involved.

There have been instances where spiteful people have given a product a bad review because of jealousy or hatred, not because the product was actually bad. I've had guest-book posts that were forums for immature people to play pranks, insult our company, or insult other people's companies.

There's a big rule to community, and it isn't widely understood. You can't let them run themselves; someone has to be monitoring them for irresponsible behavior. There are times, in fact, when Amazon.com will remove a review that seems spiteful, uninformed, or just plain mean. Many listservs have supervision and rules. If you break the rules, you get kicked off! This can be an unexpected expense for running a site with community features, but the payoff is well worth it.

To make your site a place that people want to visit and return to, make them feel a part of your community or purpose, treat them respectfully, and don't market to them or invade their privacy in distracting ways. Community is a great tool for creating brand loyalty and return visitors.

COMMUNITY FEATURES REQUIRE SCRIPTING

A tremendous amount of custom programming goes into a site like Amazon.com. Every feature, from personalization to wish lists and reviews, requires custom scripts and complex database tables that track relationships among purchases and available products. One can learn good community practices from a site like Amazon.com, but few small companies have the programming resources that can accomplish a feat of Amazon.com's magnitude.

If you want to add community features to your web site, you have four choices: create custom scripts, buy or download a free script, hire someone to modify an existing purchased or free script, or use a packaged solution such as Ecobuilder (http://www.ecobuilder.com).

In order to download a free script or purchase one, you must know what kind of scripting language you want to use. The three most popular are Perl, CFM, and PHP.

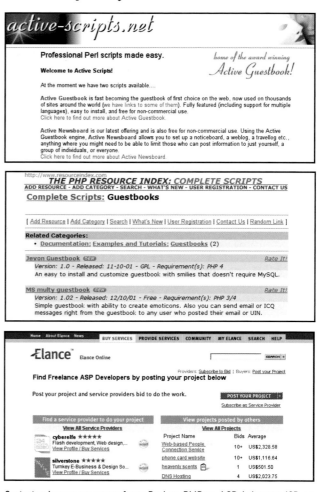

Scripting languages range from Perl to PHP to ASP. Ask your ISP or site administrator if you don't know what kind of scripts will work on your web site. These examples are taken from (top to bottom) http://www.active-scripts.net, http://php.resourceindex.com, and http://www.elance.com.

EXAMPLES OF COMMUNITY

When you want to build a community or add community features, think about the topic of your site and how people traditionally interact around that topic. For example, on the topic of movies, the Internet Movie Database (http://www.imdb.com) allows users to enter reviews of the movies they have seen and discuss the movies in a discussion forum. The web site Slashdot (http://www.slashdot.org) bills itself as "News for Nerds" and allows its users to post new stories to the main page.

Other sites that are not focused solely on community have used community features to increase functionality and satisfaction for visitors. Amazon.com is one of the most successful examples of this hybrid approach that combines traditional sales and marketing with a community component.

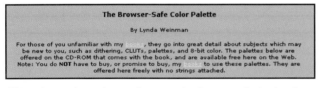

This snippet of a web page from our lynda.com web site is where our web-safe palettes are given away for free. This page is still one of the most highly trafficked areas of our web site even after being up for more than five years. Offering something for free will bring visitors to you, and it's a great technique to use if you want to increase traffic or brand loyalty.

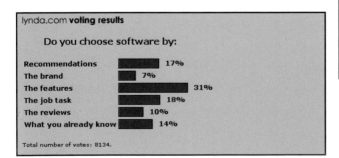

Adding polls is a way to bring people back again and again, and let them know they are a valuable voting member of your community.

When you arrive at **Amazon.com**, the site remembers whether you have shopped there before. Through sophisticated database queries and scripting, the site observes where you go and what you shop for, and it builds a list of suggestions for you on the front page. While this can be seen as an invasion of privacy (and it is!), it is also a great convenience to busy people who might want to quickly know about new products of interest.

If you have purchased from Amazon.com before, the site makes recommendations in categories for which it has kept a history on you. In this example, I was searching for a book to buy for my teenage daughter. Amazon had knowledge of what books I had purchased for her in the past, so it knew to check its database to see which books other people who bought the books I had bought were reading. It then made a recommendation based on these facts.

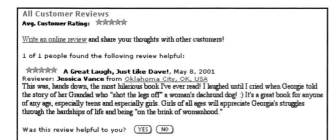

Not trusting Amazon.com completely, I went to the reviews of the book they recommended. I found a lot of favorable comments there. But I wasn't ready to buy that day... I was in "browse" mode.

I clicked on another great Amazon.com feature: the *Wish List*. This allowed me to store my discovery of the book that I thought I might want to buy my daughter at some point in the future. As you can see, I had other items in my Wish List that were put there on an earlier visit. Don't you wish you could have a Wish List in physical stores? How many times have you wanted to buy something but haven't been able to that day, only to wish that you could remember what it was that you wanted and where you had seen it? The Wish List is a great shopping convenience that creates loyalty to Amazon.com.

Another great idea that is implemented at Amazon.com is the *Recent History* link. This lets you review all the different links you've clicked on during a shopping session. I have used this many times when I've forgotten where I saw something of interest and wanted to return to it.

note

PRIVACY ISSUES

Community often requires permission to use cookies, email addresses, or other personal information as identifiers. A privacy policy is extremely important to include on your site. As well, if someone has their cookies disabled (some people do!), this can cause your community to be closed to them. Read up on Privacy in Chapter 26, *"Adding Programming Features."*

GUEST BOOKS

One of the oldest and simplest community-building tools is the guest book. An online guest book is basically the same concept as the paper guest book you might sign at a wedding reception. Online, each guest makes an entry, providing some combination of name, date, and comments, or whatever else the site designer chooses to include. When a visitor views the guest book, he or she is presented with a long list of entries, usually with a given number of entries per page.

In this instance, the guest book is a great tool to help designer **Etan Rozin** (http://www.rozin.com) get feedback about his work. As well, if a potential client came to the guest book, he or she would see that people really like Etan's work. The risk is if someone posts something negative here, it might work to counteract the positive reviews. Guest books have their pros and cons, like other community features.

Because guest books are easy to implement and have been around a long time, they are very common. They don't allow a lot of interaction, though, so a guest book may be of limited value for anything but a personal site or maybe a fan site. You can search for guest book scripts on the Internet or look to your hosting company to supply a script.

The downside to a guest book is the fact that people can leave nasty messages there. If you do use a guest book on your site, it is a good idea to know how to remove posts and/or restrict certain people from posting.

EMAIL NEWSLETTERS

Email newsletters are much like physical newsletters. You collect addresses from your site visitors (in this case, email addresses) and periodically send a newsletter to all the addresses on your list.

Email newsletters are an effective way of keeping your business fresh in the mind of your market. It is common to experience a large jump in traffic in the 24 hours after a newsletter is sent out.

```
Delivered-To: lynda@lynda.com
From: Info from Second Story <info@secondstory.com>
To: Info from Second Story <info@secondstory.com>
Subject: News from Second Story Interactive Studios
Date: Tue, 8 May 2001 11:41:03 -0700

Second Story Interactive Studios (http://www.secondstory.com/) announces the
launch of three new Web sites covering a full spectrum of topics from
American history to music entertainment to geographic exploration.

Remembering Pearl Harbor
http://www.nationalgeographic.com/pearlharbor/
To commemorate the 60th anniversary of Pearl Harbor, this site transports
visitors into the hours and minutes of the day through an interactive Attack
Map containing archival photos, text, sound effects, and personal accounts
from more than 30 survivors. You can also post your own story and search the
entries in the online Memory Book.

Janet Jackson: All For You
http://www.janet-jackson.com/
Pull back the sheets on Janet Jackson's new album, All For You. Designed to
reflect the new Janet: sexy, full of curves and ready for fun, the site is
both a beautiful, dreamy world of Janet images and a futuristic music club
layered with interactive features. Create your own mix of Janet's hit single
in the Soundboard, listen to 11 rare songs in Remix Radio, and make your own
dance video in Video Creator.

Xpeditions
http://www.nationalgeographic.com/xpeditions/
Improving upon the award-winning 1998 Xpeditions site that featured a
virtual hands-on museum of activities, the redesigned site includes many new
exciting activities and lesson plans and more than 1,800 printable maps —
all of which are made easily accessible through a global navigation system
that enables quick cross-linking between sections. In addition to receiving
several awards, the site was inducted into the Smithsonian's permanent
collection in 1999.
```

I subscribe to the newsletter for **Second Story**, a multimedia creation company (http://www.secondstory.com). Every time they send me one of these newsletters, I take great pleasure in looking through their newest works. This is a great marketing device for them, even though it's still one-way publishing.

Although an email-based newsletter does not provide a mechanism to publish its audience's responses, it is still a community-building feature. Those who belong to the mailing list feel as if they are getting special treatment as part of an elite group.

There are all kinds of challenges to creating email newsletters. One decision is related to whether you use HTML or ASCII text, as you saw in the Second Story example.

I, personally, am not a fan of HTML or Macromedia Flash-based emails. They are much larger in download size and can cause subscribers on slow modems a lot of grief. I prefer the approach of leaving links in email text and letting the subscriber make the decision to look at pages with graphics or plug-in content.

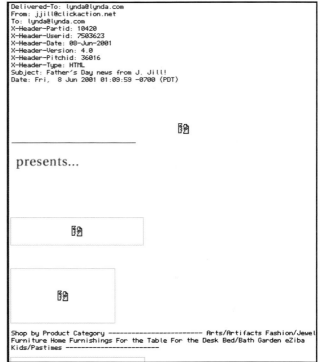

One of the disadvantages to sending image-based emails is that they take longer to load and they sometimes don't format properly in all email software. Wouldn't you rather have your subscriber see the information easily and click links to learn more?

If you are planning to create an email newsletter for your web site, it is important to understand the difference between a newsletter and spam. Spam (not the Hormel canned meat product) is the word used to describe messages sent to people without their permission, and the practice is so widely hated that you could get yourself booted from your ISP and have your web site shut down if you do it.

Unfortunately there is so much spam today, and some people are so sensitive to it, that it's easy to get accused of sending spam even when you never intended to do so. Here are some tips for avoiding the problem:

> Be sure to use a confirmation procedure in your newsletter subscription process. When a person subscribes, an automated confirmation message should be sent to the new subscriber. The subscription should be activated only after the subscriber replies to the confirmation message.

> Include information in each newsletter message that clearly identifies the web site associated with the newsletter and how to unsubscribe.

> Never add a subscriber to your newsletter manually. If someone says they cannot subscribe via the automated mechanism, try to help but don't do it manually. If a subscriber has a problem with the confirmation process, then there is a reason for it. Most likely, the email address was typed incorrectly (in which case you could end up subscribing a third party without their permission).

Email newsletters can be an excellent way to keep in touch with your customers and users. When used responsibly, an email newsletter will help build brand loyalty and encourage repeat business. Your customers will look forward to hearing from you periodically, and you will look forward to the boost in traffic that you get every time you send out a newsletter.

EMAIL LINKS

http://www.clickz.com/em_mkt/b2b_em_mkt/article.php/844161

http://www.web-marketing-tutorial.com/email-newsletters.html

http://www.microsoftfrontpage.com/usingfp/newsletters/bonus/tutorial1.html

LISTSERVS

If you have a small list of subscribers, it might work to enter their email addresses into email software by hand entry. Most sites that have larger lists (let's say more than 500 people) use listserv software instead.

A special computer program called a "list server" collects the addresses into a list for delivery. When it's time to send your newsletter, you compose the newsletter as an email message and send it to a special address. Depending on the list server, you may be able to paste it into a form on a special web page for this purpose. Then the newsletter is automatically delivered to all the addresses on the list. List server software should also provide archiving, spam filters, bounce detection, and digest delivery, as well as subscribe and unsubscribe features.

LISTSERV SOFTWARE

You can install and manage your own listservs by procuring listserv software:

http://www.list.org

http://www.lsoft.com/products

http://www.greatcircle.com/majordomo

LIST SERVER COMPANIES

You can also hire a company to run your listserv for you:

http://email.webbie.net
A newsletter delivery company run by my brother, Bill Weinman.

http://www.sparklist.com
Another reputable newsletter delivery company.

DISCUSSION LISTS

An email-based discussion list is similar to an email newsletter, but it's not the same. The big difference is that when the list is run as a discussion list, each subscriber has a way to post a message to the rest of the subscribers. That makes it much more interactive and fosters community.

What is surprising to most newbies using discussion lists is the fact that you will get a separate email for each post. This makes for a lot of extra email! I have had days where hundreds of emails have come into my inbox because of a discussion list subscription. For this reason, many people who do subscribe to discussion lists prefer digest versions. These digests include all the email posts from a single day, so that it arrives as one giant email instead of lots of small individual posts.

```
Gentle Beezers,

I've gotten a couple of e-mails expressing concern about what was considered
a personal attack on the list. We do not filter out personal attacks unless
they're
REALLY obvious, since a lot of that can be seen as being in the eye of the
beholder.

When posting messages, please err on the side of courtesy. I'm not asking you to
type
with your keyboard set on a tea saucer and your little finger sticking out , but
just think twice if you're
going to make sweeping statements about people (or refer to List Nazis, for that
matter.)

Your Mom Thanks You.

Mom

---
You are currently subscribed to cbp as: [lynda@lynda.com]
To unsubscribe, forward this message to leave-cbp@ls.studiob.com
```

I subscribe to the **Computer Book Publishing** discussion list that is monitored by Tara Calishain (http://www.studiob.com). She's referred to as the *List Mom*, a popular term (even for guys!) who supervise listservs. As shown, a List Mom's job is not always fun.

If you decide to run a discussion list, note that you will need to monitor it pretty closely. Tempers do flare, and the list can get out of control with rage if you don't nip it early and swiftly. The interesting thing is that nice people who would normally not do this face to face might be found acting totally differently in the online community world. Running and setting up a discussion list is a lot easier than managing the personalities and tempers.

DISCUSSION FORUMS

The online discussion forum (sometimes called a bulletin board) is a natural succession from the email discussion list. You can think of a discussion forum as "pull," whereas an email discussion list is a "push." The email discussion list message arrives in the user's mailbox without intervention (it is "pushed" by the list server), where users must go to the web site and look for new messages on a discussion forum (and intentionally "pull" them).

```
Forums
▼ interactive design (106)
     Design in the West (Dayle) 9/26/2001 (1)
   ▶ Know any website showcases? 9/9/2001 (7
   ▶ Do they have the right to STOP you? 8/26/
   ▶ Interactive Design Schools 7/27/2001 (7)
   ▶ PleaseReviewMyFlashSiteOnColorTheory 8/
     a new online charity organisation (Jay) 8/2
     Adobe Plugin Help (punk5150) 8/18/2001
   ▶ theories of design 8/24/2001 (4)
   ▶ Technology and art 8/25/2001 (3)
   ▶ New personal project 8/28/2001 (2)
   ▶ schools 9/3/2001 (2)
     Re: Question (Von Glitschka) 9/4/2001 (1
   ▶ search engines 9/5/2001 (2)
   ▶ Harley Davidson and Sundt 9/6/2001 (4)
```

A discussion forum posts everything to the Web instead of sending each person's post via email like a discussion list. One great advantage is that it is all archived in a place that all participants can easily find and reference.

Using a discussion forum, a user may select from a list of topics or, if allowed, create a new topic and post messages to the web site on that topic. Other users will then see that topic when they come to the site and can post new messages or reply to other messages on the same topic.

All the messages on a given topic are typically listed by subject or author, in the form of a list or a table for users to browse. In some cases messages are arranged by replies in an outline format. This is called a "threaded" display format, because a chain of replies to a message is often called a "thread."

BLOGS

A relatively new phenomenon in the web community is the "blog" (a contraction of Web Log).

A blog is to a newsletter what a discussion forum is to a discussion list. A blog is simply a running log of writings by a person or group on a web page. Of course, pages with periodic updates have been around since the inception of the Web, but today there are a number of software and service products available, many of them free, that make this activity so cheap and easy that blogs are popping up all over.

Blogger.com is one of the most popular blog software publishers.

All three of these sites (http://www.joemaller.com, http://www.flazoom.com, and http://www.designforcommunity.com) were made from a Blogger template.

BLOG LINKS

Slashdot (http://www.slashdot.org) a hybrid of a blog and a discussion list. Users post articles and then comment on the articles. What's neat is that participants are rated on the quality of their comments almost a review of the reviewer system.

http://www.blogger.com
Blogger is an excellent service for running blogs on your web site. Blogger either maintains the blog on their server or updates yours via FTP.

http://www.weblogger.com
A blogger designed for use by a team.

http://www.pitas.com
Another blogger, this one seems to host the blogs for you on their server.

http://www.flutterby.com/software/newwwsboy
A set of Perl scripts for running your own blogs.

http://www.portal.eatonweb.com
A huge catalog of blogs.

http://www.weblogs.com
Another catalog of blogs. This one lists the most recently changed blogs.

http://www.robotwisdom.com/weblogs
A FAQ about blogs.

The attraction of the blog is in its content and its frequency. In order to help build community, a blog must be compelling. Sometimes that means it's particularly well written; other times it may mean that it's candid and extemporaneous. You need to ask yourself (and perhaps your audience): Is it compelling? Will people read it? Will it bring them back to the site every day? There are a lot of blogs out there. How does mine stand out?

OTHER IDEAS

Here are a few other widgets you can add to your site to help build a community:

> **Free Stuff:** Give away free stuff. Do you make weird icons? Desktop wallpaper? Perl scripts? Articles? Whatever it is, if you can afford to give some away (and make sure you include your URL prominently in every copy), people will talk about it and flock to your site.

> **Reviews:** If you have an online catalog on your site, give people a place to post reviews. It worked for Amazon.com, and it's worked for a lot of other sites as well.

> **Polls:** What do you think? Are polls popular? Enter your opinion here! There are lots of free polling servers that will host your polls as well as freely available scripts to host them on your own site. Just think up a new topic every day, or once a week. People love to voice their opinion, and polls make it so easy! Click! Click!

There are lots of other ideas out there, and you may even think of some new ones. The main criterion is to get your users involved doing something or communicating in some way.

COMMUNITY LINKS

http://dmoz.org/computers/internet/cyberspace/
online_communities
A large directory of online community resources.

http://www.userland.com
Userland content-management software is popular. It includes a blogger and a number of other community-building tools.

COMMUNITY BOOKS

Design for Community: The Art of Connecting Real People in Virtual Places
by Derek M. Powazek
New Riders Publishing
ISBN: 0735710759

Online Communities: Designing Usability and Supporting Sociability
by Jenny Preese
John Wiley and Sons
ISBN: 0471805998

Community Building on the Web: Secret Strategies for Successful Online Communities
by Amy Jo Kim
Peachpit Press
ISBN: 0201874849
http://www.naima.com/community

CREATING COMMUNITY

SUMMARY

In this chapter you've learned about a number of different techniques and tools for building a community around your web site. Anything that involves your audience in some common activity will help build a community.

You can use a simple guest book for a start, or a newsletter or email discussion list. Online forums and blogs can help rally people around a common subject. You can give away something free, provide a place for reviews of your products, provide online polls, or think up something new!

> Anything that involves your audience or makes a place for visitors to congregate builds community.

> Make sure that you monitor your communities. People, even nice people, have a habit of getting upset online. Words can easily be misconstrued, so it's best if you have someone supervising at all times!

> Make sure that you don't spam or push too much marketing at people. They don't like it, and they won't like you or your site as a result.

> Community requires a lot of scripting. Either learn how to do it or hire a professional.

Adding Programming Features

Introduction

Even though the focus of this book is on graphics and the design side of web creation, it's a natural progression for designers to need and want to add programming features on professional sites. Two terms have become commonplace in the web site development arena: "static" and "dynamic." A static site is a site that you build page by page. A dynamic site interacts with a database, and gets information automatically without having to program anything. To create a dynamic site requires programming, however, and programming that extends beyond what HTML or XHTML alone can do.

For many applications, static web pages are just not enough to accomplish your goals for your web site. If you are selling something, or wish to interact with your users, or you want to provide personalized content, you will quickly find that you need to add programming features that will enable dynamic content.

There are a number of programming technologies that allow this level of interaction with users. This chapter will cover some of them and point you to resources that will give you more information that expands beyond the scope of this book. Shown on the following page, are some examples of programming that extend beyond HTML and XHTML.

introduction continued

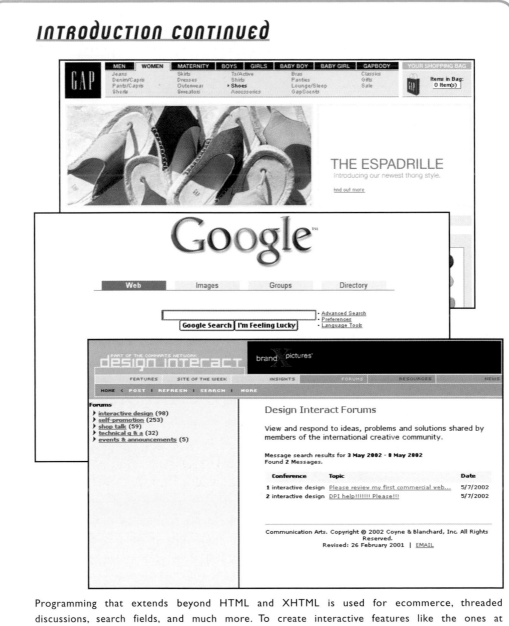

Programming that extends beyond HTML and XHTML is used for ecommerce, threaded discussions, search fields, and much more. To create interactive features like the ones at http://www.gap.com, http://www.google.com, and http://www.designinteract.com, you'll need to work with a programmer, hire a service, or learn programming on your own.

FORMS PROCESSING

HTML forms, combined with CGI (**C**ommon **G**ateway **I**nterface) scripts, are a powerful combination—simple to implement and supported by virtually every web browser on the planet. Forms provide various types of buttons, including text boxes, checkboxes, radio buttons, scrolling lists, drop-down lists, and buttons made from graphics. These controls allow the user to make selections and type text that can then be processed by a program running on the server, sometimes called a CGI script or a CGI program.

The form elements that display on the screen are created with HTML, and they will work just fine without any further programming. But to provide any useful data, they will require at least a simple program to gather results. The results must usually be gathered in a database, passed on to another person (via email or some other delivery method), or processed to generate another page for the user. All of those functions require a program.

There is one exception to this rule. It is possible, though of limited usefulness, to create a form that sends results directly to an email address, using the browser's built-in email feature (if it has one, and it's enabled). This is commonly called a "mailto" form, named after the "mailto" URL that's used in the **FORM** tag to make it happen. It's not often used anymore because too many users don't use their browser's email function.

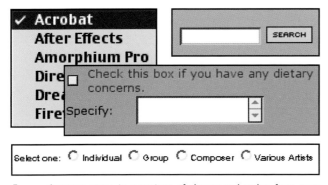

Forms elements come in a variety of shapes and styles, from text fields, to menus, to checkboxes and radial buttons.

HOW FORMS WORK

When a web form is filled in and submitted, a number of things happen behind the scenes. Here's how the process works: First, a web page is presented with the necessary form elements on it.

An example web form. (Courtesy of webmusicdb.com.)

The user can fill in the form, check the appropriate boxes, select items from lists, and eventually, when it's all filled out, press a button to send it off on its merry way.

After the button is pressed, the browser makes a connection to the web server and transmits the contents of the form to the server. The web server then passes the form data on to another program (called a "CGI script") that processes the form data. Once the data is processed, the CGI script generates a web page and gives it back to the server, which in turn transmits the new page back to the browser for display. That web page often has more **FORM** elements in it, allowing the cycle to continue until whatever task you are programming has been completed.

CGI

CGI is the **C**ommon **G**ateway **I**nterface. (In the film industry, CGI stands for "Computer Generated Imagery," but that's another book!) CGI provides a way for the web server to communicate with the script that processes the form submission. Once the script has processed the form, it can respond with another web page. When you have a multi-page form, this process can go back and forth indefinitely, creating a very interactive web experience.

CGI is not a language. CGI is a set of rules and definitions that allows a program and a web server to interact with each other. Programs that use CGI are written in many languages, and while they do not always fit the strictest definitions of the word "script," they are usually referred to as "CGI scripts" anyway. Some of the languages for CGI scripts include Perl, PHP, Python, C, C++, ASP, CFM, and Visual Basic.

CGI and HTML forms can be used to create many interesting and useful applications. The applications are limitless! Here are a few applications people commonly use HTML forms for:

> Shopping cart   > Games

> Survey/poll   > Email/contact form

> User registration   > Search engine

> Site personalization   > Dictionary

> Guest book   > Discussion forum

> Online petition   > Mailing list subscription

Of course, this list is anything but exhaustive. These are the sorts of things currently being done with CGI and HTML, but you can certainly do much, much more with them.

This is an example of a form that spawns more forms, based on the content that is entered.

CGI & PROGRAMMING LINKS

Tom Boutell's CGI Programming FAQ
A good starting point for beginners.
http://www.boutell.com/openfaq/cgi

CGI FAQ
A more thorough (and much longer) FAQ.
http://www.htmlhelp.org/faq/cgifaq.html

The CGI Resource Index
Write your own scripts or use someone else's.
http://cgi.resourceindex.com

An Online Programming Class
Good for first-time CGI programmers.
http://www.cgi101.com/class

An Online Programming Class
Step-by-step tutorial for first-time writers.
http://www.lies.com/begperl/index.html

PERSONALIZATION

Many web sites today are personalized. When you go to a personalized web site, it may refer to you by name, remember what you were doing when you were there last and keep track of a set of preferences for you. It may even remember your address, phone number, and other personal information to make it easier to fill in forms.

A small sampling of examples of personalization (http://www.amazon.com, http://www.lynda.com, and http://www.yahoo.com). Personalization can be a powerful tool in distinguishing your site from other similarly situated sites on the Web.

Personalization of web applications can be complicated because a web browser does not normally give any unique identification to a web server when it is browsing the Web. Without any unique identification, the web server cannot know what connection belongs to what user, and each click can be from a different connection. In fact, under normal circumstances there is no way for a web server to know if one click is from the same browser as another click.

note

IP ADDRESSES

Each computer connected to the Internet has an address, called an IP address, named for the Internet Protocol that is used for addressing and routing on the Internet. In the early days of the Internet, each computer had a unique IP address. Unfortunately, the IP addressing scheme that most of us are using today has a limited number of unique useable addresses, and the Internet is running out of them.

This, and other limiting factors, has created the need for many Internet users to share addresses (through proxies and other devices). Because of this address sharing, even though a web server can detect the IP address of a browser, it cannot assume that only one user is using that IP address at any given time.

So how do web sites keep track of users? How does a web site know how many unique visitors it had in a day? How does a web site know when a user returns after a week, or a month, or several years?

The answer is cookies.

COOKIES

Imagine yourself running some errands, and you stop off at the dry-cleaning shop to drop off some clothes that need to be cleaned. The clerk at the shop gives you a claim ticket, stamped with a number and the name of the shop, so that anyone at the shop can give you the right clothes when you return to pick up your cleaning. In fact, if you want to have a friend or family member pick up your cleaning for you, they can simply take the ticket along with them and they should still get the right clothes.

The concept of cookies is the same as the dry-cleaning ticket. The idea is to give a computer a special value that it can use to identify itself, independent of any network connection or user ID. When you use your web browser to visit a web site, the site's web server can give your browser a cookie, consisting of the domain name of the site (like the name of the shop) and a unique code (like the number on the claim ticket). When your browser comes back to the site, moments later or years later, it presents the cookie to the site and the web server can then identify your browser as being the same one that was there before.

Cookies are an excellent tool for maintaining information during connections or between sessions. Unfortunately, as with any powerful tool, they are easily misused and can be a security risk.

When a cookie simply carries an arbitrary identifier, like a unique number or even a user ID, they are relatively harmless. However, some developers have used cookies to store other information, like addresses, phone numbers, government ID numbers, and even passwords and credit card numbers without explaining that they are going to keep this information on file for you without your permission.

It is important to understand that cookies, be they temporary or permanent, are transmitted over the Internet "in the clear," meaning that they are not normally encrypted. They are also "stored" on your "users' computers" and might be available to other people who may have access to that computer. You should never use cookies to store anything that may compromise your users' privacy or security. There are several different types of cookies.

Type of Cookie	Definition
Hidden Fields	Hidden fields are a type of HTML Forms control that does not display on the screen but can be used to pass information from one connection to another. These are often used as a temporary cookie that gets discarded after it completes a given task.
Persistent	Sometimes called "Netscape" cookies, because they first implemented them for their Navigator browser. Persistent cookies are stored on your computer's hard drive so that they can be useful even if your computer is turned off in between sessions.
Session	Session cookies are kind of similar to persistent cookies in that they work the same way, but because they are kept in temporary memory and are not stored on the hard drive, they disappear when the browser is closed. Unlike hidden fields, session cookies do not require HTML forms to work.

COOKIE LINKS

Netscape
Original cookie specification.
http://home.netscape.com/newsref/std/cookie_spec.html

Cookiecentral.com
Lots and lots of information. Significant paranoia, too!
http://www.cookiecentral.com

Yahoo!
Informative cookie topics.
http://dir.yahoo.com/Computers_and_Internet/Internet/World_Wide_Web/Cookies

databases

When your web site is programmed to capture and generate cookies, you can assign a unique identifier to each browser or user. Once you have that number, you can use a database to associate that number with a user, their preferences, and context.

A database is a place where data is stored and organized. The hard drive in your computer is a database. So is the phone book on your desk. But in this case we are talking about something a little more sophisticated. In this context a database is a software system that allows you to store and organize large amounts of data, and then retrieve that data quickly and easily.

The most common type of database for use on a web server is a "relational database." A relational database is a system that organizes the data in relationships. In other words, you may have a set of user records that include things like user name, address, telephone number, site preferences, shipping preferences, children, spouse, pets, cars, favorite color, etc. All of this information is related to the user ID.

Database systems are commonly accessed using the Structured Query Language (SQL). SQL is a language used just for database queries, and it is often used in combination with another language such as Perl, PHP, Python, C, C++, ASP, CFM, or Visual Basic, to name a few.

database Links

MySQL Database
Is often compared to Oracle in terms of power, speed, and reliability—but it's free!
http://www.mysql.com

GNU SQL Server
Not ready yet, but it's worth keeping an eye on. The Free Software Foundation's GNU project has turned out some excellent software over the years.
http://www.ispras.ru/~kml/gss/index.html

PostgreSQL Database
Not considered as fast as MySQL, but more feature-rich—it's powerful and also free.
http://www.postgresql.org

freshmeat.net
A great discussion of SQL databases from the point of view of a person choosing one, as well as what is currently available.
http://freshmeat.net/articles/view/305

using a Database

A database can be a powerful tool to provide a personalized experience for your visitors. Welcome the user by name. This is both friendly and informative. It lets your users know that the site recognizes them and they are "logged in." It also shows that you care enough to personalize the site. Here is a chart that lists some other uses of databases.

Database Use	Definition
Site Preferences	Provide a personalized experience for your users by storing visual preferences such as color scheme and site layout.
User Context	Remember users' last transactions, and invite them to continue when they return.
Easy Access	By storing the user's login ID in a persistent cookie, you can provide a "remember your login" feature to make logging in easier. Be careful with this one—be sure to reconfirm an ID by asking for a password before allowing access to sensitive information.
Comments & Reviews	Get user comments and reviews on your different products and offerings. The feedback will be valuable to you and to your other customers.
Suggestions	By gathering data on your customer's purchasing patterns, you can give customer suggestions like "Other people who bought this widget also liked this other widget!"

Of course, there are many other ways you can use a database, especially in combination with persistent cookies, to personalize your site. Databases can also aid personalization when used in combination with more traditional applications, like directories and shopping cart services.

SHOPPING CARTS

A shopping cart is a web application that allows a user to purchase items from a web site. It usually involves a "basket" paradigm, where a user will press buttons or links to "put an item in the basket." It also uses a "check out" process that involves entering payment and delivery information, and confirming the contents of the cart and total price.

A shopping cart is a complex web application, even more so because of the context-related problems inherent to the Web, discussed earlier in this chapter.

A shopping cart usually involves a database system, and often involves a corresponding catalog application. A set of management screens are used to maintain the contents of the catalog and to retrieve sales information to use for shipping and bookkeeping. If you want to implement a shopping cart on your site, you have three main directions you can go.

Cart Direction	Definition
Off-the-Shelf Package	There are many off-the-shelf shopping cart applications available: some free and some pay. Consider the features you need, the size of your catalog, and how much volume you expect to do.
Third-Party Service	There are a number of third-party services that provide shopping carts with "no programming." These are great if you don't want to have to install software on your server. Some of them even clear credit card payments for you.
Custom Software	If your needs are complex, your product is sufficiently unique, and you can afford the time, money, and headache associated with any large programming job, then you may want to consider having a custom shopping cart system written for you. In the long run, this can work well. In the short run, expect problems.

SHOPPING CART LINKS

Dmoz
An extensive list.
http://dmoz.org/Computers/Software/
Business/E-Commerce/Shopping_Carts

Vipcart
Has both free and paid modes.
http://www.vipcart.com

Virtual Cart
Not free, but has many features.
http://www.vcart.com

Yahoo! Store
Not very flexible, but you get a lot of extra exposure by being part of the Yahoo! system.
http://store.yahoo.com

Off-The-Shelf Shopping Cart Programs
Programs you can run on your own server.
http://cgi.resourceindex.com/Programs_and_
Scripts/Perl/Shopping_Carts

PRIVACY

Whenever you start keeping any personal information about your users, you need to also think about privacy. Develop a clear privacy policy and explain it concisely.

People tend to distrust what they don't understand, so it's always a good idea to be as candid as possible about how you will use any personal information you gather about them, including aggregate information representing groups of users.

Many sites have privacy policies that are written only to meet the minimum requirements for a written policy and do not do anything to give their users a real understanding of how their personal information is or is not used. If you want your users to trust you, make a clear and concise statement of what information you gather and how you use it.

For example, does your site use cookies? If so, what is stored in the cookie? Let users know that you store a unique ID in the cookie that can be used to identify them on your site but would be unrecognizable to anyone else. Do you ask for an email address, or a street address, or phone number? If so, let the user know how you use that information, and if you make it available to any third parties, say so and explain why. Use your statement to let the users know that you respect both their privacy and their intelligence.

> Users may opt-out of receiving future mailings; see the choice/opt-out section below.
>
> Demographic and profile data is also collected at our site.
> This information may be shared with advertisers on an aggregate basis. We use this data to tailor our visitor's experience at our site showing them content that we think they might be interested in, and displaying the content according to their preferences.
>
> **External Links**
>
> This site contains links to other sites. **webmusicdb.com** is not responsible for the privacy practices or the content of such Web sites.
>
> **Public Forums**
>
> This site makes chat rooms, forums, message boards, and/or news groups available to its users. Please remember that any information that is disclosed in these areas becomes public information and you should exercise caution when deciding to disclose your personal information.
>
> **Security**
>
> This site has security measures in place to protect the loss, misuse, and alteration of the information under our control.
>
> **Children's Guidelines**
>
> The following disclosure, and its language, are mandated by U.S. law:
>
> This site **DOES NOT ACCEPT** registration by children under the age of 13.
>
> This site **DOES NOT MEET** the Online Privacy Protection Act guidelines The following criteria are violated:

Here is an excellent example of a very clear privacy policy, found at http://www.webmusicdb.com.

PRIVACY LINKS

Electronic Privacy Information Center
Lots of privacy resources.
http://epic.org

The Electronic Frontier Foundation
Online advocacy and lobbying organization.
http://www.eff.org

TRUSTe – Privacy Central
A thorough privacy resource.
http://www.truste.org/bus/pub_privacy.html

The W3C
The Platform for Privacy Preferences Project.
http://www.w3.org/P3P

W3C P3P INITIATIVE

The **W**orld **W**ide **W**eb **C**onsortium (W3C) has an ongoing initiative to create an industry-wide standard for communicating privacy policies and allowing consumers to control how their personal information is gathered and used. They call this initiative "P3P," which roughly translates as Platform for Privacy Preferences.

The idea is to generate a set of machine-readable documents to be posted on your web site so that a browser can read them and make decisions based on a user's individual privacy preferences. For example, as of this writing some new browsers will refuse to accept cookies from sites that do not have a P3P-compatible set of privacy rules available.

Here's how it works: The browser will look for a special document. If it finds the P3P document, it will read it and decide—based on preferences that the user has set in the browser—what information (if any) to allow the site to have and whether or not to accept cookies from the site. There are already automated generators appearing that will generate the necessary documents to support this emerging standard.

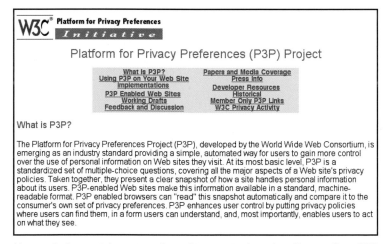

You can find more information about this initiative here: http://www.w3.org/P3P.

earning your users' confidence

If you are using your web site to gather information about your users, even if it's just a list of email addresses to send an occasional announcement, you will benefit from a policy that earns your users' confidence. Here are some specific things you can do to gain the trust of your users. These policies are not required, and are not always followed, but your users will appreciate your thoughtfulness and reward it with their loyalty.

Use double-blind confirmations.

Don't assume that just because someone entered an email address on your site that they are the owner of that address. Send confirmation email to the address in question and wait for a response before activating the account.

It is sad, but true, that there are people out there who would maliciously sign up a third-party email address to create trouble for others. You can avoid becoming a party to mischief, and the associated complaints, by using this technique.

Ask permission for each use of each email address.

When you ask for someone's permission before using their information, you gain their respect and trust. When you use their information without their permission, you achieve the opposite result.

Recently, one of the larger free-email companies changed their privacy policy and told their users that they were going to start sending out promotional email (i.e., renting out user email addresses) unless each user completed a complicated "opt-out" process. This made a lot of folks mad and created a wave of negative publicity for the company.

You can avoid this trouble by asking permission and waiting for a positive response before using your customer's information. As new revenue streams evolve in the marketplace, the good will generated will prove valuable.

Ask permission for use of all personal information.

Any time you ask for a piece of new information from your users, ask their permission explicitly. For example, "In order to offer you this new service, we will need your ZIP code. We promise to use your ZIP code only for this service and for statistical analysis. We will never use it for any other purpose without first asking your permission."

Users are understandably afraid of the misuse of their personal information. When you acknowledge that fear and show them that you have the same concerns, it puts you on the same side of the table as your users, and they will be more likely to become loyal friends.

SECURITY

Any time you increase the complexity of a system, you increase the security risks proportionally. Expect to spend as much time and resources dealing with the security implications as you do on the design and programming of each new feature.

Like other classes of bugs, security holes usually pop up where you least expect them, so telling you what to look for is a little like warning you to look left before crossing the street in England. The danger is likely to come from another direction. Nevertheless, I would like to point out some of the most obvious dangers.

Most of these suggestions assume that you are running a dedicated server. If you are running on a shared server from a hosting company, read this anyway. Some of these suggestions will still apply to you, and the rest are good to think about anyway.

Use secure passwords on your server.

Be sure that the passwords you use on your server are not simple passwords. Don't use words that are found in the dictionary; mix up letters and digits, mix up upper- and lowercase; use some punctuation. Change your passwords frequently.

Insecure passwords can lead to break-ins, which can lead to much larger problems.

Watch out for security bulletins.

Keep up with all the security bulletins from all your software vendors. Also, keep up with the CERT (CERT Coordination Center, Carnegie Mellon University) bulletins from http://www.cert.org. Make all patches as quickly as possible.

Limit server access.

Limit access to your server to only those who actually need it. Use a different machine for user mail and any other services that require access by large numbers of people. Enforce good passwords and change them often.

Have a plan.

Have a good plan for locking down the server in the event of abuse.

Check your logs.

Check *all* your logs for suspicious login activity, repeated failed attempts at anything (e.g., repeated 404 errors, repeated failed logins, repeated DNS queries), core dumps, or anything else out of the ordinary.

Watch what you store in cookies.

We mentioned this above, but in a different context. Only store keys in the cookie, never actual usernames or passwords, or any other information. To do so is not only a risk to the user, but a risk to the site as well. Cookies are easily intercepted, and one of the primary rules of security is to keep your cards close to your chest. In other words, never give away more information than necessary.

Revalidate your users.

Don't assume that just because a user has the right cookie that they are the right user. Ask for their password now and then anyway, especially when accessing sensitive information or making purchases with stored credit card numbers.

Encrypt sensitive data.

Use SSL (**S**ecure **S**ockets **L**ayer; when a URL has "`https://`" at the beginning, it is secure) for all sensitive information, including usernames, passwords, names and addresses, age, ID numbers (Social Security numbers, driver licenses, passports, credit cards, etc.), or anything else personal.

Also, just as important, encrypt this data when it's stored as well as when it's transmitted. If someone breaks into your system or steals your system (or even your backups!), another barrier cannot hurt.

Use care with passwords.

Do your users lose their passwords? You can email it to them at the address they registered with. That works for most applications, but if your data is particularly sensitive (e.g., a credit card number), require a confirmation phrase before sending the password. For example, "your mother's maiden name," "your childhood pet," or "the name of the first person you ever kissed." Something personal. Perhaps give them a choice.

Be paranoid!

This is probably the most valuable security advice: Expect disasters. Think about worst-case scenarios and plan for the contingencies. Remember that most true disasters are compounded problems. The *Titanic* didn't just hit an iceberg; it hit it too fast and too far from any other ships. Its "unsinkable" design did not account for a 248-foot series of rips and gashes spanning five compartments, it didn't have enough lifeboats, and its communications system failed.

Think about what can go wrong, and think about what happens if several things go wrong at once. And then think some more. Remember, there is no such thing as an unsinkable ship.

SECURITY LINKS

The WWW Security FAQ
http://www.w3.org/Security/Faq/

The CERT Coordination Center
A major reporting center for Internet security problems, this is the place to go to find up-to-the-minute security bulletins. Funded by the U.S. Department of Defense, CERT is run by the Software Engineering Institute at Carnegie Mellon University. CERT used to stand for **C**omputer **E**mergency **R**esponse **T**eam; now they consider that definition dated and simply use CERT as a proper noun.
http://www.cert.org

The CERT Mailing Lists
If you want to be informed of the latest security issues, this is a must.
http://www.cert.org/contact_cert/certmaillist.html

RFC 2828
This glossary of security terms is a very good reference to have around.
http://www.faqs.org/rfcs/rfc2828.html

adding programming FEATURES

SUMMARY

As you can see, the addition of programming features can add a lot of dynamic functionality to your site.

> Programming features like forms, CGI, and databases can be immensely valuable. They can help you offer more services and more value to your visitors, but like any powerful technology, they can also offer new challenges and potential pitfalls.

> Privacy issues are also compounded by the complexity of your system. The more data you deal with, the more potential there is for abuse of that data. Treat other people's personal information as a sacred trust. Your users will thank you for that with their loyalty.

> Whenever you add programming features, you add more potential for security problems. Be alert to any activity that appears out of the ordinary, and pay attention to the security of your system.

26

Usability

Introduction

Since the last edition of <designing web graphics> (.3), perhaps the most buzz-worthy term to hit the mainstream design and development community is "usability." In that past, when the Web was new, most authors focused on how to write the HTML or create the graphics. Now that the medium has matured, it's not just a matter anymore of "how" the functionality and success of a web site has come to the forefront of many creators' efforts.

The term usability, at its core, has to do with your users and how easy it is for them to access your site. Hybrid terms such as "user-friendly," "user-based," and "user-centered" have entered the vocabulary of those who develop and design web sites for good reason. If you ignore your users and how they interact with your site, then you will likely create something that works neither for you or for them.

USER-CENTERED DESIGN

As a designer or developer, it's easy to focus on your own goals when you create a web site. You might think, "I want to make money selling books and CD-ROMs. I want to have 5,000 unique visitors per day. I want to be at the top of search engine results. I want to be written up in magazines. And be profiled on *Oprah*." These are "your" goals, and they are entirely different from the goals of your user.

Your user does not come to your site thinking, "How can I give my money to this web site? Visit it all the time and tell my friends? Or make the person who developed it rich and famous?" Instead he or she comes thinking, "I want to find the book or CD that I'm looking for. I want to make sure I'm paying a fair price. I want the e-commerce system to work in a way that's understandable to me. I want to make sure that my private information isn't given to other companies or marketers. I want recommendations that match my taste, and to learn about newly released books and CDs that are of interest to me."

You can easily see how, if you meet the goals of the end user, that your goals are more likely to be met. Maybe not the part about "Oprah" and getting famous, but the part about making money and having frequent visitors is possible if your site is really usable to your end user.

Practicing user-centered design means spending a lot of time thinking in the shoes of your end user. It requires that you take yourself out of your own head and try to get into the heads of others.

You actually have a lot of experience understanding end users, because it's likely that you are one yourself, even if you develop web sites. You can look to your own tastes, likes and dislikes, and learn a lot about what other people might like and dislike. Be sure to visit your competitors' web sites and evaluate what you like and don't like. Next, conduct a little research, and ask others to share what they like and don't like. There's no way to please everyone, but it is relatively easy to determine whether something is mostly your taste and not others, and whether you're on the right track with your line of thinking.

easy is good

One key to good usability, in addition to being sensitive to your audience's goals, is to make your site easy to use. The more clear you are about where to click, how to order, how to check out, when to expect shipping, etc., the more appealing your site will be to all who use it.

The **Gap** web site has easy access to whatever department you need. It's very direct, very simple, and hence very usable.

Abercrombie & Fitch (http://www.abercrombie.com) is trying hard to identify with its audience of young, body-conscious, and label-conscious crowd. The focus of the site however, is not on luring shoppers. While they have men's and women's clothes, there is no Men or Women link at the front-end of the site. In fact, the label "SHOP A&F" is the last item on the navbar. How many people think of Abercrombie & Fitch as A&F? This navigation bar was developed thinking from the inside out, not from the user's perspective.

When visiting **yellowratbastard.com**, a youth culture clothing store, the department names are a little less direct. Instead of Men's and Women's, it's Homeys and Chicks. This is fitting for their audience, and still direct and easy for that crowd to understand. True, they're likely alienating grandparents and the conservative crowd, but with a name like "Yellow Rat Bastard," this choice was made long ago.

note

USABILITY BOOKS

Don't Make Me Think
Steve Krug
New Riders
ISBN: 0-7897-2310-7
Contains a lot of clear examples and very good ideas related to user-centered design.

Homepage Usability
Jakob Nielsen and Marie Tahir
New Riders
ISBN: 0-7357-1102-X
Site critiques of 50 websites from a usability standpoint.

Web Site Usability Handbook
Mark Pearrow
Charles River Media
ISBN: 1-58450-026-3
Contains lots of user testing guidelines and forms.

THE JAKOB NIELSEN FACTOR

For years, usability and usability testing was a niche subject with one leader's voice: Dr. Jakob Nielsen. He's written articles in numerous magazines, created a web site, and written books on this subject. You'll find that many people refer to his work as a starting point, so you might want to investigate his publications further.

Designing Web Usability: The Practice of Simplicity

Jakob Nielsen

New Riders

ISBN: 1-56205-810-X

useit.com: usable information technology		Search

useit.com: Jakob Nielsen's Website

Permanent Content	News
Alertbox Jakob's bi-weekly column on Web usability Improving Usability Guideline Compliance (June 24) Over the last 1.5 years, the average compliance with established usability guidelines increased by 4%. If we can sustain this level of improvement, we'll reach the ideal of 90% guideline compliance in 2017. Reduce Redundancy: Decrease Duplicated Design Decisions (June 9) Supporting Multiple-Location Users (May 26) Top Ten Guidelines for Homepage Usability (May 12) All Alertbox columns from 1995 to 2002 Subscribe to get a short email when a new Alertbox is published	**Examples of Flash-Based Applications and Tools Wanted for User Testing** Please nominate good examples of Internet-based applications and tools implemented in Flash. We need to test a wide variety of sample designs in order to derive the usability guidelines for functionality-oriented Flash design. My working definition is that an **application** is a complete user interface to an integrated set of features, which most often will operate on some data objects and modify them. In contrast, a **tool** will typically only have one feature (or maybe a very small number) and will be presented as an element on a web page that contains additional content (or other tools). Examples:

Useit.com is Nielsen's site. A lot of his examples of poor usability have to do with graphics and Flash (both of which are clearly absent on his own web site). Recently, Jakob has aligned himself with Macromedia (or vice versa). See the following link for more information: http://www.macromedia.com/macromedia/proom/pr/2002/macromedia_nielsen.html.

While much of what Jakob Nielsen preaches is useful and practices good common sense, he has created a lot of enemies in the design community because of his hard stand on standardized content and the lack of value he places on design or graphics. He especially angered a lot of designers by stating that 99% of all Flash sites were bad.

I believe that design and artwork have a lot to do with making information more usable and engaging. While I find some of what Nielsen writes about to be helpful, I too take objection to his lack of attention to the importance of design. An interesting book that questions and counters a lot of Jakob Nielsen's theories is *Train of Thoughts* by John Lenker.

Train of Thoughts

John Lenker

New Riders

ISBN: 0-7357-1174-7

John Lenker describes how important creativity and psychology are in web design. His question, *"Is creativity the enemy of usability?"* speaks to the Jakob Nielsen factor directly and raises very good arguments in favor of originality, innovation, and risk taking.

Here are a few other usability terms that you might hear in the professional work environment:

Human Factors: The psychology of perception. Often refers to the study of people in certain environments or situations and how they respond.

Human Factors and Ergonomics Society
http://hfes.org/

Human/Computer Interaction (HCI): The application of human factors to the way people interact with computer systems. Historically, HCI has focused on interfaces of computer programs, ergonomics, and how people interact with computer devices like mice or screens, etc.

HCI Bibliography site
http://www.hcibib.org

User-Centered Design (UCD): Approaching design from the user's perspective.

IBM's User-Centered Design pages
http://www-3.ibm.com/ibm/easy/eou_ext.nsf/Publish/570

Heuristic Evaluations: The process of evaluating a site based on clear measurements. For example, in the case of a *Cancel* button, the user would need to know with confidence that he or she had cancelled an order successfully. Having a *Cancel* button doesn't necessarily achieve the same thing as the customer confidence gain when the button worked and he or she received the proper feedback to that effect.

Jakob Nielsen's Heuristic Evaluation Program
http://www.useit.com/papers/heuristic

USER TESTING

Once you've been working on a site for a while, you will no longer be objective. One of the most important aspects of good usability practices is making sure that what you think is usable is really usable. The only way to test this is to see how users react to your content.

There are many different ways to conduct usability testing, from inexpensive to expensive, and formal to informal. You will likely know which end of the spectrum you are on this scale. Here's a chart that outlines the choices:

User Testing	Identifying Tester
Inexpensive	Recruit people who already use your site and offer to pay them directly or trade a product or subscription.
Expensive	Hire a marketing research firm to help you get testers.
Formal	Conduct marketing research on who best represents your demographics.
Informal	Recruit random people who might or might not be your target audience.

As Steve Krug writes in his excellent book *Don't Make Me Think*, "Testing one user is 100 percent better than testing none. Even the worst user will show you something that you can do to improve your site."

WHAT & HOW TO ASK

Impartiality is key when you test. It's very important that you don't ask leading questions or interject your judgments or perspectives into the process.

The process should not be viewed as one that validates what you did right, but instead should be thought of as a hunt for problems. It's also very important to test again after you've fixed problems based on the first test. It's amazing how many times something new breaks when something gets changed.

Coming up with the test plan is the first step. Every site is different, but here are some sample types of questions to ask a tester:

> What is the first thing that stands out when you look at the home page?

> Do you know what the site is about?

> Do you know how to find out more about the site or find contact information?

> Is there anything that seems unclear or confusing?

> If you wanted to find a _____ product, where would you click?

> How would you evaluate the check-out procedure?

> If you were searching for something, how would you find it?

As the user answers these questions, you will likely find lots of stumbling blocks along the way. Encourage the person doing the testing to speak what they are thinking aloud while you document what they say so you can make a report in the end to help track all the changes that you will want to make. As you do this process with many testers, you will compile a lot of different ideas and problems. Collating all the responses will vary in difficulty depending on how many testers you query and the depth of your site. Here are a few valuable usability links: useit.com, usableweb.com, and usablesites.com.

key usability issues

Things that can make your site more usable are covered throughout this book and are not necessarily addressed in detail in this chapter alone. Here's a quick list of potential issues, in no particular order of importance:

> Is the site clearly branded with your logo?

> Do you have a tag line, and does it make sense to most people?

> Can users tell by your navigation categories what the scope of your site is?

> Do you use certain fonts and styles for specific types of links and buttons to establish graphics consistency?

> Do you always have a way to navigate back to where you want to go?

> Is the search function clearly marked, or do you need to add a Search function?

> If something is not finished or not available, remove it from the site. All sites are forever under construction! Nothing is more frustrating than an "Under Construction" warning when you want to go somewhere that it isn't ready.

> Do you have a clear privacy policy?

> Do you have a clear way for people to locate your address and phone number?

> Use language that "your" customers will understand.

> Avoid animation if it isn't an important area of the page or piece of content that you're trying to draw attention to.

> Make sure that the graphics are small enough in file size so the download time isn't prohibitive to people on slow connections.

> Does your color scheme offer enough contrast to be easily readable?

> Do you have a clear hierarchy of information to help direct users to areas most trafficked?

> Have you checked your logs to make sure you understand your browser and platform demographics?

> Are all of your links clearly delineated from static graphics?

> Avoid icons without text callouts.

> Make sure your customer can easily access his/her cart or continue shopping at all times.

> Make sure your cancellation system is easily understood.

> Make sure there's a way for visitors to easily contact you with questions, comments, or problems.

> Put critical information "above the fold."

> Make sure that all pages have titles.

> Make sure that you follow accessibility practices.

> Make sure that your headlines are succinct and make sense.

> Avoid pop-up ads—people hate them.

> Is your page visually noisy (too busy)?

USABILITY

SUMMARY

Usability is an often overlooked component of good web design. This chapter outlined important guidelines to consider when implementing and testing your site for usability concerns.

> Practice user-centered design, and your personal or company goals are likely to succeed.

> Ease of use is key. People don't like to struggle to understand something or make it work as expected. Web users are in a hurry; make it easy and quick for them to make decisions.

> Test your site and look for problems, not validation that your ideas were right.

> Understand the issues that make content more clear and easy to use, and use a checklist to ensure that you've covered all the potential problems.

browser standards

introduction

When I wrote the first edition of this book in 1995, there was a chapter called "Browser Hell." It showed 11 different browsers and how each one displayed the same HTML page differently. Since then, the term "browser standards" has emerged, because the latest browsers actually attempt to follow the same guidelines. Web development for current browser software is undeniably much less "hellish."

While current and emerging standards hold much promise, there is an underlying problem that throws true stability into question. The reality is that new web technology and authoring platforms continue to change, making the process of defining and adhering to standards difficult. Most likely, the Web will always evolve, technologies will always change, and true standards and browser compatibility might always be at risk of changing. Meanwhile, what can you do to ensure that your web sites look as you intended across platforms and browsers? This chapter covers the key issues and how best to address them in your web development practices.

A BRIEF HISTORY OF BROWSER STANDARDS

Back when the Web was young, say 1993 to about 1994, there were no standards for web pages and browsers. The major computer companies were mostly ignoring the Web. At first the Web was all text-based, but in 1993, a visual web browser called Mosaic (written by Marc Andreessen and several other students from the University of Illinois) took the Web by storm.

Then came the "Browser Wars," and the "bad old days" of conflicting standards and pages with buttons that said, "Best Viewed with Browser X." Big Companies like Microsoft and Netscape, with stockholders and directors to answer to, tried to chase each other out of the market by creating features that didn't work on their competitor's browsers and encouraging people to use those features. (They even provided those *Best Viewed with…"* buttons.)

The W3C (**W**orld **W**ide **W**eb **C**onsortium) was founded in 1994, at least partly in response to the Browser Wars. The W3C became the Web's de facto standards organization and began formulating standards for browsers. One of their first tasks was to define a standard version of HTML so that people could write web pages and expect them to work on a variety of browsers.

Starting in 1995, a progression of additional specifications and recommendations for standards have been issued by the W3C. The chart on the following page shows a chronology of specifications released by the W3C in its effort to bring order to the chaos of the Web.

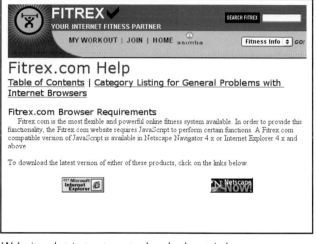

Web sites that instruct you to download certain browsers are common on the Internet, like the above site at http://www.fitrex.com.

web standards links

http://www.w3.org
The World Wide Web Consortium.

http://www.w3.org/MarkUp
The W3C's HTML-related activities.

http://wp.netscape.com/browsers/future/standards.html
Dated (and biased) but interesting discussion of the need for web standards from one of the major players in the Browser Wars.

http://www.alistapart.com
Jeffrey Zeldman's excellent 'zine about browser standards is full of tips, tricks, and examples.

http://www.webstandards.org
The Web Standards Project is full of tips and techniques for creating good-looking web sites while adhering to cross-platform standards.

Date	Specification	Description
1995	**HTML 2.0**	Intended as a minimum requirement for HTML. Contained no "layout" features, not even tables.
1996	**HTML 3.2**	A documentation of "best current practice." This specification was meant to reflect what people were actually doing with HTML at the time.
1997	**HTML 4.0**	Intended to set the future direction for HTML. Contains definitions for three types of documents: strict, transitional, and frameset. It also includes improvements in support for international documents, accessibility, multimedia, scripting, style sheets, and printing.
1998	**XML 1.0**	A framework for defining document types, XML (eXtensible Markup Language) was designed to provide a platform for future markup languages, including the intended successor to HTML called XHTML.
1999	**XHTML 1.0**	XHTML (eXtensible HTML) is a "reformulation" of HTML as an application of XML. Effectively, XHTML is a stricter, more narrowly defined replacement for HTML that works in all current browsers. That means that you can start using it today without sacrificing the size of your current audience.
1999	**HTML 4.01**	Contains minor editorial update to HTML 4.0, and is the basis from which XHTML 1.0 was developed.
2001	**XHTML 1.1**	A reformulation of XHTML to break it down into modules. This allows support for things like forms, tables, frames, multimedia extensions, and accessibility features for platforms that require them, while also supporting a subset of features for platforms that don't support all the features in a given document. Breaking XHTML into modules helps developers of devices other than browsers (cell phones, PDAs, and things yet not invented) to use standards, but not have to make huge applications just in order to satisfy the specification. It lets them use smaller bits of the standard to make smaller, yet compliant, Internet applications.

HTML & XHTML SPECIFICATIONS

The current recommendation for document markup is XHTML 1.1. This version of XHTML is very rigorous, so most people don't use it. Instead, the most commonly used versions of HTML and XHTML are HTML 4.01 and XHTML 1.0. These specifications include all the elements that are commonly used on the Web, as well as extensions for style sheets, scripting, embedded objects, right-to-left as well as left-to-right text, forms, and support for accessibility by people with disabilities.

The HTML 4.01 and XHTML 1.0 specifications are divided into three document types: strict, transitional, and frames. A given page may use one of the three document types, and a **DOCTYPE** declaration at the beginning of the document indicates which document type a given page uses. The chart found on the following page describes the three document types.

By far the most common document type is the transitional document type. It is useful because, as the name implies, it allows you to use new features like style sheets, while still incorporating presentation markup that works for older browsers that do not support style sheets.

The **strict** document type is for documents that use style sheets for all "presentation." The term presentation relates to how content is visually formatted, not the structure of the content. The specification for the strict document type does not include presentation attributes or any elements that the W3C expects to phase out as support for style sheets matures, such as the **FONT** element. Use the following **DOCTYPE** declaration at the top of your document to specify that your document uses the strict document type. It means that phased-out HTML like the **FONT** element would be totally disregarded by the browser.

```
<!DOCTYPE html PUBLIC
"-//W3C//DTD HTML 4.01//EN"
"http://www.w3.org/TR/html4/strict.dtd">
```

The **transitional** document type is for documents that use HTML and style sheets for presentation. The specification for the transitional document type includes all of the elements and attributes of the HTML 4.01 specification, including those that are excluded from the strict document type definition. Use the following **DOCTYPE** declaration at the top of your document to specify that your document uses the transitional document type:

```
<!DOCTYPE html PUBLIC
"-//W3C//DTD HTML 4.01 Transitional//EN"
"http://www.w3.org/TR/html4/loose.dtd">
```

The **frameset** document type is for documents that use frames. Use this document type for the document that contains your **FRAMESET** tags. Use the following **DOCTYPE** declaration at the top of your frameset documents:

```
<!DOCTYPE html PUBLIC
"-//W3C//DTD HTML 4.01 Frameset//EN"
"http://www.w3.org/TR/html4/frameset.dtd">
```

HTML LINKS

http://www.w3.org/TR/html4
The W3C's HTML 4.0 Specification Page.

http://validator.w3.org
W3C's HTML Validation Service.

http://www.blooberry.com/indexdot
Brian Wilson's (a.k.a. Blooberry, not a Beach Boy) excellent online HTML reference.

While HTML is the markup language of the past, XHTML is positioned to become the markup language of the future. It has the dual advantages of supporting future technology more elegantly than HTML, while still being recognized by older browsers as if it were HTML. Whereas XHTML 1.0 works exactly like HTML 4.01 in terms of having three document type definitions, XHTML 1.1 introduces the concept of modularization. What's more, by XHTML 1.1, there's only one public DTD—and it's based on the XHTML 1.0 Strict DTD. That means if you use XHTML 1.1, you have to separate presentation from structure or customize the language by writing your own DTD—something reserved for advanced developers.

XHTML 1.0 is functionally equivalent to HTML 4.01, so if you are looking to support existing browsers, you probably want to stick with XHTML 1.0. Just like HTML 4.01, XHTML 1.0 is divided into three document types: strict, transitional, and frames. A given page may use one of the three document types. Which document type a page uses is indicated by a **DOCTYPE** tag at the beginning of the document. The **DOCTYPE** declarations for XHTML are slightly different from those for HTML.

XHTML 1.0 Document Types	
Strict	`<!DOCTYPE html PUBLIC "-//W3C//DTD XHTML 1.0 Strict//EN"` `"http://www.w3.org/TR/xhtml1/DTD/xhtml1-strict.dtd">`
Transitional	`<!DOCTYPE html PUBLIC "-//W3C//DTD XHTML 1.0 Transitional//EN"` `"http://www.w3.org/TR/xhtml1/DTD/xhtml1-transitional.dtd">`
Frames	`<!DOCTYPE html PUBLIC "-//W3C//DTD XHTML 1.0 Frameset//EN"` `"http://www.w3.org/TR/xhtml1/DTD/xhtml1-frameset.dtd">`

The great thing about XHTML is that it was designed to work in place of HTML in existing browsers. Even the oldest of browsers should work fine with XHTML. That makes it perfectly okay to start using XHTML today. XHTML is an important bridge to the future for users of HTML. It is a good idea to start to use XHTML on your new projects. Because it is so new, however, many people don't yet know how to write XHTML and so it won't be nearly as prevalent as HTML.

XHTML LINKS

http://www.w3.org/TR/xhtml1
The W3C's XHTML specification.

http://www.nypl.org/styleguide/xhtml
The New York Public Library's XHTML Style Guide has excellent discussion of the transition from HTML to XHTML. Be sure to *view source,* the page itself is written in valid XHTML.

http://validator.w3.org
W3C's Validation Service also for XHTML.

http://www.w3.org/People/Raggett/tidy
Tidy is a wonderful utility for validating and formatting HTML and XHTML documents. It was written by Dave Raggett, one of W3C's main contributors to the HTML specifications.

STYLE SHEETS

The specification for style sheets is formally called **C**ascading **S**tyle **S**heets, or CSS. Style sheets are used to apply various properties to the appearance of a document. For example, CSS can be used to select fonts, colors, background images, borders, even rollover effects. (For more detailed information on how to implement CSS, see Chapter 23, *"Cascading Style Sheets."*) The W3C has defined two different levels of CSS so far: CSS Level 1 and CSS Level 2. Work is currently underway on CSS Level 3.

CSS-1 deals with things like fonts, colors, spacing, and positioning. It was designed to replace the functionality of all the disparate presentation markups that have been patched onto HTML over the years—things like **FONT**, **CENTER**, **BGCOLOR**, and the like. CSS-1 gives you the power to create a style, define it in a .css file, and use it for all the documents on your site. Then when you feel like updating the style, you can simply change the style sheet and the entire site will have a new look.

CSS-2 builds on CSS-1 by supporting media-specific style sheets. That way, you can have one style for the screen and another style for when the document is printed on a printer. Using CSS-2, you can have one page that looks right on the screen, prints well on a printer, and even displays well on a PDA, a Braille device, or whatever else is invented next week. CSS-2 also has improvements over CSS-1 in the areas of content positioning, table layout, internationalization, automatic numbering, and downloadable fonts.

CSS-3 will be modular, allowing easier extensibility. This fits with the philosophy of future work on XML and XHTML.

Note: CSS-1 is supported by most modern browsers today. Support for CSS-2 is planned for upcoming browsers from all the major browser vendors.

CSS LINKS

http://www.w3.org/Style/CSS
W3C's CSS home page. Intentionally gaudy. Be patient. It has massive amounts of information, combined with truly screwy navigation.

http://jigsaw.w3.org/css-validator
A CSS validator.

http://www.alistapart.com/stories/sizematters
A good article about CSS-support in version 4 browsers.

http://www.meyerweb.com/eric/articles/webrev/200001.html
A good tutorial on creating a separate style sheets for printing in CSS-2.

document object model

The **D**ocument **O**bject **M**odel (DOM) is an interface that allows a language like JavaScript to access the inner workings of a browser so that it can do things such as change the colors, fonts, positioning of objects, or even the contents of a document, on-the-fly.

The term "Dynamic HTML" was originally used by some browser vendors to describe the combination of HTML, style sheets, and scripts that allows objects to be animated. The various specifications for early versions of these browsers were used as a starting point, and eventually the W3C came up with one specification that has been embraced by all the major vendors for their future browsers.

DOM Level 1 specifies processes to address the various properties of a document. This enables software developers and web script authors to access and manipulate existing HTML content, such as change its location, color, border, etc.

DOM Level 2 expands on DOM-1 and modularizes it to allow for more extensibility. That means that the specification can be broken into smaller modules, allowing developers for Internet devices like cell phones or PDAs to use DOM without having to write large code-compliant applications.

You need DOM to create pages with dynamic features that work on a variety of platforms and browsers. Trying to create something as simple as a drop-down menu can be extremely difficult without DOM, if you want it to work on more than one platform.

The very latest browsers available today (beginning with version 6 browsers) have built-in support for DOM-1 in their JavaScript implementations and have included some limited support for DOM-2.

DOM LINKS

http://www.w3.org/DOM/
DOM pages on the W3C web site.

http://architag.com/tag/Article.asp?v=12&i=10&p=1&s=2
"The DOM for Non-Programmers," by Elaine Brennan. This article explains what DOM is and why it's important in terms that are a little less technical than any of the other articles I've run across.

javascript (ecmascript)

JavaScript is a client-side language (which means it runs inside the browser) that is used for manipulating the browser. It can do useful things like simple calculations, validate forms, update styles, and swap images for rollovers. It can also be used for scrolling text along the status bar at the bottom of the browser (which is most likely going to annoy your user, rather than be that beneficial to your site).

The current standard for JavaScript is called ECMAScript. It cannot be called JavaScript because Netscape's license for the name does not extend to anyone else's browser. ECMA (**E**uropean **C**omputer **M**anufacturers **A**ssociation) is the name of the standards organization that formalized the specification for the language. ECMAScript is not easy to pronounce. I predict people will continue to pronounce it "JavaScript" for the foreseeable future.

JavaScript (and Jscript on Microsoft browsers) has been a sticky area for browser compatibility. Both Microsoft and Netscape spent a lot of time during the Browser Wars trying to make important things work only on their own browsers. The latest versions of both browsers claim compatibility with the ECMA specification, but compatibility with older browsers will still be an issue for a while.

javascript/ecmascript links

http://www.ecma.ch/ecma1/STAND/ECMA-262.htm
The downloadable ECMAScript standard in PDF format.

http://developer.netscape.com/docs/manuals/index.html?content=javascript.html
Old (pre-ECMA) JavaScript documentation.

http://www.webreference.com/programming/javascript/
Lots of JavaScript articles.

http://javascript.internet.com
Literally hundreds of free JavaScript examples.

CURRENT BROWSERS

Currently the major browsers are Microsoft Internet Explorer 6, Netscape Navigator 6 (and version 7, which is in beta as of this writing), Opera 6, and AOL 8.

Microsoft Internet Explorer (MSIE) version 6 is the latest version of the browser that is bundled with the Windows operating system. Explorer version 5.1 is loaded by default on Macintosh systems and is the default browser with AOL. That gives MSIE the lion's share of the market, with between 85% and 95% of the browser market, depending on the survey you listen to.

Netscape Navigator 6 (and 7, which is in beta as of this writing) is based on the Mozilla browser, and new versions of the AOL browser will be based on Mozilla as well. Mozilla is an open-source browser project started by Netscape after the "Browser Wars". It has taken several years, but the version Mozilla 1.0 browser is emerging as a full-featured major player in the browser business. As an open-source project, it is possible for many other companies to embed the Mozilla rendering engine (called Gecko) in their browsers. Expect a new crop of products to emerge over the next few years that take advantage of this capability.

Opera is a shareware browser that is lean, fast, and extremely standards compliant. Opera doesn't take up as much space as the larger browsers from Microsoft and Netscape.

BROWSER LINKS

http://www.microsoft.com/ie
Microsoft's Internet Explorer pages.

http://www.netscape.com/computing/download
Netscape's download page.

http://www.opera.com
The Opera browser lives here.

http://www.mozilla.org
The Mozilla open-source browser that is the basis for Netscape's and AOL's latest.

http://free.aol.com/tryaolfree
Just in case you've haven't received one.

compatibility

The two major browsers both support the latest standards in their current offerings, and both have flaws that make them work a little differently from each other. Currently, it is a good idea to test your web pages on at least Microsoft and Mozilla browsers.

The browser compatibility issue is not as bad as it once was, but it is still not good as it could be. Currently, if you want your site to work on the majority of browsers, you will need to test your site on MSIE 5, 5.5 and 6, and Mozilla. Additionally, you should be aware that there are significant differences between MSIE on a Macintosh and MSIE on Windows. Mozilla uses the same rendering engine (called Gecko) for all supported platforms.

There are two general areas in which you will run into trouble: HTML layout and plug-in support. The HTML layout issues can be dealt with fairly easily. The plug-in issue may be more of a problem.

HTML Layout Compatibility

Current versions of HTML 4.01 and CSS 1 and 2 specify many details about how images and tables are to align when rendered on a web page. Older versions of HTML did not specify so much detail, so pages did not render the same on different browsers.

When you include a valid **DOCTYPE** with a valid URL (see the *"HTML Standards"* section earlier in this chapter that outlines **DOCTYPE**), newer browsers (MSIE 6 and Mozilla) will use a more strict rendering engine that follows the standards for rendering the page. For new web pages, you should use a complete **DOCTYPE** declaration, with a URL. Be sure to run your page through a validator. Then test your page on MSIE (both Windows and Mac) and Mozilla. It should look the same in both browsers on both platforms.

Both MSIE and Mozilla use a "quirks mode" for pages that do not specify the full **DOCTYPE** declaration. Unfortunately, the quirks mode of both browsers emulates the layout behavior of old versions of the same browsers, so all the incompatibilities in layout are still there. This means that your pages will look different on different browsers, and you will not have the visual control that you could have if you used the **DOCTYPE** declaration.

Wherever possible, use the full form of the **DOCTYPE** declaration, and your web pages will have more longevity and compatibility with current and future browsers.

The most popular HTML validator is located at http://validator.w3.org. Enter your web address, choose what you want to check, and click the *Validate this page* button. You'll know if your code is compliant.

```
HTML: The Web Standards Project
<!DOCTYPE html PUBLIC "-//W3C//DTD XHTML 1.0 Strict//EN"
    "http://www.w3.org/TR/xhtml1/DTD/xhtml1-strict.dtd">

<html xmlns="http://www.w3.org/1999/xhtml">

<head>
<meta name="MSSmartTagsPreventParsing" content="true" />
<title>The Web Standards Project</title>
<style type="text/css">
 @import "/inc/css/wsp.css";
</style>
<link rel="stylesheet" type="text/css" href="/inc/css/print.css" media="print" />

<script type="text/javascript" src="/inc/js/wsp.js"></script>
<!--
```

The source code here (viewed from http://www.webstandards.org) shows what a **DOCTYPE** declaration looks like in the code.

LAYOUT COMPATIBILITY LINKS

http://www.hut.fi/~hsivonen/doctype.html
An excellent page for helping decide what **DOCTYPE** to use.

http://developer.netscape.com/evangelism/docs/articles/validate
A good article about the value of a valid **DOCTYPE**.

PLUG-IN COMPATIBILITY

In the browser world, plug-ins are used for virtually all multimedia effects on a web page. Audio, video, Shockwave, Flash, and even Java are implemented in plug-ins. The fact that plug-ins have been distributed in an open-standard format (called Netscape plug-ins, because they were first implemented by Netscape) has helped make it possible for everyone to use them.

Beginning with version 3.0, Microsoft has stopped supporting the standard format for plug-ins and developed its own ActiveX proprietary plug-in format. Vendors are scrambling to produce "ActiveX" versions of their plug-ins so that their products will continue to work.

If they want to continue to support other browsers, they will have to make both ActiveX and plug-in versions of their products. With MSIE having such a huge share of the market, many will likely forgo the Netscape plug-in version all together.

Another unfortunate effect of Microsoft's decision to remove plug-in support from MSIE is that it has become more difficult to code multimedia for web sites. Most of the major sites now use complex JavaScript solutions to detect what version of what browser and what operating system is being used so that they can deliver the proper media support code.

BEST PRACTICES

Just as standards are valuable in the larger community, they are valuable for many of the same reasons on a smaller scale. Using a style guide, external style sheets, and external JavaScript files will help you centralize the aspects of your site that are most sensitive to browser compatibility issues.

Wherever possible, it's a good idea to test your new site on the latest versions of the major browsers, and it's also a good idea to keep the previous couple of versions available. Check your server logs now and then to see what browsers people are using to visit your site. Keep in mind that browsers are often different on the different computing platforms, so if you have a lot of visitors that use Macs, or Windows, or Linux, you may want to test on those platforms as well.

Last 20 Visitors			Unique Visitors
27 Jun, Thu, 15:13:19	24.244.201.186	MSIE 6	Windows XP
27 Jun, Thu, 15:27:21	netcache-1113.public.svc.webtv.net	WebTV 1	WebTV
27 Jun, Thu, 15:48:36	64.61.9.254	MSIE 5	Macintosh
27 Jun, Thu, 15:55:52	lvl-mac016.usc.edu	MSIE 5	Macintosh
27 Jun, Thu, 16:21:49	adsl-66-121-58-65.dsl.lsan03.pacbell.net	MSIE 6	Windows XP
27 Jun, Thu, 16:27:36	undefinedhost.cingular.com	MSIE 5	Windows 2000
27 Jun, Thu, 16:58:13	fw.telecomnetlinx.com	MSIE 6	Windows XP
27 Jun, Thu, 17:06:28	207.149.74.238	MSIE 5	Windows 98
27 Jun, Thu, 17:08:29	zzz-209254032151.splitrock.net	MSIE 5	Macintosh
27 Jun, Thu, 17:16:13	129.207.225.51	MSIE 6	Windows 2000
27 Jun, Thu, 17:17:19	209.79.108.202	MSIE 5	Windows 95
27 Jun, Thu, 17:18:36	modem-220-45-60-62.vip.uk.com	MSIE 5	Windows 98
27 Jun, Thu, 17:42:32	A17-216-30-68.apple.com	MSIE 5	Macintosh
27 Jun, Thu, 17:45:19	12-248-78-241.client.attbi.com	MSIE 6	Windows XP
27 Jun, Thu, 17:59:16	atif28o3y56nc.bc.hsia.telus.net	MSIE 6	Windows 98
27 Jun, Thu, 18:17:33	pool-141-157-176-199.bos.east.verizon.net	MSIE 5	Macintosh
27 Jun, Thu, 18:53:42	pm443-17.dialip.mich.net	MSIE 6	Windows XP
27 Jun, Thu, 19:02:00	med102-119.ucsd.edu	MSIE 5	Macintosh
27 Jun, Thu, 19:04:11	12-224-36-65.client.attbi.com	MSIE 5	Windows 98
27 Jun, Thu, 19:20:24	nycmny1-ar1-4-43-243-032.nycmny1.elnk.dsl.genuity.net	MSIE 6	Windows XP

Your web stats will take away the mystery of who is coming to your site. You should be able to see which browsers to target and test from by studying the results.

BEST PRACTICES LINKS

http://www.nypl.org/styleguide
An excellent example of a working style guide.

http://www.zeldman.com
Many links and resources about compatibility issues, style guides.

http://browsers.evolt.org
An archive of old browsers to download for testing purposes.

http://www.webstandards.org
Information about supporting both new standards and old browsers.

http://www.webalizer.com
A statistics program for Apache servers.

http://www.netiq.com/webtrends
A web statistics program for Microsoft servers.

BROWSER STANDARDS

SUMMARY

The process of creating web pages that work well on a variety of platforms and browsers is getting better, but it's not perfect yet. It is still a good idea to try your new pages on a number of different browsers and to continue downloading new browsers as they are released to make sure your site still works well with the latest versions.

> Web technologies continue to change quickly, making standards difficult to achieve.

> XHTML hasn't been fully embraced yet, but using it will not cause content to break on current browsers, and will make your site more forward compatible to future standards.

> Using external style sheets and external JavaScript files will help you centralize the parts of your site that may need tweaking as you try to keep up with the changing world of browser compatibility.

> Always test your content in the major browsers as well as on the different platforms.

HOSTING

INTRODUCTION

After you are finished with the planning, coding, graphics creation, and troubleshooting aspects of web design that this book has described so far, you will be ready to put your web site online. But first, you need a place to put it. And an address, also known as a URL, so people will know what to type in order to find it (like www.lynda.com). Then, you'll need to know how to upload all the files. You'll probably need to use a variety of services to accomplish these tasks, such as web hosting, FTP clients, domain registration services, and possibly more. The process of selecting all these services is daunting to most newcomers, due largely to the lack of formal documentation on this topic.

This chapter will guide you through the different types of services that you will need employ in order to get your content online. Since everyone's site is different and no "one-size-fits-all" solution works for everyone, this chapter covers a variety of options to help you make your own decisions.

WHAT IS WEB HOSTING?

A web site has to be stored somewhere—on a hard drive, to be exact. As you build a web site, you work off the hard drive on your computer, which will be referred to as the "local computer" in this chapter. Generally speaking, people will not be able to see your web site on your local computer unless you are running your own private web server. In most cases, in order for the rest of the world to see your web site, you will need to upload all your files from your local computer to a remote web server.

In the most simple terms, a web server has a hard drive that is housed on a computer that has FTP software installed that allows others access. Web hosting companies usually have a bunch of servers that are directly connected to the Internet via a super high-speed connection. When people type in your URL, they are directed to the web hosting company's server, where they can download and view your web site.

Web hosting companies offer all kinds of agreements and services. In order to pick a web hosting company, it's a good idea to understand all of the potential options they might offer to see if you need them or not. The following sections of this chapter will cover these options in order to help you make informed choices.

GET YOUR DOMAIN NAME!

If you are building a professional site, you will most likely want to get your own domain name, such as www.lynda.com. Of course, you couldn't have lynda.com because that's already taken! ;-) The domain name is part of the URL to your web site, and it's unique to your web site only. For example, www.somethingcool.com is an example of a domain name. The URL http://geocities.yahoo.com/lynda is an example of a URL without a unique domain name. Most professional web sites prefer to have a unique domain name that won't be confused with someone else's business or service.

You can check to see if the domain name that you want is available at any number of sites. For example, I like to use http://www.register.com, for no good reason except that the word "register" is part of the domain name. Most domain registration sites charge about the same fee for the registration, which is typically $35/year. For those on a tight budget, http://www.godaddy.com registers domains for $8.95/year. If the name you want is taken, you'll most likely have to pick another. Sometimes people pay (or sue each other for the right) for a web site name that is taken.

note

DOMAIN NAME SERVER (DNS)

Once you secure the domain name, you will want to have your web site content available if someone types the URL into a browser. In order to do that, a few more steps will need to be taken. First, you'll need to use a web server to house your web site. Most people will hire a web hosting company for this service. The web hosting company will need to make sure that the domain name you have secured will be tied to the IP address of your web site. (An IP address is a numeric identifier that is assigned to a web server, such as 192.168.1.30) No one could possibly remember the IP address of every site they want to visit, as domain names are much easier to remember than a bunch of numbers. Your web hosting company will assign an IP address to you, and they will take care of making sure the DNS records point your domain name to their IP address.

your web hosting needs

Before you go signing up for just any hosting account you should take some time to consider your current needs and give some thought to your possible future needs. For example, if you never intend on selling any products on your web site, then why would you need a plan that provides an e-commerce solution? (Unless it's free, of course.) Typically, the more services offered by the hosting company, the more you will pay, so analyzing your current needs and projecting future needs is important.

The **lynda.com** web site is an example of a virtual web site (http://www.lynda.com). Notice the URL has its own unique domain name. This web site is an example of a non-virtual web site (http://www.geocities.com/willemsgunther/bonsai/index.html). Notice that this URL does not have a unique domain name.

On the following pages are some choices that you'll need to make before you begin looking for a hosting company.

Dedicated versus user accounts

When choosing the kind of web server account you want, you can either have a user account or a dedicated account. A dedicated account is one that lets you lease space on a web server and requires that you have secured your own domain name. For example, http://www.lynda.com is our dedicated account. A dedicated account requires a fee and offers numerous services. A user account is one in which you don't have to secure your own name or pay a fee. For example, http://geocities.yahoo.com/lynda/ would be an example of a user account. These types of accounts are almost always free, but have a limited number of services available.

How much do you want to spend?

If you are making a web site for your local Moose-head lodge, then you might not want to spend a large amount of money each month to host the lodge's web site. In fact, a non-virtual account like those found at GeoCities would work great here. On the other hand, if you are promoting your own portfolio site and you expect potential clients to visit the site, then you should budget a reasonable amount of money so you can get the hosting services you need, like email addresses, logs, extra server space to place client work, and access to scripts. How much should you budget? That will depend on your exact needs, as services can range from $10–$500/per month.

Some web sites, like **CNET Internet Services**, let you specify the type of hosting you want and the amount of money you want to spend and it will display web hosting companies that match those criteria. Very cool (http://webservices.cnet.com/cgi/scompare.asp?stable=Hosting_Plans)!

It's easy to get a web page designed, even if you are using a free service like **GeoCities** (http://geocities.yahoo.com/v/pb.html). They offer a collection of templates and even an online web page builder to help get you started! These can be a good place to start if you are unsure about your design skills.

note

WARNING: YOUR HOSTING NEEDS

We highly recommend that you look into all of the issues covered in this section before signing up with any hosting company. You may want to call and test some of their services, it's not a bad idea to give a ring to their technical support department. See if you can get through during odd hours and what the experience is like. Chances are if it goes well the first time, it will go well the next time, when you really need help.

Technical support

This is one of the most important services a hosting company can provide for you. It doesn't matter if you are a technical expert or a complete beginner; it's a huge issue to consider. If your site goes down, you are going to want answers immediately! So make sure the hosting company you choose has awesome technical support, or you might regret it later.

Here are some things to consider about technical support services:

> *Availability:* Is someone available 7-days a week, 24-hours a day, including holidays? This is an absolute must. The Web does not sleep or take vacations; and neither should your technical support team. If they offer limited hours, look elsewhere.

> *Contact Method:* Is there a phone number you can call, or do you have to fill out some lame online form and wait for a callback? I have seen some companies respond within minutes of sending an email for technical support, but never consistently. You need to talk to a real person who knows what they are doing. Also, make sure they have a toll-free number. I mean, do you really want to pay for being on hold for 40 minutes?

> *Size of staff:* Make sure you check and find out how many tech support people they have on staff. A friend of mine called her hosting company during a normal work day, and do you want to know who answered the phone? It was the owner of the company! This is not a good sign that there was sufficient tech support on hand to take care of all the customers.

> *Size of customer base:* Ask the hosting company how many people they provide hosting for. It's important to know this and the size of their support staff. If they are servicing 10,000 customers and have one tech support person, it's probably going to be a hassle getting the support you need when you need it.

Traffic

Traffic (also referred to as "Data Transfer") is the amount of information that can be downloaded from your web site. For free accounts, there usually aren't any published limitations. However, if you have people download two or more gigabytes of information in a single month, I am sure you will get an email asking why! For virtual hosting accounts, there is almost always a limit to the amount of information that can be downloaded from your site each month. For example, if your entire web site was exactly 1 megabyte and 1,000 users visited every single page, your traffic for the month would be 1 gigabyte (1,000 megabytes). If your traffic limit was 2 gigabytes, you would be fine, but if it was 500 megabytes, you could have some issues. Some hosting companies will charge you for the extra traffic while others will simply pull the plug on your site until the first of the next month. So make sure you know what your traffic limit is and what your web hosting company's policy is if you exceed that amount. If you are paying around $25–$100 bucks a month for a user account, you should expect to get at least 10–20 gigabytes of traffic each month.

Who is going to design your site?

If you don't currently have a web site designed, then this may be something you need to consider. Many hosting companies offer web design services to their customers. Even the non-virtual hosting site, like GeoCities Tripod and others, offer free web page design templates. Of course, in most cases you will get what you pay for, so don't expect to win any Communication Arts awards using a GeoCities template.

How big is your web site?

Are you going to have a small (fewer than 20 pages) web site, or is it going to be a larger site with streaming multimedia? Take an inventory of the types of things you will have on your web site. You need to know this so you can determine how much traffic (the amount of data downloaded from your site) you expect to get each month. Most hosting companies restrict the amount of data that can be downloaded from your site each month. If you exceed this limit, the hosting company will either block access to your site or charge you more money than you agreed to spend with them. For example, if I were going to post a bunch of QuickTime movies on my site, I would need to get a hosting account that allowed for a lot of data transfer at an affordable price.

Email accounts

Do you need to have an email account set up that relates to the web site? For example, you might want yourname@someplacecool.com and you may want info@someplacecool.com. Look into the costs and availability of this service, as well as how easy it is to set up.

Server space

Server space refers to the amount of hard drive space your account is given on the hosting company's server. This space is where you will upload all the files for your web site. Most free hosting services give you more web space than many of you will ever need, typically between 3 and 15 megabytes. For example, if you subscribe to AOL or Earthlink, you already have a non-virtual account as part of your monthly fee (I bet some of you didn't even know that)! Now, 3–15 megabytes is really a lot if you figure that typical web page is under 100k. If you are paying for a hosting account, then you should expect to get somewhere between 20–50 megabytes of server space. Even though you might not need that space now, there might come a day when you want to expand your web site to include large media files, such as QuickTime, etc., and then you will need that much space!

Web server logs

Once your web site has been up for a while, you will want to find out some important things about it, such as how many visitors have come, what parts of your site they are visiting the most, what browser they are using, what operating system they are using, and so on. This is critical information to help you make decisions on how to update your site. This type of information can be obtained through the web server logs. These reports will give you detailed information about your site, which is important for its current and continued success. These reports can also help you spot problem areas of your site, such as broken links, etc. Make sure the hosting company you choose offers a comprehensive online reporting system for you web site.

Scripts

There are so many things that you will want to add to your site, such as forms processing, e-commerce solutions, connecting to a database and so much more, and these require special scripts. Sometimes JavaScript can be used for some of these tasks, but most of the time a CGI script is the more stable and preferred way to add these features. For example, if you want to add a form that sends the information to an email address, a CGI script would be the best way to go. But I bet most of you don't know how to program a CGI script, huh? Me either. So this is where a hosting company can step in and earn some of its monthly rates. You should check to make sure the hosting company has a collection of CGI scripts that you can use on your site. For example, they should offer scripts for setting up guest books, mail processing, page counters, search engines, and more. And, they should be willing to help you set up these scripts for no additional charge! They should also be willing to let you add your own CGI scripts in the event you need to add a script for something they don't already offer, such as an e-commerce solution.

DreamHost (http://www.dreamhost.com) offers a great set of services, including an e-commerce solution for $59.95 a month.

If the hosting company does not have a collection of CGI scripts for you to use, are they willing to help you set them up for no charge and willing to let you add your own CGI scripts? If not, then you need to look someplace else! And if you are paying more than $40–$50 bucks a month for a virtual hosting account, they should offer some type of basic e-commerce shopping cart for your site as well. Don't be afraid to demand and expect these services from your hosting company.

FTP—uploading your site

Once you have decided on your domain name and where your web site will be hosted, the next thing to do is upload your web site so the rest of the world can see it. To do this, you need an FTP (**F**ile **T**ransfer **P**rotocol) program. Don't let that term scare you—as you will see, using an FTP program to upload your web site is a pretty simple process.

If you are looking for an FTP program, be sure to check out some of the links below. These aren't the only FTP programs available, but they are a good place to start. Almost all of them have free trial versions available on their web sites, so don't be afraid to download one and take it for a test drive. Also, most popular WYSIWYG HTML editors, such as Dreamweaver, GoLive, and FrontPage, have FTP functions built into them, so you won't need any of the programs listed below to upload your site. Check the manual that came with these programs for instructions on how to use this feature.

Here is an example of Fetch on the Macintosh.

Here is an example of 3DFTP in Windows.

Macintosh FTP Programs

Fetch
http://www.fetchsoftworks.com

Transmit
http://www.panic.com/index-l.html

Vicomsoft FTP
http://www.vicomsoft.com

Hefty FTP
http://www.ziggy.speedhost.com/bdhefty.html

Windows FTP Programs

CuteFTP
http://www.cuteftp.com

3DFTP
http://www.3dftp.com

FTP Voyager
http://www.rhinosoft.com

WS FTP
http://www.ipswitch.com

Once you have downloaded your FTP program of choice, you will need to configure it to connect to your web hosting company. This will vary widely from program to program, but some basic information will be needed. Here is a list of the things you will need to enter into the FTP program, at a minimum:

FTP Host Address: This will often start with "ftp," but that is not a requirement. For example, `ftp.lynda.com` would be one example of an FTP host address, or you could use `www.lynda.com` or simply `lynda.com`. Your hosting company will tell you exactly what you need to enter here.

User Name: This is something you typically choose during the sign-up process with your hosting company. In some cases, the user name will be assigned by the hosting company. Either way, this is really important information and something you should keep in a safe and accessible place. You will need this each time you log on to the web host server.

User Password: This is a password that you will need to access the web hosting server to upload, download, and/or make changes to your web site. Again, this is something that you want to keep in a very safe and accessible place. Most FTP programs will save the user name and password for you so you don't have to enter them each time you connect to the web server.

FTP OPTIONAL INFORMATION

Local directory: This refers to a location on your computer, typically the location of your web site. When you start your FTP program, you will be placed in this directory by default. In almost all cases, this information is optional and not required to connect to your web server.

Remote directory: When you connect to the web server, you will automatically be placed in this directory, as opposed to the root directory (the first directory), by default. This can be helpful and save you time if the folder structure on your web server is complex. If you leave this option blank, in most cases you will be placed in the root directory of the web server.

Once your FTP program has been set up, you simply connect to the web server and click an upload button to transfer your files to the correct directory. Your hosting company will give you the necessary information so you can do this properly. That's all there is to it. Now you can sit back and watch the people flock to your site. Well, at least we all hope that's what happens! Be sure to read Chapter 30, *"Getting Listed"* to learn how to publicize your site, now that it has found a true home on the Internet.

HOSTIN9

SUMMARY

This chapter covered the process of getting a domain name, finding a web hosting company, and uploading your files. Here's a summary of its contents.

> Securing your domain name is important, even if you plan on using a non-virtual account. Once a domain name is gone, it's most likely gone for good.

> If you need web space for non-professional reasons, you should consider a non-virtual account. If you are developing a professional site, however, you should have a virtual account with its own domain.

> Make an inventory of services you want, or think you might need, for your web site and compare them to the services offered by different hosting companies before you sign up with one of them.

> When comparing web hosting companies, technical support should be at the top of your list. You never know when you will need it!

> FTP programs are used to transfer the files from your computer to the web server. There are many available for both Mac and Windows platforms. Many software applications, such as Dreamweaver and GoLive, already include FTP functionality.

29

GETTING LISTED

INTRODUCTION

Most of this book has described the process of designing a web site, either with code, graphics, animation, sound, type, layout, color, or navigation. As a designer, however, you might be surprised at how many clients also expect you to have some expertise and experience in getting their sites listed in search engines.

In this short but important chapter, you'll learn how to get the word out about your web site. You'll learn how to get listed on the search engines and, just as important, how to get your listing positioned near the top of search results.

DIRECTORIES & SEARCH ENGINES

In the early days of the Internet, if you wanted to find a new site, you simply went to one of the directories and looked it up. The most popular directory of that era, called **Yahoo!**, has evolved into a huge conglomeration of sites, but originally it was just a directory of web sites kept on a university computer by a couple of Stanford students.

Eventually, Yahoo! grew into a very large (by many accounts, unmanageably large) directory managed by a staff of about 100 full-time employees (that is, just for the directory). Users submit their URLs along with a category, and a Yahoo! staff member verifies the site and adds it to the directory, usually within 6 to 8 weeks. It's a tedious process that yields a directory with useful links that the public has learned to trust.

Eventually, the Web grew too large for a directory like Yahoo! to keep up with it. Search engines like **Lycos**, **Excite**, **Google**, and **HotBot** emerged as a way to find new sites in a growing, sprawling Web.

Search engines differ from directories in how they collect and present their data. In a "directory," users submit URLs to be listed. In a search engine, an automated process (called a robot or a spider) surfs the Web—continually following links from one page to another, carefully recording information about each page that it visits. When a user wants to find something with a search engine, he or she enters search terms and is presented with a list of sites that match the searched-for terms.

Today, the names have changed but the principals remain the same. The hottest search engine today is Google. With its advanced searching and cataloging technology, Google quickly built a database several times larger than its nearest competitors, and it continues to improve. Today, it's so popular that even the popular media uses the word "Google" as a verb for "search the Web."

Likewise, the hottest directory is no longer Yahoo!, although Yahoo! is still a very important resource. The hottest directory today is the **ODP** (dmoz.org). Most of the other directories, including the modern incarnations of Lycos and Excite use data from ODP, so you are probably using the ODP directory without even knowing it.

SEARCH ENGINE LINKS

Google
The most popular (and powerful) search engine today.
http://www.google.com

ODP (**O**pen **D**irectory **P**roject)
The premier directory today.
http://dmoz.org

Yahoo!
The empire of web sites.
http://www.yahoo.com

Yahoo! is a directory-based portal, whereas **Google** is a spider-based search engine.

GETTING LISTED

It is important to understand that, while there may be many directories and search engines, getting listed in just the few most popular can be all it takes to get your site noticed. Because so much of the Web now gets data from the ODP, once your site gets listed there, most of the major directories will list it alongside their own data. Likewise, once your site gets listed at Google, it's likely that the rest of the search engines will soon list it as well.

Search Engine Submissions

Attract more customers with bCentral Submit It! Register your site for a guaranteed* listing on top search engines and directories.

→ **Sign Up**
→ **Features & Pricing**
→ **Product Demo**

Starting at only $49!

Get noticed more often

zoom in

- Get a guaranteed listing for your site on search engines and directories including AOL, HotBot and MSN.
- Stay listed with the most popular sites at all times; Submit It! continuously updates its list of engines and directories.
- Optimize your Web site with Readiness Check, which examines your site for common failures and provides solutions.

There are lots of different listing services on the Web—**Submit It!** is shown above (http://www.submit-it.com). These services work just fine, but you can probably do what they do with better success by following many of the principles found in this chapter.

If you are in a hurry to have your site listed far and wide, there are services that will take care of listing it for you, by automatically submitting your site to hundreds of directories and search engines. But this kind if service is of limited, long-term value. You may get your site listed in a lot of places, but if you don't understand how the process works, your site will never show up near the top of any search results anyway. On the other hand, if you know the rules of the game and you work it intelligently, you can have your site well listed in the search engines without having to submit it to a lot of search engines in the first place.

Most of the search engines, and even some directories, have a way of ranking their results by popularity. For example, Google ranks results by the number of other sites that link to it. In other words, as Google's robots search the Web, they keep track of what other sites link to any given site, like lynda.com for example. Then, when a search result includes lynda.com, those sites with the most links to them will be listed first in the search results. So if you want your site listed first in search results, you will need to get other sites to link to you.

If you want to get your site in the directories and search engines, the first thing you need to do is to write a description of your site and choose some keywords. Your description should be about 20–25 words, and you should choose 10–15 keywords. Be prepared to edit your description and prioritize your keywords if necessary.

GETTING LISTED LINKS

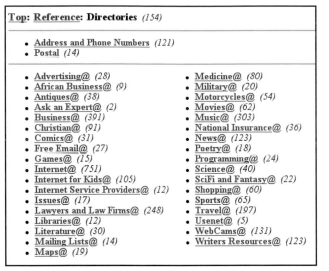

Top: Reference: Directories *(154)*

- Address and Phone Numbers *(121)*
- Postal *(14)*

- Advertising@ *(28)*
- African Business@ *(9)*
- Antiques@ *(38)*
- Ask an Expert@ *(2)*
- Business@ *(391)*
- Christian@ *(91)*
- Comics@ *(31)*
- Free Email@ *(27)*
- Games@ *(15)*
- Internet@ *(751)*
- Internet for Kids@ *(105)*
- Internet Service Providers@ *(12)*
- Issues@ *(17)*
- Lawyers and Law Firms@ *(248)*
- Libraries@ *(12)*
- Literature@ *(30)*
- Mailing Lists@ *(14)*
- Maps@ *(19)*
- Medicine@ *(80)*
- Military@ *(20)*
- Motorcycles@ *(54)*
- Movies@ *(62)*
- Music@ *(303)*
- National Insurance@ *(36)*
- News@ *(123)*
- Poetry@ *(18)*
- Programming@ *(24)*
- Science@ *(40)*
- SciFi and Fantasy@ *(22)*
- Shopping@ *(60)*
- Sports@ *(65)*
- Travel@ *(197)*
- Usenet@ *(5)*
- WebCams@ *(131)*
- Writers Resources@ *(123)*

DMOZ is the directory of directories! To find all the directories within your specified niche, give them a visit at http://dmoz.org/ Reference/Directories.

dmoz.org

Instructions for adding a site to this directory.
http://dmoz.org/add.html

Yahoo!

How to suggest (submit) a site to them.
http://docs.yahoo.com/info/suggest

Google

"Submit your site" form.
http://news.google.com/addurl.html

Internet.com

This Search Engine Watch provides news and other content about search engines.
http://searchenginewatch.com

Now, select a handful of popular sites to submit to. I recommend a few general sites, like Yahoo!, Google, and ODP, plus a few select directories specific to the subject your site focuses on. Chances are, you already know where you would like your site listed. If not, try searching for "directories" on ODP or Yahoo! for a starting point.

Each site will have a unique submission policy and procedure. Read the instructions carefully and follow them as closely as you can. Incorrectly filled-in forms or incomplete information can delay your request. A person must review your submission before it can be added to the directory, so be clear and succinct.

META TAGS

Once you submit your site to directories and search engines, automated processes (called robots or spiders), start visiting your site to update their databases. You can help them by including **META** tags in your web pages with helpful information for the search engines.

HTML includes a tag called **META** for providing information that's readable electronically but doesn't display on the web page. **META** tags belong in the **HEAD** part of the document. It's a good idea to just put them right after the **TITLE** tag so you can make sure they always go in the right place. Here's an example:

code
```
<head>
<title>The David Bowie List</title>
<meta name="description"
content="A complete list of every
song David Bowie ever sang.">
<meta name="keywords"
content="david bowie, ziggy stardust,
major tom, spiders from mars, rebel
rebel, diamond dogs">
</head>
```

There are two **META** tags here: the first contains a description of the document, and the second contains keywords. The **NAME** attribute is for the type of **META** tag ("description" or "keywords"), and the **CONTENT** attribute is for the actual data that goes with it. Note that in XHTML the **META** tag is terminated with a trailing slash: `<meta/>`.

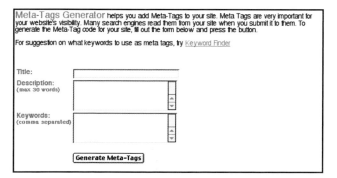

If you don't want to write your own **META** tags, here's a site that will do it for you: http://www.addme.com/meta.htm.

The search engines will blindly catalog every page on your web site, even pages that you may not want indexed, like email forms, legal statements, etc. It will also continue to list old pages, even after you've removed all the links to them.

For this unwanted situation, there is another kind of **META** tag that tells the search engines to ignore a certain page, without indexing it or following the links in it. Use this **META** tag for pages that you still want to leave on the web server but don't want showing up in the search engines:

code
```
<meta name="ROBOTS"
content="NOINDEX,NOFOLLOW">
```

By using **META** tags correctly, you will find your site listed in search engines you didn't even know about and that those listings have picked up the description and keywords from your **META** tags.

META TAGS LINKS

searchenginewatch.com
A good introduction to **META** tags with a focus on search engines.
http://searchenginewatch.com/webmasters/meta.html

webdeveloper.com
A more general discussion of **META** tags.
http://www.webdeveloper.com/html/html_metatags.html

addme.com
A **META** tag generator. Just put your description and keywords in the form, and copy and paste the result!
http://www.addme.com/meta.htm

TRADING LINKS

You can get higher ranking in the search engines by getting other sites to link to you. One popular way to do that is by trading links with other sites. You can create a special page on your site with links to other sites you have traded with, or you can create a "sponsored links" section in the margins of the main parts of your site.

With some popular sites, all you have to do is create a selection of banners and buttons and offer them to your visitors. Many people will put them on their web sites just to be associated with something they identify with. This technique works well for fan sites, gaming sites, and other subjects with strong cultural identity.

Here's an example of a banner site that offers banners and then links to anyone who uses them http://the-tech.mit.edu/Macmade. This is one great way to get links.

In other cases you may want to try one of the popular banner exchange programs. A banner exchange program is a program where you agree to run banners on your site, in exchange for getting your banner in the rotation of banners on all the other sites in the program. Each site generally earns "points" for each banner impression or click, and those points are used to get your banner in heavier rotation on the other sites.

About 123Banners
123Banners is a free public service designed to help web sites advertise each other. The concept is simple: by joining, you agree to display advertising banners for other members, and they agree to display banners for you. You can decide what type of sites to advertise on and advertise for so you don't need to worry about inappropriate material showing up on your pages.

The amount of free advertising you receive from the 123Banners is directly proportional to the amount you give to others. Our system will automatically display your banner on our network of member web pages. In addition to giving you instant access to free banner advertising, we also provide you with up-to-the-minute statistics.

There are lots of banner exchange programs on the Web—just search for "banner exchange" at http://www.google.com. These sites trade links and banners for a living.

Banner exchange programs may work to drive traffic to your site, but they won't necessarily get you better ranking on the search engines. Ad banner links are generally not counted as links in the computation used by the search engines to assign a rank to your site.

To be honest, while trading links is one way to get more links, most of the schemes out there are rather random. Although they might get you a few more links, the true way to get links is to have the best site in your category so that people find it so useful they actually want to link to you. Be sure to read Chapter 25 , *"Creating Community"* to get ideas about how to make a genuinely useful and magnetic site.

TRADING LINKS RESOURCES

dmoz.org
A large selection of banner exchange sites.
http://dmoz.org/Computers/Internet/Web_Design_and_Development/Promotion/
Banner_Exchanges
The ODP's section on web site promotion.
http://dmoz.org/Computers/Internet/Web_Design_and_Development/Promotion/

SUMMARY

In this chapter you've learned how the search engines work and how to get a listing positioned near the top of search results.

There are a great many ideas out there for promoting your web site, so use your imagination! Take a little time with the search engines and directories, and look for new and interesting ways to promote your site. Above all: Keep your site interesting and fresh so that when people do find it they'll want to spread the word. Here's a short summary of what was covered in this chapter:

> Know the difference between a directory-based and spider-based search site. You go about listing your site differently depending on what type of site it is.

> Write a concise description of your web site, as well as a short list of keywords. Have this copy handy so you can enter it into different search engine directories.

> Know your **META** tags and use them!

> Investigate portal sites that are related to the subject matter of your site. See if you can trade a link to get posted on their resource links.

Designing Web Graphics.4

index

Where is it?

dwg

X – Z

informIT

www.informit.com

VISIT OUR WEB SITE

WWW.NEWRIDERS.COM

On our web site, you'll find information about our other books, authors, tables of contents, and book errata. You will also find information about book registration and how to purchase our books, both domestically and internationally.

EMAIL US

Contact us at: **nrfeedback@newriders.com**

- If you have comments or questions about this book
- To report errors that you have found in this book
- If you have a book proposal to submit or are interested in writing for New Riders
- If you are an expert in a computer topic or technology and are interested in being a technical editor who reviews manuscripts for technical accuracy

Contact us at: **nreducation@newriders.com**

- If you are an instructor from an educational institution who wants to preview New Riders books for classroom use. Email should include your name, title, school, department, address, phone number, office days/hours, text in use, and enrollment, along with your request for desk/examination copies and/or additional information.

Contact us at: **nrmedia@newriders.com**

- If you are a member of the media who is interested in reviewing copies of New Riders books. Send your name, mailing address, and email address, along with the name of the publication or web site you work for.

BULK PURCHASES/CORPORATE SALES

The publisher offers discounts on this book when ordered in quantity for bulk purchases and special sales. For sales within the U.S., please contact: Corporate and Government Sales (800) 382-3419 or **corpsales@pearsontechgroup.com**. Outside of the U.S., please contact: International Sales (317) 581-3793 or **international@pearsontechgroup.com**.

WRITE TO US

New Riders Publishing
201 W. 103rd St.
Indianapolis, IN 46290-1097

CALL/FAX US

Toll-free (800) 571-5840
If outside U.S. (317) 581-3500
Ask for New Riders
FAX: (317) 581-4663

New Riders

WWW.NEWRIDERS.COM

VIEW CART ⊟

| | search ⊙

▸ Registration already a member? Log in. ▸ Book Registration

OUR AUTHORS

PRESS ROOM

| ▦ web development | ▦ design | ▦ photoshop | ▦ new media | ▦ 3-D | ▦ server technologies |

EDUCATORS

ABOUT US

CONTACT US

You already know that New Riders brings you the **Voices that Matter**.

But what does that mean? It means that New Riders brings you the

Voices that challenge your assumptions, take your talents to the next

level, or simply help you better understand the complex technical world

we're all navigating.

Visit **www.newriders.com** to find:

▸ *Discounts* on specific book purchases

▸ Never-before-published chapters

▸ Sample chapters and excerpts

▸ Author bios and interviews

▸ Contests and enter-to-wins

▸ Up-to-date industry event information

▸ Book reviews

▸ Special offers from our friends and partners

▸ Info on how to join our User Group program

▸ Ways to have your Voice heard

W W W . N E W R I D E R S . C O M

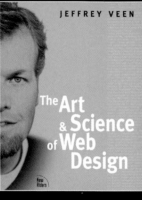

Photoshop 7 Killer Tips
Scott Kelby
0735713006
US$39.99

**Photoshop 7
Down & Dirty Tricks**
Scott Kelby
0735712379
US$39.99

Photoshop 7 Magic
Sherry London,
Rhoda Grossman
0735712646
US$45.00

Photoshop 7 Artistry
Barry Haynes,
Wendy Crumpler
0735712409
US$55.00

Inside Photoshop 7
Gary Bouton, Robert Stanley,
J. Scott Hamlin, Daniel Will-Harris,
Mara Nathanson
0735712417
US$49.99

**Photoshop Studio with
Bert Monroy**
Bert Monroy
0735712468
US$45.00

**Photoshop Restoration
and Retouching**
Katrin Eismann
0789723182
US$49.99

**Photoshop Type Effects
Visual Encyclopedia**
Roger Pring
0735711909
US$45.00

**Creative Thinking in
Photoshop**
Sharon Steuer
0735711224
US$45.00

**Photoshop 7
Power Shortcuts**
Michael Ninness
0735713316
US$19.99

New
Riders